Walt Whitman and His Caribbean
Interlocutors: José Martí,
C.L.R. James, and Pedro Mir

Historical Materialism Book Series

The Historical Materialism Book Series is a major publishing initiative of the radical left. The capitalist crisis of the twenty-first century has been met by a resurgence of interest in critical Marxist theory. At the same time, the publishing institutions committed to Marxism have contracted markedly since the high point of the 1970s. The Historical Materialism Book Series is dedicated to addressing this situation by making available important works of Marxist theory. The aim of the series is to publish important theoretical contributions as the basis for vigorous intellectual debate and exchange on the left.

The peer-reviewed series publishes original monographs, translated texts, and reprints of classics across the bounds of academic disciplinary agendas and across the divisions of the left. The series is particularly concerned to encourage the internationalization of Marxist debate and aims to translate significant studies from beyond the English-speaking world.

For a full list of titles in the Historical Materialism Book Series available in paperback from Haymarket Books, visit:
https://www.haymarketbooks.org/series_collections/1-historical-materialism

Walt Whitman and His Caribbean Interlocutors: José Martí, C.L.R. James, and Pedro Mir

Song and Countersong

Rafael Bernabe

Haymarket Books
Chicago, IL

First published in 2021 by Brill Academic Publishers, The Netherlands
© 2021 Koninklijke Brill NV, Leiden, The Netherlands

Published in paperback in 2022 by
Haymarket Books
P.O. Box 180165
Chicago, IL 60618
773-583-7884
www.haymarketbooks.org

ISBN: 978-1-64259-766-0

Distributed to the trade in the US through Consortium Book Sales and Distribution (www.cbsd.com) and internationally through Ingram Publisher Services International (www.ingramcontent.com).

This book was published with the generous support of Lannan Foundation and Wallace Action Fund.

Special discounts are available for bulk purchases by organizations and institutions. Please call 773-583-7884 or email info@haymarketbooks.org for more information.

Cover art and design by David Mabb. Cover art is a detail from *Painting 35, Rhythm 69, (William Morris Block Printed Pattern Book, with Hans Richter Storyboard, developed from Richter's Rhythmus 25 and Kazimir Malevich's film script Artistic and Scientific Film – Painting and Architectural Concerns – Approaching the New Plastic Architectural System)*. Paint and wallpaper on canvas (2007).

Printed in the United States.

10 9 8 7 6 5 4 3 2 1

Library of Congress Cataloging-in-Publication data is available.

For Natalia

Contents

Introduction 1

1 Marx and the 'Transformation of History into World History' 5

2 'Within Me Latitude Widens, Longitude Lengthens': Whitman and the World Created by Capital 11

3 'In Paths Untrodden': Whitman, Nature, Democracy and the 'Average Man of To-day' 37

4 The 'Emptiness' of the Present: Marx, the 'Bourgeois Viewpoint' and Its 'Romantic Antithesis' 52

5 'This All-Devouring Modern Word': Whitman's Critique of Business 71

6 From Brooklyn Ferry to Brooklyn Bridge: José Martí and the 'Modern Multiple Life' 102

7 'The Final Culmination of This Vast and Varied Republic': Whitman's Failed Transcendence of the Present 136

8 Whitman: Inconsistent Democrat, Yet More Than a Democrat 155

9 A 'Damaged and Alien Civilization': Martí's Search for an Alternative Modernity 183

10 C.L.R. James's *Notes on American Civilization*, or the Song of the C.I.O. 218

11 'Now Has Come the Hour of the Countersong': Pedro Mir and Walt Whitman 250

References 273
Index 286

Introduction

Allow me to begin with two statements. The first will initially seem both outlandish and reductionist, though I hope the readers will revise their opinion as the book proceeds. The other was Whitman's preferred description of his own work, an appreciation many others have embraced while giving it a celebratory tone I do not share.

To formulate the first claim rather bluntly: Walt Whitman was the poet of an expanding capitalist economy, of the rise of modern industry and of the formation of a capitalist world market. Formulated by a Marxist, this statement may read as an indictment. It is not. The only passages that can rival Whitman's celebration of the world created by capital are to be found in the introductory portions of Marx and Engels's *German Ideology* (1845), the first section of their *Communist Manifesto* (1848), and some of the more inspired passages of Marx's *Grundrisse* (1857–8). In fact, one could illustrate many passages of these canonical texts of Marx's critique of neo-Hegelian philosophy and of classical political economy with portions of *Leaves of Grass*. That non-Marxist critics have overlooked this, and that anti-Marxist critics may deem it outrageous, is understandable. That Marxists or authors sympathetic to Marxism have largely ignored this is more puzzling. I contend that reading Whitman and Marx side by side, contrapuntally, to borrow a term from Edward W. Said, enriches our understanding of these two prophets of modernity, of modernity as such, and, thus, of ourselves.[1]

Turning from the provocative to the commonplace: Whitman was the poet of the American experience, of the United States. Whitman's poetic voice sought to encompass the multitudes bubbling within the confines of a new nation and sought to give them unity of vision and purpose. As Jerome Loving puts it, he wished to celebrate the 'American character'.[2] This was the way he thought of himself and how he wanted to be remembered. As he concluded the 'Preface' to the first edition of *Leaves of Grass*: 'The proof of the poet is that his country absorbs him as affectionately as he has absorbed it'.[3] Or, as he urged in

---

1 Betsy Erkkila has pointed out some 'uncanny overlappings' of Marx's and Whitman's trajectories: born a year from each other (May of 1818 and of 1819), both became youthful newspaper editors in the early 1840s, while exhibiting an early concern for radical democratic politics and the condition of the labouring classes. The differences between them are, of course, equally significant. This work can be read as a further exploration along the path suggested by Erkkila. Erkkila 2007, p. 36. See Erkkila 1989.
2 Loving 1982, p. 77.
3 'Preface' in Walt Whitman. *Complete Poetry and Collected Prose*, edited by Justin Kaplan (New

'Starting from Paumanok': 'Take my leaves America / ... / for they are your own offspring'.[4] But while seeking America's distinct poetic expression, Whitman also claimed a special role for the United States. In any period, he proclaimed in 'By Blue Ontario's Shore', 'one nation must lead, / One land must be the promise and reliance of the future'.[5] The same idea and even the same words reappear in *Democratic Vistas*: 'The individuality of one nation must then, always, lead the world. Can there be any doubt who the leader ought to be?'[6] Similarly, in the preface to the 1872 edition of *Leaves of Grass* he presented the United States as nothing less than the 'culmination' of 'history and humanity'.[7] More often than not, Whitman thought of this leading role in moral and spiritual rather than military or political terms. He thus argued that the United States could not take on the leading role he assigned to it without first creating truly 'noble men and women', capable of exercising a spiritual and comradely influence over the world. But beyond all the qualifiers we may tack on to our description of his vision of America's privileged destiny, there is no doubt that, whatever else he was, the good gray poet was also an American nationalist, deeply convinced of the special, central and unique place the United States was called upon to occupy in the affairs of the modern world.

Formulated by a critic of US imperial policies, of the global assertion of US political, economic and military power and a supporter of his country's political independence from the United States, this may seem to be a definition of Whitman as the enemy. It is not. Anti-imperialism need not be based on a crude anti-Americanism. In fact, anti-imperialism is perfectly compatible with admiration for more than one dimension of modern American society. The author of this book is by no means the first critic of US imperialism from the Caribbean who has been seduced by the idea of exploring the work of Walt Whitman as one of the ways of coming to terms with metropolitan culture, with 'American civilization', while seeking a more equal and freer relationship with it. Such was also the case of the Cuban José Martí (1853–95), the Trinidadian C.L.R. James (1901–89) and the Dominican Pedro Mir (1913–2000). This work brings their contributions to bear on the conversation it imagines between Marx and Whitman. It explores how they read Whitman and some of

---

York: The Library of America, 1982), p. 26. All quotes from Whitman, unless otherwise indicated, are taken from this collection. I have chosen it because it is readily available, and conveniently includes both the first (1855) as well as the last (1892) edition of *Leaves of Grass*, and also key prose works such as *Democratic Vistas* (1871) and *Specimen Days* (1882).
4 'Starting from Paumanok', p. 177.
5 'By Blue Ontario's Shore', p. 471.
6 Whitman [1871], p. 981.
7 'Preface, 1872', p. 1001.

the things that may tell us about them and Whitman and about the relations of US and Caribbean cultures.

The study is organised as follows. Chapters 1 and 2 explore the celebrations of the modern in Marx and Whitman. Chapter 3 continues the discussion of Whitman initiated in Chapter 2. Thematically, the two chapters are one. Given its length, the presentation has been split, hopefully making the argument clearer and its consideration less burdensome for the reader. Chapters 4 and 5 examine Marx's and Whitman's critique of modernity and some of the alternatives they envisioned as part of that critique. Chapter 6 addresses Martí's reading of Whitman as it relates to his celebration and critique of an emergent modernity in its American, late nineteenth-century, New York City embodiment. Chapters 7, 8 and 9 explore how Whitman and Martí sought a way out, or around, the contradictions they increasingly detected at the very centre of the modern world. Chapter 10 discusses C.L.R. James's reading of Whitman, as well as the conception of US history of which it is part, as presented in his unfinished manuscript *Notes on American Civilization* (1949–50) and in his book on *Moby Dick* (1953). The study concludes with a commentary on Pedro Mir's poetic tribute and response to Whitman, *Countersong to Walt Whitman* (1952).

Books and articles about Whitman could fill a fairly large library. There are journals exclusively dedicated to him and his writing. There are glossaries, indexes and companions to his works. There is a Whitman encyclopedia. By now it is impossible to say something *entirely* new about *Leaves of Grass* and its author. Yet this vast critical literature is full of ideas suggested but not developed, insights formulated in passing, clues mentioned but not explored, and, above all, varied readings not integrated with each other. Part of what follows argues that much of what is best in that effort can be brought together most productively and coherently within a Marxist framework, which also allows for further insights. This is not to say that only Marxists can say interesting things about Whitman. My many references to the contributions of non-Marxist scholars should make my position on this clear.

In what follows I sometimes pursue insights suggested by others, and often attempt a synthesis of diverse contributions, sources which I readily acknowledge. There are cases, of course, in which I challenge past interpretations of Whitman, Martí, James and Mir and of the relationship between some of them, including those of influential specialists such as Julio Ramos, Laura Lomas and Donald E. Pease, among others. I have similarly sought to specify the relationship of my argument with those of important predecessors such as Newton Arvin (in the 1930s), Betsy Erkkila, Ed Folsom and M. Wynn Thomas, for example. In order to facilitate the exposition, in some cases this work is carried out in the notes to the main text.

In the case of José Martí, besides the English version, I provide the Spanish original if the passage quoted has been the object of different and disputed readings, if I felt that much was lost in translation or if consulting the original source would be difficult for most readers. In all cases I indicate the location in his *Obras Completas*. I have not provided the Spanish original for some texts that are readily available on the Internet, such as his articles on the Brooklyn Bridge, Coney Island, among others, unless the conditions regarding to divergent readings or unavoidable loss in translation apply.

Little did the author suspect that between the completion of the bulk of this text and its publication, a major movement would arise in the United States to protest police and other abuses against African Americans and other communities, to be followed by the election of Donald Trump to the presidency and the renewed visibility of racist and white-supremacist groups. These events include a reignited debate on the memory and the legacy in the United States of slavery, the Confederacy, the Civil War, Emancipation, segregation, and more mutedly, of the defeat of Reconstruction. These issues are all too present in what follows.[8] Whitman's life and work cannot be separated from them, nor was he oblivious to them: quite the contrary, more often than not he engaged them consciously and actively. I can only hope that these unforeseen changes in the present political and social context add interest to this exploration of Whitman and his Caribbean interlocutors and hope, as well, that this study, in turn, makes a contribution, however small, to the renewed struggle for justice.

I wish to thank Danny Hayward of the Historical Materialism Series for his help and patience in the final preparation of this text.

---

8   These words, written in January 2018, referred to the protests sparked by the police assassination of Michael Brown in Ferguson, Missouri, and the rise of the Black Lives Matter movement. As this text is readied for publication, the global protests against racism in response to the assassination of George Floyd in Minneapolis have posed these issues in a wider, sharper, and more urgent fashion.

CHAPTER 1

Marx and the 'Transformation of History into World History'

Marx was an anti-capitalist thinker. As far as it goes, this statement is undoubtedly true. It describes a dimension of his thought without which it would be impossible to make any sense of his life and work. But it does not go far enough if we wish to grasp his unique place in the evolution of the socialist critique of capitalist civilisation. For that, we need to recall that capitalism, for Marx, brutal and destructive as he deemed it to be, was also a creative, enabling, and, if compared to previous forms of exploitation, a liberating force.

For him, two characteristics set capitalism apart from previous class societies: the immersion of all social relations in the circuits of commodity production and exchange, and the tendency toward a constant development of humanity's productive potential. The relationship that according to Marx existed between these characteristics of capitalism need not detain us now: we will return to it later. Let us simply underline the resulting features that Marx singled out as key components of capitalism's revolutionary drive: the relentless undermining of relations of personal dependence, as well as of inherited customs, rituals and traditions; the constant transformation of the material basis of production and, thus, of all human activity, including the creation of a new type of urban experience; the unprecedented extension of science and its practical applications; the creation of new and more varied needs, even among the exploited; the consolidation, on the basis of ever more effective means of transportation and communication, of a truly international economy and, with it, of material and intellectual exchanges between formerly unconnected cultures. This transformation brought forth a type of human being that had never existed before: what the young Marx called 'a world-historical individual'.

Capitalism, Marx explained, dissolves 'fixed personal (historic) relations of dependence'.[1] It shatters 'fixed, fast-frozen relations' along 'with their train of ancient and venerable prejudices'.[2] Under its impact, 'patriarchal', 'ancient',

---

1 Marx 1993, p. 156.
2 Marx and Engels [1848], p. 487.

'feudal' conditions decompose.³ Loyalties 'resting on blood ties or on ... master-servant relations'⁴ disintegrate. Individuals are no longer 'imprisoned within a certain definition, as feudal lord and vassal, landlord and serf, etc., or as members of a caste ... [or] estate'.⁵ Pre-capitalist societies separated themselves from existing forms of production and consumption slowly and incompletely. Capitalism, by way of contrast, cannot 'exist without constantly revolutionizing the means of production' and it cannot revolutionise the means of production without unsettling 'the relations of production, and with them the whole relations of society'.⁶ Marx minced no words: capitalism 'has accomplished wonders far surpassing Egyptian pyramids, Roman aqueducts, and Gothic cathedrals; it has conducted expeditions that put in the shade all former Exoduses of nations and crusades'.⁷ It had made possible the 'universal development of the forces of production'.⁸ Only thus had humanity discovered its true productive and scientific potential: capitalism had been 'the first to show what man's activity can bring about'.⁹ Capitalism, Marx proclaimed, 'has created more massive and more colossal productive forces than have all preceding generations together. Subjection of nature's forces to man, application of chemistry to industry and agriculture, steam navigation, railways, electric telegraphs, clearing of whole continents for cultivation, canalization of rivers, whole populations conjured out of the ground – what earlier century had even a presentiment that such productive forces slumbered in the lap of social labour?'¹⁰

Change, under capitalism, is not a one-time occurrence, but constant. 'Modern industry', Marx explained, 'never views or treats the existing forms of a production process as the definitive one. Its technical basis is therefore revolutionary, whereas all earlier modes of production were essentially conservative'.¹¹ Capitalist production develops the social division of labour to unprecedented levels of complexity. It creates a 'totality of real kinds of labour, of which no single one is any longer predominant'.¹² This constant transformation of production and the complex articulation of different activities within a deep-

---

3   Marx 1993, p. 158.
4   Marx 1993, p. 161.
5   Marx 1993, p. 163.
6   Marx and Engels [1848], p. 487.
7   Marx and Engels [1848], p. 487.
8   Marx 1993, p. 540.
9   Marx and Engels [1848], p. 487.
10 Marx and Engels [1848], p. 489.
11 Marx 1977, p. 617.
12 Marx 1993, p. 104.

ening division of labour require and create a new kind of labourer: 'large-scale industry, by its very nature, necessitates variation of labour, fluidity of functions, and mobility of the worker in all directions'.[13]

For Marx, writing in the late 1850s, the supreme example of economic expansion, technical innovation, and of the articulation of different activities in an intricate division of labour was none other than the United States: 'We can see this versatility, this perfect indifference towards the particular content of work and the free transition from one branch of industry to the next, most obviously in North America, where the development of wage-labour has been relatively untrammeled by the vestiges of the guild system, etc'.[14] For Marx, the United States was the best example of a 'totality' of different kinds of labour 'in which no single one is any longer predominant'. It was, for him, 'the most modern form of existence of bourgeois society': 'Indifference towards any specific kind of labor', he argued, 'presupposes a very developed totality of real kinds of labour, of which no single one is any longer predominant ... Such a state of affairs is at its most developed in the most modern form of existence of bourgeois society – in the United States'.[15]

Marx agreed with, and derived some of his ideas from, de Tocqueville's *Democracy in America*, which presented the United States as the land of variability of occupations, of openness to innovation, and of a conception of progress as an incessant process. In the United States, argued de Tocqueville, 'One comes across men who have been by turn lawyers, farmers, businessmen, ministers of the Gospel, doctors. If the American has less skill than the European in each particular craft, there is almost no skill which is entirely foreign to him'.[16] Thus, he added, 'They are no more attached to one way of working than any other; they do not feel more tied to an old than a new method'.[17] Americans, he explained, 'consider society as a body making progress, humanity as a changing picture in which nothing is ... permanently fixed and they acknowledge that what they hold as good today may be replaced tomorrow by something better that is as yet hidden'.[18] For Marx, such was the outlook nurtured by *capitalism*. There was nothing inherently 'American' about it, even if, as he also argued, the United States embodied it in its purest, most vibrant form.

---

13   Marx 1977, p. 617.
14   Marx 1977, p. 1034.
15   Marx 1993, p. 104.
16   Tocqueville 2003, p. 474.
17   Tocqueville 2003, p. 474.
18   Tocqueville 2003, p. 439.

Capitalism transforms production incessantly while also promoting the 'expansion of existing consumption', the emergence of '*new* needs'.[19] It does away with the 'traditional, confined, complacent, encrusted satisfaction of present needs, and reproductions of old ways of life'.[20] It creates not only a more complex network of 'different kinds of production' but also a parallel 'constantly enriched system of needs'.[21] Past societies, argued Marx, condemned humans to 'local and national seclusion and self-sufficiency',[22] to 'national onesidedness and narrow-mindedness'.[23] They gave life a 'limited national, religious, political character'.[24] Capitalism joins 'loosely connected provinces' into 'one nation, with one government, one code of laws, one national class-interest, one frontier and one customs-tariff'.[25] But it does not stop there: such jurisdictions crystallise within an expanding *world* market. Capitalism consolidates 'universal intercourse founded upon the mutual dependency of mankind'.[26] 'The need of a constantly expanding market', Marx argued, 'chases the bourgeoisie over the whole surface of the globe'.[27] It develops 'intercourse in every direction' and with it, the 'universal inter-dependence of nations'.[28] It gives 'a cosmopolitan character to production and consumption in every country'.[29] This cosmopolitan, 'universalizing tendency' distinguishes capitalism 'from all previous stages of production'.[30] As a result of this 'in place of the old wants, satisfied by the production of the country, we find new wants, requiring for their satisfaction the products of distant lands and climes'.[31]

Driven by forces we shall later discuss, capitalism is thus pushed into the path of an unceasing transformation of both production and consumption, of constant technological innovation and geographical expansion. Marx summarised the process and the resulting 'cultivation' of a new type of 'many-sided' human being:

---

19 Marx 1993, p. 408.
20 Marx 1993, p. 410.
21 Marx 1993, p. 409.
22 Marx and Engels [1848], p. 488.
23 Marx and Engels [1848], p. 488.
24 Marx 1993, p. 488.
25 Marx and Engels [1848], p. 489.
26 Marx [1853a], p. 225.
27 Marx and Engels [1848], p. 487.
28 Marx and Engels [1848], p. 488.
29 Marx and Engels [1848], p. 488.
30 Marx 1993, p. 540.
31 Marx and Engels [1848], p. 488.

> Hence exploration of all of nature in order to discover new, useful qualities in things; universal exchange of the products of all alien climates and lands; new (artificial) preparation of natural objects ... The exploration of the earth in all directions ...; the development ... of the natural sciences to their highest point; likewise the discovery, creation and satisfaction of new needs ...; the cultivation of all the qualities of the social human being, ... – production of this [human] being as the most total and universal possible social product, for, in order to take gratification in a many-sided way, he must be capable of many pleasures, hence cultured to a high degree.[32]

Universal material intercourse cannot but bring forth universal intellectual ferment: 'as in material, so also in intellectual production'.[33] The *Manifesto* thus rushed to celebrate how 'from the numerous national and local literatures there arises a world literature'.[34]

Now all nations and peoples come to depend 'on the revolutions of the others'.[35] The term 'revolution' here refers not so much to political rebellions as to productive and commercial upheavals. A new machine in England has an immediate impact on India. Such an invention ceases to be a local or a national event. It 'becomes a world-historical fact',[36] just as the troubles produced by the absence of sugar and coffee from the world market during the Napoleonic wars demonstrated the 'world-historical importance' of these commodities.[37] It is, therefore, with capitalism that one may first truly speak, argued Marx, of human history becoming 'world history'.[38] Capitalism, he argued, 'produced world history for the first time, in so far as it made all civilized nations and every individual ... dependent for the satisfaction of their wants on the whole world, thus destroying the former natural exclusiveness of separate nations'.[39] This growing interdependence implied the emergence of a new type of individual: 'world-historical, empirically universal individuals in place of local ones'.[40] This individual's universality is not a result of their intellectual elaborations, cosmic visions, or imaginative energies. Rather, it resides in the fabric of the material relations that underlie human life under an increasingly cosmopolitan capit-

---

32 Marx 1993, p. 409.
33 Marx and Engels [1848], p. 488.
34 Marx and Engels [1848], p. 488.
35 Marx and Engels [1845], p. 49.
36 Marx and Engels [1845], p. 51.
37 Marx and Engels [1845], p. 51.
38 Marx and Engels [1845], p. 51.
39 Marx and Engels [1845], p. 73.
40 Marx and Engels [1845], p. 49.

alism: the 'transformation of history into world history is by no means a mere abstract act on the part of "self-consciousness", the world spirit, or any other metaphysical spectre, but a quite material, empirically verifiable act, an act the proof of which every individual furnishes as he comes and goes, eats, drinks, and clothes himself'.[41]

Even the proletariat, the collective agent called upon by Marx to replace capitalism, was an exploited class like no other before it: versatile and adaptable to an ever-changing labour process, forced to sell its labour power to the capitalist class, but not bound to any particular employer, free to determine how to spend its wages and driven to collective independent action to defend its interests, it was as active and as full of initiative as its antagonist. If in the proletariat capital creates its gravedigger, it does so after its own dynamic image. Young Marx and Engels thus explained that 'communism is for us not ... an *ideal* to which reality [will] have to adjust itself. We call communism the real movement which abolishes the present state of things. The conditions of this movement result from the now existing premise'.[42] That premise is 'the universal development of productive forces and the world intercourse bound with them'.[43]

Marx felt that the world created by capital demanded a new type of 'imagination' from the artist.[44] He asked his readers if classical Greek art, or Shakespeare, are 'possible with self-acting spindles and railways and locomotives and electrical telegraphs? ... What becomes of Fama alongside Printing House Square?'[45] Is 'Achilles possible with powder and lead? Or the *Iliad* with the printing press, not to mention the printing machine? Do not the song and the saga and the muse necessarily come to an end with the printer's bar, hence do not the necessary conditions of epic poetry vanish?'[46] The world of self-acting spindles, locomotives, and electrical telegraphs, of powder and lead and the printing press would thus require a new poetry. The following chapter explores how *Leaves of Grass* and many of Whitman's prose works bear witness to his agreement with Marx's conclusion.

41 Marx and Engels [1845], p. 51.
42 Marx and Engels [1845], p. 49.
43 Marx and Engels [1845], p. 49.
44 Marx 1993, p. 110.
45 Marx 1993, p. 110.
46 Marx 1993, p. 111.

CHAPTER 2

'Within Me Latitude Widens, Longitude Lengthens': Whitman and the World Created by Capital

The preceding chapter considered some key features of the world created and of the processes unleashed by capitalism as described by Marx: the creation of 'massive and ... colossal productive forces'; the interlocking of the world through 'steam navigation, railways, [and] electric telegraphs'; the 'clearing of whole continents for cultivation'; the increase 'of the urban population as compared with the rural'; the conjuring 'of whole populations ... out of the ground'; the creation of a 'totality of real kinds of labor, of which no single one is ... predominant'; 'the variation of labor' and 'fluidity of [its] functions'; the 'mobility of the worker in all directions'; the lumping together of 'loosely connected provinces' into 'one nation, with one government, one code of laws, one national class interest, one frontier and one custom tariff'; the increasingly 'cosmopolitan character' of production and consumption; the growth of 'intercourse in every direction'; the end of 'national seclusion and self-sufficiency'; the 'universal interdependence of nations'; the emergence of a truly *world* history, and of an individual connected by material threads to events and processes in the farthest corners of the world.

What is this world, if not the world of *Leaves of Grass*? Whatever else it may be, what is *Leaves of Grass* if not also the song of that nascent 'world-historical individual' described by Marx? What is it that 'widens' within Whitman, 'a kosmos, of Manhattan the son', if not that 'totality of labors, of which no single one is ... predominant', if not that 'variation of labor', the 'fluidity of [its] functions' and the 'mobility of the worker in all directions'; if not the growth of 'intercourse in every direction' and the increasingly 'cosmopolitan character' of production and consumption, on the basis of expanding 'steam navigation, railways, [and] electric telegraphs'? Of course, Whitman's poetry cannot be reduced to this.[1] But neither is this one feature of his work among many: it is from its tapping into the experience made possible by capitalism that his verse draws its unprecedented energy, its restless rhythm, its defiance of pre-

---

1 Reduction is probably not the right word, since, far from reducing, this description can only expand its reach and significance far beyond the experience of life in the United States.

vious limits and prescriptions. *Leaves of Grass* was itself an accumulative text, repeatedly reconfigured over several decades, which only ceased evolving with the poet's death.

While Whitman wrote and rewrote *Leaves of Grass* from 1850 to 1890, the United States was also remade as a nascent capitalist industrial power. This transformation, the outcome of momentous class struggles and shifts, included four major chapters, as discussed by Charles Post: (1) the transition from the domination of merchant/bank capital (which made profit connecting slave, artisan and small-farmer production to the world market and each other) to the domination of manufacturing capital linked to the transformation of artisan into industrial production and the subordination of the small farmer to market imperatives (including growing technical innovation and crop specialisation); (2) the growing clash of northern manufacturing capital and the market agriculture that provided its internal market (both as buyer of manufactured goods and as a provider of materials to be processed) with the territorial expansion of the South's slave-based economy, a clash rehearsed in the conflicts over the organisation of the new states and territories to the West (1820–60) and settled through the Civil War (1860–65); (3) the Civil War itself, leading to (4) the accelerated expansion of industrial capitalism in the North (after 1865) and the clash over the social and economic reorganisation of the South (1865–75), which concluded with the establishment, not of capitalist or small-farmer production, but of a new form of semi-capitalist exploitation (share-cropping) and of institutionalised racism (after 1875).

New York, the birthplace of *Leaves of Grass*, was at the centre of these transformations: as the main hub of merchant capital, which remained dominant until the 1840s, with major commercial links to the South; as a major port, linking internal producers to each other and to external markets; as the site of an early process of 'metropolitan industrialisation', from the 1830s on; and as the home of far-reaching and unprecedented concentrations of capital, after the Civil War.[2]

Whitman once described *Leaves of Grass* as the result of his life in Brooklyn and New York between 1838 and 1855 (two separate cities at the time), or, in his words, of 'absorbing a million people for fifteen years'.[3] *Leaves of Grass*, he explained in 1888, grew out 'of the multitudinousness, vitality, and the unprecedented stimulants of to-day and here'.[4] This poetry of 'to-day and here' was

---

2 The concept of 'metropolitan industrialization' is elaborated in Wilentz 2004, Chapter 3.
3 Bucke 1970, p. 67. For New York in this period see Wilentz 2004 and Spann 1981.
4 'A Backward Glance o'er Travel'd Roads', p. 661.

very much the poetry of the emergent capitalist metropolis.[5] By the 1850s, New York harbour had become the centre of one of the world's major industrial zones, a region that included eleven counties located in three states: New York, New Jersey and Connecticut.[6] By the 1840s it 'was probably the fastest-growing large industrial area in the world'.[7] Manhattan, itself the site of important industrial activities, was the most significant point of shipment and arrival of goods to and from Europe. Without shedding past functions, the mercantile city was becoming an industrial city. It was undergoing a process of 'metropolitan industrialisation' that implied the combination and coexistence of both machine and hand-tool industrial production with the putting-out system and small workshops as well as artisan activity.[8] During this period the New York area, including the Jersey shore, became the chief centre of eastern steamboat development.[9] New York State became the state with most railroad mileage.[10] Its ports received most immigrants into the United States. Wall Street was already a key credit and banking hub. Manhattan was a major media centre, as a publishing platform of newspapers, magazines, and books. It had the daily with the largest public in the world, the *New York Tribune*, with 200,000 readers (Karl Marx was one of its correspondents).[11] In 1860 it had close to one million inhabitants, more than 20 of the 33 states of the Union at the time.[12]

As early as 1842, as editor of the daily *New York Aurora*, young Whitman had proclaimed: 'New York is a great place – a mighty world in itself'. He added:

---

5   As Andrew Lawson has pointed out, 'Whitman identifies with the multitudinous acts of exchange he sees going on around him: what fascinates him is the dynamic movement of persons and things in the marketplace'. Lawson 2006, p. 13. Jill Wacker points out that Whitman's early pieces as editor of the *New York Aurora* in 1842 were already 'observations on city life, garnered from the many strolls ... he took outside of his newspaper office in Lower Manhattan'. Wacker 1994, p. 87. For a similar point Stacy 2008, p. 57.
6   Spann 1981, p. 402.
7   Wilentz 2004, p. 107.
8   Wilentz 2004, p. 112.
9   Taylor 1968, p. 58.
10 Taylor 1968, p. 79.
11 Ledbetter (ed.) 2007, pp. xvii–xviii. An interesting question: Did Whitman ever read Marx? It is very hard to think he did not. Whitman was an assiduous reader of the press. He was also interested in a very wide range of topics, including those pertaining to current affairs and debates. The *New York Tribune* had the largest circulation in New York. Marx wrote 350 articles for the *Tribune* between 1852 and 1862, plus twelve more he co-authored with Engels. It is hard to think Whitman never came across any of these articles. Ledbetter (ed.) 2007, p. xviii.
12 Spann 1981, pp. 121, 402, 405. For a summary description of New York around the time of publication of *Leaves of Grass*, see 'Metropolis', chapter 15 of Spann's book. Spann 1981, pp. 401–27.

'Here are people of all classes and stages of rank – from all countries on the globe – engaged in all the varieties of avocations – of every grade, every hue, of ignorance and learning, morality and vice, wealth and want, fashion and coarseness, breeding and brutality, elevation and degradation, impudence and modesty'.[13] A week later, he was back on the topic: '"our city" is the great place of the western continent, the heart, the brain, the focus, the main spring, the pinnacle, the extremity, the no more beyond, of the New World'.[14] The young Whitman was thus the first to proclaim the centrality for his work of a new type of city which was itself central to the rise of the new world capitalist economy. It was an expanding universe: Brooklyn almost doubled in size between 1846 and 1847, two years that Whitman spent as editor of the *Brooklyn Eagle*.[15] Since that time, he had a sense of ongoing transformation. Steamships that had been a sensation five years before, he remarked in 1847, now went unnoticed: 'Steam navigation has made a monstrous stride within the time above mentioned'. That year he witnessed the launching of the vessel *Washington*, the first American transatlantic steamer.[16]

New York/Brooklyn was fundamental to Whitman in at least five ways, as the site of: (1) diverse, interdependent, concurrent, incessant activities; (2) ever-changing productive forces (means of production, transportation, communication and trade); (3) the cultivation of new tastes and forms of consumption; (4) the emergence of new types of human contact and interaction; and (5) the crystallisation of a key hub of an expanding world market. Whitman was enthralled with the movement of city life, the ebb and flow of the crowded streets.[17] He was captivated by the railroad, the steamboat and the telegraph: inventions that enabled the transformation of hitherto unconnected regions into provinces of an emergent world economy.[18] He was especially attracted to harbours and docks, where ships connected his city of residence to the rest of

---

13   Whitman [1842], p. 17.
14   Whitman [1842a], p. 19.
15   Brasher 1970, p. 65.
16   Brasher 1970, pp. 54, 55. The New York-New Jersey area was the centre of eastern steamboat construction between 1815 and 1860.
17   Whitman, as Chaffin has argued, 'was the first major American poet to affirm the city as a proper subject of romantic poetry – of any poetry, for that matter'. Chaffin 1977, p. 119. The relationship of the city and the young Whitman is ably discussed in Chapter 5 of Kaplan's well-known biography. Kaplan 2003, pp. 95–113.
18   Allen has pointed out that the key years in the composition of *Leaves of Grass*, 1850 to 1855, were a period of feverish prosperity in both New York and Brooklyn. Allen 1955, p. 106. This rapid expansion was brought to a halt by the crisis of 1857.

the world, while buses and ferries were among his favorite points of observation. The latter in particular – the ferries connecting Brooklyn and New York and Camden and Philadelphia, the two sets of adjacent cities separated by rivers where he spent much of his life – became for him exciting vantage points: ferries allowed him to both immerse himself in the moving crowd while simultaneously contemplating the city from a distance as a vast, shifting, urban landscape, with the rim of sail and steamships linking it to countless other cities in the foreground. The moving ferry could bring together the experience of the city street, including the sense of incessant movement, the 'feeling', as one critic has described it, 'of being propelled by a strong and constant artificial force' with the vision of the city as an internally differentiated whole, and the voyages and contacts evoked by the harbour, like no other spot in the urban landscape.[19] It is no coincidence that 'Crossing Brooklyn Ferry' is one of Whitman's masterpieces.[20]

The city, as seen from the ferry, suggests a grand perspective into a wider national and international division of labour within an expanding capitalist economy. Whitman cannot be divorced from the experience enabled by this. This is true not only of his much maligned 'Song of the Exposition', written very rapidly in 1871 as a commission for an industrial exposition, but also of 'Song of Myself', 'A Song for Occupations', 'Starting from Paumanok', 'Song of the Broad-Axe', 'Crossing Brooklyn Ferry', 'Salut au Monde', 'Passage to India', not to mention 'To a Locomotive in Winter', 'Give Me the Splendid, Silent Sun', 'Mannahatta', among many other texts.

Whitman himself invited us to seek in his poetry 'the broad show of artificial things, ships, machinery, politics, creeds, modern improvements, and the interchange of nations'.[21] The list bears repetition: artificial things, modern improvements, ships, machinery, and 'interchange' of nations. These are perfect keywords for the new world created by capital, as described by Marx in the first pages of the *Manifesto*. 'The shapes arise!' Whitman tells us in 'Song of the Broad-Axe':

> Shapes of factories, arsenals, foundries, markets,
> Shapes of the two-threaded tracks of railroads,
> Shapes of the sleepers of bridges, vast frameworks, girders, arches,

---

19 The quote is from Geffen 1984, p. 7. On Whitman and the New York ferries see Chapter 4 of Thomas 1987, pp. 91–116.
20 As early as 1847 Whitman wrote an article for the *Brooklyn Eagle* entitled 'Philosophy of Ferries'. Whitman [1847c], pp. 159–66.
21 'I Was Looking a Long While', pp. 512–13.

> Shapes of the fleets of barges, tows, lake and canal craft, river craft,
> Ship-yards and dry-docks, along the Eastern and Western seas, and in many a bay and by-place,[22]

The poet proclaims in 'A Song for Occupations' that he will sing of 'manufactures ... commerce ... engineering ... the building of cities, and every trade carried on there ... and the implements of every trade'.[23] Whitman invites us to see in his poems 'cities, solid, vast, inland, with paved streets, with iron and stone edifices, cease-less vehicles, and commerce'. See, he commands us, 'steamers steaming through my poems':[24]

> See the many-cylinder'd steam printing-press – see the electric telegraph stretching across the continent,
> ...
> See, the strong and quick locomotive as it departs, panting, blowing the steam whistle,
> See ploughmen ploughing farms – see miners digging mines – see the numberless factories,
> See mechanics busy at their benches with tools[25]

There is a pleasure in gazing at, or rather imagining, this vast elaborate landscape of interdependent pursuits, 'of which', in Marx's words, 'no single one is ... predominant'. Four typically Whitmanian verses include references to nine occupations:

> The clean hair'd Yankee girl works with her sewing-machine or in the factory or mill,
> The paving-man leans on his two-handed rammer, the reporter's lead flies swiftly over the note-book, the sign-painter is lettering with blue and gold,
> The canal boy trots on the tow-path, the book-keeper counts at his desk, the shoemaker waxes his thread,

---

22 'Song of the Broad-Axe', p. 339.
23 'A Song for Occupations', p. 95.
24 'Starting from Paumanok', p. 187.
25 'Starting from Paumanok' 187. In an editorial of the *Brooklyn Eagle*, dated 13 October 1847 and titled 'The Current Exhibition at Castle Garden', the young journalist proclaimed 'That new and powerful steam-engine, alone, is an almost sublime subject for observation'. Quoted in Brasher 1970, p. 44.

> The conductor beats time for the band and all the performers follow him,[26]

Whitman constructs his poetic voice as part of that 'interlink'd' landscape. He is but an individual sum of those social relations:

> And these tend inward to me, and I tend outward to them,
> And such as it is to be of these more or less I am,
> And of these one and all I weave the song of myself.[27]

This is the song of the 'totality of labors', to use Marx's phrase: 'I hear America singing, the varied carols I hear', the poet proclaims, and in the following six verses he mentions seven crafts: mechanics, carpenters, masons, boatmen, deck hands, woodcutters, and ploughboys plus 'the young wife at work' and the 'girl sewing or washing'.[28] Or take the list which precedes his affirmation quoted above that 'all these tend inward to me', a catalogue which includes singers ('contraltos'), carpenters, pilots, deacons, 'spinning girls', farmers, machinists, reformers, deckhands, pavingmen, 'canal-boys', conductors, drivers, peddlers, prostitutes, opium eaters, fare collectors, flatboatmen, crews of the fishing boats, and floormen. Or take Section 5 of 'A Song for Occupations', where Whitman's verse moves briskly over home-building, blacksmithing, glass-blowing, tin-roofing, dock-building, fish-curing, stone-cutting, coach-making, boiler-making, distilling, electroplating, electrotyping, among other activities – the dominance of the present participle giving a sense of ongoing movement – as well as coal mines, ironworks, blast furnaces, 'great mills and factories', breweries, sugarhouses, flour works among other productive installations.[29] The 'I' in the 'Song of Myself' is 'weaved' from all of these. Whitman's poetic voice dwells with each, but not for long. It embraces all, but is not permanently attached to any.

Whitman imagines himself as an engineer: 'O the engineer's joys! / to go with a locomotive!' As a fireman: 'O the fireman's joys! / I hear the alarm at dead

---

26 'Song of Myself', pp. 201–2.
27 'Song of Myself', p. 203.
28 'I Hear America Singing', p. 174.
29 Newton Arvin pointed out long ago that Whitman was the poet of 'process, of movement, of endless becoming and growth'. His verses were full of 'things "rocking", "gliding", "tossing", "ascending", "soaring", etc'. Whitman was in love with 'the mobile and the mutable'. While Arvin largely attributes this dynamic vision to the impact of nineteenth-century science, we would argue it was far more directly nurtured by the incessant renovations and transformations of capitalist expansion. Arvin 1938, pp. 256, 257.

of night'. As a miner and iron worker: 'O to work in mines, or forging iron'.[30] He goes on to the 'farmer's joys', the 'whaleman's joys', the 'orator's joys', in a series too long to summarise. His voice takes on a fluid identity that can be imagined on the basis of the 'variation of labour', the 'fluidity of functions', the 'mobility of the worker in all directions',[31] the 'free transition from one branch of industry to the next',[32] which Marx described as the product of capitalist industry and as 'a historic product of the United States'.[33] This ample web of differentiated labours gives Whitman's voice its distinctive combination of concreteness and vastness. 'My ties and ballasts', he announces in 'Song of Myself', 'leave me, my elbows rest in sea-gaps / I skirt sierras, my palms cover continents, I am afoot with my vision'. This is followed by yet another list of different pursuits (camping with lumbermen, weeding, hoeing, crossing savannas, trailing in forests, prospecting, gold-digging, girdling trees, hauling boats):[34] Whitman's vision is that of the vast 'totality of labors' described by Marx, of a vast network of interconnected and differentiated labours. In a poem first included in *Leaves of Grass* in 1871 the poet insists in his fluid persona: 'Myself effusing and fluid, a phantom curiously floating, now here absorbed and arrested' as he watches a knife-sharpener at work.[35]

Many stretches of the poet's early life were not far from this dynamic, as Whitman went from one occupation to another: office boy, clerk, schoolteacher, several occupations in the print trades (typesetter, compositor) and the publishing business (journalist, columnist, editor), manager of a book and stationery store, while trying his hand at carpentry and house painting and public lecturing. This enumeration similarly reminds us of the 'variation', 'fluidity' and 'mobility' of labour under capitalism, as described by Marx, and of de Tocqueville's description quoted in Chapter 1.[36] This process, which Marx described as 'a historic product of the United States', enabled a form of representation that we have learned to recognise as Whitmanian – the type of enumeration formulated from a perspective improbably mixing the imagination of the poet and the meticulousness of a census-taker.

---

30 'Song of Joys', pp. 323, 324, 326.
31 Marx 1977, p. 617.
32 Marx 1977, p. 1034.
33 Marx 1993, p. 105.
34 'Song of Myself', p. 219.
35 'Sparkles from the Wheel', p. 514.
36 Andrew Lawson suggests as much, we think, when he writes: 'This fluid self ... is a feature of a market society characterized by the notion of exchange'. Lawson 2006, p. 2. For an insightful discussion of Whitman and the dynamics of market exchange, different but compatible with our argument here, see Lawson 2006, p. 14.

During the Civil War, the third-floor window of Whitman's residence in Washington D.C. became the observation post from which he attempted to encompass the life of a human collective split into different but interconnected activities, in this case an army camp that emerges in a nearby field as a temporary miniature city:

> The little wall-tents and shelter tents spring up quickly. I see the fires already blazing, and pots and kettles over them. Some among the men are driving tent-poles, wielding their axes with strong, slow blows. I see great huddles of horses, bundles of hay, groups of men ... a few officers, piles of wood ... The smoke streams upward, additional men arrive and dismount – some drive in stakes, and tie their horses to them; some go with buckets for water, some are chopping wood, and so on.[37]

Whitman wants us to share his joy in observing a 'hundred little things going on':

> Still the camp opposite – perhaps fifty or sixty tents. Some of the men are cleaning their sabers ... some brushing boots, some laving off, reading, writing – some cooking, some sleeping. On long temporary cross-sticks back of the tents are cavalry accoutrements – blankets and overcoats are hung out to air – there are squads of horses tether'd ... I sit long in my third story window and look at the scene – a hundred little things going on.[38]

To grasp the whole panorama of the many 'little things going on', to capture what a critic has called 'the all-encompassing power of the panoramic': this is what Whitman sought to do with the city and the vast network of market-connected varied labours, of the industry and trade of which it was part.[39] This perspective is also anticipated in some passages of Whitman's earlier writings. As early as 1842, he had referred to what he called his 'observative mood' and the search for a vantage point from which the city could be contemplated as a vast, rushing spectacle. The young editor thus informed his readers that 'on an afternoon ... as we sauntered out of the west gate of the Park, feeling in an observative mood, we recollected an old custom of ours ... – we went up the stairs of the American Museum, entered the first room, took a chair ... – and in

---

37 Whitman [1882], p. 730.
38 Whitman [1882], p. 730.
39 Wacker 1994, p. 87.

that chair ensconced we ourselves. Out before us was the busiest spectacle this busy city may present. One mighty rush of men, business, carts, carriages, and clang'.[40]

In 1846, he similarly praised the area around Fort Greene in Brooklyn, which he wanted to save from demolition, as a place from which the viewer could contemplate 'the metropolis like a map beyond'.[41] Jill Wacker has correctly pointed out that for Whitman, 'views were the inalienable right of the average city-dweller', and that he sought 'the higher ground as a spot from which one ... could behold the workings of the world's greatest capitalist city and derive pleasure from it'.[42] Beyond his early years, this possibility of contemplating the intricate web of activities characteristic of the modern metropolis was always to retain its appeal for Whitman.

But Whitman did not only cherish mapping the metropolis from an all-encompassing vantage point. He similarly celebrated the direct experience of the city street and sidewalk, the diversity and excitement of which he contrasted to the isolation of rural spaces. Whitman famously described himself as 'a kosmos, of Manhattan the son', 'One of the roughs', as the verse had originally proclaimed. He is the proud, defiant, street-smart, son of the modern metropolis 'hurrying with the modern crowd as eager and fickle as any'.[43] Whitman, as Justin Kaplan has pointed out, refused to 'sentimentalise' country life, which he associated with incessant toil, isolation and ignorance.[44] Indeed, some of his descriptions of rural life make Marx's references to 'rural idiocy' seem mild by comparison. In an 1840 letter written in rural Long Island, he despaired: 'Down in these parts, people understand as much of political economy as they do the Choctaw language. I never met with such complete, unqualified, infernal jackasses, in all my life'.[45]

By way of contrast, Whitman described himself as 'Looking in at the shop-windows of Broadway the whole forenoon'.[46] In 1846 he had already described Broadway as 'a fascinating chaos'.[47] 'This is the city', he proclaims in 'Song of

---

40 Whitman [1842b], p. 26.
41 Whitman [1846], p. 49.
42 Wacker 1994, p. 91.
43 'Song of Myself', p. 223.
44 Kaplan 2003, p. 157.
45 Stacy 2008, p. 24.
46 'Song of Myself', p. 222. Describing the streets of New York in 1846, Whitman commented: 'activity never flags. Surely there can be no town on earth that has less of a sleepy look than that. It is always "wide awake", and the throbbings of its pulse beat forever'. 'Gayety of Americans' (September, 23 1846), quoted in Brasher 1970, p. 40.
47 Whitman [1846b], p. 142.

Myself', 'and I am one of the citizens': 'Whatever interests the rest interests me, politics, wars, markets, newspapers, schools, / The mayor and the councils, banks, tariffs, steamships, factories, stocks, stores, real estate and personal estate'.[48] It is to the 'mighty, many-threaded wealth and industry', the 'complicated business genius' gathered there that he attributed his realisation 'that not Nature alone is great ... but ... the work of man ... is equally great'. In *Democratic Vistas* Whitman explains:

> The splendor, the picturesqueness, and oceanic amplitude and rush of these great cities ... the lofty new buildings, facades of marble and iron ... the endless ships, the tumultuous streets, Broadway, the heavy, low, musical roar, hardly ever intermitted, even at night; the jobbers' houses, the rich shops, the wharves, the great Central Park, and the Brooklyn Park of hills ... – the assemblages of the citizens in their groups, conversations, trades, evening amusements, or along the by-quarters – these, I say, and the like of these, completely satisfy my senses of power, fulness, motion ... and give me, through such senses and appetites, and through my esthetic conscience, a continued exaltation and absolute fulfilment. Always and more and more, as I cross the East and North rivers, the ferries, or with the pilots in their pilot-houses, or pass an hour in Wall street, or the gold exchange, I realize ... that not Nature alone is great in her fields of freedom and the open air ... – but in the artificial, the work of man too is equally great – in this profusion of teeming humanity – in these ingenuities, streets, goods, houses, ships – these hurrying, feverish, electric crowds of men, their complicated business genius ... and all this mighty, many-threaded wealth and industry concentrated here.[49]

The 'many-threaded wealth and industry': the notion, and the whole passage, cannot but remind us of Marx's description of capitalism as a 'comprehensive system of different kinds of labour' to which a 'constantly enriched system of needs corresponds'.[50] Indeed, this passage celebrates what Marx described

---

48 'Song of Myself', p. 235. Emerson reacted favourably to the first edition of *Leaves of Grass*. In some passages of his own writings he had suggested a similar wish to join the 'resounding tumult' of the world: 'The world – this shadow of the soul, or *other me*, lies wide around. Its attractions are the keys which unlock my thoughts and make me acquainted with myself. I launch eagerly into this resounding tumult. I grasp the hands of those next me, and take my place in the ring to suffer and to work, taught by an instinct that so shall the dumb abyss be vocal with speech'. Emerson [1837], 58–59.
49 Whitman [1871], pp. 938–9.
50 Marx 1993, p. 409.

as the emergence of an individual 'capable of many pleasures' and of 'gratification in a many-sided way' and of the 'material elements' that make such a 'rich individuality' possible.[51]

Similarly, many sections of Whitman's *Specimen Days*, published in 1882, are descriptions of the life of the city street. The titles are suggestive enough: 'My Passion for Ferries', 'Broadway Sights', 'Omnibus Jaunts and Drivers', 'Manhattan from the Bay', 'Human and Heroic New York', 'Delaware River – Days and Nights', 'Scenes on Ferry and River – Last Winter's Nights', 'The First Spring Day on Chestnut Street', 'Two City Areas, Certain Hours', 'A Fine Afternoon, 4 to 6'.

Whitman characteristically celebrates the crowd of a New York afternoon, 'its countless prodigality of locomotion, dry goods, glitter, magnetism, and happiness'.[52] Describing New York as the 'world's city',[53] he praises its 'great seething oceanic populations'.[54] He similarly celebrates 'the hurrying and vast amplitude' of its 'never-ending human currents'.[55] But he is fascinated not only with Broadway – 'New York's (perhaps the world's,) great thoroughfare'[56] – but also with Chestnut Street in Philadelphia, 'St. Charles street in New Orleans, Tremont street in Boston, and ... Pennsylvania avenue in Washington'.[57] He was, he proclaimed in 'Starting from Paumanok', a 'lover of populous pavements'.[58] He was, as indicated above, particularly attracted by docks and harbours: 'The departing of the big steamers, noons or afternoons – there is no better medicine when one is listless or vapory'.[59] Ferries are the perfect place to feel the pulse of the city as it moves through the day:

> Take a March picture I jotted there two or three weeks since. Afternoon, about 3 ½ o'clock, it begins to snow. There has been a matinee performance at the theater – from 4 ¼ to 5 comes a stream of homeward bound ladies ... [along with them come] ... mothers with bevies of daughters, (a charming sight) – children, countrymen – the railroad men in their blue clothes and caps – all the various characters of the city and country represented or suggested ... Towards six o'clock the human stream gradually thickening – now a pressure of vehicles, drays, piled railroad crates –

---

51 Marx 1993, pp. 409, 325.
52 Whitman [1882], p. 844.
53 Whitman [1882], p. 860.
54 Whitman [1882], p. 823.
55 Whitman [1882], p. 701.
56 Whitman [1882], p. 838.
57 Whitman [1882], p. 838.
58 'Starting from Paumanok' p. 176.
59 Whitman [1882], p. 847.

now a drove of cattle, making quite an excitement ... Inside the reception room, business bargains, flirting, love-making, eclaircissements, proposals.[60]

'All the various characters of the city and country represented or suggested': Whitman's description of the sight at the dock can also double as a description of vast expanses of *Leaves of Grass*. One of Whitman's finest songs to city life is his poem 'Give Me the Splendid Silent Sun'.[61] It opens with a heartfelt celebration of 'rural domestic life', linked to the 'primal sanities' of Nature and protected from the 'noise of the world'. 'Give me', the poet pleads, the 'sun with all his beams full of dazzling', the 'serene-moving animals', 'perfectly quiet nights', 'for marriage a sweet-breathed woman of whom I should never tire' and 'a perfect child'. This passage is followed by tense, confused and confusing verses in which the vision of the city pulls the poet in the opposite direction. By the end of this transition the appeal of the city cannot be resisted. The cries of the poet are 'reversed': 'O I see what I sought to escape, confronting, reversing my cries'. The attempt to flee the city becomes a celebration of it:

> Keep your splendid, silent sun,
> Keep your woods, O Nature, and the quiet places by the woods,
> Keep your fields of clover and timothy, and your corn-fields and orchards,
> Keep the blossoming buckwheat fields where the Ninth-month bees hum,
> Give me faces and streets, give me these phantoms incessant and endless along the trottoirs!
> Give me interminable eyes! – give me women – give me comrades and lovers by the thousand!
> Let me see new ones every day! – let me hold new ones by the hand every day!
> Give me such shows! – give me the streets of Manhattan!
> Give me Broadway, with the soldiers marching – give me the sound of the trumpets and drums!
> ...
> Give me the shores and the wharves heavy-fringed with the black ships!

---

60 Whitman [1882], p. 834. In 1846 Whitman had already commented: 'what mortal could wish a better-managed mode of passage than appertains our Brooklyn ferries'. Whitman [1846b], p. 142.
61 Chaffin 1977, pp. 109–20.

> O such for me! O an intense life, full to repletion, and varied!
> The life of the theatre, bar-room, huge hotel, for me!
> The saloon of the steamer! the crowded excursion for me! the torch-light procession!
> ...
> People, endless, streaming, with strong voices, passions, pageants.
> Manhattan streets, with their powerful throbs, with beating drums, as now,
> The endless and noisy chorus, the rustle and clank of muskets, (even the sight of the wounded,)
> Manhattan crowds, with their turbulent musical chorus!
> Manhattan faces and eyes forever for me.[62]

'Give Me the Splendid Silent Sun' is a war poem, a poem of mobilisation, but this does not detract from our reading: it is the city, as a site of 'intense life, full to repletion, and varied' that Whitman seeks to mobilise. 'Mannahatta' is yet another portrait readers may consult. It contains three typically Whitmanian ingredients: the crowded street, the varied activities concentrated in the city, the movement of the harbour. But a city is never isolated or self-sufficient: it is typically the hub of a wider production and trade system. Manhattan faced both inland and seaward. To the west it drew from the many different agricultural and industrial labours of a nascent American capitalism (with an agro-industrial complex at the centre of its internal market, as discussed by Post).[63] As Whitman describes it in 'Starting from Paumanok':

> Interlink'd, food yielding lands.
> Land of coal and iron! land of gold! land of cotton, sugar, rice!
> Land of wheat, beef, pork! land of wool and hemp! land of the apple and the grape!
> Land of the pastoral plains, the grass-fields of the world![64]

Whitman embraces the steamboat and the railroad, tunnels and canals, and the telegraph, means of welding different regions into parts of a differentiated whole.[65] Like many others, Whitman took the railroad as an 'emblem of

---

62 'Give Me the Splendid Silent Sun', pp. 446–7.
63 Post 2012.
64 'Starting from Paumanok', p. 184.
65 In 1860 the steamer *Great Eastern* arrived in New York. It was five times larger than the next largest existing vessel, a veritable triumph, as Kaplan describes it, of nineteenth-century

the modern'.⁶⁶ Like the ferry, the railroad afforded the opportunity to fuse personal immersion in the modern landscape with the panoramic contemplation of it. Vehicle of quickened life, purveyor of new sensations, it was a machine of imposing size and unprecedented speed and power, and a new type of window into real or imagined landscapes. In *Specimen Days*, published in 1882, Whitman described a voyage west, pulled by a Baldwin locomotive:

> What a fierce weird pleasure to lie in my berth in the luxurious palace-car, drawn by the mighty Baldwin – embodying and filling me, too, full of the swift motion, and most resistless strength! It is late, perhaps midnight or after – distances join'd like magic – as we speed through Harrisburg, Columbus, Indianapolis. The element of danger adds zest to it all. On we go, rumbling and flashing, with our loud whinnies thrown out from time to time, or trumpet-blasts, into the darkness. Passing the homes of men, the farms, barns, cattle – the silent villages.⁶⁷

Whitman does not actually *see* the homes, farms, and villages: he imagines them as 'we fly like lightning through the night', as he also imagines women and children, sleeping in their berths.⁶⁸ In the 1876 poem 'To a Locomotive in Winter', Whitman had similarly described this invention as the '[t]ype of the modern', as an 'emblem of motion and power'. The poem is a song to the locomotive and a declaration that the world created by it demands a new poetry: 'Roll through my chant, with all thy lawless music', the poem demands of this 'Fierce-throated beauty'.⁶⁹

'engineering hubris' (Kaplan 2003, p. 257). Whitman did not allow the event to go unrecorded in the pages of *Leaves of Grass*: 'Nor forget I to sing of the wonder, the ship as she swam up my bay'. 'Year of Meteors', p. 381.

66   In his classic study of the 'transportation revolution' in the United States, Taylor argued that, as the internal economy of the United States expanded over the century, eastern cities, including New York, although to a lesser extent than others, turned inward, or, as he put it, more towards the train station than the docks. Taylor 1968, p. 398.

67   Whitman [1882], p. 851.

68   Whitman [1882], p. 851.

69   'To a Locomotive in Winter', p. 583. Arvin pointed out that in an epoch in which most poets were indifferent or hostile to the machine, Whitman embraced its 'unromantic beauty', Arvin 1938, pp. 211–12. Whitman criticised Ruskin's attacks on railroads: 'Without railroads, where would our civilization be?' Traubel 1964, p. 485. According to G. Ferris Cronkhite, 'Despite Emerson's dictum in 1844 that the railway, along with the factory-village, constituted proper material for poetry, the first major American poet to make more than a fleeting and fragmentary use of it was Walt Whitman'. Cronkhite 1954, p. 164. See also Collier 2005, p. 205.

Manhattan was not only connected by railroad to an internal 'system of labors'. It was plugged into an increasingly *international* circuit of production and consumption. Whitman was not a kosmos *and* a son of Manhattan. He was a kosmos *because* he was a son of Manhattan: Manhattan was not just any city. It was, to use the young Marx's terms, a 'world-historical', an 'empirically universal' place: a place where individuals could not avoid being aware of the cosmopolitan foundation of modern life as they stepped out on the street and 'ate, drank, and clothed' themselves. 'Through Mannahatta's streets I walking', Whitman proclaimed in 'Our Old Feulliage', 'these things gathering ...' In a passage unearthed by M. Wynn Thomas, Whitman, criticising Thoreau, uses *city* as a synonym of *universe*: 'The great vice in Thoreau's composition', Whitman commented to his friend Horace Traubel, 'was his disdain of the universe – his disdain of cities, companions, civilization. I have very little room for the man who disdains the universe'.[70] He thus conflated universality with the modern city created by capital in a way that recalls Marx's description of how capitalism creates a new humanity 'as the most total and universal possible social product'.[71]

In 1860, a Japanese delegation visited the United States to ratify a commercial treaty: the 'opening' of Japan, largely as a result of US pressure, had been a signal chapter in the formation of a capitalist world market. In 'A Broadway Pageant' Whitman steps onto the streets of Manhattan to witness this moment in the transformation of history into *world*-history, as Marx described it in 1847. As Edward Whitley has pointed out, in this poem Whitman 'presents New York as the central node in a global network connected to the world'. If in other texts Whitman is able to 'transcend national boundaries as a "kosmos"', this poem makes transparent 'that his global vision is based on the expanding networks of international trade that converge upon New York City'. Indeed, as Whitley correctly underlines, Whitman as 'a kosmos' cannot be detached from 'the machinery of international trade that makes him feel as if lower Manhattan were the center of the world'.[72] The self as a 'kosmos' and a product of Manhattan: this is the poetic birth cry of Marx's 'empirically universal individual'.[73] New York was a 'city of the world':

---

70 Brought to our attention by Thomas 1987, p. 148. Original in Traubel 1982, p. 201.
71 Marx 1993, p. 409. The more pedestrian type of example of this can be culled from a description in the *New York Evening Mirror* of the Fulton market in Whitman's time: 'We saw ... fruits, vegetables, and flowers from all parts of the world ... Messina oranges; a heap of pineapples from the Bahamas, and bunches of ripe bananas from Cuba ... Alpine strawberries ... There were ... hams smoked in Westphalia; sausages stuffed in Bologna'. Spann 1981, p. 124.
72 Whitley 2006, p. 457. See also Welty 1979.
73 Marx and Engels [1845], p. 49.

> City of Ships!
> (O the black ships! O the fierce ships!
> O the beautiful sharp-bow'd steam-ships and sail-ships!)
> City of the world! (for all races are here,
> All the lands of the earth make contributions here;)
> City of the sea! city of hurried and glittering tides!
> ...
> City of wharves and stores – city of tall facades of marble and iron!
> Proud and passionate city – mettlesome, mad, extravagant city![74]

From 'world-historical' Manhattan, as with the train pulled by the Baldwin locomotive through a darkened landscape, Whitman could envision a vaster panorama:

> I see the tracks of the railroads of the earth,
> I see them in Great Britain, I see them in Europe,
> I see them in Asia and in Africa.
> I see the electric telegraphs of the earth,
> I see the filaments of the news of the wars, deaths, losses, gains, passions, of my race.[75]

The steamship, along with the locomotive, also came to embody the new combination of power and motion:

> I behold the sail and steamships of the world, some in clusters in port, some on their voyages,
> Some double the cape of Storms, some cape Verde, others capes Guardafui, Bon, or Bajadore,
> Others Dondra head, others pass the straits of Sundra, others Cape Lopatka, others Behring's straits,
> Others Cape Horn, others sail the Gulf of Mexico or along Cuba or Hayti, others Hudson bay or Baffin's bay,
> ...
> Others wait steam'd up ready to start in the ports of Australia,
> Wait at Liverpool, Glasgow, Dublin, Marseilles, Lisbon, Naples, Hamburg, Bremen, Bordeaux, the Hague, Copenhagen,
> Wait at Valparaiso, Rio Janeiro, Panama.[76]

---

74   'City of Ships', pp. 429–30.
75   'Salut au Monde', p. 290.
76   'Salut au Monde', p. 290.

The results of the industrial harnessing of steam now made it possible to salute all corners of the world. In the first volume of *Capital*, Marx described 'river steamers, railways, ocean steamers and telegraphs' as the adaptation of the inherited means of transport and communication to the specific needs of capitalist large-scale industry, their adaptation, as he described it, to 'the feverish velocity' of capitalist industry, to its 'enormous extent', to its 'constant flinging of capital and labor from one sphere of production into another'.[77] And it is this feverish, expanding, shifting world of 'river steamers, railways, ocean steamers and telegraphs', to quote Marx, that Whitman both celebrates and recognises as the enabling material premise of his verse.

The poet can now think of himself moving, not only from one occupation to another, but from one port or one city to the next, not unlike the steamship, the railroad and the telegraph he celebrated:

> I see the cities of the earth and make myself at random a part of them,
> I am a real Parisian,
> I am an inhabitant of Vienna, St. Petersburg, Berlin, Constantinople,
> I am of Adelaide, Sidney, Melbourne,
> I am of London, Manchester, Bristol, Edinburgh, Limerick,
> I am of Madrid, Cadiz, Barcelona, Oporto, Lyons, Brussels, Berne, Frankfort, Stuttgart, Turin, Florence,
> I belong in Moscow, Cracow, Warsaw, or northward in Christiania or Stockholm, or in Siberian Irkutsk, or in some street in Iceland,
> I descend upon all those cities, and rise from them again.[78]

It is not only America, but the world that Whitman can hear. 'What do you hear Walt Whitman?', he asks, and his answer includes: 'echoes from the Thames', 'French liberty-songs', recitatives by an 'Italian boat-sculler', the 'Coptic refrain toward sundown', 'the chirp of the Mexican muleteer', the voice of 'the Arab muezzin', the 'cry of the Cossack', 'the Hebrew reading his record and psalms'.[79] Gay Wilson Allen, in a classic biography, argues that the ultimate subject of Whitman's poetry was '*himself*' or '*the self*', a notion endorsed by many readers.[80] But capitalism, as Marx pointed out, creates, or at least makes possible,

---

77   Marx 1977, p. 506. For a classic study of this transportation revolution in the United States in the epoch of Whitman see Taylor 1968.
78   'Salut au Monde', p. 293.
79   'Salut au Monde', p. 288.
80   Allen 1955, p. 134.

a new kind of 'self', an unprecedented 'empirically universal individual':[81] it is this historically specific 'self' that we encounter in Whitman's writing.

As early as 1847, Whitman's journalistic texts suggested a connection between his global vision and the emergence of dense patterns of world trade. In a youthful a defence of free trade he argued that, while protectionists were focused on local markets, 'we free traders are striking out in the mighty game of the world for our market, and distant kingdoms for our commercial tributaries!'[82]

Whitman portrayed himself 'roaming many lands, lover of populous pavements'.[83] But he roamed less than he proclaimed. With the exception of stays in New Orleans and Boston and some brief forays into the west of the United States and into Canada, Whitman spent his life in the New York area (Long Island, Brooklyn, Manhattan), Washington D.C. and Camden-Philadelphia:[84] the continental and overseas vision of *Leaves of Grass* was the result of an extraordinary act of imagination, made possible by the spread of the railroad, the telegraph, and the structuring of vast internal and world markets.[85] Whitman imagines the world as it would look from a plane or a spaceship. He becomes what a critic has described as a 'flaneur in orbit':

> What do you see Walt Whitman?
> ...
> I see a great round wonder rolling through space,
> I see diminute farms, hamlets, ruins, graveyards, jails, factories, palaces, hovels, huts of barbarians, tents of nomads upon the surface,
> I see the shaded part on one side where the sleepers are sleeping, and the sunlit part on the other side[86]

The transformation of the built environment of human life had created a new subjectivity – a new internal landscape, so to speak. Hence Whitman's famous question: 'What widens within you Walt Whitman? / What waves and soils exuding? / What climes? what persons and cities are here?'[87] And his answer:

---

81   Marx and Engels [1845], p. 49.
82   Whitman [1847d], p. 64.
83   'Starting from Paumanok', p. 176.
84   Reynolds 1996, p. 18. In 1848 Whitman travelled to New Orleans via the Ohio and Mississippi Rivers. He returned by way of the Mississippi and the Great Lakes, with brief stops in St. Louis, Chicago, Milwaukee, and Cleveland. Allen 1955, p. 214.
85   Dickstein 1991–2, p. 187.
86   'Salut au Monde', p. 289.
87   'Salut au Monde', p. 287.

> Within me latitude widens, longitude lengthens,
> Asia, Africa, Europe, are to the east – America is provided for in the west,
> ...
> Within me zones, seas, cataracts, forests, volcanoes, groups,
> Malaysia, Polynesia, and the great West Indian islands.[88]

This is a new type of 'teeming' individual, connected to the world by many threads, 'hurrying' in Manhattan, Paris, Berlin or Manchester 'with the modern crowd as eager and fickle as any'.[89] 'Do I contradict myself?' the poet asks no less famously. 'Very well then', he responds, 'I contradict myself / (I am large, I contain multitudes.)'[90] He has discovered a wider outside world, and thus new forces, stirring *within*: 'I will sleep no more but arise, / You oceans that have been calm within me! how I feel you, fathomless, stirring, preparing unprecedented waves and storms'.[91]

Whitman described himself as 'a kosmos' and argued that 'America demands a poetry that is bold, modern, and all-surrounding and kosmical, as she is herself'.[92] But America was 'kosmical', Marx would argue, as the result, not of the working out of some expansive American spirit, but of the differentiated structure of its industrial, agricultural, transportation and communication networks and of the nodal place it increasingly claimed in an expanding capitalist world market. What critics have called Whitman's 'cosmic flights'[93] should not be divorced from the new ways of being in the world made possible by the productive, transport and communication revolutions launched by capitalism.

Our discussion has so far ignored 'Song of the Exposition', a poem that probably deserves the harsh treatment it has received from critics.[94] Yet, there is one dimension of the text that deserves attention: its celebration of modern industry could be attributed all too easily to its origin as a poem commissioned by the organisers of the National Industrial Exposition of the American Institute in 1871. A logical interpretation were it not for the fact that its content and

---

88 'Salut au Monde', pp. 287–8.
89 'Song of Myself', p. 223.
90 'Song of Myself', p. 246.
91 'Starting from Paumanok', p. 187.
92 Whitman [1871], p. 979.
93 Allen 1955, p. 166.
94 For a scathing judgment of 'Song of the Exposition' as a failed, bathetic poem and of Whitman's performance as verging on the ridiculous, see Allen 1955, pp. 434–5.

tone also can be found in earlier texts and in other poems written in or around 1871 or later.

In 'Passage to India', for example, Whitman pays homage, just as he does in 'Song of the Exposition', to the inventions and structures – the intercontinental railroad, the Suez canal and the trans-Atlantic telegraph cable – that underpinned his notion of 'lands welded together', of a world 'connected by network', a vision we had already encountered in earlier poems, such as 'Salut au Monde', to take an evident example. *Inter*continental railroad, *trans*-Atlantic cable, *inter*-oceanic channel: the prefixes spoke of the transformation, as the young Marx put it, of history into world history.[95] Like Marx, Whitman feels these achievements put to shame all the wonders of the past:

> Singing my days,
> Singing the great achievements of the present,
> Singing the strong light work of engineers,
> Our modern wonders, (the antique ponderous Seven outvied)
> In the Old World the east the Suez Canal,
> The New by its mighty railroad spann'd,
> The seas inlaid with eloquent gentle wires;[96]

Whitman imagines the intercontinental railroad reaching for the Pacific coast. He envisions the Suez Canal and the 'procession of steamships' moving through it. He imagines he is there, panning as a camera over it:

> I mark from on deck the strange landscape, the pure sky, the level sand in the distance,
> I pass swiftly the picturesque groups, the workmen gather'd,
> The gigantic dredging machines.[97]

As Leo Marx pointed out in a classic study, the poem is penetrated by 'a sense of buoyant power that arises from the sight of the machine's motion across the landscape'.[98] And the poet, with his readers, seeks to take off, gliding through the new routes and circuits created by industry:

---

95   According to Allen, 'Passage to India' was composed around 1868–9. Allen 1955, pp. 411–13. Allen has noted how Whitman enthusiastically followed the attempts to lay a trans-Atlantic cable beginning in 1858. Allen 1955, p. 212; Leonard 1980; Doudna 1977.
96   'Passage to India', p. 531.
97   'Passage to India', p. 532.
98   Leo Marx 1964, p. 223.

> Passage, immediate passage! the blood burns in my veins!
> Away O soul! hoist instantly the anchor!
> Cut the hawsers – haul out – shake out every sail![99]

In 'Song of the Redwood-Tree', Whitman similarly imagined new industrial cities replacing the ancient forests of the West:

> Ships coming in from the whole round world, and going out to the whole world,
> To India and China and Australia and the thousand island paradises of the Pacific,
> Populous cities, the latest inventions, the steamer on the rivers, the railroads, with many a thrifty farm, with machinery,
> And wool and wheat and the grape and diggings of yellow gold[100]

There is, therefore, little or nothing new or exceptional found in the references in 'Song of the Exposition' to world trade, to the sea and 'on its limitless, heaving breast, the ships'[101] or to 'Manhattan steamboats and clippers taking the measure of all seas'.[102] In the 'Song of Joys', Whitman had already portrayed himself as a sailor, and his book as a joyous ship 'bound for all ports': 'O to sail in a ship' he proclaimed:

> To be a sailor of the world bound for all ports
> A ship itself, (see indeed these sails I spread to the sun and air,)
> A swift and swelling ship full of rich words, full of joys.[103]

The ship is a key trope for Whitman, a fact that confirms his status as the poet of the 'world-historical individual'. The book, the body and the soul are all encompassed by the same image: 'But O the ship, the immortal ship! Oh ship aboard the ship! / Ship of the body, ship of the soul, voyaging, voyaging, voyaging'.

Whitman's catalogues do not describe a uniformly industrialised capitalism. While mills and factories, iron works, blast furnaces, locomotives are already

---

99   'Passage to India', p. 539.
100 'Song of the Redwood-Tree', p. 354.
101 'Song of the Exposition', p. 348.
102 'Song of the Broad-Axe', p. 338. It is startling that Erkkila's path-breaking work on Whitman discusses 'Passage to India' extensively, for example, without once mentioning capitalism. Erkkila, pp. 265–73.
103 'Song of Joys', p. 330.

present, the world of carpenters and blacksmiths still corresponds to that of the *skilled* workers and their *hand* tools. His poems, written over four decades, record an industrial*ising*, and thus, *not yet* fully industrialised, United States.[104] The choice he gives between 'the clean hair'd Yankee girl' working with *either* 'her sewing-machine or in the factory or mill' corresponds to this transitional moment. Capital's tendency to replace hand-tools with machines guided the poet as he revised his texts: by 1881, as Alan Trachtenberg has acutely pointed out, Whitman replaced 'the anvil and the tongs and hammer' that had figured in a passage of the 1855 version of 'A Song for Occupations', with the 'blast-furnace and the puddling-furnace'.[105] In the final organisation of *Leaves of Grass*, Whitman placed 'Song of the Exposition' right after 'Song of the Broad-Axe': a sequence that suggests the passage from a built environment largely constructed with wood and shaped by hand tools such as the ax, to a mechanised world of iron and steel.[106] In 'Song of the Exposition', the poet promises the Muse a magnificent spectacle of multiple, varied, industrial activities:

---

104   Factories did not dominate manufacturing in the United States before 1860. Laurie 1997.
105   Trachtenberg 1994, p. 124.
106   Marx described manufacture as the stage of capitalist production just preceding the emergence of machine production. It was characterised by the joint action of diverse workers, each wielding specialised tools within a complex division of labour. One could hardly come up with a better description of it than Whitman's:
   The house-builder at work in cities or anywhere,
   The preparatory jointing, squaring, sawing, mortising,
   The hoist-up of beams, the push of them in their places, laying them regular,
   Setting the studs by their tenons in the mortises according as they were prepared,
   The blows of mallets and hammers, the attitudes of the men, their curv'd limbs,
   Bending, standing, astride the beams, driving in pins, holding on by posts and braces,
   The hook'd arm over the plate, the other arm wielding the axe,
   The floor-men forcing the planks close, to be nail'd,
   Their postures bringing their weapons downward on the bearers,
   The echoes resounding through the vacant building;
   The huge store-house carried up in the city well under way,
   The six framing-men, two in the middle and two at each end, carefully bearing on their shoulders a heavy stick for a cross beam,
   The crowded line of masons with trowels in their right hands, rapidly laying the long side-wall, two hundred feet from front to rear,
   The flexible rise and fall of backs, the continual click of the trowels striking the bricks,
   The bricks one after another each laid so workmanlike in its place, and set with a knock of the trowel-handle,
   The piles of materials, the mortar on the mortar-boards, and the steady replenishing by the hod-men
'Song of the Broad-Axe', pp. 332–3.

> Materials here under your eye shall change their shape as if by magic,
> The cotton shall be pick'd almost in the very field,
> Shall be dried, clean'd, ginn'd, baled, spun into thread and cloth before you,
> You shall see the hands at work at all the old processes and all the new ones,
> You shall see the various grains and how flour is made and then bread baked by the bakers,
> You shall see the crude ores of California and Nevada passing on and on until they become bullion,
> You shall watch how the printer sets type, and learn what a composing-stick is,
> You shall mark in amazement the Hoe press whirling its cylinders, shedding the printed leaves steadily and fast,
> The photograph, model, watch, pin, nail, shall be created before you.[107]

Perhaps Whitman's emphasis shifted from the labourers to the machines to be exhibited (just as capitalism becomes increasingly mechanised), but the fascination with a social whole composed of many different activities can hardly startle us: the celebratory enumeration of such sets of diverse activities can be traced through many of his key texts, beginning with 'Song of Myself' and its long lists of skills, trades, work sites and tools.

Almost two decades before the National Industrial Exposition in Philadelphia, and two years before the first edition of *Leaves of Grass*, Whitman visited the New York Crystal Palace exposition of 1853. Organised to rival the London Exposition of 1851, it 'enclosed', as Kaplan describes it, 'nearly five acres of ... steam and electric engines; bridge elements; printing presses; guns; gold bars from California; lighthouse lenses; lifeboats; grain separators; apple parers; furniture ... works in precious metals; and painting and sculptures'.[108] Such exhibitions, Ed Cutler points out, sought 'to create a sense of global totality'.[109] The exhibition was itself 'a deeply rhetorical project in its own right, one that sought to ... portray favorably the sweeping social transformations brought about by an emerging international industrial capitalism'.[110] According to Cutler, the rhetoric of the exhibition can be traced within *Leaves of Grass*: 'Although ... not overtly cast as an exhibition, its heterogeneous catalogues draw upon a

---

107   'Song of the Exposition', p. 345.
108   Kaplan 2003, p. 180.
109   Cutler 1998, p. 68.
110   Cutler 1998, p. 66.

technique of presentation common to the exhibition gallery'.[111] Whitman visited the exhibition dozens of times. Like its organisers, he was searching 'for a method of enclosing the heterogeneity of modern experience'.[112] Whitman's 'poet-Kosmos', Cutler concludes, thus becomes 'a type of the Crystal Palace itself'.[113] Not unlike the way in which the exhibition attained its totality-effect by placing diverse products, machines, and works of art side by side in contiguous galleries, Whitman reached for metonymic connection as a central feature of *Leaves of Grass*. Cutler argues that 'While Whitman is often credited with popularising free-verse poetry, his most celebrated poem departs just as radically from nineteenth-century poetic convention in its virtual abandonment of metaphorical and symbolic figures. Metonymic connectivity, not metaphorical comparison or symbolic representation, best describes the figurative structure of the poem'.[114]

In 1846, Whitman already had commented on the exhibits in a more modest industrial fair in Brooklyn. They convinced him of the capacity of American industry to compete in the world market. He thus proudly pointed to the 'little mountains of fine cheap cotton and worsted cloths, linens, silks, and specimens of raw material – those wares of glass, leather, cutlery, iron, and wood – with and-so-forths as long as a comet's tail'.[115]

Cutler's argument regarding the possible connection between Whitman's metonymies and the structure of industrial expositions can and should be placed along other connections of *Leaves of Grass* with innovations of the rising capitalist metropolis.

Simon Parker, for example, has linked Whitman's verse to some features of the first mass newspapers, as they emerged in the 1840s. Whitman's catalogues parallel the cheap daily's forms of representation of city life, including 'those columns of the newspaper which are most repetitive in appearance – that is, the classified advertising columns'.[116] Further studies link certain features of *Leaves of Grass* to his contact with Italian opera companies that regularly visited New York, and to other spectacles, such as the Egyptian Museum of

---

111 Cutler 1998, p. 65.
112 Cutler 1998, p. 76.
113 Cutler 1998, p. 76. Whitman's interest in such expositions was long-lasting. In the 1889 he thus sent 'America's applause, love, memories and good will' to the Paris Exposition. 'Bravo, Paris Exposition', p. 693. Martí, as we shall see, also wrote his own salute to this exposition.
114 Cutler 1998, p. 77. M. Wynn Thomas has similarly pointed out that Whitman's 'favorite device is parataxis: the arranging of perceptions side by side'. Thomas 1987, p. 154.
115 Whitman [1846d], p. 61. Whitman describes it as the 'Great Fair' at Castle Garden.
116 Parker 1999, p. 168.

Dr. Henry Abbot, to mention two examples.[117] The point of our catalogue of these varied readings is not to determine which process had a larger impact on Whitman. It is rather to insist that they are *all* connected to the economic and cultural trends unleashed by an emergent capitalism. What is described here, if not the cultural crossings (Italian opera and Egyptian antiquities in Manhattan) made possible by the circuits of an emergent capitalist world market, if not the new media (cheap daily newspapers) made possible by modern industry (the modern printing press), linked to the varied interdependent activities (registered in the classified ads) of a capitalist city? If *Leaves of Grass* shares its metonymic inclinations with the Crystal Palace, what is the Crystal Palace, as Cutler and others have rightly pointed out, if not a microcosm of industrial capitalism, if not an attempt to turn the latter into a dazzling concentrated spectacle?

The preceding discussion poses two further issues. Whitman, the poet of 'modern improvements', also claimed to be the poet of nature. He also considered himself to be the poet, not only of 'modern improvements' but also of equal rights, of democracy. How is that apparent paradox (the celebration of both 'artificial things' and nature) to be interpreted, and how is the song of modern industry and of expanding internal and world markets linked to the celebration of democracy? We turn to these questions in Chapter 3.

---

117   Kaplan 2003, p. 170.

CHAPTER 3

'In Paths Untrodden': Whitman, Nature, Democracy and the 'Average Man of To-day'

Whitman was the singer of the steamboat and the telegraph, of the transcontinental railroad and the trans-Atlantic cable, of 'great mills and factories'. Yet he also thought of himself as the poet of nature, 'of the retreat from the clank of the world'. He was furthermore the poet of democracy. How are these features – industry, which we have already discussed, nature and democracy, which we will examine now – connected in his work? For Marx the premise of that triple articulation must be sought in the fundamental dynamics of capitalist civilisation and its ideological and cultural consequences.

Whitman was the poet of 'the modern' and 'the artificial'. He asked, not for 'quiet places by the woods', but rather for 'faces and streets', for the 'phantoms' of the sidewalks. Yet, Whitman also thought of himself as the poet of nature and of the liberation of humanity into nature: 'A morning-glory at my window satisfies me more than the metaphysics of books'.[1] He would not allow the 'perfumes' of 'houses and rooms' to 'intoxicate' him:

> Houses and rooms are full of perfumes, the shelves are crowded with perfumes,
> I breathe the fragrance myself and know it and like it,
> The distillation would intoxicate me also, but I shall not let it.

Instead, 'undisguised and naked', he turns to nature and goes 'to the bank by the wood':

> The atmosphere is not a perfume, it has no taste of the distillation, it is odorless,
> It is for my mouth forever, I am in love with it,
> I will go to the bank by the wood and become undisguised and naked,
> I am mad for it to be in contact with me.[2]

---

1 'Song of Myself', p. 212.
2 'Song of Myself', pp. 188–9.

He will yield to the sea's 'inviting fingers'. He will undress. He wishes to be 'integral' with it.[3] It is not the 'trills of shrieks' and the 'lawless music' of the locomotive that he now wishes to recruit for his song, but the 'undulation of one wave'.[4] He feels the need to turn 'away from the clank of the world', to escape 'from the life that exhibits itself', to move into the 'margins of pond waters':

> In paths untrodden,
> In the growth by margins of pond-waters,
> Escaped from the life that exhibits itself,
> From all the standards hitherto publish'd, from the pleasures, profits, conformities,
> Which too long I was offering to feed my soul[5]

'Paths untrodden': the image suggests *both* an excursion into unexplored nature and, paradoxically, the pursuit of the inventions of the modern; a 'world primal again', yet also *new* politics and a *new* art:

> A world primal again, vistas of glory incessant and branching
> A new race dominating previous ones and grander far, with new contests,
> New politics, new literatures and religions, new inventions and arts.

There is a *new* voice here, 'unprecedented', which has, nevertheless, *also* been there all along: 'These, my voice announcing – I will sleep no more but arise, / You oceans that have been calm within me! how I feel you, fathomless, stirring, preparing unprecedented waves and storms'.[6] For Marx, this double anchoring of Whitman in the industrial and the 'primal', the modern and the natural, would not have been surprising at all. On the contrary, he argued that it is typical of modern capitalist social relations to present themselves – to appear to us, immersed in them – as the spontaneous, natural order of human interactions, and to project their relatively recent historical emergence as the removal of artificial constraints on human nature, and thus as the adjustment of social and political arrangements to a seemingly natural order.

---

3 'Song of Myself', p. 208.
4 'Had I the Choice', p. 618.
5 'In Paths Untrodden', p. 268.
6 'Starting from Paumanok', p. 187.

'Natural man', Marx pointed out playfully in the first page of the *Grundrisse*, was not an outgrowth of nature, but the *historical* product of the eighteenth century in some parts of Europe. The break-up of the feudal forms of society between the sixteenth and the eighteenth centuries detached individuals from the bonds that in the past made them, as he put it, 'accessory of a defined and limited human conglomerate'.[7] As producers and exchangers of commodities, they were freed to collide with each other in pursuit of their private interests. They were no longer subordinated to lord or master, village custom or guild regulations. Instead, they had to abide by the terms of individually or privately negotiated contractual agreements and to, more generally, obey the market indicators and market discipline resulting from the sum of their private initiatives. Past social regulations were replaced by market interactions as an objective, impersonal, and self-regulating mechanism. Seen from the logic of that seemingly self-correcting market mechanism, feudal, guild, village, or state rules and regulations now seemed as arbitrary and artificial – unnatural – restrictions on the isolated individual's initiative: once generalised as the fundamental means of social regulation, market relations fostered the image of their own expansion as the removal of artificial constraints on human interactions and as the institution of, or the return to, a freer, spontaneous, natural order. For American poet and editor William Cullen Bryant, to take an influential figure of nineteenth-century US liberalism, the 'laws of trade' constituted 'a fixed, eternal order' that the state should not tamper with: to remove such government interference was to open the path for the 'natural way'.[8] Marx pointed out how Adam Smith and David Ricardo, and their many disciples, thus projected into the past a modern isolated individual, naturally inclined to trade and barter, which, far from being a natural basis or starting point of social evolution, was in fact a recent historical result of both 'the dissolution of the feudal forms society' and the 'new forces of production developed since the sixteenth century'.[9] From the perspective nurtured by the movement of market society, to modernise was to remove artificial, inherited restraints, but to remove such restraints was to deliver humanity into its undistorted nature: modernisation could thus be conceived as both a break with the past *and* as a return to nature. Whitman could thus celebrate both the creation of a 'new art' *and* 'a world primal again'. He embraced New York with all its bustling newness, yet argued that Mannahatta was the city's most 'fit and noble name': an act of naming or

---

7 Marx 1993, p. 83.
8 For quotes and discussion see Spann 1972, pp. 101, 105, 106.
9 Marx 1993, pp. 83–4.

renaming that, as M. Wynn Thomas has pointed out, allowed him to embrace its 'thronging, variegated life as simultaneously uniquely modern and primevally old'.[10]

But Whitman did not only think of himself as the poet 'of artificial things, ships, machinery, politics, creeds, modern improvements' and/or, however paradoxically, of the return to nature. Whitman was also the self-proclaimed poet of democracy, of the 'average man of to-day':

> I was looking for a while for Intentions,
> For a clew to the history of the past myself, and for these chants – and now I have found it,
> ...
> It is in the present – it is this earth today,
> It is in Democracy – (the purport and aim of all the past,)
> It is the life of one man or one woman to-day – the average man of to-day
> It is in languages, social customs, literatures, arts,
> It is in the broad show of artificial things, ships, machinery, politics, creeds, modern improvements, and the interchange of nations,
> All for the modern – all for the average man of to-day.[11]

Whitman was the poet of equal rights. He could not understand why some objected to the concept 'Of Equality – as if it harm'd me, giving others the same chances and rights as myself – as if it were not indispensable to my own rights that others possess the same'.[12] 'Song of Myself' proclaims: 'Whoever degrades another degrades me'.[13] Grass itself became the sign of a democratically non-discriminating attitude:

> Or I guess it is a uniform hieroglyphic,
> And it means, Sprouting alike in broad zones and narrow zones,
> Growing among black folks as among white
> Kanuck, Tuckahoe, Congressman, Cuff, I give them the same, I receive them the same.[14]

---

10 Thomas 1987, p. 152. The same point formulated in Chaffin 1977, p. 116.
11 'I was looking a long while', pp. 512–13.
12 'Thought', p. 414.
13 'Song of Myself', p. 210.
14 'Song of Myself', p. 193.

As in the case of the double celebration of the industrial and the natural, the modern and the 'primal', Marx would not have been surprised by this celebration of equal rights, on the one hand, and of an array of diverse and interconnected labours, on the other, such as we find in *Leaves of Grass*. The generalisation of commodity production and exchange, he argued, has a deep, cumulative and, for him, a liberating, impact on the prevalent notions of human equality and inequality. Market exchange as the dominant means of economic regulation, he argued, implies the presence of private agents that are driven to demand what they consider a fair equivalent or price for their products, an equivalent or price that is subject to constant fluctuations and renegotiations. As exchangers demand the value of their product (or labour power) in the market and are made to recognise the right of others to do the same, the notion of formal equality, of a mutual recognition of equal rights as a fair and just framework for conducting transactions, becomes a generally accepted opinion. This idea, in turn, can nurture the notion of the fundamental equality of all individuals. Marx thus argued that it had been through the emergence of a society in which people relate fundamentally 'as possessors of commodities' that the 'concept of human equality' had acquired the 'permanence of a fixed popular opinion'.[15] As we have seen, Marx considered the United States to be the foremost exponent of a nascent capitalist civilisation. Whitman's attachment to equal rights cannot be divorced from the generalisation of commodity production in the non-slave economy of the northern states, a process which was completed by the 1820s in New England and the Middle States, and spread to the mid-western territories through the 1840s and 1850s. The fact that slavery had been allowed to survive within the frontiers of the new republic, and that, instead of withering away, it soon entered a period of expansion, burdened the United States with an internal economic, political and ideological antagonism that was only settled through a new and bloodier war.[16]

Whitman's notion of the 'average man', of the 'average man of to-day', of the 'averaging' of human differences is also connected to the dynamics of commodity production as deciphered by Marx. Sacrificing the many nuances of Marx analysis, the argument can be briefly summarised as follows. In the act of exchanging, say two hats for a pair of shoes, or of fixing the relative values and prices of both commodities, say $20 for a hat and $40 for a pair of shoes, commodity producers *abstract* from their product's concrete features. As *concrete* objects, as use values, hats and shoes are, quite evidently, *not* the same,

---

15 Marx 1977, p. 152.
16 For the interactions of small independent, small commodity and slave-production in the emergence of US capitalism in the period leading to the Civil War, see Post 2012.

yet in commodity exchange an equivalence is established between them. In the example provided two hats are considered to be equal to a pair of shoes.

Marx argued that exchange fixes the relative value of different commodities by reducing them to quantities of the same shared substance, and he argued further that the shared social substance, to be found in different quantities in all commodities, was none other than human labour. Values and prices correspond to the amount of labour required for the production of diverse commodities. If a pair of shoes is worth twice as much as a hat it's because twice as much labour is required for its creation. But the value of a particular type of product is *not* determined by the amount of labour *actually* employed in the elaboration of any specific item, but rather by the time *normally* required for its production. If it normally takes two hours to manufacture a hat that sells for $20, a lazy hatmaker that employed four hours would not thereby obtain $40 for his hat: like all other hatmakers, he would have to settle for $20. In other words, in the market, individual producers count as *average* producers, their labour is validated as average labour, according to the evolving situation in the particular line of work. They are all taken as average men or women that possess an equal value-producing capacity to labour. They each count as 'a socially average unit of labour-power' and, if they do not wish to work in vain, they must make sure their actual labour conforms to that social average.[17] Diversity of labours, equal rights, and the 'average man', differently employed but equal to their fellow men: what are these if not three of the main threads that run through Whitman's texts? As Whitman explained to Richard M. Bucke: 'I represent vast averages'. This is what, according to Marx, values and prices represent in a capitalist economy.[18] In this sense, too, it is fair to describe Whitman as the poet of an emergent capitalist economy and of the ideological consequences of generalised commodity production.

Yet it would be unfair to say that Whitman simply poetised a popular and generalised democratic attitude. He did not simply sing what had already become a 'fixed popular opinion'. He carried it farther than most of his contemporaries. His sympathies are with the commonest and the cheapest: 'What is commonest, cheapest, nearest, easiest, is Me'.[19] Indeed, in spite of inconsistencies we shall consider below, Whitman's vision of democracy, certainly in the mid-1850s, when he published the first edition of *Leaves of Grass*, and in many ways throughout his life, was strikingly and exceptionally inclusive. He

---

17   Marx 1977, p. 129.
18   Bucke 1970, p. 67.
19   'Song of Myself', p. 200.

was not satisfied with equal rights and some form of representative government. The elected officials of republican governments, and not only monarchs, could become enemies and dangers to democracy. He admonished citizens to see government officials, not as their rulers, but as their agents. The truly great city stands:

> Where the men and women think lightly of the laws,
> Where the slave ceases, and the master of slave ceases,
> Where the populace rise at once against the never-ending audacity of elected persons,
> ...
> Where the citizen is always the head and ideal, and President, Mayor, Governor and what not, are agents for pay[20]

Those holding higher office must be brought down to a common level. As Lincoln would famously proclaim in his Gettysburg address, government was there 'for the people', an idea which Whitman mixed with a more irreverent, levelling tone. He thus called on his readers not to forget:

> The President is there in the White House for you, not you here for him,
> The Secretaries act in their bureaus for you, not you here for them,
> The Congress convenes every Twelfth-month for you,
> Laws, courts, the forming of States, the charters of cities, the going and coming of commerce and mails, are all for you.[21]

Whitman celebrates the power of public opinion over elected or appointed officials and what he hopes is a growing willingness to challenge and question established rules and doctrines. He thus speaks of public opinion:

> Of a calm and cool fiat, sooner or later, (how impassive! how certain and final!)
> Of the President with pale face, asking secretly to himself, *What will the people say at last?*
> Of the frivolous Judge – of the corrupt Congressman, Governor, Mayor – of such as these, standing helpless and exposed,

---

20 'Song of the Broad-Axe', p. 336.
21 'A Song for Occupations', p. 359.

> Of the mumbling and screaming priest, (soon, soon deserted,)
> Of the lessening, year by year, of venerableness, and of the dicta of officers, statutes, pulpits, schools,
> Of the rising forever taller and stronger and broader, of the intuitions of men and women, and of Self-esteem, and of Personality,
> Of the true New World – of the Democracies resplendent en-masse[22]

His notion of equal rights, and what is more, of equal participation, included not only men but women. The great city also stands: 'Where women walk in public processions in the streets the same as the men, / Where they enter the public assembly and take places the same as the men'.[23] Nor was Whitman's notion of equal rights and citizenship limited to the skilled, the honourable or the able bodied:

> I will not have a single person slighted or left away,
> The kept-woman, sponger, thief, are hereby invited;
> The heavy-lipp'd slave is invited, the veneralee is invited;
> There shall be no difference between them and the rest.[24]

All are beautiful to him, including the stammerer, the sick, the homely, the consumptive, the idiot.[25] Nobody will be denied:

> To cotton-field drudge or cleaner of privies I lean,
> On his right cheek I put the family kiss,
> And in my soul I swear I never will deny him.[26]

To 'a common prostitute' he proclaims: 'Not till the sun excludes you do I exclude you'.[27] To the despised he affirms: 'I at least do not shun you, / I come forthwith in your midst, I will be your poet'.[28] He will stand besides the condemned: 'Not a mutineer walks handcuff'd to jail but I am handcuff'd to him and walk by his side'.[29] The poet wishes to give voice not only to the oppressed,

---

22 'Thoughts', pp. 589–90.
23 'Song of the Broad-Axe', p. 336.
24 'Song of Myself', p. 205.
25 'The Sleepers', p. 114.
26 'Song of Myself', p. 232.
27 'To a Common Prostitute', p. 512.
28 'Native Moments', p. 266.
29 'Song of Myself', p. 230. In his wonderful 'The City Dead House' Whitman lovingly contemplates the body of a dead prostitute. As J.M. Tyree has written: 'The poem represents

the repressed, and the despised, of which he gives specific examples (slave, prisoner, dwarfs), but also to themes related to areas considered indecent: sex and forbidden desires in their material, bodily form. This is not sublimated love, but copulation:

> Through me many long dumb voices,
> Voices of the interminable generations of prisoners and slaves,
> Voices of the diseas'd and despairing and of thieves and dwarfs,
> ...
> Through me forbidden voices,
> Voices of sexes and lusts, voices veil'd and I remove the veil,
> Voices indecent by me clarified and transfigur'd.
> ...
> Copulation is no more rank to me than death is.[30]

Published in 1855, as the debate on slavery entered its acutest phase leading to civil war, the first edition of *Leaves of Grass* proclaimed the worth and dignity of African Americans. This was a perspective that Whitman had not consistently defended in the past and from which he began to retreat soon afterward. But in the pages of that first edition his vision of human equality reached beyond that of most of his fellow white citizens. The poet makes the point that grass, central image of his work, grows 'among black folks as among white'.[31] As Martin Klammer has pointed out, his image of a 'calm and commanding' black dray driver recognised in the black person the quality that racists and the defenders of slavery would most emphatically deny: the black person's capacity for 'self-sovereignty'.[32] Whitman admires this man and declares his love for him:

> The negro holds firmly the reins of his four horses – the block swags underneath on its tied-over chain;
> The negro that drives the dray of the stone-yard – steady and tall he stands, pois'd on one leg on the string-piece;
> His blue shirt exposes his ample neck and breast, and loosens over his hand;

---

      a determined communing with what America and New York have trampled and used and spat out'. Tyree 2006, p. 73.
30 'Song of Myself', p. 211.
31 'Song of Myself', p. 193.
32 Klammer 1995, p. 126.

> His glance is calm and commanding – he tosses the slouch of his hat away from his forehead;
> The sun falls on his crispy hair and moustache – falls on the black of his polish'd and perfect limbs.
> I behold the picturesque giant, and love him – and I do not stop there;
> I go with the team also.[33]

The poet, Whitman proposed in the 1855 preface to *Leaves of Grass*, was bound to help the 'furtherance' of 'escaped slaves'.[34] In a well-known passage, he imagines himself encountering a runaway slave, curing him and sheltering 'before he recuperated and pass'd north'.[35] Elsewhere in 'Song of Myself' the poet's perspective fuses with that of the runaway: 'I am the hounded slave, I wince at the bite of the dogs'.[36] The 1855 version of 'The Sleepers' included a passage (often referred to as the 'Lucifer passage') which also adopted the perspective of the slave, wronged, but actively waiting for the occasion to strike back at the oppressor:

> I have been wronged .... I am oppressed .... I hate him that oppresses me,
> I will either destroy him, or he shall release me.
> Damn him! how he does defile me,
> How he informs against my brother and sister and takes pay for their blood,
> How he laughs when I look down the bend after the steamboat that carries away my woman.
> Now the vast dusk bulk that is the whale's bulk .... it seems mine,
> Warily, sportsman! though I lie so sleepy and sluggish, my tap is death.[37]

'Salut au Monde' similarly upholds racial equality: 'You dim-descended, black, divine-soul'd African, large, fine-headed, nobly-form'd, superbly destin'd, on equal terms with me!'[38] And in a much commented section of 'I Sing the Body

---

33 'Song of Myself', pp. 198–9.
34 'Preface', p. 22.
35 'Song of Myself', p. 197.
36 'Song of Myself', p. 225.
37 'The Sleepers', p. 113.
38 'Salut au Monde', p. 294.

Electric', the poet pushes aside the slave auctioneer to sing the praise of black male and female bodies.[39]

In a very clever exploration, Ed Folsom has pointed out that in some places Whitman may have experimented with the construction of black poetic voice. He indicates that the inspiration for the episode in 'Song of Myself' in which an injured fireman is rescued was an actual event witnessed by Whitman and recorded in one of his notebooks. The poem reads:

> I lie in the night air in my red shirt, the pervading hush is for my
>   sake
> Painless after all I lie exhausted but not so unhappy,
> White and beautiful are the faces around me, the heads are bared of
>   their fire caps,
> The kneeling crowd fades with the light of the torches.

Folsom indicates that the injured fireman in the event recorded in Whitman's notebooks was black. At first it may seem that Whitman erased the race of the fireman when he poetically reconstructed the event. The jarring mention of the whiteness of the surrounding faces could then be read as a symptom of racism. But what if Whitman adopted the perspective of the injured black fireman after all? Such a poetic voice, Folsom argues, would feel no need to describe itself as black, but would find it remarkable and noteworthy that the surrounding faces were white. In other words the mention of the whiteness of those around the speaker would not be a mark of racism but of the opposite: Whitman's attempt to write from the perspective and the voice of the black fireman. Folsom concludes that there is 'ghost-black speaker' in this passage, a result of Whitman's attempt to fully identify with a black subjectivity.[40] The force of Folsom arguments regarding these lines cannot be denied. He extends this reading to several other poems, such as 'When Lilacs Last in the Dooryard Bloom'd' (in particular the passage written from the perspective of the men in charge of recuperating the remains of dead soldiers from battlefields and improvised cemeteries). In the case of the poem 'Reconciliation' the argument is weaker, and we shall return to it when we discuss Whitman's retreat from the anti-racist positions that prevail in the first editions of *Leaves of Grass*.

---

39   Klammer 1995, p. 147. Klammer points out how Whitman included black faces in his poem 'Faces', a 'remarkable gesture' at the time. Klammer, p. 145.
40   Folsom 2014, p. 23. Folsom speaks of Whitman's attempt at 'race crossing', p. 20.

Of course, Whitman did not invent his democratic ideas or inclinations. His credit lies in having responded and at times extended them. If he could and did sympathise with runaway slaves it was because slaves were constantly running away and making their way to the northern states: a form of resistance, less spectacular than rebellions perhaps, but nevertheless a constant pressure which undermined the attempts by the dominant parties of the time to keep the explosive issue of slavery outside the national political debate.[41] Meanwhile, the early women's rights movement branched out of the anti-slavery movement and led to the Seneca Falls convention in 1848 and similar initiatives in the following years.[42] Women's rights were in the air, and it is Whitman's merit that he was among those embracing them and not the many who opposed them. Here he extended them, as indicated, not the least by portraying women as active sexual subjects, just as interested in enjoying their bodies as men.

Whitman, singer of American democracy, was also eager to detect a similar democratic spirit abroad. 'Resurgemus' had been his early homage to the defeated European revolutions of 1848.[43] The news of the proclamation of the first Spanish republic in 1873 makes him conclude that democracy is a force waiting to emerge everywhere.[44] As he explained in the programmatic preface to the 1855 edition of *Leaves of Grass*: 'The attitude of great poets is to cheer up slaves and horrify despots'.[45]

One of Whitman's distinctive ideas was the notion of democracy as a process that both required and produced a new type of personality. Democracy, in that sense, was not, or was not merely, a set of procedural rules or an institution, but a *practice*, a transformative practice. This is what stands behind Whitman's notion of an 'athletic democracy'. Democracy both creates and demands 'athletes', that is to say, *active* participants. It is, as he argued in *Democratic Vistas*, 'a training-school for making first-class men. It is life's gymnasium … fit for freedom's athletes'.[46] Citizens remake themselves through the practice of demo-

---

[41] It eventually provoked the crisis around the Fugitive Slave Law of 1850, for example, in which Whitman intervened forcefully. See Chapter 8.
[42] Reynolds 1996, pp. 218–22.
[43] In 1856 he similarly composed to revolutionaries of all lands the poem that later became 'To a Foil'd Revolutionary'. The original title was truly all-encompassing: 'Liberty Poem for Asia, Africa, Europe, America, Australia, Cuba, and the Archipelagoes of the Sea'. See Gohdes 1959, p. 5.
[44] 'Spain, 1873–4', p. 591.
[45] 'Preface', p. 17.
[46] Whitman [1871], p. 952. See on this Henkel 2010.

cracy, just as athletes become such through their own activity. Whitman is a teacher of athletes who feels stronger through his disciples' assertion of their independence against him:

> I am the teacher of athletes,
> He that by me spreads a wider breast than my own proves the width of my own,
> He most honors my style who learns under it to destroy the teacher.[47]

Whitman wants his readers to become active agents. He demands that readers join him at the active centre of his poems. As he explained to Bucke: 'In my poems all ... revolves around myself. I have put one central figure, the general human personality typified in myself'. But, he adds, 'my book inevitably necessitates that its reader transpose him or herself into that central position, and become the actor, experiencer, himself or herself, of every page, every aspiration, every line'.[48]

At his most radical, Whitman envisaged a republic ruled by 'mechanics', that is to say, by skilled manual labourers. In 'Starting from Paumanok' he invites us to 'See mechanics busy at their benches with tools – see from among them superior judges, philosophs, / Presidents, emerge, drest in working dresses'.[49] In an article entitled 'Rulers strictly out of the masses' he returns to this idea: 'I expect to see the day when ... qualified mechanics and young men will reach Congress and other official stations, sent in their working costumes, fresh from their benches and tools, and returning to them again with dignity'.[50] For Whitman the labouring classes were the ideal source for government personnel: 'There is more rude and undevelopt bravery, friendship, conscientiousness, clear-sightedness, and practical genius ... now among the American mechanics and young men, than in all the official persons in these States, legislative, executive, judicial, military, and naval, and more than among all the literary persons'.[51]

Far from rejecting mass production, Whitman detected a democratic dimension within it: modern industry enabled a truly democratic civilisation. He complained that William Morris's books, beautifully produced through costly

---

47   'Song of Myself', p. 242.
48   Bucke 1970, p. 63.
49   'Starting from Paumanok', p. 187.
50   'Rulers Strictly Out of the Masses', p. 1070.
51   'Rulers Strictly Out of the Masses', p. 1070.

artisan methods, 'are not books for the people. They are books for collectors'.[52] Similarly, medieval illuminated books may be beautiful but 'they are exclusive: they are made by slaves for masters'.[53] Whitman wants 'that beautiful book cheap':[54] democracy is enabled by mass production.

The discussion in this and the previous chapter suggests some correspondences between Whitman's formal innovations and the lived experience of capitalist expansion and democracy. Consider, for example, how capitalism takes no form of production or consumption as permanent. It thrives, as Marx put it, on the 'constant overthrow of ... presuppositions',[55] and refuses to abide by any '*predetermined* yardstick'.[56] Is this not a description of Whitman's relation to inherited poetic forms as he ran against 'predetermined forms' and 'preestablished molds'?[57] Abandoning regular rhyme and conventional stanza forms, Whitman pioneered what came to be known as free verse and used it flexibly, shunning just about any 'predetermined yardstick' and overthrowing formal 'presuppositions'.[58] This operation had a democratic dimension. Whitman was a 'leveller of style', as Doris Sommer puts it. He wished to incorporate 'everyday speech' into his verse. He tended, she argues, 'to cancel the privilege of poet over reader'.[59] His greatest innovation, David Reynolds has argued, was the 'prose like nature of his verse'.[60] Erkkila had made the same points earlier.[61] Whitman said as much: 'In my opinion the time has arrived to essentially break down the barriers of the form between prose and poetry'.[62] As he had explained in 1855: 'The messages of great poets to each man and woman are, Come to us on equal terms, Only then can you understand us, We are no better than you, What we enclose you enclose, What we enjoy you may enjoy'.[63]

The absence of end-verse rhyme deprive Whitman's much commented catalogues of a sense of completeness: one feels there is always a new item that could be added.[64] Not unlike capitalism, *Leaves of Grass* seems to be con-

---

52   Traubel 1953, p. 20.
53   Traubel 1953, p. 20.
54   Traubel 1953, p. 20.
55   Marx 1993, p. 541.
56   Marx 1993, p. 488.
57   Crawley 1970, pp. 18–19.
58   Reynolds considers Whitman the father of free verse. Reynolds 1996, p. 314.
59   Sommer 1999, pp. 49–50. Also Reynolds 1996, p. 156.
60   Reynolds 1996, p. 314.
61   Erkkila 1989, pp. 3, 5, 84, 87.
62   'Notes Left Over', p. 1056.
63   'Preface', p. 14.
64   Erkkila makes the point that his poems sought to appear as 'open-ended'. Erkkila 1989, p. 117.

stantly evolving, expanding, any particular configuration being a temporary order soon to be transgressed. Whitman kept remaking it, adding, subtracting, rearranging, rewriting. *Drum-taps, Sequel to Drum-Taps, November Boughs*, and *Two Rivulets*, which at first appeared as independent books, were incorporated into *Leaves of Grass* (and remade in the process). How can we fix the text of *Leaves of Grass*? Despite Whitman's wish that the 1892 edition be taken as definitive, many readers prefer the first 1855 edition, even if some key sections, such as 'Calamus', only made it into the book in 1860.[65] The fact is that *Leaves of Grass* must be taken as a *process*.[66] Even Whitman's favorite rhetorical figure – the anaphora – corresponds to this attempt to organise and expanding totality: repetition of sounds at the beginning of verses allows the poet to suggest unity without closure, unity deprived of the feeling of completeness that end rhyme tends to promote, a sense of both internal correspondence and open-endedness.

So far we have encountered Marx and Whitman as singers of the world created by capital – of the incessant expansion of production, the emergence of new needs, the transformation of history into world history – and of the generalisation of 'the concept of human equality'. Yet for both Marx and Whitman the achievements of the present were incomplete, and, in many ways, contradictory. Both envisioned a transcendence of the present. This issue is explored in Chapters 4 and 5.

---

65 Loving points out how Pearce considers the third (1860) to be the best edition of *Leaves of Grass*, while Malcolm Cowley prefers the first (1855) edition. Loving favours the first, second (1856) and third, taken as an evolving whole. Loving 1982, p. 146. On a lighter tone, Francis Murphy comments that 'Whitman's revisions of *Leaves of Grass* were so numerous that their study has almost become an American form of small business'. Whitman 1975, p. 21.

66 As Jerome Loving has argued, Whitman 'wrote the same book over and over again, expanding it but always returning to the same essential theme'. Loving 1982, p. 42.

CHAPTER 4

The 'Emptiness' of the Present: Marx, the 'Bourgeois Viewpoint' and Its 'Romantic Antithesis'

Regarding Marx, we have so far focused our attention on his appreciation, even celebration, of the achievements of capitalism. Capitalism creates unprecedented productive forces and links all nations in a world circuit of material and cultural exchange. It develops science and its applications to production as no other previous society, dissolves past relations of personal subordination and dependence and dismantles guild restrictions and the limits of small town and village life. Market society forces individuals to pursue their own interests and pushes them to rely on their own initiative. Capitalism promotes the emergence of a new type of dynamic, adaptable personality, open to cultural change, willing to challenge prescribed or inherited customs, rituals, and traditions. It opens a wider horizon for the satisfaction of human needs through the better understanding and conscious manipulation of nature, in turn the basis for the flourishing of other artistic and cultural pursuits. But the achievements of capitalism have their underside. Here it is easy to loose sight of the subtleties of Marx's analysis, and hard to do it justice in just a few pages. It is essential to his perspective that capitalism's brilliance cannot be detached from its more sinister dimensions. For him it is impossible to explain one without considering the other. What follows is a brief look into some aspects of this dialectic. The discussion will send us back to Whitman, and later to Martí, James and Mir, with some interesting questions.

We will successively focus on four interrelated features of capitalism as analysed by Marx: first, its fetish-like functioning as a self-regulating objective mechanism, beyond the control of any social agent; second, the puzzling, mysterious appearance that those mechanisms present to the social agents immersed in them, a feature which corresponds to the fact that the latter, far more than controlling, are controlled by the former; third, the imperative toward constant quantitative expansion – the pursuit of accumulation for accumulation's sake – beyond any desire for *personal* consumption by its ruling classes; fourth, the one-sided and alienating form of capitalist progress and the limits it poses to the very same possibilities for human development that it creates. This will allow us to summarise Marx's description of what he considered two opposite but inseparable perspectives nurtured by capitalist development: the *apology* of capitalist progress, on the one hand, and the *romantic* yearning for pre-capitalist social forms, on the other, as well as Marx's alternative to both. This leads to a brief discussion of how Marx's general perspective informed his analysis of the spread of capitalism beyond its birthplaces, an aspect of his work that will be relevant both to our further discussion of Whitman and to our exploration of the work of José Martí, C.L.R. James and Pedro Mir and their reading of Whitman.

Capitalism is, to begin with, a system of commodity production. Some of its features can be discerned in their simplest form if we first imagine a society of independent artisans and small farmers, that is to say, of small commodity producers.[1] Such producers depend on each other for the goods and services they need to survive. They are pieces of a social division of labour. Yet they are also autonomous agents, engaged, as 'mutually indifferent individuals', in the pursuit of their respective, private interests.[2] Their relations of mutual dependence are not regulated by communal, village or guild rules, or through bonds of personal subordination to lord or master. Nor are those relations under their collective control as associated producers. Instead, their private activities are regulated through the market, that is to say, through the exchange of their products and the results of those exchanges. Such producers must sell in order to buy, but there is no guarantee they will be able to sell at the expected price or, for that matter, to sell at all. Commodity producers may have no lord or master, but each must constantly monitor their own activity and adjust it to value and price fluctuations: their mutual dependence, the social dimension of their activity, the necessary interconnection of their individual pursuits, becomes an autonomous, objective mechanism – the shifting and fluctuating market – that imposes on them a discipline that can be as strict as it is impersonal. Market indicators are the result of their interactions, of the balancing-out of number-

---

1   Marxists have long debated whether the notion of small commodity production refers to an actual stage in the history of at least some societies or was rather an explanatory device deployed by Marx to present some general aspects of a market economy while abstracting from its specifically capitalist features. The debate may have much to do with the use of different definitions of small commodity production. Small producers that sell a portion of their output, but are not forced to do so to retain access to the land, have certainly existed in many societies. But they are not fully market-dependent and therefore not fully under market discipline. Small producers disciplined by capitalist markets have also existed. But small producers fully disciplined by the market, as the ones in our example, without the presence of other tendencies typical of capitalism do seem to us to be a construction used by Marx to explain the more basic aspects of market regulation and coercion while not considering other elements. For a discussion relevant to the United States in Whitman's epoch see Post 2012. We return to this topic in Chapter 8 in our discussion of Whitman's participation in some key debates of his time.
2   Marx 1993, p. 157.

less private decisions coordinated through exchange, but this ongoing social evaluation of their private initiatives asserts itself as their subordination to an economic process that now appears as an '*alien* social power standing above them'.[3] Or, as the young Marx had put it in 1844: 'In this way the medieval saying *nulle terre sans seigneur* [no land without a lord] gives way to the modern saying *l'argent n'a pas de maitre* [money has no master], which is an expression of the complete domination of dead matter over men'.[4]

Commodities have prices, which are expressions in money of their values, which in turn correspond to the socially necessary *labour time* required for their production: exchange and price fluctuations are a means regulating production and, more specifically, of allocating and re-allocating the many private labours among different productive activities. The value of a product includes the last labour performed in its production and the value of the tools and materials employed, which is labour previously performed. Contrary to what some commentators have argued, Marx does not think labour should be recognised or honoured as the legitimate source of value. He is by no means arguing a moral case for the value of labour or human toil. He argues instead that commodity exchange actually and objectively compares different commodities by reducing them to quantities of socially necessary labour time, represented as their value and price.

But values and prices do not appear transparently in exchange as different amounts of socially necessary labour time but rather as one of the characteristics, a quality, an attribute inherent in each product, a veiling of the relations between the producers which Marx famously called the fetish-like dimension that products acquire once they become commodities: value created by socially necessary labour appears as something, as an aspect of the product, independent of labour. Gold and silver, to take the more evident examples of commodity fetishism, seem as valuable, as mysteriously 'precious' in and of themselves, for reasons unrelated to the labour required for their production. It seems as if it is worth performing much labour to obtain these 'valuable' things, when, in fact, it is the reality that much labour is required to obtain them that explains their high value.

But this fetishistic representation of value (of gold or any other commodity) as something or an attribute independent of labour, of social relations as objects or as the qualities of objects (as the values and prices of commodities), of relations between people as the relations between things (as relations

---

3 Marx 1993, p. 197.
4 Marx [1844], p. 319.

of commodities and money, of the movements of prices, for example) is but one aspect of the wider fact that commodity producers, as participants in a system of many private labours, are indeed under the rule of an objective self-regulating mechanism of shifting values and prices which is beyond their individual or collective control, and, increasingly, beyond their understanding. In fact, the determination of the values and the prices of commodities, the nature and origins of money (and, with the coming of capitalism, of profit, interest, rent, the causes of unemployment and crises, and much more) become the object of a particular discipline – political economy and later 'economics' – and of heated polemics, a clear indication that the economic process – the interaction between private producers – has become a mystery to those immersed in it.

Commodity production thus implies both the affirmation of individual freedom and 'the most complete suspension of individual freedom'.[5] It dissolves past 'ties of personal dependence', but imposes the 'subjugation of individuality under social conditions which assume the form of objective powers'.[6] This 'fixation of social activity' as a 'material power' acting independently of all social agents, subordinating their individual actions to its impersonal dictates, becomes all the more evident when we shift our analysis from small to *capitalist* commodity production.[7]

Capitalism is both a form of commodity production and a system of class domination and exploitation. Under capitalism, workers are free to pursue their interests as 'mutually indifferent individuals' in the market. But given their separation from the means of production – monopolised by capital – to ensure a livelihood, they are forced to sell their capacity to work for a wage. As in all class societies, the producers create a surplus beyond what is required for their own reproduction, a surplus appropriated by the exploiting classes. Under capitalism this mechanism is obscured by the value form. Marx elegantly unveils it through a consistent application of his theory of value: he assumes all commodities are sold at their value. He also introduces a fundamental clarification: workers do not sell their labour, but their *capacity* to labour, their labour power. In the case of the commodity labour power, bought by the capitalists and sold by the workers, its value is determined like that of all commodities, by the labour required for its production, which in this instance corresponds

---

5   Marx 1993, p. 652.
6   Marx 1993, p. 652.
7   Marx [1845], p. 47. It is only through the transformation of most labourers into wage-workers, that is to say, through the rise of capitalism, that commodity production and exchange become the prevalent forms of production and circulation.

to the value of the commodities necessary for the reproduction of the workers and their offspring. Capital pays this in accordance with the rules of commodity exchange: with their wages workers obtain the goods necessary for their reproduction. But while employed by capital, workers produce more new value than the value of their labour power, represented by their wage. In other words, wages are equal to only part of the new value created by labour. Upon selling the commodities containing it, also at their value, the capitalist can obtain a profit, an extra value, a surplus value, which is nothing but unpaid labour. Marx's explanation, based on the fundamental distinction between the value of labour power and the value created by it, thus reconciles the exchange of equivalents in the market (of all commodities, including labour power) and the exploitation of labour, the appropriation of unpaid labour, by capital.

As indicated above, the value of a product includes the last labour performed in its elaboration and the value of the tools and materials employed (the machines, tools, materials, energy bought by the capitalist), which is the product of labour previously performed: the capitalist recuperates the cost of the latter as part of the selling price. Machines and tools have value, product of previous labour, which is transferred to the new product, but they are not the source of new value, or of surplus value, or of profit.[8]

Of course, Marx also explores how the wage form generates the impression that workers are paid for their *labour*, and not the value of their labour *power*, in other words, the appearance that they receive a pay equivalent to all the value they produce, and not part of it: it hides the surplus value extracted from labour by capital. And if the origin of profit in unpaid labour is hidden, then it cannot but seem to emanate from capital itself, which in turn appears as an amount of value, somehow pregnant with more value. In the case of industrial capital, profit seems to arise from technology itself, or it may appear as the wage of a particular kind of supervisory 'labour'. In the case of commercial capital, profit seems to emerge, not from production, but from the sphere of

---

8 Through a mechanism that need not detain us here Marx explains how improved machinery may help capitalists capture a surplus profit, which is nevertheless also unpaid labour. Nor does Marx's theory imply that under capitalism commodities are sold at their value. Indeed it argues the opposite: under capitalism the tendency toward the equalisation of the rate of profit ensures that individual products are not sold at their values but rather at prices of production that diverge from them. But he still argues that while value is transferred from one sector to another and while surplus value created in one sector may be transferred to and realised in another, labour is still the only source of value: it is to quantities of socially necessary labour that commodities are reduced when they are exchanged. A fully automated sector, for example, will still obtain a profit which is in its totality created in and transferred to it from non-automated sectors.

circulation of capital, from the mere buying and selling of goods. In the case of interest (one of the forms taken by capitalist profit), capital seems to grow at a certain rate (5 percent a year, for example) just on account of the passage of time. Capital becomes, as Marx puts it, an automatic fetish. Thus, just as certain social relations (relations between commodity producers) are turned into a characteristic of certain objects (the value or price of each commodity), a social relation of exploitation between classes (the extraction of surplus labour by capital) masks itself as the, always somewhat mysterious, capacity of capital, of an amount of money, for self-expansion.

Insofar as it is a system of extraction of surplus labour from the producers, capitalism is not different from class societies before it, such as slavery or serfdom, even if, compared to them, the process of capitalist exploitation – the extraction of surplus – may be less evident or visible. But the fact that capitalism is a form of commodity production in which labour power itself has become a commodity has a momentous consequence, which sharply differentiates it from past systems of exploitation. To begin with individual capitalists do not directly consume the product of that surplus labour. It takes the form of commodities that capitalists must sell in order to realise their profit. Like all commodity producers, capitalists are in no way guaranteed to find buyers or to obtain the expected price from them. Capitals do not only exploit labour, they also compete for customers. Competition, 'as an alien social power standing above them', forces all capitals to constantly reduce costs and increase productivity, as they battle to increase their profits while lowering their prices to lure buyers and increase their share of the market. Secondly, due to the fact that labour power is a commodity bought and sold as much as the means of production, the search for lower costs can and does take the form of the displacing of labour with improved machinery. No capital can opt out of this race, under threat of extinction: in the capitalist war of all against all, only the capitals with lower costs will be able to survive. In the midst of capitalist competition, any particular capital can survive only by 'increasing itself',[9] 'by driving beyond its quantitative barrier' and by constantly increasing its productivity.[10] Capitalism is thus characterised by unprecedented growth rates.

Needless to say, money is the ruling power of such a society, and money is the abstract form of wealth – wealth reduced to mere quantity, devoid of any concrete form, unable to stimulate any sense, embodying the possibility of enjoyment, but not enjoyment itself. It is not strange to hear people wonder why

9   Marx 1993, p. 270.
10 Marx 1993, p. 270.

one or another magnate pursues further investments and profits, even if they already manage and own a fortune larger than they could spend in several lives. Is not this seeming transformation of money from means of obtaining concrete goods into an end itself, this apparent accumulation for accumulation's sake, somewhat absurd and irrational? It is, of course, irrational from the perspective of *personal* consumption, but not according to the logic of capitalist accumulation. The mistaken assumption implicit in that perfectly reasonable question (why do they still want more money?) is the idea that the drive of capitalist accumulation can be explained in terms of the will or the, rational or irrational, personal or subjective desires of capitalists, when, in fact, it is fuelled by an objective, impersonal dynamic: regardless of whether the capitalist is personally a gluttonous spender or an austere miser, their capital must quantitatively grow, or be crushed by other capitals.

This drive to accumulate, which differentiates capitalism from past societies, underlies the boundless as well as the one-sided nature of capitalist progress. Precisely because it is impersonal, this dynamic is both limitless, and altogether unconcerned with anybody's, including the capitalist's, possible attachment to existing social norms, inherited traditions, past rituals or personal loyalties. Any particular capitalist may very well be a conservative admirer of tradition. They may yearn for the rhythms and rituals of country or village life, may sincerely respect the skills, pride, and accomplished work of the artisan, or cherish the personal loyalties that were part of pre-capitalist hierarchies: but the imperatives of capitalist accumulation inexorably pull them to destroy and supersede all of these practices.[11]

The other side of this limitless expansion is its one-sidedness. Capital has an unlimited hunger, but that hunger has only one object: monetary profit. All of humanity's capacities are enhanced, but only to be funneled in one dir-

---

11 Marx's description of the 'clearing of estates', of the refashioning of the British countryside by capital, exemplifies the attitude of capital toward inherited or existing productive conditions and social practices. Noting that the British term 'clearing of estates' will not be found in any continental country, Marx asks: 'But what is the meaning of this "*clearing of estates*"? It means that without any consideration for the local inhabitants, who are driven away, for existing village communities, which are obliterated, for agricultural buildings, which are torn down, for the type of agriculture, which is transformed ... none of the conditions of production are accepted as they have traditionally existed but are historically *transformed* in such a way that ... they will provide the most profitable investment for capital'. The quote is from Chapter XI of *Theories of Surplus Value*, 'Ricardo's Theory of Rent'. It may be consulted online at: http://www.marxists.org/archive/marx/works/1863/theories-surplus-value/ch11.htm.

ection: the quantitative expansion of capital.[12] Nowhere is the subordination of humanity to the both limitless *and* one-sided imperatives of capital more in evidence than in the evolution of the capitalist production process. The combination of exploitation and competition means both that capitalists are incessantly driven to innovate *and* that each step in the evolution of production is also a step in the material subordination of labour to an alien, despotic power. Labour is divided and fragmented, and with the coming of machine production increasingly reduced to a repetitive gesture, deprived of most intellectual, not to speak of creative, effort. Capital seeks to transform the workers into a living appendix of a material process beyond their control.[13] Labourers can hardly find satisfaction in such a work process – besides obtaining a wage – as it is anything but a process of self-determined investment of the their abilities or faculties. The machine confronts them as the property of another, which, wielded by capital, controls the pace of their work, and even threatens to make any particular worker redundant. All the potential blessings of increased productivity – satisfaction of the basic needs of all, the reduction of the working-day with the freeing of time for other pursuits – turn into their opposites: job and income insecurity, unemployment, extension of the working day and intensification of labour. Potential versatility of functions and diversity of employments become universal insecurity. 'Capitalist production', argued Marx, 'is the first to develop

---

12 Capital is only interested in 'that which increases, multiplies and hence preserves it as capital'. Marx 1993, p. 271.

13 'It converts the worker into a crippled monstrosity by furthering his particular skill as in a forcing-house, through the suppression of a whole world of productive drives and inclinations'. Marx 1977, p. 481. Or, as Emerson argued in 1837: members of society 'have suffered amputation from the trunk, and strut about as so many walking monsters, – a good finger, a neck, a stomach, an elbow, but never a man' (Emerson [1837], p. 52). David Herreshoff has pointed out the parallels between Marx and some of Emerson's texts in Herreshoff 1967, pp. 11–30. Marx succinctly describes how this process unfolds as capitalist industry moves from simple cooperation (bringing many workers under one roof), manufacture (division and fragmentation of labour among workers) and machine production: 'What is lost by the specialized workers is concentrated in the capital which confronts them. It is a result of the division of labor in manufacture that the worker is brought face to face with the intellectual potentialities of the material process of production as the property of another and as a power which rules over him. This process of separation starts in simple co-operation, where the capitalist represents to the individual workers the unity and the will of the whole of the body of social labor. It is developed in manufacture, which mutilates the worker, turning him into a fragment of himself. It is completed in large-scale industry, which makes science a potentiality for production which is distinct from labor and presses it into the service of capital'. Marx 1977, p. 482.

the conditions of the labor process ... on a large-scale'. But it 'develops them as powers that control the individual worker and are alien to him'.[14]

But, as we saw, it is in the nature of capitalism that not only the workers but *capitalists* themselves are subjected to economic processes beyond their control. If capitalists lord over labourers, the market lords over them. This mechanism does not only force them to constantly innovate but, in the form of crashes, crises, and depressions it comes to haunt even those that normally profit from it. As the young Marx argued: 'Estrangement appears ... in the fact that ... – and this goes of the capitalists too – an *inhuman* power rules over everything'.[15] Market fluctuations and indicators are followed not unlike the weather report: as means of anticipating and of trying to adapt to the possible course of a natural process. Recessions and depressions are endured as natural disasters beyond human control. Metaphors used to describe economic processes – financial tsunamis, to mention a recent example – attest to this transformation of the activity of 'mutually indifferent' economic agents into 'something alien and objective'.[16] Individuals are free, but, even in the case of capitalists, their economic relations appear as alien, autonomous process. Instead of controlling they are controlled by them. Instead of directing, they experience them as 'their fate',[17] as 'chance', or as 'natural force', to use Marx's terms.[18] Starkly put: 'It is not individuals who are set free by free competition; it is, rather, capital which is set free'.[19] It is the impersonal will of capital that rules, not of any individual or individuals.[20]

---

14   Marx 1977, p. 1056.
15   Marx [1844], p. 366.
16   Marx 1993, p. 157.
17   Marx 1993, p. 158.
18   Marx 1993, p. 197.
19   Marx 1993, p. 650.
20   Tocqueville, discussing the United States in the 1830s, spoke of 'aristocratic' and 'democratic' societies, but many of the features he attributed to 'democracy' were in fact consequences of the emergence of capitalism. He thus referred to the fundamental role of money, to the tendency toward constant innovation, and to recurrent crises as features of democracy. He wrote: 'In aristocracies, rents are not paid in money alone but in respect, affection, and service. In democracies money is the only payment'. And in another passage: 'In aristocracies, money leads to a few points only on the vast circles of men's desires; in democracies, it leads to them all'. Regarding innovation we find the following anecdote: 'I meet an American sailor and ask him why his country's vessels are constructed to last for so short a time; he answers ... that the art of navigation is making such rapid progress that the finest ship would soon outlive its usefulness if it extended its life for more than a few years'. Early on he had pointed out 'recurrent crises', again ascribing to democracy what is in fact a feature of capitalism: 'I believe that the recurrence of industrial crises is an endemic sickness of all democracies in our days'. (Tocqueville 2003, 672, 713, 523, 645.)

There is a cruel irony embedded in the remaking of society by capitalism: it is as if humanity could only be made aware of its full potential under the pull of an objective, impersonal, inhuman force – the incessant movement of capitalist accumulation – a force that can only reveal that potential while emptying labour of all content and reducing human pursuits to the quest for profit, a force that can only reveal that potential while thwarting and distorting it. The many-sided and unprecedented expansion of human capacities under capitalism thus 'appears as a complete emptying-out'.[21] The incessant application of those capacities beyond all previous limits emerges as the 'sacrifice of the human end-in-itself to an entirely external end':[22] the limitless expansion of capital. Progress, as the young Marx argued, had taken the form of an 'impoverishment' of 'human nature': 'Therefore *all* the physical and intellectual senses have been replaced by the simple estrangement of all these senses – the sense of *having*. So that it might give birth to its inner wealth, human nature had to be reduced to this absolute poverty'.[23]

Such are the wrenching results of capitalist development. On the one hand it develops the productive and scientific capacities of human beings, on the other it reduces the labourer's activity to an empty gesture subordinated to the machine; it links up all peoples into a web of international trade and exchange, but it subordinates them to the fluctuations of a world market beyond anybody's control; it undermines the notion that people must submit to inherited customs and nurtures the conviction that they can shape and reshape their culture and habits, but it creates an unstable and insecure world, in which change often takes the form of a disorienting imposition and not of an act of self-determination or self-definition. We are no longer limited by the bonds or relations of personal subordination to lord or master, prince or village elders or to the morals or rules of our community or the culture into which we were born, but, in turn, we find ourselves immersed in the cold world of mutual indifference and competition of the market. Cultures are opened to change and are placed into closer contact with each other, but all aspects of culture are turned into commodities, and subordinated to capital's pursuit of its own expansion – and that which cannot be bent to such purposes is marginalised or discarded. Science allows us to better control natural processes, but we neither understand nor control the movements of capitals and markets that rule our lives. This system compels all capitalists to mobilise all human technical, artistic,

---

21   Marx 1993, p. 488.
22   Marx 1993, p. 488.
23   Marx [1844], p. 352.

cultural resources within their reach, but it has only one index to measure the result of their combination: the quantitative expansion of capital through increased profit.[24]

Given that contradictory, impersonal, isolating and vulgarly commercial (as it reduces everything to dollars and cents) character of capitalist progress, it is possible that pre-capitalist societies – with their more stable social structures, their relations of domination mixed with personal loyalties, the lesser role of money and competition in their midst, their closer communal rules and attachments – may appear as more balanced, harmonic, noble and lofty worlds. Human relations may seem denser, as they are not reduced to the cash nexus. Life's activities may seem fuller of meaning since they are not solely directed to the pursuit of monetary profit. But Marx insists that we should *not* yield to this nostalgic temptation. Such pre-capitalist worlds may seem fuller and more balanced: compare, for example, an artisan, master of his skill, proud of a product that carries his personal stamp, with the factory operator, or the egalitarian ethos and person-to-person contact of some peasant communes with the precarious, unsettled, antagonistic aspects of life in the capitalist metropolis, or classical literature with the superficiality of capitalist publicity. But those past worlds, Marx warns us, were also narrow and static. Humanity could feel fuller within their confines because it was yet unaware of possibilities and potentials beyond them. 'In earlier stages of development', Marx argued, 'the single individual seems to be developed more fully, because he has not yet worked out his relationships in their fullness'.[25] He adds 'This is why the childish world of antiquity appears on one side as loftier. On the other side, it really is loftier in all matters where closed shapes, forms and given limits are sought for. It is satisfaction from a limited standpoint'.[26] Against this, Marx wants us to seize the possibilities brought about by science and the machine, by the large city and international trade, *without* thereby reconciling ourselves with the capitalist, alienated form under which they were first brought about. It would be as absurd, he argued, to yearn for the narrow plenitude of the pre-capitalist world as to reconcile ourselves with the one-sidedness of capitalist progress: 'It is as

---

24 Or as Emerson puts it: 'This is the good and this the evil of trade, that it would put everything into market; talent, beauty, virtue, and man himself'. Recognising the polarised results of capitalist progress, Emerson argued: 'The science is confident, and surely the poverty is real. If any means could be found to bring these two together!' Emerson [1844], pp. 160, 162.
25 Marx 1993, p. 162.
26 Marx 1993, p. 488.

ridiculous to yearn for a return to that original fullness as it is to believe that with this complete emptiness history has come to a standstill'.[27]

In this fashion, Marx differentiated his perspective from two rival visions whose interplay, he argued, characterises capitalist civilisation: the romantic yearning for a pre-capitalist past as a refuge from the more destructive aspects of capitalist progress, on the one hand, and the uncritical apology for capitalist development as the only possible form of human progress, on the other. Unable to imagine a *post-capitalist* world, capitalist civilisation will always carry *both* perspectives in its midst: 'The bourgeois viewpoint', he argued, 'has never advanced beyond this antithesis between itself and this romantic viewpoint, and therefore the latter will accompany it as legitimate antithesis up to its blessed end'.[28]

Marx wants us to step out of this polarity. While recognising the charm that the limited worlds of the past may still exercise on us, Marx bid us to renounce the nostalgic idealisation of the past while also repudiating any notion of capitalism – of this 'complete emptiness' – as the final stop in human social arrangements. If romantics would prefer to undo many aspects of capitalist modernity, its apologists hope to perpetuate it intact.[29] Marx favours a third option: he wishes to transcend capitalism, transforming the potentialities it has revealed into the basis for a radically different society. Marx thus argued that under capitalism 'the working-out of the productive forces, of general wealth etc., knowledge etc., appears in such a way that the working individual alienates himself; ... But this antithetical form is itself fleeting, and produces the real conditions of its own suspension'.[30] Or, as he put it in his earlier works: industry had 'prepared the conditions for human emancipation, however much its immediate effect was to complete the process of dehumanization'.[31]

By turning the productive forces created by capitalism into collective property, to be democratically administered by the producers themselves, it would be possible to satisfy the basic needs of all, to radically reduce the working day and to eliminate the more alienating forms of the capitalist division of labour. With the extension of free time, all would be able to participate actively in political processes, in the determination of economic priorities, in scientific,

---

27 Marx 1993, p. 162.
28 Marx 1993, p. 162.
29 This does not deny the insights and at times liberating nature of the romantic critique of capitalist modernity, a tradition I have explored in the case of Puerto Rico by drawing on the work of Michael Lowy. See Bernabe 2002; Lowy and Sayre 2001; Lowy 1993.
30 Marx 1993, pp. 541–2.
31 Marx [1844], p. 355.

professional or artistic pursuits, according to each person's inclinations. Freed from the obsessive pursuit of moneyed wealth, social agents could enter into a fuller relationship with themselves, with others, and the world. If capital had estranged the senses, reducing them to the 'sense of having', the abolition of the rule of the market and of capital – and the consequent guaranteed satisfaction of the basic needs of all and the extension of free time – would open the path to 'the complete *emancipation* of all human senses and attributes'.[32]

This perspective has nothing to do with the subordination of the individual to the interest of the community, as even sympathetic commentators often mispresent Marx's views. For Marx socialism meant the freeing of the *individuals* through their association with others, so as to claim control over the economic interactions that shape their lives. He thus wrote repeatedly of the 'universal development of the individual', the 'real development of the individuals', of the 'free development of individualities'.[33] He often referred to the future society he considered both possible and desirable as a free association of individuals, for example, as 'individuals associated on the basis of common appropriation and control of the means of production'.[34] Thus, from the vantage point that capitalism opens on both the non-capitalist past and a post-capitalist future, Marx proposed a division of human history into three epochs:

1) the emergence and evolution of several types of relations of personal dependence and subordination (serfdom, slavery, etc.), in which productivity developed slowly and discontinuously.
2) the rise, under capitalism, of relations of mutual indifference and 'personal independence' regulated by an objective, impersonal market mechanism in which human capacities, needs, and interconnections develop as never before, 'in which a system of general social metabolism, of universal relations, of all-around needs and universal capacities is formed for the first time',[35] if only as an alien force controlling, instead of under the control of individuals.
3) the reign of 'free individuality' through the placing of the means of production under the control of the associated producers, which in turn makes the 'universal', 'many-sided' development of each person possible.[36]

---

32   Marx [1844], p. 352.
33   Marx 1993, pp. 542, 706.
34   Marx 1993, p. 159. For Marx it is capitalism, not socialism that develops social productive capacity at the expense of the individual worker.
35   Marx 1993, p. 158.
36   Marx 1993, p. 158.

It was, he argued, the second stage that made passage to the third possible.[37] Nor was Marx a participant of a cult of labour, as he is often presented: committed to the full growth of the individual, he considered the extension of *free* time to be the necessary enabling condition of it. His appreciation of time freed from enforced labour was the other dimension of his often forgotten individualism. He explained that the 'free development of individualities' depends on a 'general reduction of the necessary labour of society to a minimum, which then corresponds to the artistic, scientific etc. development of the individuals in the time set free'.[38] Real wealth, he quoted from an 1821 text, consists of '*disposable time* outside that needed in direct production, for *every individual* and the whole society'.[39] Such 'social disposable time' would 'free everyone's time for their own development'.[40] Free time was 'time for the full development of the individual'.[41] It was the 'true realm of freedom' within which there could unfold a 'development of human energies which is an end in itself': beyond labour time, people could engage in activities (manual, intellectual, artistic, scientific, etc.), not forced upon them by material needs or class oppression, but for their own sake. Through the exploitation of the majority, past class societies had created 'disposable' time for small minorities.[42] Capitalism, through its

---

37   Again, as Herreshoff has pointed out, Emerson seems to echo Marx's views: 'Trade was one instrument, but trade is also but for a time, and must give way to somewhat broader and better, whose signs are already dawning in the sky'. Emerson [1844], p. 161. The signs Emerson referred to were 'beneficient socialism', the 'Communism of France, Germany and Switzerland', the Trade Unions and the Utopian and Fourierist communities, among others. See Herreshoff 1967, pp. 11–30. While there are interesting coincidences between Marx and Emerson, they should not be exaggerated, a danger present when isolated passages are placed side by side. In the same text that Emerson speaks of 'beneficient socialism' he also argues that interference with the market provokes the opposite of the intended effects: charity increases pauperism, relief for the unemployed does not prevent the 'principle of population' from reducing wages to the lowest level. He similarly criticises those who attack the new aristocracy of trade that has replaced the feudal aristocracy, since the former, according to him, is built on 'toil and talent', is a result of merit, and is constantly renewed. He similarly anticipates that in the future public operations, such as the post office, would be displaced by private interests, such as the private telegraph and express companies. Emerson [1844], pp. 158, 160, 165.
38   Marx 1993, p. 706. See also his considerations in *Capital*, Volume III, on the 'realm of freedom' residing beyond the realm of labour imposed by necessity, and thus requiring the progressive shortening of the working day. Marx 1981, pp. 958–9.
39   Marx 1993, p. 706.
40   Marx 1993, p. 708.
41   Marx 1993, p. 711.
42   Marx 1993, p. 708.

incessant increase in productivity, had created the *possibility* of combining the general satisfaction of basic human needs and a reduction of the working day *for all*.

But as long as the new productive forces remained locked into the logic of capitalist accumulation that emancipatory potential would *not* be realised: the purpose of capitalist innovation is the further extraction of profit, that is to say, of surplus *labour*. Under capitalism innovation is thus combined with the push not to relax, but to intensify the pace of work; not to reduce, but to extend the working day as much as possible. Only the transformation of modern industry into the collective property of the producers could turn the productive forces created by capital into the source of 'disposable time' for all.

Present and passionate debates justify this brief aside: this perspective does not imply that the liberation of the means of production from the grip of capitalism should lead to their constant expansion regardless of ecological consequences. Quite the contrary: it is the unrelenting drive of capital to self-expansion that inevitably leads to growth beyond all limits imposed by nature, while the transition from the private to the social property of technology is a precondition of its use and reconfiguration according to such limits.[43]

This double refusal by Marx of both *capitalist apology* and *romantic nostalgia*, also framed his pronouncements on the impact of European imperial expansion on the rest of the world. This aspect of the problem is no less pertinent, as we shall see, to our further discussion of Whitman's poetic representation of the world created by capital, as well as to the exploration of the work of José Martí, C.L.R. James and Pedro Mir. We explore it briefly in the following paragraphs.

Marx's views on this question, his writings on British imperialism in India and China, for example, are often portrayed as Eurocentric celebrations of the spread of 'progressive' modern civilisation at the expense of Oriental isolation and immobility. But such readings, to be found in influential texts such as Edward W. Said's *Orientalism*, fail to register the nuances of Marx's complex approach to this question.

Most of Marx's texts on British imperialism in India and China were prepared as articles for the *New York Tribune* in the mid-1850s. Yet, even these brief journalistic interventions were structured by Marx's grand historical perspective, as summarised above: as the attempt to transcend both capitalist apology and romantic nostalgia. They embraced capitalist progress (against the romantics), while at the same time denouncing its horrors (against its apo-

---

43   See among others Foster 2000 and 2009; Lowy 2015; Tanuro 2013.

logists); rejected a romantic idealisation of the precolonial past, while exposing the base motives and brutal means of colonial and imperial agents; welcomed the spread of the elements of modern society in the colonies (against the romantics), but warned that social revolution, including colonial rebellions, would be necessary if those elements were to become the source of well-being for all (against the apologists of capitalism). Often misread, these texts progressed by adding nuance upon nuance, constantly shifting perspective to encompass the opposite poles of a process Marx described as the 'tragical couplet' of past limitations and exploitative progress. Descriptions of progress brought about by imperial rule (against the romantics) are followed by indications of their social cost (against its apologists). Mentions of social costs are coupled with descriptions of the limits of precolonial structures. It is quite easy to lose sight of one or another side of Marx's analysis.

Referring to the destruction of Indian village life under British rule, Marx described how 'sickening … it must be to human feeling to witness those myriads of industrious and inoffensive social organizations disorganised and dissolved into their units, thrown into a sea of woes, and their individual members losing at the same time their ancient form of civilization, and their hereditary means of subsistence'.[44] But before we have fully assimilated this moving portrait, Marx enjoins us to not forget that these idyllic communities

> … had always been the solid foundation of Oriental despotism, that they restrained the human mind within the smallest possible compass, making it the unresisting tool of superstition, enslaving it beneath traditional rules … We must not forget … this undignified, stagnatory, and vegetative life … this passive sort of existence … We must not forget that these little communities were contaminated by distinctions of caste and by slavery, and that they subjugated man to external circumstances.[45]

The notion that Marx is being racist here overlooks the fact, as Aijaz Ahmad has pointed out, that his attitude to traditional Indian society (stagnant, fatalistic, passive, bound by tradition, resigned to received limits and restrictions) coincided with his views on feudal and pre-capitalist *Europe*: against the slow-pace of productive and cultural change in the pre-capitalist world, Marx spoke of the 'civilizing influence' of capitalism in Europe as much as Asia.[46]

---

44   Marx [1853], p. 218.
45   Marx [1853], p. 218.
46   Marx 1993, pp. 409–10; Ahmad 1992, pp. 224–5. This was, Ahmad adds, a judgment shared by a 'whole range of reformist politics and analysis in India', p. 225.

For Marx it was not a question of European civilisation relieving Asian immobility, but of capitalist dynamism replacing the relative immobility of pre-capitalist structures. If this process often took the form of European incursions into non-European societies it was a consequence of the fact that capitalism arose first in Europe and not elsewhere: *capitalism*, not Marx, was Eurocentric. And neither in Europe, India or China, did Marx lose sight of the destructive, 'sickening', dimension of capitalist modernisation.[47] This is not to argue that Marx's comments on Asian societies were always accurate, far from it. But his mistakes cannot be attributed to an alleged uncritical embrace of the colonial or imperial project.[48]

Similarly, Marx decried the isolation of China, denounced its traditional rulers, discounted their claim to cultural superiority, saw a liberating dimension in the breakdown of Chinese isolation and inherited social structures. But his description of the process, in his articles, for example, on the Opium Wars and similar incidents, is not a one-sided celebration of change under imperialist compulsion. If this was progress, it was tragical nonetheless:

> That a giant empire ... insulated by the forced exclusion of general intercourse, and thus contriving to dupe itself with delusions of Celestial perfection – that such an empire should at last be overtaken ... on occasion of a deadly duel, in which the representative of the antiquated world appears prompted by ethical motives, while the representative of overwhelming modern society fights for the privilege of buying in the cheapest and selling in the dearest markets – this, indeed, is a sort of tragical couplet, stranger than any poet would ever have dared to fancy.[49]

But this, according to Marx, is the nature of capitalist progress: it is one-sided, it is progress to buy and sell, progress with which we should not be reconciled, yet progress after all.

'Tragedy', in these texts, to quote Ahmad's illuminating article on this, refers to 'a sense of colossal disruption and irretrievable loss, a moral dilemma wherein neither the old nor the new can be wholly affirmed, the recognition that the sufferer was at once decent and flawed ... and the glimmer of hope ... that something good might yet come of this merciless history'.[50] The only

---

47 Nor did he overlook the ecological cost of capitalist development, another aspect of his work that is often misunderstood. See Foster 2000.
48 Ahmad 1992, p. 241.
49 Marx [1858], p. 27.
50 Ahmad 1992, p. 228.

way out of the 'tragical couplet' enacted by an 'antiquated world' and 'overwhelming modern society', lay beyond the precolonial past and, thus, *through* the path enabled by a predatory colonialism at an appalling human cost. Through political unification, the creation of a native army, a free press and a scientifically educated class; the establishment of regular external communication and the construction of railroads within the subcontinent, Britain, while animated by the 'vilest interests', was creating the basis for modern society in India.[51] Had those changes improved the life of the majority? Not necessarily. Was it not better, then, to speak of *potential* and not actual enjoyment of the fruits of modernity? Absolutely. But that, argued Marx, is how capital proceeds everywhere: it creates the groundwork for human emancipation, the completion of which, in turn, requires the abolition of capitalism. 'All the English bourgeoisie may be forced to do' in India, he explained, 'will neither emancipate nor materially mend the social condition of the mass of the people'. That emancipation depended 'not only on the development of the productive powers, but on their appropriation by the people'. But what the English bourgeoisie 'will not fail to do', he added, 'is lay down the material premises for both'. Marx concluded: 'Has the bourgeoisie ever done more? Has it ever effected progress without dragging individuals and people through blood and dirt, through misery and degradation?'[52] In the end, he predicted that 'The Indians will not reap the fruit of the new elements of society scattered among them by the British bourgeoisie, till in Great Britain itself the ruling classes shall have been supplanted by the industrial proletariat, or till the Hindoos themselves shall have grown strong enough to throw off the English yoke altogether'.[53]

Marx thus struggled, as Ahmad describes it, to 'carve out a position independent both of the Orientalist-Romantic and the colonial-modernist'.[54] This was an extension to the colonial world of his general perspective which sought to escape the polarity of capitalist apology and its romantic shadow.[55] In other words, for Marx, not only the history of India under English rule but the history of humanity as a whole (to the extent that the conditions of human emancipation are created at a tremendous human cost) can be thought of as a

---

51   Marx [1853], p. 219. Marx [1853a], pp. 220, 223.
52   Marx [1853a], p. 223.
53   Marx [1853a], p. 224.
54   Ahmad 1992, p. 235.
55   Ahmad 1992, p. 235. Achcar argues convincingly that Marx's views shifted in time toward a more critical view of the destructive impact of colonial rule. See Achcar 2013.

tragedy, a tragedy, to quote Ahmad, that still allows 'the glimmer of hope ... that something good might yet come of this merciless history'.[56]

Marx considered the celebration of capitalist progress and the romantic yearning for a fuller past as the twin opposites between which bourgeois thought inevitably oscillated. To move beyond that cycle it was necessary to see further than bourgeois society as such: Marx thought of socialism as transcending both the apology of capitalist progress and its romantic counterpart, or as transcending, beyond the developed countries, both the colonial-modernist project and the Orientalist-romantic reaction to it, to use Ahmad's terms. We can now ask ourselves: where did Whitman stand in that map of the present, of its apologists and of its backward and forward looking discontents? Where did he stand in the map of the apologists and critics of imperial expansion? We address the first question in the following chapter and the second in Chapter 7.

---

56 The tragedy implicit in this – the fact that liberation can only be wrenched from a process marked by tremendous injustices and suffering – applies not only to the colonial world but to humanity as a whole. Marx had a tragic vision of human history, as Eagleton has remarked, not because it ends badly, but due to its immense and irreparable human cost, which not even the best future outcome can mend (Eagleton 2011, p. 61).

CHAPTER 5

'This All-Devouring Modern Word': Whitman's Critique of Business

Marx argued that capitalism nurtures both celebrations of its achievements and romantic yearnings for a lost plenitude. He refused both options for the vision of a post-capitalist future, built on the mixed appropriation and negation of the world created by capital. Where is Whitman in this map? His celebration of the modern puts him out of the romantic continent. But nor does it amount to an uncritical celebration of capitalist progress. Whitman too wished to transcend the existing forms of progress, if not by the means favoured by Marx. Poetry, for Whitman, was the means for that transcendence: for him poetry was no mere aesthetic exercise, or rather, aesthetics was no mere secondary result of the modern. 'No one will get at my verses', he warned, 'who insist upon them as a literary performance ... or aiming mainly toward art or aestheticism'.[1] Without a new poetics, the modern would not only be unsung: it would be truncated. The task of the poet was to complete the modern. Marx argued that capitalism develops the 'universality and the comprehensiveness' of human 'relations and capacities', but does so through the operation of impersonal market imperatives, through the subordination of all to the objective rules of capitalist expansion, that is to say, through 'the alienation of the individual from himself and from others'.[2] Whitman celebrates the modern, but in his own way he also sensed the alienation from oneself and from others, the emergence of an objective, alien manmade landscape, animated by, but seemingly independent of, human labour and agency, and the reduction of human pursuits to their monetary, profit-seeking dimension.[3] Betsy Erkkila was thus right when she argued that we can find in *Leaves of Grass* a 'poetic resistance' to the 'dependence, dispossession, commodification, and merchandising of the self fostered by capitalism'.[4]

---

1 'A Backward Glance O'er Travell'd Roads', p. 671.
2 Marx 1993, p. 162.
3 Whitman's concern with the alienation of the producer from his activity, his product and from others has been suggested by Erkkila 2007, p. 44. We attempt to extend these ideas here.
4 Erkkila 1989, p. 48. She similarly argued that *Leaves of Grass* 'might be read as a response to the essentially unpredictable workings of a new market economy' (76). While offering many

Whitman was the poet of multitudes. But what if the multitude, as Marx argued, was made up of mutually indifferent individuals? Whitman was fascinated by the powers and capacities embodied in modern industry. But what if those powers, as Marx explained, become an alien, impersonal force? Whitman was enthralled with the tapestry of different occupations created by the capitalist market. But what if they are all reduced to one aim: profit? What if the joy of labour turned into an enslaving work discipline? In that case, the multitude could also generate a sense of isolation; expansion could produce a feeling of emptiness; and progress could appear as both limiting and one-sided. The celebration of progress could then include the notion of a separation still to be bridged, of a unity not yet forged, of a conflict to be reconciled, of a one-sidedness to be completed, of a promise or potential to be honoured, of a lack, an absence, or a void, in the centre of material progress, still to be filled. This is what we find in Whitman.

Whitman was the poet of the individual, of the many pursuits of the modern metropolis, of material progress, the poet of occupations, of artificial objects and of modern tools. But there is an unsettled tension in his discourse, even at its most celebratory. He was the poet of the individual, but also came to see individualism as destructive of the cohesion he yearned for. He celebrated diversity, but also saw it as a potential purveyor of chaos and disintegration. He was a poet of material progress, but came to see it as one-sided and deadening. He was the poet of occupations, but worried about work encroaching on free time. He was the singer of the expanding national and world market, but sensed they harboured a personal void: they knitted together a wider but 'unloving earth'. Through his work Whitman sought a new vocabulary to designate his uneasiness with the present. Soullessness was one of his terms to describe the one-sided reduction of the self to some of its faculties and of its pursuits to the search for monetary gain.

To the reign of mutual indifference he opposed a catalogue of neologisms or of redefined terms: friendship, compaction, adhesiveness, comradeship, love, fraternisation, friendliness, companionship, attachment, annealing, identifying, fusing, kneading, to mention a few. Thus, he neither wished a return to the past, nor did he feel, to use Marx's words, 'that with this complete emptiness history has come to a standstill'. Separate interests, he argued, must be compacted. The material must be spiritualised. The world of dead objects must be 'vitalized'. Free time must be regained.[5] What underlies these demands is

insights, Erkkila's pioneering work did not pursue these formulations in a systematic way, nor did she make consistent use of what I consider to be Marx's very useful categories.

5 Neil Larsen has argued that Whitman's ideology was adapted to that of an emergent indus-

the threefold desire for a human bond above and beyond the cash-nexus, for free time beyond an implacable work discipline and for a goal for human activity besides profit-making. Thus, the poet of the individual becomes the poet of comradeship. The poet of the material is also the singer of the soul. The poet of occupations, as Robert Shulman has argued, is also the poet of loafing.[6] The poet of artificial things, of tools and all their products, is also the poet of human agency. Whitman wishes to be the poet of the reconciliation – the de-alienation, to use Marx's terms – of the self and of the self with others.[7] Poetry was the means for attaining that compaction, spiritualisation and vivification: without it there would be no reconciliation of the self and of the self with others and with the world of objects. Without it there would be no culmination of the modern.

There is, of course, an erotic dimension, and more specifically, a homoerotic dimension to Whitman's discourse of friendship, comradeship, companionship, attachment and adhesiveness. There is also a national dimension to his affirmation of compaction: his poetry sought to forge the 'true nationality of the States'.[8] The discourse of union, fusion and adhesiveness also has what we may call an ontological side: it refers to his conception of the unity and nature of the universe. Many of his poems can thus be read as operating on any number or all of these seven levels: as love poems; as a vindication of homoerotic desire and same sex love; as a vision of social unity beyond the rules of the market; as the positing of a spiritual, moral, aesthetic realm beyond the mere pursuit of monetary wealth or profit; as the cement of national American unity and consciousness; as a statement of the role of poetry in the modern world; and as a speculation on the ultimate nature of the universe and the world. It is not hard to imagine how terms such as fusion, compaction, adhesiveness, attachment among others, could operate simultaneously in any and all of these areas.

---

trial bourgeoisie. It amounted to a 'lyricising' of the status of proletarian labour under nascent capitalist relations. As such Whitman sought to mediate the contradictions between the individual and the collective, the egocentric and the humanitarian, the somatic and the intellectual, the subjective and the objective. It is true that Whitman sought to reconcile these extremes. But there was in him far more concern and anxiety about the lack of an appropriate synthesis than Larsen's thesis allows. His emphasis on comradeship thus betrayed the absence of such relations in the existing social interactions. Larsen and Sousa 1983, p. 97.

6 Shulman, p. 1982.
7 For a discussion of the concept of alienation as it evolved from the early to the mature works of Marx, see Mandel 2015.
8 Whitman [1871], pp. 935–6.

His vision of social compaction and of the spiritualisation of material progress came together in his notion of a future 'Religious Democracy'. The term religious did not designate a theocratic plan but rather *social* relations that would enable humans to move beyond their merely monetary pursuits and their mutual isolation. The religious and the social were thus fused in his vision of a new epoch to be ushered in by the work of the poet: 'View'd, to-day … the problem of humanity … is social and religious, and is to be finally met and treated by literature. The priest departs, the divine literatus comes. Never was anything more wanted than … the poet of the modern is wanted'.[9]

Whitman's fear of disunion and desire for social reconciliation should not be reduced to his concern, before 1860, with the approaching Civil War, or his aspiration, after 1865, for national and sectional reunion. Both are, of course, aspects of his work. Poems such as 'Out of the Cradle Endlessly Rocking' and as 'I Ebb'd with the Ocean of Life', speak, at least in part, as Betsy Erkkila, David S. Reynolds and other have argued, to the sense of approaching national disintegration on the eve of the Civil War. Similarly, poems such as 'Over the Carnage Rose a Prophetic Voice' posed the problem of postwar reconciliation (in a text that can also be read at several of the seven levels mentioned above). But Whitman was not only distressed with the specifically American problems leading to and arising from the Civil War. He was concerned with the social contradictions characteristic, not only of American society, but of capitalist civilisation as a whole.

As early as 1841, Whitman denounced how 'men go on from year to year with their pitiful schemes of business and profit, and wrapped up and narrowed down in those schemes, they never think of the pleasant and beautiful capacities that God has given them'.[10] In 1842, Whitman denounced the 'strife for gain'. He described it as 'an unholy spirit' that 'seems to have no bound or check'. This was not a minor problem, but rather the threat of 'greatest evil to the land'. The young editor wrote:

> If we were asked the particular trait of national character from which might be apprehended the greatest evil to the land, we should unhesitatingly point to the strife for gain which of late years has marked, and now marks, the American people. This unholy spirit seems to have no bound or check. It leads yearly to the commission, among us, of the most abominable actions. It has built up those paper money bubbles … It forms

---

9   Whitman [1871], p. 932.
10 Whitman [1841], p. 47.

insolent and selfish cliques, that stand out against the government itself, and laugh at punishment. It imbues the popular mind with a disposition to connive at villainy, if joined with wealth – to palliate crime, if its consequences are estate – to smile gently at a swindler, if he has only been a swindler of millions.[11]

Three elements of Whitman's early attitude toward the 'strife for gain' and the 'pitiful schemes of business and profit' must be underlined: the description of the race for monetary gain as '*unholy*', as an *ever-expanding* current threatening to devour all social practices, and as a '*narrow*' path, impeding the cultivation of human capacities.

Under capitalism accumulation is not driven by the capitalist's desire to consume. It's a limitless impersonal process. It has one aim: profit. It is both limitless and narrow. Whitman seems to have sensed this when he described the 'rich man' as a 'dismal and measureless fool': as an agent of the constant expansion of capital, of its growth beyond all measure, he made his life and the life of others dismal.[12] There was wealth, but not enjoyment of life. Led by an impersonal current, people became living objects or moving corpses: 'I do not believe people of these days are happy. The public countenance lacks its bloom of love and its freshness of faith. – For want of these, it is cadaverous as a corpse'.[13]

The notion of business as a soulless, unholy, ungodly, deadened force encroaching on our fuller development is a constant in Whitman's pronouncements on the issue. His vindication of the sacred, the holy and the soul cannot be divorced from this aversion to the all-devouring 'strife for gain' or from his yearning for a full flourishing of our 'capacities' and liberation from a 'cadaverous' existence.

In an 1846 editorial, Whitman denounced the 'feverish anxiety after riches', the 'unholy wish for great riches' that, according to him, 'enters into every transaction of society, and more or less taints its moral soundness'.[14] Against those who would demolish a structure – Fort Greene – vested with patriotic significance as the site of important events of the Revolutionary War, Whitman protested against the limitless cult of the 'Dollar-god'.[15] Subordination to this

---

11   Whitman [1842c], p. 41.
12   Whitman [1847?], p. 68.
13   Whitman [pre-1855], p. 90.
14   Whitman [1846a], p. 133. This text is discussed by Arvin 1938, p. 109; Erkkila 1989, p. 37.
15   Whitman [1846], p. 47. Discussed by Erkkila 1989, p. 41. Wacker refers to the 'cautiously anti-capitalist ... rhetoric' of this editorial. Wacker 1994, p. 90.

unholy 'Dollar-god' also implied a crippling of the human faculties: Whitman's 'religion' was a protest against a 'crushing' of the human faculties. Whitman thus asked his readers: 'Is the Dollar-god so ruthless that he grudges a few poor acres ... to the service of health, of refinement, of *religion*? Is nothing to be thought of on earth, but cash? O, let us be more just to the faculties God has given us! Let us not deliberately crush them out and forbid their development in this way'.[16] The destruction of Fort Greene was not only an unholy act, a 'desecration': it also 'deprives us ... of the finest and purest enjoyment human beings are capable of'.[17]

Whitman, it should be pointed out, was arguing against an editorial of the *New York Tribune* which warned that opposition to the planned demolition was 'hopeless' since 'Trade and commerce are an irresistible power, and before their necessities nothing can stand'.[18] Against this, Whitman argued that the fort should be kept as 'a Place of the Ideal'.[19] Ideal was thus another notion that Whitman opposed to the rule of 'trade and commerce' that the *Tribune* considered irresistible.

A few years later, in his 1851 lecture to the Brooklyn Art Union, Whitman denounced Americans for 'viewing most things with an eye to pecuniary profit – more for acquiring than for enjoying'. Americans were 'ambitious of the physical rather than the intellectual'. They were 'a race to whom matter of fact is everything, and the ideal nothing – a nation of whom the steam engine is no bad symbol'.[20] Whitman enumerated some unflattering traits of a typical member of that American 'race':

> His contempt for all there is in the world, except money can be made of it; his utter vacuity of anything more important to him as a man than success in 'business' – his religion what is written down in books, or preached to him as he sits in his rich pew, by whom he pays a round sum, and thinks

---

16 Whitman [1846], pp. 47–8.
17 Whitman [1846], p. 48.
18 Whitman [1846], p. 46.
19 Whitman [1846], pp. 48–9.
20 Whitman [1851], p. 241. In the 1830s, in his famous observations about American society, de Tocqueville had already diagnosed the tendency of capitalism to sacrifice the cultivation of the intellect in the pursuit of 'self-interest'. He thus wrote: 'Greed is always in a breathless hurry; the human mind, constantly diverted from the pleasures of imaginative thought and the labors of the intellect, is swayed by the pursuit of wealth'. Also: 'That instinctive drive which draws the mind to the highest realms of the intellect fights a vain battle against self-interest which draws it down to the average'. (Tocqueville 2003, pp. 52, 534) See also note 96 in Chapter 6 below.

it a bargain, – his only interest in affairs of state, getting office or jobs for himself or someone who pays him – so much for some points of character.[21]

In the 1855 preface to *Leaves of Grass*, Whitman returned to his critique of 'moneymaking' as leading to social inequality ('shameless stuffing while others starve') as well as the blunting of the senses and the impoverishment of human interactions. He denounced as 'the great fraud upon modern civilization' what he described as the 'abandonment ... to ... years of moneymaking with all their scorching days and icy nights and all their stifling deceits and underhanded dodgings ... or shameless stuffing while others starve: and all the loss of the bloom and odor of the earth and of the flowers and atmosphere and of the sea and of the true taste of the women and men you pass'.[22] This description of 'the loss of the bloom and odor of the earth ... and of the true taste of the women and men',[23] along with the earlier description of the 'contempt' of a business civilisation 'for all there is in the world, except money can be made of it' cannot but remind us of the young Marx's description of the replacement of 'all the physical and intellectual senses ... by the simple estrangement of all these senses – the sense of *having*'.[24]

These concerns reemerge in Whitman's writings after the Civil War. Such is the case of *Democratic Vistas*, his book-long rant on the failings of American society, published in 1871, at a time when the reshaping of American society by industrial capitalism was accelerating.[25] There, as in other texts, Whitman employed images such as 'hollowness', 'void', and 'blank' to describe the lack that threatened modern progress from within. Marx would have not been surprised: he had described how the 'working out' of human capacities under capitalism is experienced as 'a complete emptying-out',[26] as an 'impoverishment' of 'human nature',[27] as a 'process of dehumanization',[28] as the 'sacrifice of the human end-in-itself to an entirely external end'.[29] 'Never', proclaimed Whitman, 'was there ... more hollowness at heart than at present'.[30] Whitman

---

21 Whitman [1851], p. 245.
22 'Preface', p. 21.
23 'Preface', p. 21.
24 Marx [1844], p. 352.
25 Allen 1955, pp. 411–13. For an interesting study of *Democratic Vistas*, see Haddox 2004.
26 Marx 1993, p. 488.
27 Marx [1844], p. 352. Marx's words: 'reduced to this absolute poverty'.
28 Marx [1844], p. 355.
29 Marx 1993, p. 488.
30 Whitman [1871], p. 937.

described American cities, despite their material achievements, as failures in the creation of a fuller personality: 'But sternly discarding', he warned his readers, 'shutting our eyes to the glow and grandeur of the general superficial effect, coming down to what is of the only real importance, Personalities ... we question, we ask, Are there indeed, men here worthy of the name?'[31]

Whitman was the enthusiastic poet of the city crowd, of the shuttling ferries and the restless harbour, but this world teeming with activity now presents itself as a void, as a vast emptiness, or as a meaningless, grotesque stage: according to Whitman it was necessary to 'Confess that to severe eyes, using the moral microscope upon humanity, a sort of dry and flat Sahara appears, these cities, crowded with petty grotesques, malformations, phantoms, playing meaningless antics'.[32]

Whitman warned against a merely material, soulless progress: 'It is as if we were somehow being endow'd with a vast and more thoroughly-appointed body, and then left with little or no soul'.[33] Money-making is the ruling power in that hollow, soulless world. It is a force that penetrates and dominates all social activities: a 'serpent' that eats all other serpents.[34] According to Whitman, 'The magician's serpent in the fable ate up all the other serpents; and money-making is our magician's serpent, remaining today sole master of the field'.[35] Whitman protested against business, 'this all-devouring modern word'.[36] Business creates the modern world, and then devours it. Whitman saw the results of this dialectic everywhere. In spite of its 'unprecedented materialistic advancement – society, in these States', Whitman proclaimed,

> is canker'd, crude, superstitious, and rotten ... the element of moral conscience, the most important, the verteber to State or man, seems to me either entirely lacking, or seriously unfeebled or ungrown ... The depravity of the business classes of our country is not less than has been supposed,

---

31 Whitman [1871], p. 939.
32 Whitman [1871], p. 939.
33 Whitman [1871], p. 938. He argued elsewhere that the United States was in danger of turning into 'a more and more expanded and well-appointed body, and perhaps brain, with little or no soul' ('Poetry To-Day in America – Shakspere – The Future', p. 1014).
34 It seems to us that M. Wynn Thomas suggests as much in this passage: 'That nebulous word "soul" is invoked to communicate to others his conviction that they have allowed themselves to be devalued, silently demoralized by accepting the current market prices for their lives and by relying on the crude descriptive terms of social classification for their self-identity'. Thomas 1987, p. 13. See also Higgins 2002.
35 Whitman [1871], p. 937.
36 Whitman [1871], p. 937.

> but infinitely greater. The official services of America, national, state, and municipal, in all their branches and departments, except the judiciary, are saturated in corruption, bribery, falsehood, mal-administration; and the judiciary is tainted. The great cities reek with respectable as much as non-respectable robbery and scoundrelism ... In business, (this all-devouring modern word, business,) the one sole object is, by any means, pecuniary gain ... The best class we show, is but a mob of fashionably dress'd speculators and vulgarians.[37]

Whitman minced no words in his descriptions of 'persons arrived at high positions'. They appeared to him 'full of the rotten excrement of maggots'. They were 'sad, hasty, unwaked sonnambules'.[38] This critique of 'our materialistic, self-assertive, money-worshipping, Anglo-Saxon races' runs through Whitman's work, from the early 1840s to the 1880s.[39] He denounced the 'materialistic and business vortices, in their present devouring relations, controlling and belittling everything else'.[40] Where the soul, or a moral conscience should be, he lamented, a 'blank', 'a barren void exists'.[41] The United States enjoyed 'unprecedented material wealth, industrial products'.[42] It was 'a vast varied community, prosperous and fat with wealth of money and products and business ventures', but it was 'utterly without the sound, prevailing, moral and aesthetic healthaction beyond all the money and mere intellect of the world'.[43] The images of deformation, one-sidedness and incompleteness abound: with a 'barren void' within, Whitman had warned in *Democratic Vistas*, the 'triumphant modern civilizee, with his all-schooling and his wondrous appliances, will show himself but an amputation'.[44]

Against all this, Whitman insisted that material progress should not be an end but a means to an end. Business should not be the all-devouring vortex, the

---

37 Whitman [1871], p. 937. One cannot but be reminded of the present age of Trump.
38 'Thought', p. 513. Andrew Lawson summarises Whitman's perspective: 'What is missing from the rich man's house is pith, substance, reality – in short, soul. The encompassing structures of finance capitalism, with their mortgages and bonds, libraries and paintings, conceal a spiritual vacuum and spread a pervasive unreality. The possessions of the rich are mere husks'. Andrew Lawson 2006, p. 58. The description strikes me as correct, excepting the notion of a soulless world as lacking reality, which I think departs from Whitman's perspective.
39 'Death of Longfellow', pp. 917–18.
40 'The Spanish Element in Our Nationality', pp. 1146–7.
41 'Poetry To-Day in America – Shakspere – The Future', p. 1014.
42 'Poetry To-Day in America – Shakspere – The Future', p. 1027.
43 'Poetry To-Day in America – Shakspere – The Future', p. 1026.
44 Whitman [1871], p. 964.

serpent that rules all fields. Progress should create fuller, rounder personalities. This should be the measure of progress. This should take the place of measureless expansion pursued by 'measureless fools'. He presented the hollow, void, blank personalities so far created by modern progress as soulless: soullessness was an amputation of the self. There was, as he wrote in one of his earlier notebooks, an 'ossification of the spirit'.[45] Spiritualisation or the reconciliation with the soul was Whitman's means of expressing his vision of a fuller, many-sided self, of a wider path for our faculties and capacities. For this, the work of the poet was indispensable.

Whitman's summarised his wager: 'we of the States are the most materialistic and money-making people ever known. My own theory, while fully accepting this, is that we are the most emotional, spiritualistic, and poetry-loving people also'.[46] Nothing less than the very promise of modernity as a step forward in human progress was at stake: 'this ... play of solely materialistic bearings upon current life in the United States ... must either be confronted ... by ... an equally subtle and tremendous force-infusion for purposes of spiritualization, for the pure conscience, for genuine esthetics, and for absolute and primal manliness and womanliness – or else our modern civilization, with all its improvements, is in vain'.[47] Whitman hoped that the 'seething materialistic and business vortices' would prove to be a transitional stage to a fuller civilisation: 'The seething materialistic and business vortices, in their present devouring relations, controlling and belittling everything else, are, in my opinion, but a vast and indispensable stage in the new world's development, and are certainly to be follow'd by something entirely different – at least by immense modifications'.[48]

But the rejection of the 'business vortices, in their present devouring relations' is only one side of Whitman's aversion to a 'money-worshipping'[49] civilisation: the other is his protest against the lack of what he called adhesiveness or compaction.[50]

---

45   Whitman [pre-1855], p. 90.
46   'Poetry To-Day in America – Shakspere – The Future', p. 1024.
47   Whitman [1871], p. 992.
48   'The Spanish Element in Our Nationality', pp. 1146–7.
49   Whitman [1882], p. 898; 'Death of Longfellow', pp. 917–18.
50   As Betsy Erkkila has pointed out, even his beloved and celebrated ferries could at times embody the relentless impersonal flow of the metropolis: 'Perhaps some one has been crushed between the landing and the prow – ... still no matter, for the great business of the mass must be helped forward as before. A moment's pause – the quick gathering of a curious crowd, (how strange they can look so unshudderingly on the scene!) – the paleness of the more chicken hearted – and all subsides, and the current sweeps as it did the moment

The poet of the self thus proclaimed himself to be the poet of comrades. Friendship, comradeship, adhesiveness, companionship, attachment were all terms deployed to name his search for a non-market, non-monetary link between social agents, a vision that he often mixed with the vindication of same-sex love. 'Comradeship', he proclaimed, must be the 'twin' of democracy:

> Many will say it is a dream ... but I confidently expect a time when there will be seen, running ... through all the ... worldly interests of America, threads of manly friendship, fond and loving, pure and sweet, strong and life-long, carried to degrees hitherto unknown – not only giving tone to individual character ... but having the deepest relations to general politics. I say democracy infers such loving comradeship, as its most inevitable twin or counterpart, without which it will be incomplete, in vain, and incapable of perpetuating itself.[51]

Whitman thus explained that he looked forward to 'personal comradeship' as 'the subtlest, strongest future hold of this many-itm'd Union'.[52] A true Union, he argued, required the 'double ties not only of intertrade barter, but human comradeship'.[53]

In 1841, in the same article in which he derided the narrowing of human pursuits to business schemes, Whitman had counterposed the flourishing of human affections to the world of bank stocks, 'corporation scrip', bonds and mortgages, dollars and cents:

> I would have men cultivate their disposition for kindness to all around. To be sure, it may not bring in a percentage like bank stock, or corporation scrip, or bonds and mortgages, but it is very valuable, and will pay manifold. It is a faculty given to every human soul, though in most it is dormant and used not. It prompts us to be affectionate to all men. It leads us to scorn the cold and heartless limits of custom, but moves our souls to swell up with pure and glowing love for persons or for communities. It

---

previously. How it deadens one's sympathies, this living in a city'. Whitman [1847c], p. 160; Erkkila 1989, p. 38.

51 Whitman [1871], p. 982. Adhesiveness, a term which Whitman adapted from the pseudo-science of phrenology, became for him a 'socially condoned concept for communicating both personal love and social bonding'. Reynolds 2010, p. 639. According to Loving, in *Leaves of Grass* the term adhesiveness first appears in 'Song of the Open Road'. Loving 1982, p. 157.

52 Whitman [1882], p. 824.

53 'President Hayes's Speeches', p. 870.

makes us disdain to be hemmed in by the formal mummeries of fashion, but at the kiss of a sister or a brother, or when our arms clasp the form of a friend, or when our lips touch the cheek of a boy or girl whom we love, it proves to us that all pleasures of dollars, and cents are dross to those of loving and being beloved.[54]

Conscious of possible misunderstandings or trivialisations, the young Whitman attempted to explain his use of the word 'love': 'By "love" ... I do not mean the sickly sentimentality which is so favorite a theme with novelists and magazine writers. What I would inculcate is that healthy, cheerful feeling of kindness and good will, an affectionate tenderness, a warm-heartedness, the germs of which are plentifully sown by God in each human breast; and which contribute to form a state of feeling very different from the puerile, moping love, painted by such trashy writers as Byron and Bulwer, and their more trashy imitators'.[55] Solidarity was yet another term Whitman embraced to describe his aspiration to a social union built on a basis other than the clash of private business interests. Late in life he explained to Horace Traubel: 'The older I grow, the broader, deeper, larger that word Solidarity is impressed on my convictions – Solidarity: where can one produce its substitute? To me, the largest word in human resources – the largest word in the catalogue – fullest of meaning, potential, all inclusive'.[56]

The problem posed was not solely American, or provoked by post-Civil War sectional resentments: Whitman entertained the vision of an international comradeship. He called for the emergence of a new generation of 'bards of adhesiveness' and of 'international poems'. It was this, not the mere expansion of industry and material interconnection of the world, which could bring about the 'culmination of the modern':

> Indeed, the peculiar glory of our lands, I have come to see, or expect to see, not in their geographical or republican greatness, nor wealth or products, nor military or naval power ... but more and more in a vaster, saner, more surrounding Comradeship, uniting closer and closer not only the American States, but all nations, and all humanity. That, O poets! is not that a theme worth chanting, striving for? ... Perhaps the most illustrious culmination of the modern may thus prove to be a signal growth of joyous,

---

54 Whitman [1841], p. 47.
55 Whitman [1841], p. 48.
56 Traubel 1964, p. 342.

more exalted bards of adhesiveness, identically one in soul, but contributed by every nation, each after its distinctive kind ... I would inaugurate from America, for this purpose, new formulas – international poems ... I have thought that ... we have adhered too long to petty limits, and that the time has come to enfold the world.[57]

This vision reemerges in his introduction to a projected Russian edition of his poems. The work of material interconnection had to be completed by 'an internationality of poems and poets, binding the lands of the earth closer than all treaties and diplomacy'.[58]

To the money-worshipping individualistic civilisation Whitman opposed the dual vision of spiritualisation and comradeship, elements which nurtured each other: by creating a non-monetary link between individuals, comradeship revealed the path to 'spiritualisation', while the recognition of the spiritual, non-monetary needs enabled the possibility of a non-commercial comradely link between social agents. Whitman thus explained that '[i]t is to the development ... of that fervid comradeship (the adhesive love, at least rivaling the amative love hitherto possessing imaginative literature, if not going beyond it,) that I look for the counterbalance and offset of our materialistic and vulgar American democracy, and for the spiritualization thereof'.[59] Other texts present adhesiveness as the inclination that can, and must, curb an individualism 'which isolates' and religion as the force that 'vitalizes' both. The modern world thus needs:

> Not only that half only, individualism, which isolates. There is another half, which is adhesiveness or love, that fuses, ties and aggregates, making the races comrades, and fraternizing all. Both are to be vitalized by religion (sole worthiest elevator of man or State,) breathing into the proud, material tissues, the breath of life. For I say at the core of democracy, finally, is the religious element.[60]

---

57 'Poetry To-Day in America – Shakspere – The Future', pp. 1024–5.
58 'Two Letters', p. 1049.
59 Whitman [1871], pp. 981–2.
60 Whitman [1871], p. 949. Cross-examined during the trial of the anti-war activists known as the Chicago Seven, Allen Ginsberg offered a wonderful summary of Whitman's vision, brought to our attention by Magaril 2010, p. 74: 'THE WITNESS: As part of our nature, as part of our human nature, we have many loves, many of which are denied, many of which we deny to ourselves. He said that the reclaiming of those loves and the becoming aware of those loves was the only way that this nation could save itself and become a democratic and spiritual republic. He said that unless there were an infusion of feeling, of tenderness,

Religion in Whitman was not a mere reference to a spiritual beyond. It also refers to the constitution of the individual self and its relations with others. It refers both to the reconciliation of an otherwise fragmented self and to a new type of relations between individuals.[61] Whitman's use of the term religion reminds us of the literal meaning of its Latin root: to bind again and/or to bind tightly. It is the vehicle of Whitman's rejection of a society ruled by the mutually indifferent and one-sided pursuits of monetary gain. He claimed to find this double and conjoined affirmation of a spiritual dimension and of human comradeship in the main religious leaders of the past. He explained that 'intense and loving comradeship, the personal and passionate attachment of man to man … underlies the lessons and ideals of all the profound saviours of every land and age'. The 'most substantial hope and safety of the future of these States', he added, depended on the cultivation 'in manners and literature' of that 'intense and loving comradeship'.[62] Thus, when Whitman claims that a religious purpose underlies his poems, this must not be seen as an affirmation of a mere concern with God or a spiritual other-world: it also refers to his vision of poetry as an agent of *social* transformation.[63]

This is a major flaw in Newton Arvin's pioneering Marxist study of Whitman. Arvin rightly perceived the dynamic nature of Whitman's world-view, but he links this above all to the changes in the conception of nature brought about by the achievements of nineteenth-century science (evolution and natural selection, uniformitarian geology, molecular biology). Arvin thus calls him the poet of Scientism.[64] Whitman's religiosity is then understood as a conservative retreat into philosophical idealism.[65] But Whitman's vision was largely

---

of fearlessness, of spirituality, of natural sexuality, of natural delight in each other's bodies into the hardened, materialistic, cynical, life denying, clearly competitive, afraid, scared, armored bodies, there would be no chance for a spiritual democracy to take place in America. And he defined that tenderness between the citizens as, in his words, an adhesiveness, a natural tenderness flowing between all citizens, not only men and women but also a tenderness between men and men as part of our democratic heritage, part of the adhesiveness which would make the democracy function; that men could work together not as competitive beasts but as tender lovers and fellows'. Available in http://law2.umkc.edu/faculty/projects/ftrials/chicago7/ginsberg.html.

61   This idea is suggested by Magaril 2010, p. 62. This is the best overview of the impact of Whitman on the Spanish-speaking world.
62   Whitman [1871], p. 981.
63   'Preface, 1872', pp. 1002–3.
64   Arvin 1938, p. 213.
65   Arvin 1938, pp. 216, 224–6. This does not invalidate other aspects of Arvin's analysis, such as his discussion of Whitman's drift from pantheism toward a more traditional theism in his later years (226).

enabled by the observable, lived consequences of capitalist accumulation and not solely or even largely by the scientific discoveries of his time. The consequences of capitalism are, in turn, decisive to understand Whitman's religiosity. 'Religious Democracy' and similar notions cannot be reduced to a retreat from science into idealism or a mystical escapism: they also registered his aspiration to new *social* relations, beyond the atomisation of market competition and the imperatives of the pursuit of profit.

Whitman considered literature as the means of achieving that double objective of compaction and spiritualisation: literature would bring men and women together while also raising them above mere material, monetary pursuits.[66] Of the poet, he proclaimed in 1856 in 'By Blue Ontario's Shore' (originally entitled 'Poem of Many in One'): 'He is the arbiter of the diverse, he is the key, / He is the equalizer of his age and land, / He supplies what wants supplying, he checks what wants checking'.[67] In the 1855 preface to *Leaves of Grass*, he had already proclaimed of the American people: 'Their Presidents shall not be their common referee so much as their poets shall'. In *Democratic Vistas* he insisted it was the task of 'a class ... of native authors', of the 'prophetic literature of these States', to bring forth the 'religious and moral character beneath the political and productive and intellectual bases of the States'.[68] The United States needed not a political, but a social redefinition, and the road to it went through a new literary project: we, explained Whitman, 'are not to look so much to changes ... in Politics as to those of Literature and (thence) domestic Sociology'.[69]

Whitman described a form of material progress that must be 'vivified' by poetry, and that would otherwise, implicitly, remain dead.[70] He thus warned

---

66   Reynolds points out that Whitman had already claimed this special role for the artist as early as his 1851 speech to the Brooklyn Art Union. Reynolds 1996, p. 300.

67   'By Blue Ontario's Shore', p. 475. Erkkila has underlined how in this poem Whitman presents the poet as the 'fuser' of the nation. Erkkila 1989, p. 133. As Andrew Lawson and other critics have pointed out, 'Whitman offers poetry as a cohesive force in a divided society'. Lawson 2006, p. 52. He thus wished to 'provide the connecting tissue that will reconstitute the dismembered society into a whole, organic body' (Thomas 1987, p. 19).

68   Whitman [1871], pp. 932, 984. It was, argued Whitman, necessary to attain the 'fusion of the States into the only reliable identity, the moral and artistic one'. Whitman [1871], p. 935.

69   'Preface to "Democratic Vistas" with Other Papers, – English Edition', p. 1195.

70   Whitman's notion of 'vivification' reminds us of the young Marx's description of capitalism as the 'domination of dead matter over men' (Marx [1844], p. 319). M. Wynn Thomas has argued that 'Depending partly on his social situation, the individual is either fascinated (like the possessive bourgeois) or dominated (like the laborer) by the commodified world of objects, and the commodified objective world, he has brought into existence' (Thomas 1987, p. 26). But this contrast between bourgeois 'fascination' and working-class

that '[w]ithout that ultimate vivification – which the poet or other artist alone can give – reality would seem incomplete, and science, democracy, and life itself, finally in vain'.[71]

The historical periodisation that corresponded to Whitman's critique of the limits of democracy and material progress posited three stages. The first stage had been the political revolution, including the creation of democratic structures and the proclamation of equal rights. In the United States this corresponded to the revolution of 1776. The second comprised the expansion of industry within that framework. The third, 'without which the first two were useless', was to be the instauration of a 'Religious Democracy':

> The First stage was the planning and putting on record the political foundation rights of immense masses of people – indeed all people – in the organization of republican National, State, and municipal governments ... The Second stage relates to material prosperity, wealth, produce, labor-saving machines, iron, cotton, local, State and continental railways, intercommunication and trade with all lands, steamships, mining, general employment, organization of great cities, cheap appliances for comfort, numberless technical schools ... The Third stage, rising out of the previous ones ... I, now, for one, promulge ... a sublime and serious Religious Democracy sternly taking command, dissolving the old, sloughing off surfaces, and from its own interior and vital principles, reconstructing, democratizing society.[72]

Whitman felt that the third stage, 'arising out of the previous ones', could not come about without the work of 'original authors and poets to come', of singers, preachers and orators. Not surprisingly, in 1855 the very first three lines of 'Song of Myself' had proposed a reconciliation of the self with others:

> I celebrate myself, and sing myself,
> And what I assume you shall assume,
> For every atom belonging to me as good belongs to you.

'subordination', while not entirely objectionable, is not entirely accurate: capitalists may and do enjoy class privileges, but are no less subordinated to objective imperatives of capitalist accumulation than those they exploit. Indeed, the perpetuation of their privileges hinges on their strict adherence to those imperatives.

71   'A Backward Glance o'er Travel'd Roads', p. 659. This notion of 'vivification' or 'vitalisation' reappears in many passages.
72   Whitman [1871], pp. 976–7.

The poet celebrates himself, but immediately turns this into a celebration of the other. The celebration of the self becomes a reciprocal act: whatever the poet claims, the other can also claim. As M. Wynn Thomas argues, this was an 'open challenge' to the 'system of selfishness'.[73] This fusion of the self with others runs through Whitman's major texts, such as 'Crossing Brooklyn Ferry', to mention an obvious example, a poem that strives to close the 'breach' between writer and reader, the self and others, both present and future.[74] The concept of comradeship makes an early appearance in 'Song of Myself'. Whitman describes a diversity of labours and regions and binds them together through his comradely identification with each and all: 'Comrade of Californians, comrade of free North-Westerners, (loving their big proportions,) / Comrade of raftsmen and coalmen, comrade of all who shake hands and welcome to drink and meat'.[75] In time, Whitman would add dozens of poems to the 1855 version of *Leaves of Grass*. Yet the inscription that opened the final 1892 edition, not unlike the first lines of 'Song of Myself', combined the affirmation of the individual self and its connection with others: 'One's-self I sing, a simple separate person, / Yet utter the word Democratic, the word En-Masse'.[76]

Whitman was the self-proclaimed 'poet of comrades', of 'companionship', of 'friendliness', and 'adhesiveness'.[77] Among other things, this clearly made him

---

[73] Thomas 1987, p. 47.
[74] Thomas 1987, pp. 96–7.
[75] 'Song of Myself', p. 204.
[76] 'One's Self I Sing', p. 165.
[77] A few passages where these terms appear: (1) 'I will sing the song of companionship, / I will show what alone must finally compact these, / I believe these are to found their own ideal of manly love, indicating it in me, / ... / I will write the evangel-poem of comrades and of love, / ... / And who but I should be the poet of comrades?' ('Starting from Paumanok', p. 179). (2) 'I believe the main purport of these States is to found a superb friendship, exalté, previously unknown, / Because I perceive it waits, and has been always waiting, latent in all men' ('To the East and to the West', p. 285). (3) 'The prairie-grass dividing, its special odor breathing / I demand of it the spiritual corresponding / Demand the most copious and close companionship of men' ('The Prairie-Grass Dividing', p. 281). (4) 'I dream'd in a dream I saw a city invincible to the attacks of the whole of the rest of the earth, / I dream'd that was the city of Friends, / Nothing was greater there than the quality of robust love, it led the rest, / It was seen every hour in the actions of the men of that city, / And in all their looks and words' ('I Dream'd in a Dream', p. 284). (5) 'This moment yearning and thoughtful sitting alone, / It seems to me there are other men in other lands yearning and thoughtful, / It seems to me I can look over and behold them in Germany, Italy, France, Spain, / Or far, far away, in China, or in Russia or Japan, talking dialects, / And it seems to me if I could know those men I should become attached to them as I do to men in my own lands, / O I know we should be brethren and lovers, / I know I should be happy with them'

the singer of same-sex love, affections and desire.[78] Examples could be easily multiplied, with texts such as 'In Paths Untrodden', 'O Tan-Faced Prairie Boy', 'A Glimpse', 'Behold This Swarthy Face', 'To a Western Boy', 'Among the Multitude', 'City of Orgies', some of which are 'evocative', as Sylvia Molloy has pointed out, not so much of lasting relations, as of the urban 'male cruising scene'.[79] But this homoerotic dimension of Whitmanian comradeship, friendliness, companionship and manly attachment does not exhaust the function and meaning of these terms in his texts: they also correspond to his aversion toward the mutual indifference characteristic of the capitalist metropolis. The vindication of comradeship, friendliness, adhesiveness is both an affirmation of same-sex love, affection and desire *and* a vision of human solidarity to supplement the cash-nexus.[80] The 'love of strangers' functions as both a reference to homosexual encounters *and* as an affirmation of the need to counter the 'individualism, which isolates' with the 'adhesiveness' that 'fuses, ties and aggregates'. Whitman thus fuses his erotic, homoerotic and social vision:

> Come, I will make the continent indissoluble,
> I will make the most splendid race the sun ever shone upon,
> I will make divine magnetic lands, with love of comrades,
> with the life-long love of comrades.
> I will plant companionship thick as trees along all the rivers
> ....
> I will make inseparable cities with their arms about each other's necks,
>   by the love of comrades.
> For you these from me, O Democracy, to serve you ma femme!
> For you, for you I am trilling these songs.[81]

('This Moment Yearning and Thoughtful', pp. 280–1). See also, among other poems: 'These I Singing in Spring', 'Not Heaving from My Ribb'd Breast Only'.

78   For an interesting discussion of the way in which Whitman's sexuality has been approached, see Kaplan 1989.
79   Molloy 1996, p. 87.
80   Erkkila has argued that Whitman sought to turn 'homoerotic feelings into bonds of democratic comradeship'. He 'sought to reconnect his private homosexual feeling with the public culture of democracy'. Erkkila 1989, pp. 145, 179. While not incompatible, my point here is slightly different: Whitman's perspective went *beyond* 'democratic comradeship' or the 'culture of democracy' as commonly understood in the United States (individual freedoms, elected government) and suggests a desire to transcend some of the consequences of capitalist social relations. Arvin comes closer to our thesis, but his argument is marred by his conception of homosexuality as an 'aberration' incompatible with a 'healthy society'. Arvin 1938, pp. 273–5, 278.
81   'For You O Democracy', p. 272.

Thus, while Whitman at times sought to discourage the bolder homoerotic readings of the 'Calamus' cluster, he was not deceiving his readers when he argued that its 'special meaning ... mainly resides in its political significance'.[82] It was *both* homoerotic and political, and political not only because defying existing sexual norms is political, but in terms of envisioning an alternative to the mutual indifference of a 'business' civilisation: 'In my opinion', he explained, 'it is by a fervent, accepted development of comradeship, the beautiful and sane affection of man to man ... that the United States ... are to be effectually welded together, intercalated, anneal'd into a living union'.[83]

As Robert Shulman has forcefully argued, nothing could be farther from 'the competitive acquisitiveness' and the 'isolating, divisive tendencies of market society'.[84] What Whitman offers, M. Wynn Thomas adds, is a 'nonpossessive Self'.[85] He invites us to define ourselves 'in terms other than those of the cash nexus and of market relations'.[86] Similarly and much earlier, Newton Arvin had detected Whitman's 'deep antagonism to the whole ethic of utility and possessiveness'.[87] In the same or similar line, Richard Pascal has read 'Song of the Banner at Day-break' as a presentation of the clash between the logic of 'self-enrichment' and of 'trans-individual unity'.[88]

If the first three lines of 'Song of Myself' already proclaim the fusion of the self and others, the fourth verse seeks a reconciliation of the self with itself, a completion of a fragmented self, presented as a reconciliation with its soul: 'I loafe and invite my soul'. To the individualistic soulless world of business Whitman opposed a reunion of comrades and the recuperation of the soul, or, at times, of reconciliation with God. Whitman was not a systematic thinker. It would be wrong to attribute to him a conceptual consistency he did not exhibit, or seek. The search for a fuller human development beyond the reign of the 'Dollar-god' he described with different terms in various texts and sometimes in the same text: as a personal reconciliation of the individual with their *soul*; as the discovery of the identity of the observable material world with the *divine*; as a more commonplace theistic connection of humanity with *God*; as a vindica-

---

82   'Preface, 1876', p. 1011.
83   'Preface, 1876', p. 1011.
84   Shulman 1982, pp. 19, 20. Shulman nicely summarised his argument: Whitman 'explicitly criticizes and enacts an alternative to the world of possessive individualism. He perceptively connects and exposes its work ethic respectability, its chronic dissatisfaction and mania for ownership, its class differences and deference, and its religious guilt' (p. 24).
85   Thomas 1987, p. 89.
86   Thomas 1987, p. 13.
87   Arvin 1938, p. 112.
88   Pascal 1989, p. 164.

tion of *Religion*. Beginning around 1860, religion emerged as a recurrent theme in his poems. 'Starting from Paumanok' proclaims:

> I say that the real and permanent grandeur of these States must be their religion,
> Otherwise there is no real and permanent grandeur;
> (Nor character nor life worthy the name without religion,
> Nor land nor man or woman without religion.)[89]

The poem similarly affirms:

> My comrade!
> For you to share with me two greatnesses, and a third one rising inclusive and more resplendent,
> The greatness of Love and Democracy, and the greatness of Religion.[90]

But, as indicated, in Whitman religion does not only refer to the relation with a spiritual beyond, it also designates a new type of relation between the self and others. The soul, the divine, Religion and God are the invisible threads joining an otherwise social fragmented universe. A divine link allows the poet's spirit to find 'equals' in all lands:

> My spirit has pass'd in compassion and determination around the whole earth,
> I have look'd for equals and lovers and found them ready for me in all lands,
> I think some divine rapport has equalized me with them.[91]

Grass itself stands for both the hidden but decipherable transcendent dimension of the observable world and for a comradeship that included all:

> Or I guess it is the handkerchief of the Lord,
> A scented gift and remembrancer designedly dropt,
> Bearing the owner's name someway in the corners, that we may remark, and say *Whose*?
> ...

---

89 'Starting from Paumanok', p. 180.
90 'Starting from Paumanok', pp. 180–1.
91 'Salut au Monde', p. 296.

> Or I guess it is a uniform hieroglyphic,
> And it means, Sprouting alike in broad zones and narrow zones,
> Growing among black folks as among white, Kanuck, Tuckahoe, Congressman, Cuff, I give them the same, I receive them the same.[92]

The poet is a brother of both God and of all men and women:

> And I know that the hand of God is the promise of my own,
> And I know that the spirit of God is the brother of my own,
> And that all the men ever born are also my brothers, and the women my sisters and lovers,
> And that a kelson of the creation is love[93]

At times, comradeship becomes the all-encompassing category: God becomes a comrade and seems to either stand alongside or fuse with the lover the poet yearns for:

> My rendezvous is appointed, it is certain,
> The Lord will be there and wait till I come on perfect terms,
> The Great Camerado, the lover for whom I pine will be there.[94]

Consider again the fourth line of 'Song of Myself'. 'I loafe and invite my soul'. Reconciliation with the soul occurs in a moment of idleness, a fact which leads to a third aspect of Whitman's challenge to capitalist civilisation, namely, his self-description as a 'loafer', his celebration of 'loafing', his vindication, as others have suggested, of free time over and against the demands of capitalist accumulation.[95] For capital, as Marx explained, the purpose of increased productivity is not the extension of free time through the reduction of the working day, but rather the extraction of greater quantities of surplus value, that is to say, of surplus *labour*, from workers. Capitalism combines a constant push to

---

92 'Song of Myself', p. 193.
93 'Song of Myself', p. 192.
94 'Song of Myself', p. 241.
95 See Hunnicutt 2008. Whitman's celebration of loafing was already pointed out by Arvin. Arvin 1938, p. 112. He similarly pointed out, in relation to this, that while swimming was Whitman's favourite exercise, floating (loafing in the water, so to speak) was his favourite activity. Arvin 1938, p. 29.

increase productivity (and thus reduce the time required for the elaboration of any particular product) with a pursuit of the maximum extension of the working day: only biological barriers (the need for at least a minimum of rest) and labour's organised resistance have put a limit on capital's tendency to lengthen the working day. Limiting and reducing working hours has been a central issue of the labour movement since its birth in the nineteenth century, during which it engaged in struggles first for the ten-hour, then for the eight-hour day.[96] But the resistance of labour against capital's voracity was inevitably a holding operation. For Marx, only the transformation of the means of production into the collective property of the associated producers can turn the former from means for the exploitation of labour into means for reducing the working day and thus generating free time for all. Only thus can the liberating potential of modern industry be realised.

Guaranteed satisfaction of the basic necessities of all, reduction of the required working time and the extension of free time were three key aspects of socialism, as envisioned by Marx: a liberating constellation made possible by capitalism yet unattainable within it. There is much in *Leaves of Grass* that also runs contrary to the capitalist logic of incessant accumulation and endless toil. As Benjamin K. Hunnicutt has pointed out, for Whitman, the 'joining together' of people 'in free *activities* would be the acme of progress'.[97] Whitman understood progress as the extension of free time, not as an incessant, measureless, accumulation of profit and capital. He did not reject labour-saving machinery. Like Marx, he saw it as the basis for further human progress as long as it was employed, not to perpetuate, but to lessen the burden of work.[98] In *Democratic Vistas*, Hunnicutt points out, Whitman describes the time freed from labour for other pursuits as the 'main thing':[99] 'I can conceive such a community organized in running order, powers judiciously delegated – farming, building, trade, courts, mails, schools, elections, all attended to; and then the rest of life, the main thing, freely branching and blossoming in each individual, and bearing golden fruit'.[100] 'The rest of life, the main thing' unfolded as voluntarily chosen activities, pursued for their own sake, in the free time made available by the

---

96   For the struggle around the length of the working day in the United States, see Roediger and Foner 1989.
97   Hunnicutt 2008, p. 95.
98   As Hunnicutt argues: 'The reduction of working hours was then, as now, the obvious practical link between increasing material wealth and "higher progress"' (Hunnicutt 2008, p. 97).
99   Hunnicutt 2008.
100 Whitman [1871], pp. 968–9.

reduction of the working day. This is what Marx termed the realm of liberty, beyond the realm of labour imposed by the need to satisfy material human needs.[101]

Whitman formulated this aspiration, not through a political or economic programme but rather through his vindication of 'loafing' as one of the defining characteristics of his poetic self, which we already encounter in the fourth verse of 'Song of Myself'. In fact, as early as 1840, in the same articles in which he had denounced the atrophy of 'the pleasant and beautiful capacities' within the 'narrowed' existence ruled by pursuit of profit, Whitman had boldly proclaimed: 'How do I love a loafer!'[102] He praised 'your calm, steady, philosophick son of indolence' and placed him above 'your upstarts, your dandies, and your political oracles'.[103] Diogenes had been a loafer. Indeed, 'All the old philosophers were loafers'.[104] Adam himself, had neither worked nor 'dealt in stocks'.[105] The young Whitman's musings led to an utopian vision beyond profit-seeking and the curse of incessant labour: 'I have sometimes amused myself with picturing a nation of loafers. Only think of it! an entire loafer kingdom! How sweet it sounds! Repose, – quietude, – roast duck, – loafer'.[106] Whitman left no doubt as to which aspects of the present he wished to replace with his 'nation of loafers': 'talk about your commercial countries, and your national industry, indeed! Give us the facilities of loafing, and you are welcome to all the benefits of your tariff system, your manufacturing privileges, and your cotton trade'.[107] Whitman's praise of loafing, present in dozens of pages of *Leaves of Grass*, could not have been better chosen to offend the work discipline and entrepreneurial diligence increasingly required by an expanding capitalism.[108]

This went beyond Whitman's poetic self: biographers remind us of what many acquaintances described as his incurable 'indolence', his unwillingness to be hurried, and what his employers in particular derided as his laziness.[109] A lover of free time, a loafer by inclination and conviction, Whitman was ill-

---

101   The well-known passage on the realm of freedom is found in *Capital*, Volume III. Marx 1981, pp. 958–9.
102   Whitman [1840], p. 44.
103   Whitman [1840], p. 44.
104   Whitman [1840], p. 44.
105   Whitman [1840], p. 45.
106   Whitman [1840], p. 45.
107   Whitman [1840], p. 45.
108   The point is well made by Shulman 1982.
109   Kaplan 2003, p. 83. Even the 1849 'phrenological' chart of Whitman's head revealed a tendency toward 'Indolence'. Loving 1982, p. 62.

adapted to the logic of capitalist accumulation and its demands on both dominant capital and subordinated labour.

Another passage of 'A Song for Occupations' can be read as a thrust against the fetishistic effect – the turning of human powers into attributes inherent in objects and the subordination of social agents to an objective, impersonal, dynamic – of commodity exchange and capitalist accumulation. Under capitalism, it should be remembered, the values of commodities seem to be independent of the labour required for their production (even if exchange is precisely the act of reducing each product to a quantity of socially necessary labour time). Some commodities, such as gold and other precious metals, are endowed with half-magical powers as embodiments of value. By way of contrast with this inverted world in which commodities and money seem to have a will of their own, Whitman insists in the following passage that it is human labour (of the singers, preachers, carvers, silversmiths, bakers and masons) that stands behind the products (psalms, script, pulpit, desk, vessels, lath and plast) that surround us, while also affirming a web of human affections (friendly companions, a woman and child, the smile of the nightwatchman's daughter) against gold, the supreme fetish of commodity exchange, and the alienated objectification of human learning or of social relations in the university and the law:[110]

> When the psalm sings instead of the singer,
> When the script preaches instead of the preacher,
> When the pulpit descends and goes instead of the carver that carved the supporting desk,
> When the sacred vessels or the bits of the eucharist, or the lath and plast,
> procreate as effectually as the young silversmiths or bakers, or the masons in their overalls,
> When a university course convinces like a slumbering woman and child convince,
> When the minted gold in the vault smiles like the nightwatchman's daughter,

---

110   Ed Cutler offers a similar assessment in Cutler 1998, p. 85. For M. Wynn Thomas, this passage is an 'almost classic description of the workings of the alienated mind', of the 'reversal of cause and effect' typical of 'capitalist psychology' (Thomas 1987, p. 25). This formulation is unobjectionable, as long as the references to 'mind' and 'psychology' do not mislead us into taking this as a strictly subjective or ideological problem: for Marx the workings of the 'alienated mind' correspond to the objective, fetish-like nature of capitalist economic and social relations.

'THIS ALL-DEVOURING MODERN WORD' 95

> When warrantee deeds loafe in chairs opposite and are my friendly companions,
> I intend to reach them my hand and make as much of them as I do of men and women.[111]

And this insistence on the human labour (of singers, preachers, carvers, silversmiths, bakers and masons) that sustains the products that surround us, this affirmation of human agency against commodity fetishism and of human affections against gold, is combined by Whitman with a peek beyond the work discipline associated with the relentless pursuit of profit: a vision of the poet loafing with his 'friendly companions'. In a previous section of 'A Song for Occupations', Whitman had similarly felt the need to 'rate' the people, the love of people, and human agency over and above the world of objects, institutions, business pursuits and sacred texts:

> Old institutions, these arts, libraries, legends, collections, and the practice handed along in manufactures, will we rate them so high?
> Will we rate our cash and business high? I have no objection,
> I rate them as high as the highest – then a child born of a woman and man
> I rate beyond all rate.
>
> We thought our Union grand, and our Constitution grand,
> I do not say they are not grand and good, for they are,
> I am this day just as much in love with them as you,
> Then I am in love with You, and with all my fellows upon the earth.
>
> We consider bibles and religions divine – I do not say they are not divine,
> I say they have all grown out of you, and may grow out of you still,
> It is not they who give the life, it is you who give the life,
> Leaves are not more shed from the trees, or trees from the earth, than they are shed out of you.[112]

---

111 'A Song for Occupations', pp. 98–9. These verses bring to memory a passage from Emerson's 1837 address 'The American Scholar': 'The tradesman scarcely ever gives an ideal worth to his work, but is ridden by the routine of his craft, and the soul is subject to dollars. The priest becomes a form; the attorney, a statute-book; the mechanic, a machine; the sailor, a rope of a ship' (Emerson [1837], p. 52).
112 'A Song for Occupations', p. 359.

The poems thus affirms human agency against the threat of fetishistic subordination to its own creations in the form of traditional institutions, the world of 'cash and business', the US Constitution, or any of the many available 'bibles'.

As many authors have pointed out, Whitman was deeply moved by the experience of the Civil War. The camaraderie in field and hospital nurtured his hope that there was an alternative to the bleak 'individualism, which isolates'. 'Wartime comradeship', Erkkila has argued, seemed to prefigure his vision of a 'city of friends'.[113] The war 'represented a spark of democratic idealism in the midst of vulgar commercialism'.[114] For Whitman, according to Reynolds, the war 'accomplished for America what he had hoped his poetry would accomplish'.[115] Poems such as 'Rise O Days' clearly register this vision of the war as a demonstration that there is a shared ideal and a unity of purpose capable of generating a joint mobilisation of the many hitherto isolated social atoms.

> Long had I walk'd my cities, my country roads through farms, only half satisfied,
> ...
> But now I no longer wait, I am fully satisfied, I am glutted,
> I have witnessed the true lightning, I have witness'd my cities electric[116]

His hopes were also expressed in 'Song of the Banner at Day Break', in which the banner represents the struggle for an ideal as opposed to pursuit of material wealth and monetary gain. But Whitman's satisfaction did not last long. As Erkkila also points out, if at first he felt that the war was accomplishing 'what he had hoped his poetry would', by the early 1870s he had concluded such was *not* the case, as a reading of *Democratic Vistas* demonstrates.[117] At this time Whitman formed a new cluster within *Leaves of Grass*: 'Songs of Insurrection', a response, according to Erkkila, to the 'corruption of power and authority in the Gilded Age'.[118] (The cluster was eliminated in the next edition: a point we discuss in Chapter 8) The need to endow industry with a dimension beyond

---

113 Erkkila 1989, p. 221.
114 Erkkila 1989, p. 243.
115 Reynolds 1996, pp. 413, 420.
116 'Rise O Days From Your Fathomless Deeps', pp. 428–9.
117 Erkkila 1989, 243.
118 Erkkila 1989, p. 264. She also refers to the brief but revealing note that Newton Arvin had

profit-making continued to inform even his more celebratory visions of modern technology. In 'Song of the Exposition' he proposed the Union as the means of transcending the mere pursuit of profit. It is necessary, he proclaimed 'To fill the gross torpid bulk with vital religious fire'.[119] Addressing the Union he pleads: 'Think not our chant, our show, merely for products gross or lucre – it is for thee, the soul in thee, electric, spiritual!'[120] 'Passage to India', a celebration of several monuments of modern industry (the Suez Canal, intercontinental railroad, trans-Atlantic cable), describes how these achievements, in and of themselves, leave humanity and the world 'disjoined and diffus'd'.[121] They do not bind the earth to our 'affections'. It remains a 'cold earth, the place of graves'. The poem asks:

> Ah who shall soothe these feverish children?
> Who justify these restless explorations?
> Who speak the secret of impassive earth?
> Who bind it to us? what is this separate Nature so unnatural?
> What is this earth to our affections? (unloving earth, without a throb to answer ours,
> Cold earth, the place of graves.)[122]

The poet, the 'true son of God', must therefore complete the work of the engineers, inventors and scientists:

> After the seas are all cross'd, (as they seem already cross'd)
> After the great captains and engineers have accomplish'd their work,
> After the noble inventors, after the scientists, the chemist, the geologist, ethnologist,
> Finally shall come the poet worthy that name,
> The true son of God shall come singing his songs.[123]

---

quoted in his 1938 study, in which Whitman warns against 'all the growths corruptions and tyrannies & formalisms of Obedience (accumulating, vast folds strata, from the rankness of continued prosperity and the more insidious grip of capital)' (Erkkila 1989, p. 264). This note was written in 1870. It was commented on in Arvin 1938, pp. 138–9.
119 'Song of the Exposition', p. 341.
120 'Song of the Exposition', p. 350.
121 'Passage to India', p. 535.
122 'Passage to India', p. 534. Erkkila describes Whitman as dealing with an 'alien unresponsive world'. Erkkila 1989, p. 143.
123 'Passage to India', p. 534.

As a result, 'Nature and Man shall be disjoin'd and diffus'd no more, / The true son of God shall absolutely fuse them'.[124] The poet will fuse what would otherwise remain disjoined. Reconciliation and fusion thus emerge as key categories of Whitman's project: reconciliation of comrade with comrade, of the self with the soul, of humanity with nature, of nature with the divine.[125]

To conclude: Whitman did not yearn romantically for a past plenitude, nor was he satisfied with the emptiness of modern progress. He wanted to transcend the present. But that transcendence was not to be attained in a mere spiritual realm, nor was it to be achieved through social revolution. It had to be attained through the shared realisation that the here and now contains more than meets the eye. Whitman endeavored to bring forth the hidden dimension of the present. He wished, as M. Wynn Thomas argues, to find 'the ideal to be immanent in many aspects of contemporary life'.[126] He wished to reveal the beyond within the actual, the soul in the body, God in the world, the eternal within the transient. In 'Song for Occupations' he explains:

> A song for occupations!
> In the labor of engines and trades and the labor of fields I find the developments,
> And find the eternal meanings.[127]

The soul could be found in and through the material, not beyond it: 'Was somebody asking to see the soul? / See your own shape and countenance, persons, substances, beasts, the trees, the running rivers, the rocks and sands'.[128] He will affirm the spirit, through his affirmation of the body:

> The thin red jellies within you or within me, the bones and the marrow in the bones,
> The exquisite realization of health;

---

124 'Passage to India', p. 535. As Kaplan has pointed out, 'Passage to India' can thus be considered a 'verse counterpart' to *Democratic Vistas* (Kaplan 2003, p. 338).
125 We similarly read in 'Song of the Open Road': 'The earth is rude, silent, incomprehensible at first, Nature is rude and incomprehensible at first, / Be not discouraged, keep on, there are divine things well envelop'd' (p. 302). For a vision of 'a vast similitude' interlocking 'All nations, colors, barbarisms, civilizations, languages, / All identities that have existed or may exist on this globe, or any globe', see 'On the Beach at Night Alone', pp. 400–1.
126 Thomas 1987, p. 37.
127 'A Song for Occupations', p. 355.
128 'Starting from Paumanok', p. 183.

> O I say these are not the parts and poems of the body only, but of the soul,
> O I say now these are the soul![129]

Seeking the soul in the body, the spiritual within the industrial, Whitman's language combined the vulgar and the sublime. It was, as Charles Eliot Norton commented early on, a mix of 'New England transcendentalism' and New York 'rowdyism', or of the 'grimy' and the 'spiritual', as Reynolds describes it.[130] It combined slang with the most abstract formulas, as Matthiessen pointed out in his classic study while adding that Whitman ran into 'inordinate and grotesque failures in both directions'.[131] This mix of transcendentalism and 'rowdyism', the grimy and the spiritual, corresponds to Whitman's position as neither an opponent nor a mere apologist of capitalist progress: against all romantic yearnings, elitist disdain or mystical other-worldliness he affirmed the present in all its rowdy, grimy, bodily vulgarity, while also insisting on a poetic search that would reveal a hidden meaning, a fuller realisation of human potential, and fill the void he detected in the existing forms of modern progress. He thus mixed the language, as Emerson reportedly put it, of 'the *Bhagvat Ghita* and the *New York Herald*'.[132]

Five lines of 'Song of Myself' can be read as a compressed summary of Whitman's indictment of existing society:

> Here and there with dimes on the eyes walking,
> To feed the greed of the belly the brains liberally spooning,
> Tickets buying, taking, selling, but in the feast never once going.

---

129 'I Sing the Body Electric', p. 258.
130 Norton 1969, p. 3. Reynolds 2005, p. 31.
131 Matthiessen 1941, p. 526.
132 The judgement was attributed to Emerson by Frank B. Sanborn in 'Reminiscent of Whitman' Sanborn 1897. Also available in Schmidgall 2006. Or it could be argued that transcendentalism itself was open to a mixture of the most mundane and its hidden meanings. Whitman often seems to respond to ideas expressed by Emerson and it is not surprising that Emerson reacted positively to the first edition of *Leaves of Grass*. Consider this passage from 'The American Scholar' (1837): 'Give me insight into to-day, and you may have the antique and future worlds. What would we really know the meaning of? The meal in the firkin; the milk in the pan; the ballad in the street; the news of the boat; the glance of the eye; the form and the gait of the body; – show me the ultimate reason of these matters; show me the sublime presence of the highest spiritual cause lurking, as always it does lurk, in these suburbs and extremities of nature; let me see every trifle bristling with the polarity that ranges it instantly on an eternal law; and the shop, the plow, and the ledger referred to the like cause by which light undulates and poets sing; – and the world lies no longer

> Many sweating, ploughing, thrashing, and then the chaff for payment receiving,
> A few idly owning, and they the wheat continually claiming.¹³³

The last two lines are an obvious reference to the exploitation of labour under capitalism by the idle possessing classes. The previous three are equally interesting. The first, singled out by Richard Pascal, is particularly rich with connotations.¹³⁴ It refers, first, to people reduced to the pursuit of money. They walk with 'dimes on the eyes'.¹³⁵ But that phrase also refers to the custom of the time of placing dimes on the eyes of the dead: the image thus describes people that the pursuit of money has turned into walking dead.¹³⁶ They live in a deadened world, governed by impersonal forces. We are back to the 'cadaverous' existence he had described in the early 1850s,¹³⁷ which reminds us of 'the complete domination of dead matter over men' described by Marx in 1844.¹³⁸ The intellect is also sacrificed in the race for material accumulation, as the third line indicates. It can be read, along with the next two, as indicating that the fruits are reserved for the owning few, and not the many, who are excluded from the 'feast'. Or it can be read, along with the previous two lines, as an indication that all are immersed in the ceaseless pursuit of exchange value, of the representations of value, of abstract wealth (trading tickets) and are thus deprived of the enjoyment of concrete wealth, of the sensuous 'feast' of use value. In five dense lines Whitman's encompasses the exploitation of labour, the rule of exchange over use value, the reduction of all to the pursuit of money, the limitation of the intellect and the transformation of people into living dead. The poet was called upon to fight against these evils.

In 1887 Walt Whitman delivered his popular 'Lincoln Lecture' in Madison Square Garden in Manhattan. Cuban poet and revolutionary José Martí, who had lived in New York since 1882, took advantage of the event to write a long

---

a dull miscellany and lumber-room, but has form and order: there is no trifle, there is no puzzle, but one design unites and animates the farthest pinnacle and the lowest trench' (Emerson [1837], p. 67).

133 'Song of Myself', p. 235. A few lines later the poem refers to 'The little plentiful manikins skipping around in collars and tail'd coats'.
134 Pascal 1989.
135 Dime is the ten cent coin in US currency.
136 It seems the dimes were meant to fall or move if the person presumed dead blinked or moved their eyes: it was a means of corroborating that the person was dead.
137 Whitman [pre-1855], p. 90. Discussed in Chapter 5.
138 Marx [1844], p. 319.

review of Whitman's work.[139] His article was the first presentation of Whitman to the Spanish-speaking world.[140] Martí's approach to Whitman's poetry was part of his attempt to define and fix his own position regarding American society, and the bewildering reality of the modern metropolis. The following chapter explores the ways in which this Caribbean exile in Manhattan approached Whitman's work and its context.

---

139   Gay Wilson Allen mentions Martí's essay written on the occasion of Whitman's lecture. Allen 1955, p. 525. Almost all commentators – Kaplan and Magaril for example – assume that Martí attended Whitman's lecture. Yet that conclusion cannot be derived from Martí's text. Plus there are dozens of passages in Martí's writings in which he gives witness-like accounts of events that it is certain he did not attend. Kaplan 2003, p. 29. Magaril 2010, p. 21.
140   See the discussion of the impact of Martí's text in Alegría 1954.

CHAPTER 6

From Brooklyn Ferry to Brooklyn Bridge: José Martí and the 'Modern Multiple Life'

Cuban poet and revolutionary José Martí lived the last twelve years of his relatively brief life – he died in 1895 at 42 – in New York City. During much of this time he earned a living writing chronicles of life in the United States for newspapers in Mexico City, Caracas and Buenos Aires.[1] His writings on the United States take up more than two thousand pages and several volumes of his collected works. The debates on protectionism and free trade, the dealings of Tammany Hall and corruption scandals in Washington, painting expositions and industrial exhibitions, literature and forms of leisure, the Knights of Labor and the doctrines of Henry George, divisions within the US Catholic church and the infighting in the New York Democratic Party, the strikes against Gould's railroad empire and the 'Haymarket affair': there is hardly an aspect of American society that Martí did not attempt to convey to his Latin American readers.[2] He took on the task with the enthusiasm of one who considered himself a privileged observer of a truly unique spectacle: nothing less than the rise, in North America, of a new type of civilisation.[3] Martí was convinced that he lived in a time of transition, of 'structural change' ('cambio de quicio'), of a 'remaking of the world' ('refacción del mundo').[4] That nascent modernity rushing past his eyes filled him with a sense of fear and expectation, desolation and possibility, alienation and hope, uneasiness and admiration, 'nausea and delight', 'awe and fear'.[5]

---

1 For a discussion of the Latin American chronicle, a hybrid genre mixing journalism with the essay, see González 1983.
2 'Here we hardly have the time to look into everything that happens'. 'De año nuevo' [1886] *OC*, x, p. 364. ['Acá apenas se tiene tiempo para echar los ojos sobre todo lo que pasa'.]
3 In 1883, after a long description of the corruption of New York politics, Martí still presented the city as 'this monumental and admirable city ... in which, on foundations worthy of it, sung by voices of the workshop, and with the concert of labour and the noises of a colossal dawn, the new world is put in place'. 'Cartas de Martí' [1883], *OC*, IX, p. 350. ['esta ciudad monumental y benemérita ... donde, como en cimientos dignos de él, se asienta, coreado por voces de taller, concierto de labradores y ruidos de alba colosal – ¡el mundo nuevo!']
4 Martí [1882a], p. 48; 'El Poema del Niágara', *OC*, VII, p. 229.
5 Martí [1882a], p. 44; Martí [1885], p. 165. 'El Poema del Niágara', *OC*, VII, p. 225; 'La explosión mayor del mundo', *OC*, x, p. 331.

Such tense pairings aptly describe his attitude toward the emergent modern world in general – the world created by capital, as Marx would put it – and toward the United States in particular. But if Martí was troubled by the tensions of the present, he harboured little nostalgia for the past. He could brood over the still hidden answers to the problems of modernity, but he was convinced those answers would be equally modern: modernity could and should be reshaped, but it could not be undone. If an excessively commercial civilisation could only be completed through the work of the poet, only a thoroughly modern poet would be equal to the task. This was an important part of his reading of *Leaves of Grass*.

As he peered beyond the present, Martí embraced Nature – a central notion of his world-view and a term more often than not capitalised in his writing – as the harmonious system into which society would eventually settle. Yet this vision of nature as a regulating ideal did not imply a rejection of modernity. On the contrary, modernity, for Martí, was called upon to prepare the installation of the reign of nature through its dismantling of past conventions. The present needed a poet that was *both* thoroughly modern and in contact with nature. This too was a central aspect of his reading of *Leaves of Grass*.

Martí was convinced that the revolutions of the eighteenth century had demolished the 'old world' ('mundo antiguo') and the 'old life' ('vida vieja') and that his time – the late nineteenth century – was 'accumulating' the elements of a new 'synthesis'. But the time of preparation was not itself a time of 'synthesis'.[6] It was a grim and inhospitable time, were it not for the promise of a new, future, fuller life. Martí registered many of his views on a troubled present in his 1882 'Prologue' to Juan Pérez Bonalde's 'Poem of Niagara'. There Martí celebrates the emergence of a new, freer, wider world, liberated from the restrictions of a feudal and clerical past. A few years later, Whitman was to explain to his friend

---

6 'The last century was the time of the collapse of the old world: this century is the time of the elaboration of the new world'. 'El Presidente Garfield' [1881], *OC*, XIII, p. 199. ['El siglo último fue el del derrumbe del mundo antiguo: este es el de la elaboración del mundo nuevo'.] 'With powerful and vigorous anger, the past century cast out the elements of the old life. This century ... deals with particulars and preparations and is accumulating the durable elements of the new life'. Martí [1882b], p. 247; 'Carta de los Estados Unidos', *OC*, IX, p. 325. ['El siglo pasado aventó, con ira siniestra y pujante, los elementos de la vida vieja. Estorbado a su paso por las ruinas ... este siglo, que es de detalle y preparación, acumula los elementos durables de la vida nueva'.] 'This century is preparing the philosophy that will be established by the coming century. This is the century of particulars: the next one will be the century of synthesis'. 'Carta de Nueva York' [1882], *OC*, IX, p. 226. ['Este siglo prepara la filosofía que ha de establecer el siglo que viene. Este es el siglo del detalle: el que viene será el siglo de síntesis'.]

Horace Traubel that 'I was never made to live inside a fence'.[7] In 1882, Martí too had written of the present as a 'time of broken fences'. Martí's description fused freedom of movement with freedom of thought: 'Today there is a kind of dismantling ('desmembramiento') of the human mind. Gone are the days of high fences; now is the time of broken fences ('vallas rotas')'. And he added: 'Now men are beginning to walk across the whole of the earth without stumbling; before now, they had hardly begun to move when they ran into the wall of a gentleman's estate or the ramparts of a convent'.[8] 'We are witnessing something', Martí added, 'like a decentralization of intelligence'.[9] What used to be the privilege of a few is now available to the 'masses'. The time of the genius is now past: 'Individual geniuses are less distinguishable, for they are beginning to lack the surrounding lowliness that once heightened their stature'.[10] Such a 'decentralization of intelligence' could perhaps be regretted by the privileged few, but Martí invited his readers to embrace it:[11] 'We are witnessing a decentralization of intelligence. Beauty has become the dominion of all … Genius is moving from the individual to the collectivity. Man is losing out to men. The traits of the privileged are being diluted and expanded to the masses, which will not please those among the privileged with ignoble souls, but will gladden those of generous and gallant heart'.[12]

But the emergence of a new world was far from complete: no new 'synthesis' had yet emerged.[13] Such times of 'realignment and restructuring' ('reenquiciamiento y remolde') did not foster the elaboration of lasting works of art.[14]

---

7   Traubel 1915b, p. 19. Mentioned in Kaplan 2003, p. 70.
8   Martí [1882a], p. 45; 'El Poema del Niágara', *OC*, VII, p. 226.
9   Martí [1882a], p. 47; 'El Poema del Niágara', *OC*, VII, p. 228.
10 Martí [1882a], p. 47; 'El Poema del Niágara', *OC*, VII, p. 228.
11 Laura Lomas has rightfully emphasised this democratic dimension of Martí's introduction to Pérez Bonalde's poem. Lomas 2008, pp. 161–2.
12 Martí [1882a], p. 47; 'El Poema del Niágara', *OC*, VII, p. 229. Martí reaffirmed this idea in 1889. He argued that the time of exceptional minds was now past: 'The truly important is now in the laboratories: not in the laboratory of one, but in the laboratory of all. This is the time of putting in order and of bowing the head to acknowledge, not of raising it to prophesize. Today prophecies come from below!' 'Correspondencia especial del *Partido Liberal*' [1889], *OC*, XII, p. 163. ['La trascendencia está ahora en los laboratorios: no en el laboratorio de uno, sino en los laboratorios todos. Es época de ordenación y de bajar la cabeza para reconocer, no de alzarla para profetizar. ¡Ahora las profecías vienen de abajo!']
13 'This century is preparing the philosophy that will be established by the coming century. This is the century of particulars: the next one will be the century of synthesis'. 'Carta de Nueva York' [1882], *OC*, IX, p. 226. ['Este siglo prepara la filosofía que ha de establecer el siglo que viene. Este es el siglo del detalle: el que viene será el siglo de síntesis'.]
14 Martí [1882a], p. 44; 'El Poema del Niágara', *OC*, VII, p. 225.

Works undertaken under such circumstances were as 'restless' and 'unsettled' as their times: 'The roots of the old poetry are in decay ... personal life is full of doubt, unsettled, questioning, restless, Luciferian; and feverish inner life, dynamic, clamorous, not fully anchored, has become the principal and, with nature itself, the only legitimate subject of modern poetry'.[15] 'There are no permanent works', Martí insisted, 'because works produced during times of realignment and restructuring are shifting and unsettled in their very essence: there are no established paths'.[16] The 'once revered' models were now discredited, but the image of the future was far from clear. The modern present mixes hope and 'bewilderment', 'yearning' and 'fear': 'there is a constant yearning for some knowledge that will confirm current beliefs and a fear of learning something that will alter them ... With the spirit thus divided among contradictory and disturbed loves, and the concept of literature shaken at every moment by some new gospel, with all the images that were once revered now naked and discredited while the future's images are as yet unknown, in this bewilderment of the mind, this restless life without fixed course, definite character or certain conclusion ... it is no longer possible to produce those long and patient works, those expansive tales in verse'.[17]

Martí's description of the modern condition in his 'Prologue' to Pérez Bonalde's poem mixed anxiety and exhilaration, uneasiness and celebration. This description cannot be detached from the experience of the modern city, from the world of the railroad, the daily newspaper and the city crowd:

---

15   Martí [1882a], p. 48; 'El Poema del Niágara', *OC*, VII, p. 229.
16   Martí [1882a], p. 44; 'El Poema del Niágara', *OC*, VII, p. 225.
17   Martí [1882a], p. 45; 'El Poema del Niágara', *OC*, VII, pp. 225–6. Another example of Martí's vision of the present as the unsettled transition to a future synthesis: 'Where is the man who fails to discern, in the immensity of sorrow in his rudimentary state of being, the joyous glory awaiting him after his painful but purifying passage through the world? What peace must there be to balance such a beginning! It is a moving experience to conceive of such supreme happiness, yet how few men, satisfied with their small projects, are permitted a glimpse of it from their sack of bones'. Martí [1885a], p. 90. The reasoning is particularly dialectical: Martí is confident that the more miserable the present, the brighter and fuller must the future be to compensate for it. It should be pointed out that at least in this case Martí's original is more gender neutral than the available translation. ['¿Quién no entrevé, en la magnitud de los pesares que acarrea el estado rudimentario de la especie humana, la claridad dichosa que la aguarda, después de su acendramiento y paso doloroso por los mundos? ¡Que paz para equilibrar este comienzo! ¡Arrebata el pensar en esa suprema dicha; a cuan pocos es dado vislumbrarla, satisfechos de su pequeña máquina, desde su cáscara de huesos!' 'El General Grant', *OC*, XIII, p. 93.]

> Cities have more tongues now than there are leaves on the trees of the forest; ideas mature in the public square where they are taught and passed from hand to hand ... The ears are ready for anything; thoughts have hardly sprung up when they are already ... leaping off the page and penetrating every mind ... Trains vanquish the wilderness; newspapers, the human wilderness ... All is expansion, communication, florescence, contagion, diffusion ... Ideas do not form families in the mind, as before, or build homes, or live long lives. They go at a gallop, mounted on lighting, winged. They do not grow within a solitary mind but emerge through commerce among all ideas ... They are wrung out, placed on a pedestal, worn as a crown, stuck on a spike, worshipped as idols, overturned, raised up, and torn down ... We arise in the morning with one problem, and by the time we go to bed at night we have exchanged it for another. Images devour each other in the mind. There is not enough time to give form to thought.[18]

What was Martí's attitude to this new, unsettled and unsettling world? It was, as he put it while considering the situation of the poet in such a time, a mix of 'nausea and delight'.

> To the poets of today neither the lyric nor the epic mold comes naturally and calmly ... No one nowadays is certain of his faith, and those who believe they are deceive themselves ... All are soldiers in an army on the march. All have been kissed by the same sorceress. In every one the new blood boils. Men can tear their innermost selves to shreds, but perturbation, insecurity, vague hopes, and secret visions remain, famished and wrathful, in the most secret recesses of their beings ... Such a pounding in the brain! Such fear in the breast! Such demanding of things that do not come! Such unawareness of what one wants and in the spirit, such a sense of mingled nausea and delight, nausea for the day that is dying, delight for the dawn![19]

Martí was neither a romantic yearning for the 'day that is dying', nor an apologist proclaiming the plenitude of the present. Instead, he clung to the dimly

---

18 Martí [1882a], p. 46; 'El Poema del Niágara', *OC*, VII, p. 227. The central image of the poem introduced by Martí was the massive torrent of Niagara. Interestingly, as early as the 1840s the incessant and noisy flow of people and vehicles through Broadway had been likened to powerful falls to the north. Spann 1981, p. 95.
19 Martí [1882a], p. 44; 'El Poema del Niágara', *OC*, VII, p. 225.

discerned outline of a future 'dawn'. Martí often envisioned that future 'dawn' as the installation of a reign of nature. Yet, for him, that passage could only be enabled by modernity's removal of the deadweight of past restrictions: modernity and a latent nature were not opposing but rather complementary forces. Like Whitman, who had proclaimed 'the priest departs, the divine literatus comes', Martí felt that poets were destined to be the 'priests' of a modern religion: 'Stand up', he commanded, 'because you are the priests'.[20] For him modernity, as a point of transit between the limitations of the past and a future 'synthesis', could be described as that time 'when the priest no longer deserves the praise or reverence of the poets, but the poets have not yet begun to be priests!'[21] Whitman, as we shall see, was for Martí a prime example of the type of poet-as-priest-of-Nature that he envisioned.

Martí saw modern humanity as trapped between the 'no longer' and the 'not yet'. In that troubled, agitated, intermediate stage, the world was 'at a boil'. There was promise and hope, but no ease or comfort: 'The noise of the cars drowns the sound of the lyre. We await the new lyre, which will make chords from the axels of the cars. All the earth is now at a boil: the lyre will come later, when this ocean settles'.[22]

Martí visited the United States briefly in 1874 and again in 1880. He settled in New York City in 1882, where he lived until 1894. Martí's perception of his time was directly connected to this encounter with New York, even if some texts, such as the prologue we have just reviewed, do not mention it. It is not difficult to detect its echo in Martí's description of cities that 'have more tongues than there are leaves on the trees', where 'ideas mature in the public square', 'ears are ready for anything', where 'all is expansion, communication, florescence, contagion, diffusion'. As he explained in 1886: 'To gather the events of these days in a newspaper report is like collecting the lava of a volcano in a cup of coffee'.[23] His descriptions of the United States were a mixture, as Pedro Pablo Rodríguez puts it, of 'dynamism and uncertainty'.[24]

---

20   Martí [1887], p. 187; 'El poeta Walt Whitman', *OC*, XIII, p. 135. The point is made by Magaril 2010, p. 24.
21   Martí [1882a], p. 44; 'El Poema del Niágara', *OC*, VII, p. 233.
22   'Cartas de José Martí' [1883], *OC*, IX, p. 338. ['Ahora el ruido de los carros ahoga las voces de la lira. Se espera la lira nueva, que hará cuerdas de los ejes de los carros. La tierra está ahora en hervor: la lira se verá luego, cuando este mar repose'.]
23   Martí 1980, 'Correspondencia particular del *Partido Liberal*' [1886], p. 19. ['Poner los acontecimientos de esos días en una correspondencia de periódico es como recoger la lava de un volcán en una taza de café'.]
24   Rodríguez 1988, pp. 82–93. [dinamismo e incertidumbre.]

In one of his earlier texts on the United States, Martí had acknowledged how his observation of American city-life had from the very first moment driven him to the conclusion that the rhythms of human existence were undergoing an irrevocable alteration. Proclaiming his amazement at 'this feverish life; this astounding movement',[25] the 27 year-old Martí bid farewell to what now appeared to him as a lazy and impractical European past: 'I was never surprised in any country of the world I have visited. Here', he admitted, 'I was surprised'.[26] There was something unprecedented in New York that placed his past experience in a new light: 'As I arrived, in one of these summer-days ... when ... I saw the diligent New Yorkers running up and down, buying here, selling there, transpiring, working, going ahead; when I remarked that no one stood quietly in the corners, no door was shut an instant, no man was quiet, I stopped myself, I looked respectfully on this people, and I said good-bye for ever to that lazy life and poetical inutility of our European countries'.[27] In this 'land of railroads' even language was remade to suit new material conditions and social interactions: 'All conversation is here in a single word: no breath, no pause; not a distinct sound. We see that we are in the land of railroads. "That's all" – "didn't" – "won't" – "ain't" – "indeed" – "Nice weather" – "very pleasant" – "Coney Island" – "Excursion". That is all I can seize, when I listen with anxious attention to the average American'.[28]

Martí, overwhelmed by a new urban landscape, struggled to convey to his readers its vastness, its movement, and what he considered to be the startling transformation of the extraordinary into the commonplace. 'Nothing in the annals of humanity', he affirmed in a description of Coney Island, 'can compare to the marvelous prosperity of the United States of the North'.[29] Martí's prose tried to capture his impression of that 'sudden result of human activity':

> The amazing thing here is the size, the quantity, this sudden result of human activity, this immense valve of pleasure opened to an immense people, these dining rooms that, seen from afar, look like the encampments of armies, these roads that from two miles away are not roads at all but long carpets of heads, the daily surge of a prodigious people onto a prodigious beach, this mobility, this faculty for progress, this enterprise,

---

25   Martí [1880], p. 35. 'Impresiones de América I', *OC*, XIX, p. 109. This article (published in three parts in *The Hour*) was written in English originally.
26   Martí [1880], p. 32; 'Impresiones de América I', *OC*, XIX, p. 107.
27   Martí [1880], pp. 32–3; 'Impresiones de América I', *OC*, XIX, p. 107.
28   Martí [1880], p. 40; 'Impresiones de América III', *OC*, XIX, p. 125.
29   Martí [1881], p. 89; 'Coney Island', *OC*, IX, p. 123.

this altered form, this fevered rivalry in wealth, the monumentality of the whole ... this rising tide, this overwhelming and invincible, constant and frenetic drive to expand, and the taking for granted of these very wonders – that is the amazing thing here.[30]

The cumulative description by Martí just quoted, drifts into a Whitmanesque rhythm, anaphora included. 'The shapes arise', proclaimed Whitman:

Shapes of factories, arsenals, foundries, markets,
Shapes of the two-threaded tracks of railroads,
Shapes of the sleepers of bridges, vast frameworks, girders, arches[31]

'And there the structure rises!' exclaimed Martí in a text on the then recently inaugurated Brooklyn Bridge.[32] Here again it is the sheer 'immensity' of the achievement that 'brings joy' to the observer.[33] Unheard-of size is coupled with the continuity of movement and the diversity of those participating in it. Martí refers to the 'five broad lanes along which a hundred thousand men ... now rush from dawn to midnight' and to the crowd itself, made up of 'avid-eyed Hebrews with sharp profiles, jovial Irishmen, fleshy, robust Germans, ruddy, muscular Scotsmen, handsome Hungarians, resplendent Negroes, Russians with burning eyes, redhead Norwegians, elegant Japanese, and lean and listless Chinamen'.[34] New York, he explained elsewhere, is 'a city of cities and a sea of people and a gulf where all the currents of modern life meet, break against each other and seethe together'. It was a 'maelstrom: everything brewing in the world falls into it. Here they smile at those that flee; elsewhere they make them flee'.[35] It was 'an enormous city where the whole Universe ceaselessly sends its most agitated currents'.[36]

---

30 Martí [1881], p. 92; 'Coney Island', *OC*, IX, p. 125.
31 'Song of the Broad-Axe', p. 339.
32 Martí [1883] p. 141; 'El puente de Brooklyn', *OC*, IX, p. 424. ['¡Allá va la estructura!'] For a discussion of Martí's texts on the Brooklyn bridge and Coney Island from a perspective similar to ours see Reyes 2015.
33 Martí [1883] p. 143; 'El puente de Brooklyn', *OC*, IX, p. 426. ['Regocija lo inmenso'] Martí more than likely took both historical and technical information for his article from Conant 1883.
34 Martí [1883] p. 141; 'El puente de Brooklyn', *OC*, IX, p. 424.
35 Martí, 'Cartas de Martí' [1883], *OC*, IX, p. 388. ['Ciudad de ciudades y mar de gente y golfo donde se encuentran, rompen y hierven juntas todas las corrientes de la vida moderna'; 'vorágine: cuanto en el mundo hierve, en ella cae. Acá sonríen al que huye; allá, le hacen huir'.]
36 Martí 1980, 'Correspondencia particular del *Partido Liberal*' [1886] p. 67. ['una ciudad enorme a donde el Universo entero envía sin tregua sus más alborotadas corrientes'.]

The young Marx referred to the emergence of a 'world-historical individual' linked through countless threads to a wider world. Whitman had described the interconnection of the world through the railroad, the steamboat and the telegraph, and the sense of expansion of the self that he derived from it: 'What widens within you Walt Whitman?'[37] Contemplating the Brooklyn Bridge Martí too felt as if 'mountains were rising' within him. 'The four taut walls' of the bridge', he wrote, 'hang from the four curving cables like the doors of a grandiose world that fills the spirit with rejoicing. In the presence of this gigantic brace, we feel tidings of majesty and we yield to gratitude, as if mountain peaks were rising within our minds, which are moved by an almost religious fervor'.[38] But this was the religion and the fervor of the modern. Martí imagined Manhattan and Brooklyn as words of a 'New Gospel' and the new bridge as the hyphen joining them: 'Oh clasp worthy of these two marvelous cities! Oh steel hyphen between these two words of the New Gospel!'[39]

The scene observed from the bridge was equally interesting: 'steamboats whistle, chimneys smoke, the crowds that travel back and forth in now antiquated steamers disembark; barges unload; boats weigh anchor'.[40] This sense of wonder permeated all of Martí's references to the bridge. In a less known piece he turned the cars of the train running across the bridge into 'flying cars' and described how passengers, upon arriving – or, as he put it, 'descending' – at the opposite side, involuntarily closed their eyes 'as if they wished to not stop seeing the marvel'.[41]

The reference to the 'now antiquated steamers' points to the transformation completed between the time of Whitman's 'Crossing Brooklyn Ferry' (1860) and Martí's arrival in the United States in the early 1880s.[42] The golden age of the ferries that Whitman had celebrated belonged to a steam-powered, manufacturing capitalism that was beginning to replace hand tools with machine production. By the 1880s large scale industrial production had dwarfed its pre-bellum precursor, just as the immense bridge now overshadowed and diminished the ferries on the river.[43] Whitman, as Arthur Geffen has indicated, never

---

37 'Salut au Monde', p. 287.
38 Martí [1883] p. 143; 'El puente de Brooklyn', *OC*, IX, p. 425.
39 Martí [1883] p. 142; 'El puente de Brooklyn', *OC*, IX, p. 424.
40 Martí [1883] p. 143; 'El puente de Brooklyn', *OC*, IX, p. 426.
41 'Escena neoyorkina' [1883], *OC*, IX, p. 470. ['como si no quisiera dejarse de ver la maravilla'.]
42 Martí's term is 'añejo' which is not strictly 'antiquated' but 'aged'.
43 In an able exploration, Clayton McCarl has compared Whitman's Manhattan to Martí's New York. While the ante-bellum working population was largely made up of skilled mechanics, by the 1880s large sectors of the labouring classes were treated as living interchangeable parts of a vast industrial process. While McCarl tends to idealise the human

celebrated the bridge, as Martí did: for Martí it was a monumental expression of the promise of modernity, for Whitman, an indication that modernity as he had celebrated it was, in fact, passing from centre stage.[44]

If steel was the emblematic building material of the new metropolis, electricity was the newly found means of propelling that vaster, feverish, expansive civilisation. Martí wrote an admiring portrait of Edison, placing him alongside Emerson and Whitman as representatives of American culture.[45] Describing industrial expositions in Chicago and Boston, Martí composed his own 'Song of the Exposition', singing the praises of electricity and of the machines moved by it: 'Among the dreams of man there is a beautiful one: to suppress the night. And this seemed attained in the monumental halls of Chicago! ... How happy, smiling and beautiful, electric light is as it moves over a camp of active machines, giant wheels, fast and gasping pistons, sonorous bells, immense steam shovels ... On one side, a car moved by electricity ... on the other, a windmill, also moved by electricity ... on another, a colossal steam shovel, precise, discreet, admirable, almost intelligent'.[46] Martí's exhilaration reminds us of Whitman's praise for the Suez Canal, the trans-Atlantic cable and the intercontinental railroad in 'Passage to India' and his 1848 description of a visit to the engine room of a ferry: 'it is an almost sublime sight that one beholds there; for indeed there are few more magnificent pieces of handiwork than a powerful steam-engine, swiftly at work! ... There is a strange gratification ... [in contemplating the engine] It makes one think that man – he who can invent such powers as this – is not such an insignificant creature after all'.[47] For Martí, the variety of products from all lands at the exhibition was equally interesting: 'From Madeira, wines; from the Sandwich Islands, sugar; from Austria ... many finished art and industrial products. From everywhere, everything'.[48]

---

warmness of pre-Civil War capitalism, the contrast with the impersonality of the full-fledged industrial capitalism of the Gilded Age is largely correct. McCarl, 2006.

44 Geffen 1984.
45 Martí 1980, 'Edison' [1890], p. 135.
46 'La Exposición de Material de Ferrocarriles de Chicago' [1883], *OC*, VIII, p. 353. ['Entre los sueños del hombre, hay uno hermoso: suprimir la noche. ¡Y parecía esto conseguido en los monumentales salones de Chicago! ... ¡Qué expansiva, risueña y hermosa la luz eléctrica sobre un campamento de máquinas en acción, de ruedas girantes, de émbolos veloces, de pistones jadeantes, de campanas sonoras, de inmensas palas de vapor ... ! Por un lado, un carro movido por electricidad ... por otro, un molino de viento, por la electricidad también movido ... por otro, una pala de vapor colosal, precisa, discreta, admirable, casi inteligente'.]
47 Whitman 1920, II, 'Ten Minutes in the Engine Room of a Brooklyn Ferry Boat' [1848], pp. 210–11.
48 'La Exposición de Boston', [1883], *OC*, VIII, p. 351.

Industrial expositions gave Martí what he considered was a summary vision of modern man: 'That is modern man: standing besides the wheels of labour, he looks serenely into the future'.[49] Martí felt that modern industrial productive forces led people beyond inherited limits; they accustomed them to the hitherto unthinkable. Martí thus described an American industrial workshop:

> To see greatness, makes for greatness: – one who enters a North American workshop, where the machines roll and roar, where steam hisses and murmurs, and men walk by with mountains of artifacts on their backs, and the elevator, that modern messenger, ascends like a subtle spirit, between the walls, and hundreds of workers move back and forth, and the impetus, the effort, the frenetic and fantastic movement, the constant and colossal labour, the marvels of size and time never cease – is not surprised that such apprentices have made such a people. – The extraordinary is natural to them, since they are brought up in it. They undertake everything, because they have seen everything undertaken. Nothing marvels them, since they live surrounded by the marvelous.[50]

The passage reminds us of Marx's notion that capitalism had first revealed the unsuspected 'productive forces' that had until then 'slumbered in the lap of social labour'.[51] For Martí there was an element of defiance implicit in the modern industrial project. Tired of seeking the meaning of life from a 'hidden God', mankind had turned its attention from the heavens to earth: it was a now a 'Rebel Angel' ('Angel rebelde') defying God through its remaking of the world. The 'Rebel Angel' had, furthermore, acquired 'a new sword for the battle, –

---

49 'La Exposición de Material de Ferrocarriles de Chicago', [1883], OC, VIII, p. 352. ['Ese es el hombre moderno: de pie junto a las ruedas de trabajo, mira serenamente a lo futuro'.]

50 'Un mastodonte', [1883], OC, VIII, pp. 408–9. ['Ver grandeza, hace grande: – quien entre en un taller norteamericano, donde las máquinas ruedan y rugen, y susurra el vapor y cuchichea, y pasan hombres con montes de artefactos a la espalda, y asciende el elevador, moderno recadero, como un espíritu sutil por entre las paredes, y hormiguean centenares de trabajadores, y no cesan el ímpetu, el esfuerzo, el movimiento frenético y fantástico, la labor regular y colosal, la maravilla de tamaño y tiempo – no se asombra de que tales aprendices de taller hayan hecho tal pueblo. – Lo maravilloso les es natural, porque se crían en ello. Lo acometen todo, porque lo han visto acometer todo. De nada se sorprenden, porque viven en medio de lo sorprendente.'] In the same text Martí proclaims: 'It gladdens to see the men of today. One can be sure that the epoch of the true revelation is beginning. That of man to himself' (p. 410) ['Da gozo ver a los hombres de ahora. Puede asegurarse que ya empieza la época de la verdadera revelación. La del hombre a sí propio'.]

51 Marx and Engels [1848], p. 489.

electricity'.⁵² This notion of modern industry as a rebellion against past, even God-ordained, limits reemerged in Martí's references to specific structures in New York, to the city as a whole, and sometimes the United States in general, and to the modern world, as a new Babel that would not be frustrated through the means that had derailed its mythical namesake. In the modern Babel languages and peoples were not confounded or scattered, but, on the contrary, joined and brought together: 'In the United States', he proclaimed in 1887, 'a new humanity is now brewing; that which has been mixing through the century is already fermenting: men already understand each other in Babel'.⁵³ Martí similarly likened a new building in Broad Street to the tower of Babel, although in the modern tower, he rushed to add, 'the tongues of men are no longer confounded but rather come together, oh symbol!'⁵⁴ Martí celebrated the cranes that in New York elevated building materials 'to the edge of the clouds' and concluded that the earth was now a modern Babel, while always underlining the dimension that differentiated it from its biblical counterpart: 'The whole Earth is Babel: but the tongues are no longer confounded'.⁵⁵ Again we cannot but be reminded of Marx's 'world-historical' individual: a citizen of Martí's modern Babel. (In 1889 he similarly imagined the whole world as a ship and the recently inaugurated Eiffel tower as its mast: 'The whole world is now as if moving in the sea, with all the peoples of humanity on board, and of the ship of the world, the tower is the mast!')⁵⁶

Yet Martí derived little solace from what he took to be a new humanity in the making. The time of emergence, formation and preparation was *not* a time of synthesis, balance, harmony or reconciliation. To live in such times, Martí warned, produced 'vertigo'. There is no time to rest or look back. All must

---

52 'Noticias de los Estados Unidos' [1881], *OC*, IX, p. 45. ['nueva espada para el combate, – la electricidad –']. Martí similarly wrote of the 'cavaliers of the new type, who ride steam engines and carry a beam of electric light as their spade' 'Escuela de electricidad' [1883], *OC*, VIII, pp. 281–2. ['caballeros de la nueva usanza, que montan en máquinas de vapor, y llevan como astas de sus lanzas un haz de luz eléctrica'.]

53 'Cartas de Martí', [1887], *OC*, XI, p. 172. ['En los Estados Unidos hierve ahora una humanidad nueva; lo que ha venido amalgamándose durante el siglo, ya fermenta: ya los hombres se entienden en Babel'.]

54 '¿Cuál es el objeto de la torre?' [1883], *OC*, IX, p. 474. ['ya no se confunden ... sino que se unen ¡oh símbolo! las lenguas de los hombres'.]

55 'Cartas de Martí' [1884], *OC*, X, p. 81. ['Babel es la tierra toda: sólo que ya no se confunden las lenguas'.]

56 'La exposición de París' [1889], *OC*, XVIII, p. 414. ['¡El mundo entero va ahora como moviéndose en la mar, con todos los pueblos humanos a bordo, y del barco del mundo, la torre es el mástil!']

constantly rush forward, or risk being trampled and left behind. Martí's description of that pitiless and 'marvellous' race is an uneasy mixture of aversion and admiration:

> To live in our times produces vertigo. Neither the pleasure of looking back, nor the strength from repose is allowed to those that, engaged in this marvellous race, must perpetually look forward. Breathless, covered in dust, bloodstained, our weapons tarnished or broken, we arrive at the way station, and we drop fainting ... He who stops on the way, people or individual, is thrown on the ground, stepped upon, insulted, torn to pieces ... In vain, if still alive, regretful of his weakness, will the fallen one get up, fix his dented armor and attempt to move the rusty metal. The great fighters ... are beyond the magnificent horizon. And the lazy one has been forgotten. They are already far; very far![57]

There is progress, but there is also fear, disquiet and anxiety:

> Everything pushes, precipitates, exasperates, exacerbates, drags. One is afraid of falling behind. Because of human arrogance and to insure one's subsistence, one wishes to attain the level of everything that is on sight. Everything is railroad, telephone, telegraph. Activity is tremendous, sleep unsettled, yearning is permanent ... One feels that in these great cities life consumes itself, thins itself out, evaporates. The general situation improves; but before that favorable change in the human condition is definitely assured, many will have fallen in this break-neck war through which the change is being carried out.[58]

---

57   'Carta de Nueva York' [1881], OC, IX, p. 105. ['Vivir en nuestros tiempos produce vértigo. Ni el placer de recordar, ni el fortalecimiento de reposar son dados a los que, en la regata maravillosa, han menester de ir mirando perpetuamente hacia adelante. Sofocados, cubiertos de polvo, salpicados de sangre, deslustradas o quebradas las armas, llegamos a la estación de tránsito, caemos exánimes ... Al que se detiene en el camino, pueblo o hombre, échanlo a tierra pisoteándolo, injuriándolo, despedazándolo ... Y en vano ya, si queda vivo, arrepentido de su flaqueza, levántase el caído, repara su abollada coraza, intenta mover el oxidado acero. Los grandes batalladores ... han traspuesto el magnífico horizonte. Y el perezoso ha sido olvidado. Van ya lejos; ¡muy lejos!']

58   'Cansancio del cerebro' [1884], OC, XIII, p. 427. ['Todo empuja, precipita, exaspera, exacerba, arrastra. Se tiene miedo de quedar atrás. Se quiere ir, por arrogancia humana y por tener segura la subsistencia, al nivel de todo lo que se ve. Todo es ferrocarril, teléfono, telégrafo. La actividad es tremenda, el sueño inquieto, el ansia permanente ... Se siente que la vida en estas grandes ciudades se consume, adelgaza y evapora. La situación

The present is chaotic, the future uncertain, yet in Martí there is no yearning for a dead past: 'the past; everything is solitary castle and empty armor!; the present, everything is question, negation, rage, blasphemy of defeat, triumphant cry!; the future, everything is darkened by the dust and vapor of the battle!'[59] Life in this new Babel was a mixture of technical progress and danger, an exciting adventure and a mass spectacle. All ingredients are in evidence in Martí's 1885 chronicle of the demolition of an islet that had been an obstacle to navigation in the Hudson River: 'the islet of Flood Rock', he explained, 'flew through the air in tiny shards at the impact of 280,000 pounds of explosives, opening a clear route for ships through the mouth of the East River'.[60] 'Not in vain', he added, 'did the city gather in awe and fear' ('entre medrosa y admirada') to witness the explosion.[61] 'Awe and fear': Martí's attitude to the metropolis around him can be summarised with this phrase. Typically, Martí's report described in detail the technical preparation of the explosion (the placement and distribution of the charges, the cables and means of operating them). He also described the transformation of the event into a live spectacle for the inhabitants of New York as well as the ways it would be relayed to a wider audience by a nascent mass media: 'It is 1:15 in the afternoon; 100,000 curious onlookers crowd the riverbanks, the rooftops, and the towers. Like immense spiders perched atop their long tentacles, photographers line the river on the New York side, and the crowd makes room for them; some newspapers have as many as seven photographers here to shoot instantaneous views of the enormous explosion that they can show their readers tomorrow'.[62] But then Martí, who has taken the reader into an imaginary exploration of the tunnels that hold the explosives beneath the island, considers the possibility that progress (the freeing of navigation in the Hudson), as an explosive mixture of creation and destruction, could literally blow him, and us, to pieces:

> What if someone stumbles against the instrument that stands in a little wooden hut on the other side of the river, while we, wrapped in our rub-

---

general mejora; pero antes de que ese cambio favorable en la condición humana quede definitivamente asegurado, muchos habrán perecido en esta guerra vertiginosa en que se está haciendo la mudanza'.]

59   'El poema del Niágara', [1882], *OC*, VII, pp. 232–3. (This passage is not included in Esther Allen's excerpt of this text in *Selected Writings*.) ['lo pasado; ¡todo es castillo solitario y armadura vacía!; lo presente, ¡todo es pregunta, negación, cólera, blasfemia de derrota, alarido de triunfo!; lo venidero, ¡todo está obscurecido por el polvo y vapor de la batalla!']

60   Martí [1885], p. 164; 'La explosión mayor del mundo', *OC*, X, p. 332.

61   Martí [1885], p. 165; 'La explosión mayor del mundo', *OC*, X, p. 331.

62   Martí [1885], pp. 166–67; 'La explosión mayor del mundo', *OC*, X, p. 333.

ber capes, are seeing the tunnels! What if, over our heads the workers, who have forgotten the meaning of fear, connect the electrical wires in the cable that runs to the hut on the other bank! Ah! What if the blast is detonated before the reckless boats and steamers that are crossing the river ... are far enough away!⁶³

Martí's report concludes with the somber image of some onlookers collecting the fish killed by the explosion.

The dosage of nausea, of vertigo, of fear that Martí slipped into his description of the New Babel did not revoke his conviction that there was no turning back. In 1888 Martí wrote a piece explaining the dangers created, as well as portraying what he considered to be the ugliness and general nuisance caused, by New York's elevated trains. But he had nothing to say about *past* means of transportation, nor did he evoke a slower preindustrial city: the point of the article was to join in the celebration of the beginning of the construction of the new subway.⁶⁴

To preserve old practices was futile. Speaking of the teaching of electricity in American universities, he argued that 'To the new world corresponds a new University'.⁶⁵ It would be a crime, he insisted, to keep education divorced from the needs of the times: 'In theological times, theological university. In sci-

---

63   Martí [1885], p. 165; 'La explosión mayor del mundo', *OC*, X, p. 332.
64   'Ferrocarriles elevados' [1888], *OC*, XI, pp. 443–9. In a fragment in his notebooks Martí presented an optimistic appreciation of the evolution of New York City: 'Someone who saw New York fifteen years ago would not recognize it today: in Wall Street, for example ... buildings that seemed gigantic then are now dwarfs, and what was luxurious then must outdo itself today to keep up with the ... babylons that have grown besides it. Uptown, in the residential areas, the somber rows of brownstones have fallen ... to open the path for the original and airy houses of recent years. From all the canons [órdenes] of world architecture a new canon is in the making, in which the best of the rest is adapted to this continental scale: in twenty years there will be no city with nobler buildings'. 'Una altísima torre', *OC*, XXII, (undated), p. 150. ['Quien vio a New York hace quince años, no lo conocería hoy: En Wall Street por ejemplo ... resultan ahora enanos los edificios que parecían gigantescos entonces, y el lujo de aquel tiempo tiene que ... echar pisos nuevos para no desmerecer de las babilonias ... que les han crecido al lado. En lo alto de la ciudad, en la parte de las viviendas, aquellas hileras sombrías de piedra achocolatada han caído ... para abrir lugar a las casas originales y airosas de estos últimos años. De todos los órdenes de la arquitectura del mundo se está componiendo un orden nuevo, en que lo selecto de los demás se acomoda a estos tamaños continentales: no habrá de aquí a veinte años, ciudad con edificios más nobles'.]
65   'Escuela de electricidad' [1883], *OC*, VIII, p. 281. ['Al nuevo mundo corresponde la Universidad nueva'.]

entific times, scientific university'.⁶⁶ Journalists like him could no longer rely on their mastery of inherited literary form. They had to master a shifting, multiple experience: 'the multiple modern life, in all its forms, as it roars in the forges, as it is transformed and travels in commerce, as it becomes idea in literature and politics, as it is sublimated and painted in the arts. The journalist must know from the cloud to the microbe. Omar Khayyam and Pasteur'.⁶⁷ More generally, Latin America as a whole needed to abandon outdated cultural forms. Close observation of the United States could be a major aspect of that endeavour. As Martí wrote to Bartolomé Mitre while explaining the objective of his chronicles: 'Today, above all in some regions of our America in which Spain grew deeper roots than in others, a wrong project turned toward the stagnant old times is promoted under the banner of literature and of poetic love for tradition, – it is an urgent task to bring to light this battle of men [the United States] in all its magnificence and to place it in high relief with all its strengths'.⁶⁸ Universities in Latin America, he argued, had to abandon their almost exclusive interest in literature and the arts. What the present demanded was practical and technical instruction in accord with 'this epoch of change where each person must father himself, and there is no secure inheritance, in which houses are not built for centuries, and there is no safe place beyond the reach of social upheavals and financial catastrophes'.⁶⁹

Martí's reporting included portraits of famous or infamous Americans, a gallery that ranged from Buffalo Bill to Emerson, Jesse James to Wendell Phillips, New York political machine operator Roscoe Conkling to Brooklyn Bridge engineers John and Washington Roebling, among many others. Martí turned these literary portraits into further attempts to seize the nature, tensions and

---

66   'Escuela de electricidad' [1883], *OC*, VIII, p. 281. ['En tiempos teológicos, universidad teológica. En tiempos científicos, universidad científica'.]
67   'Cartas de Martí' [1885], *OC*, X, p. 235. ['la moderna vida múltiple, en todas sus formas, como ruge en las fraguas, como se transforma en el comercio y viaja, como se ideaifica en la literatura y en la política, como se sublima y colorea en las artes. El periodista ha de saber, desde la nube hasta el microbio. A Omar-Khayyam y a Pasteur'.]
68   'A Bartolomé Mitre y Vedia' [1882], *OC*, IX, p. 16. ['Hoy, sobre todo, en que en ciertas comarcas de nuestra América, en que arraigó España más hondamente que en otras, se capitanea, bajo bandera literaria y amor poético de la tradición, una mala empresa devuelta a los estancados tiempos viejos, – urge sacar a luz con todas sus magnificencias y poner en relieve con todas sus fuerzas, esta espléndida lidia de hombres'.]
69   Martí 1980, 'Correspondencia particular del *Partido Liberal*' [1886], p. 39. ['esta época de revuelta donde cada cual tiene que ser padre de sí, y no hay herencia segura, ni se edifican casas para siglos, ni hay forma que esté a salvo de los vuelcos sociales y de las catástrofes financieras'.]

contradictions of the modern. He thus invited his readers to examine the life of Ulysses S. Grant as a means of exploring 'the making of a great leader in a modern nation'.[70] What features, according to Martí, made Grant a typically modern figure? Grant was neither an aristocrat nor the owner or inheritor of a large fortune. He was not an academic, immersed in bookish pursuits. He was a practical man – he had been the owner of a hide and tanning business – willing and able to lend a hand in the rougher, manual aspects of production.[71] According to Martí: 'He was lacking in instruction, was little endowed with imagination and slow in conception, yet he saw the overall picture, the great contours, the reasons for enemy strength, the new approaches demanded by a kind of war never before experienced'.[72]

Martí would have agreed with Whitman's notion that Grant's trajectory proved 'how an average western farmer, mechanic, boatman'[73] could emerge in a time of crisis as a great leader. And how did such a man conduct the war? Not according to tradition or 'the book' but as his observations and appraisal of available means and of existing conditions dictated. Victory under modern conditions depended more on the efficient deployment of great numbers of men and material than on the audacity of the individual. It was a war 'of size and numbers' which could only be won 'with size and numbers'.[74]

Organising a massive, gradual, but relentless advance was ultimately more decisive than spectacular engagements and victories. Grant had commanded enormous resources, vaster than the forces marshalled by any general in the past.[75] His armies moved like a 'huge advancing mass'[76] ('mole'), not engaging in 'spectacular battles' but delivering blow after numbing blow, progress-

---

70 Martí [1885a], p. 73; 'El general Grant', *oc*, XIII, p. 84. ['Veamos cómo se hace un gran capitán en un pueblo moderno'] For a discussion of this text in terms of the debates regarding the relation of civilian and military dimensions in the Cuban struggle for independence see Díaz Quiñones 2006.

71 Díaz Quiñones has rightly pointed out the contrast drawn by Martí between Grant and his 'academic' predecessor General George B. McClellan. Díaz Quiñones 2006, p. 273.

72 Martí [1885a], p. 102; 'El general Grant', *oc*, XIII, p. 103.

73 Whitman [1882], p. 869. Whitman proclaimed that 'our leading modern Americans, Lincoln and Grant' came from the 'prairies'. Whitman [1882], p. 854. Martí: 'A railsplitter was in the White House, a tanner of hides in Galena'. Martí [1885a], p. 87; 'El general Grant', *oc*, XIII, p. 92.

74 'They do not see that this is a war of size and number, which can only be won through size and number'. Martí [1885a], p. 90; 'El general Grant', *oc*, XIII, p. 95 ['No ven que ésta es una guerra de tamaño y número, que sólo puede vencerse con el tamaño y con el número'.]

75 Martí [1885a], pp. 101, 104; 'El general Grant', *oc*, XIII, pp. 101, 104.

76 Martí [1885a], p. 101; 'El general Grant', *oc*, XIII, p. 101.

ing through incremental, unremarkable steps, taking 'a trench today, another tomorrow', but advancing nevertheless.[77] In its own grim way, the rise of Grant and the course of the war confirmed the judgment on the modern that Martí had formulated in his prologue to Pérez Bonalde's poem: 'We are witnessing a decentralization of intelligence ... Genius is moving from the individual to the collectivity. Man is losing out to men. The traits of the privileged are being diluted and expanded to the masses'.[78] Martí would have again agreed with Whitman's verdict that Grant had 'no art, no poetry – only practical sense'.[79] Or when Whitman argued that there was in Grant, 'nothing heroic, as the authorities put it', that is to say, according to inherited standards. Yet, he was 'the greatest hero'.[80] Grant's victory demonstrated how in modern war the mass overwhelmed the individual, the average weighed more than the extraordinary, dogged persistence prevailed over blazing charges. 'Oh!' Martí insisted, 'this campaign is unprecedented! What kind of warmaking is this?'[81] But if traditionalists could object to Grant's un-heroic approach, Martí relayed what he imagined his response would be: 'Is the object of war to fight brilliantly or to defeat the enemy?'[82] It is the end result, victory or defeat, which matters, at least for a 'modern captain'. And the result of Grant's war had been, not only a military victory, but the preservation of the democratic union and the liberation of four million slaves. That was the essence of the modern project as the path to a freer, fuller life: it was this that made the attempt to understand the massive impact of the career of an otherwise unexceptional individual a worthwhile endeavour.

For Whitman, as Martin T. Buinicki has argued, Grant was not only a magnificent demonstration of the capacity of the average man to perform a major historical task. His willingness to do so as his understanding, and not tradition, dictated, made him a model for the modern poet.[83] The fact that Grant, like

---

77 'Forward, forward; not battles that shine, but blows that stun'; 'Today one river and another tomorrow; one trench today and another tomorrow'. Martí [1885a], p. 101; 'El general Grant', OC, XIII, p. 102 ['Adelante, adelante; no batallas que brillan, sino golpes que aturden'; 'Hoy un río y mañana otro; una trinchera hoy y otra mañana'.]
78 Martí [1882a], p. 47; 'El Poema del Niágara', OC, VII, p. 228.
79 Whitman [1882], p. 869.
80 Whitman [1882], p. 869.
81 Martí [1885a], p. 101; 'El general Grant', OC, XIII, p. 102, ['Grant no pelea contra Lee como general que proyecta, sino como mole que avanza ... ¡Oh, aquella guerra no tiene precedente! ¿Qué manera es aquella de hacer la guerra?']
82 Martí [1885a], p. 102; 'El general Grant', OC, XIII, p. 103. ['¿El objeto de la guerra es pelear brillantemente, o vencer al enemigo?']
83 Buinicki 2008.

Napoleon, had broken with tradition and triumphed showed that the modern poet could prevail against an outdated literary canon.[84] As Whitman put it to Traubel:

> Napoleon, as a general, came up against the same class [of critics] ... When he set to and whacked away at the enemy, the tacticians, the traditionists, the canonites, all cursed him: 'God damn him! he is violating all the laws, the customs, of soldiering we were taught in the schools!' but then the fellow who was getting licked would come on and cry: 'That's true; that's all true; but, God damn him, he's knocking hell out of us anyway!' The canon proves that the poet is not a poet – but suppose he *is* a poet anyway, what can be said for the canon? ... Why – there was Grant – see how he went about his work, defied the rules, played the game his own way – did all the things the best generals told him he should not do – and won out! Suppose the poet is warned, warned, warned, and wins out?[85]

Martí also approached Grant as an emblematically modern leader. If he did not see him as a model for the poet it was perhaps because he discovered in Whitman the very same characteristics that Whitman attributed to Grant. For Martí they were parallel embodiments of the modern break with tradition, and thus they were also, paradoxically, men of nature, a point we will return to below.

But even as he attempted to convey the emancipatory impact of an emergent modernity, Martí also formulated a critique of what he considered its one-sidedness. Beginning with his first text on the United States, Martí zeroed-in on two features of the American metropolis: its reduction of all human pursuits to the race for monetary gain and the disintegration of community, the isolation of persons from each other, or, to put it in Marx's words 'the alienation of the individual from himself and from others'.[86] To this he added an awareness of the class divisions that increasingly characterised American society. Martí's

---

84 As Buinicki puts it: 'Grant was to politics and the military as Whitman was to poetry'. Buinicki 2008, p. 84.
85 Quoted in Buinicki 2008, p. 88. Originally Traubel 1915a, pp. 445–6. A few lines before, Whitman says: 'The critics are always after the style ... Nearly everybody who takes up *Leaves of Grass* stops with the style, as if that was all there is to it. Nearly everybody ... founders on that rock – goes down hopelessly – a victim of rules, canons, cultures' (p. 445).
86 Marx 1993, p. 162.

concern with an 'excessive individualism' and the 'reverence for wealth',[87] as he put it in 1889, cannot but remind us of Whitman's critical reflections on American society, as discussed in the previous chapter.

Martí noted that the United States had 'been metallized ('metalificado') to make it prosper'.[88] Its prosperity had been attained through its 'glacial metallization' ('metalificación helada').[89] A well known passage of the *Communist Manifesto* describes how capitalism 'has left no other nexus between two people than naked self-interest, than callous "cash-payment"'. It drowns all relations 'in the ice-cold water of egotistical calculation'. Martí's image of 'glacial metallization' evoked both the notion of cash payment and of cold 'egotistical calculation', as well as the distinctive building material of the modern world. North America was a land of 'cold and calculating heads' and of 'hearts made of cotton and ships'.[90] Such stunted personalities inhabited a social landscape ruled by the clash of competing, isolated individuals. Like Whitman, Martí described a life dominated by 'business' as a soulless world. The 'passion for money', he explained, killed both the 'ardent love of intellectual pleasures' and 'kindness toward men'.[91] The result was a spirit-less, fragmented civilisation, a society that reduced human contact to the clash of competing interests. 'Men', argued Martí, 'are only joined by interests, by the loving hate that those struggling for the same prize have for each other ... It is necessary that they unite for something more durable. It is necessary to create a common atmosphere for the isolated spirits'.[92]

---

87 Martí [1889], p. 264; 'Vindicación de Cuba', *OC*, I, p. 237.
88 'The American laws have given the North a high degree of prosperity and have also raised it to the highest degree of corruption. It has been metallized to make it prosper. Accursed be prosperity at such a cost!' Martí [1871], p. 22; 'Cuadernos de apuntes 1', *OC*, XXI, p. 16. ['Las leyes americanas han dado al Norte alto grado de prosperidad, y, lo han elevado también al más alto grado de corrupción. Lo han metalificado para hacerlo próspero. ¡Maldita sea la prosperidad a tanta costa!']
89 Martí [1871], p. 22; 'Cuadernos de apuntes 1', *OC*, XXI, p. 16. The whole passage reads: 'And if the general state of enlightenment in the United States seduces you, despite the corruption and the glacial metallization, can't we aspire to enlighten without corrupting?'; ['Y si el estado general de ilustración en los Estados Unidos os seduce, a pesar de la corrupción, de su metalificación helada, ¿no podemos nosotros aspirar a ilustrar sin corromper?']
90 Martí [1871], p. 21; 'Cuadernos de apuntes 1', *OC*, XXI, p. 15.
91 'If this love of richness is not tempered and dignified by the ardent love of intellectual pleasures – if kindness toward men, passion for all that is great, devotion for all that means sacrifice and glory, are not as developed as fervorous and absorbent passion for money, where shall they go?' Martí [1880], p. 33; 'Impresiones de América I', *OC*, XIX, p. 107.
92 Martí, 'El problema indio en los Estados Unidos', [1886], *OC*, X, p. 375. ['Los hombres sólo

Within that race nobody could expect help from anybody: 'Men do not stop to console and help each other. Nobody helps anybody ... Everybody marches, pushing, cursing, elbowing and biting to make their way, running over everything and anything, in order to be first'.[93] This cannot but remind one of some of Whitman's descriptions of city life.[94] In such a world, human life was terribly impoverished: in the United States, besides business matters, Martí argued, 'men have nothing to tell each other'.[95] The inhabitants of the United States were an 'astonishing people', a 'splendid people', but they were also a 'sick people'. 'This astonishing movement', Martí wrote, 'this splendid sick people, in one side wonderfully extended, in other side – that of intellectual pleasures – childish and poor ... these men too devoted to business of pocket, with remarkable neglectness of spiritual business'.[96] For Martí there was something shallow in 'these tranquil spirits, disturbed only by their eagerness to possess wealth'.[97] While Whitman criticised Americans for 'viewing most things with an eye to

       están unidos ... por los intereses, por el odio amoroso que se tienen entre sí los que regatean por un mismo premio. Es necesario que se unan por algo más durable. Es indispensable crear a los espíritus aislados una atmósfera común'.]
93 Martí, 'Cartas de Martí' [1886], *OC*, XI, p. 83. ['Los hombres no se detienen a consolarse y ayudarse. Nadie ayuda a nadie. Nadie espera en balde ... Todos marchan, empujándose, maldiciéndose, abriéndose espacio a codazos y a mordidas, arrollándolo todo, todo, por llegar primero'.]
94 For example, his description of accidents in the ferry, quoted above: 'Perhaps some one has been crushed between the landing and the prow – ... still no matter, for the great business of the mass must be helped forward as before. A moment's pause – the quick gathering of a curious crowd, (how strange they can look so unshudderingly on the scene!) – the paleness of the more chicken hearted – and all subsides, and the current sweeps as it did the moment previously. How it deadens one's sympathies, this living in a city'. Whitman [1847c], p. 160.
95 'El problema indio en los Estados Unidos' [1886], *OC*, X, p. 375. ['Los hombres no tienen nada que decirse'.]
96 Martí [1880], p. 35; 'Impresiones de América I', *OC*, XIX, p. 109. Martí similarly feared the destiny of 'a people that does not cultivate the arts of the spirit along with those of commerce'. 'Cartas de Martí' [1885], *OC*, X, p. 184. ['el pueblo que no cultiva las artes del espíritu aparejadamente con las del comercio'] As indicated in note 20 in Chapter 5 above, in 1840 de Tocqueville had anticipated both Whitman and Marx with his description of the tension between a society animated by the pursuit of profit and the intellect. Some of his formulations remind us of Martí's style and content: 'Amid this widespread upheaval, this repeated grating of opposing interests, men's unremitting progress toward wealth, where could we find that tranquility needed for deep intellectual investigations. How could the mind dwell upon one point, if everything around it was in constant movement and everyday man himself is dragged along like flotsam in the raging torrent that carries all before it?' (Tocqueville 2003, p. 531).
97 Martí [1881], p. 92; 'Coney Island', *OC*, IX, p. 126.

pecuniary profit', Martí denounced what he called the 'the mad race for simple pecuniary gain'.[98] Americans, he argued, have 'the habit of selling everything, and of not valuing anything except that which has a price'.[99] According to Martí, the typical American: 'Pays, and punches. For three things he has the fist: to hoard, to squander, to stun ... He envies nothing but fortune. He is for sale, and thinks that everything can be bought'.[100]

After describing the vibrant and exuberant life of the American cities, Whitman, asked his readers in 1871: 'But sternly discarding, shutting our eyes to the glow and grandeur of the general superficial effect, coming down to what is of the only real importance, Personalities ... we question, we ask, Are there indeed, men here worthy of the name?'[101] He answered that it was necessary to 'Confess that to severe eyes ... a sort of dry and flat Sahara appears'.[102] In the same vein, he added: 'Never was there, perhaps, more hollowness at heart than at present, and here in the United States'.[103] Where the soul should be, he argued elsewhere, a 'blank', 'a barren void exists'.[104] Contemplating the multitude in Coney Island, Martí too embraced the notion of a void at the centre of an otherwise admirable prosperity. He confessed to a '[n]ostalgia for a superior spiritual world ('un mundo spiritual superior') ... because this land is devoid of spirit ('está vacía de espíritu')'.[105] One could see this as a conservative, elitist reaction

---

98   Martí 1980, 'Correspondencia particular del *Partido Liberal*' [1886], p. 41. ['loca contienda por la simple riqueza pecuniaria'].
99   Martí 1980, 'Correspondencia particular del *Partido Liberal*' [1886], p. 69. ['el hábito de venderlo todo, y de no dar valor sino a lo que tiene precio'.]
100 'Cartas de Martí', [1884], *OC*, X, p. 131. ['Paga, y pega. Para tres cosas tiene el puño: para acaparar, para dispendiar, para anonadar ... Nada envidia, menos la fortuna. Se vende, y cree que todo se compra'.] In this article he also described Americans as 'una gente bovina', a 'bovine people' (p. 131).
101 Whitman [1871], p. 939.
102 Whitman [1871], p. 939.
103 Whitman [1871], p. 937.
104 'Poetry To-day in America – Shakspere – The Future', p. 1014.
105 Martí [1881], p. 92; 'Coney Island', *OC*, IX, p. 126. Martí similarly argued that 'there is not enough soul in this gigantic people' ['no hay alma suficiente en este pueblo gigantesco'.] 'El problema indio en los Estados Unidos', [1886], *OC*, X, p. 375. Compare the following two formulations. The first by Whitman: 'I say of all this tremendous and dominant play of solely materialistic bearings upon current life in the United States ... that they must either be confronted and met by at least an equally subtle and tremendous force-infusion for purposes of spiritualization, for the pure conscience, for genuine esthetics, and for absolute and primal manliness and womanliness – or else our modern civilization, with all its improvements, is in vain, and we are on the road to a destiny, a status, equivalent, in its real world, to that of the fabled damned' (Whitman [1871], p. 992). The second by Martí: 'But is this activity devoted in the same extent to the development of these high and noble

to modernity, as yearning for a past of moral consistency or spiritual plenitude, were it not for the enthusiasm with which Martí traced the image of a new civilisation illuminated by electricity, joined by railroads and majestic bridges, tendered and served by machines, while he also celebrated what he described as the 'decentralization of intelligence', the transformation of beauty into the 'domain of all', the movement of 'genius' from the 'individual' to the 'collectivity' and the distribution of the 'traits of the privileged' among the 'masses'.[106] Yet, over and over, he returned to what he considered to be the dual curse of one-sidedness and fragmentation afflicting the United States.

Martí had nothing but words of praise for the Brooklyn Bridge, as we have seen. The creators of the bridge, 'and those who maintain it, and those who cross it' seemed to him 'men carved out of granite, like the bridge itself'.[107] But there was an element that threatened to erode this achievement from within: 'the excessive love of wealth that gnaws at their intestines like a worm'.[108] If Whitman described 'persons arrived at high places' as 'full of the rotten excrement of maggots',[109] the image of worms as a repulsive agent undermining a healthy body, or as life in its least attractive form, appears more than once in Martí's chronicles of life in the United States: through its one-sided pursuit of

---

anxieties of soul, that cannot be forgotten by people who want to escape from unavoidable ruin, and strepitous definitive crumbling?' Martí [1880], p. 33; "Impresiones de América I", *OC*, XIX, p. 107. Barring the different attitude to 'womanliness' (see Chapter 9) there is an unmistakable affinity of content and tone.

106   For a further description of the restless and soulless city consider this passage: 'Here there is barely enough time to live. The head is a circus, and thoughts are whipped horses. "The neurosis of Paris", say the French dailies: because they have not come to see this neurosis! Nobody sleeps, nobody wakes, nobody sits: everything is race, escape, assault, noisy fall, eminent triumph. It is a procession of eager eyes, mounted on winged legs – the legs of Mercury. All follow all, as if pursuing each other, catching up, bringing each other down. The marrow twists and shrinks as a wet hide placed in the sun: the soul leaves the body as drops of liquid from a broken flask'. 'De año nuevo' [1886], *OC*, X, p. 363. But even here the concern with the loss of the soul is mixed with the exhilarating description of modern city life. ['Acá apenas se tiene tiempo para vivir. El cráneo es circo, y los pensamientos son caballos azotados. "La neurosis de Paris" dicen los diarios de Francia: ¡por qué no han venido a ver esta otra neurosis! Nadie se duerme, nadie se despierta, nadie está sentado: todo es galope, escape, asalto, estrepitosa caída, eminente triunfo. Es una procesión de ojos sedientos, montados sobre piernas aladas, – las piernas de Mercurio. Van los unos tras los otros, como persiguiéndose, alcanzándose, abatiéndose. La médula se retuerce, y encoge como un cuero húmedo puesto al sol: el alma se va del cuerpo como de un pomo roto las gotas de esencia'.]

107   Martí [1883] p. 141; 'El puente de Brooklyn', *OC*, IX, p. 424.
108   Martí [1883] p. 141; 'El puente de Brooklyn', *OC*, IX, p. 424.
109   'Thought', p. 513.

wealth the United States risked becoming 'a nation of worms'.¹¹⁰ In a formulation that combined his admiration and his qualms regarding the United States he affirmed: 'This country is like a great tree; perhaps it is a law of nature that in the roots of great trees live worms'.¹¹¹ The curve of Grant's life, with its combination of monumental and less than admirable aspects, personified the possible course of 'a republic corrupted by the predominant love of wealth':¹¹² misled by that 'love of wealth', Grant had lent his name to the promotion of shady, semi-fraudulent financial operations.¹¹³ The savior of the republic had become a speculator.

Two phrases summarised Martí's description of what he took to be the darker side of life in the United States: 'Each for himself. Fortune as the only objective in life',¹¹⁴ or, as he put it in a later text, 'excessive individualism, reverence for wealth'.¹¹⁵ 'Size', he severely proclaimed, 'is the only greatness of this land'¹¹⁶ and he similarly referred to New York as 'this great city, where people live so alone'.¹¹⁷

Martí wrote a glowing portrait of Wendell Phillips, an opponent of slavery who, according to him, had also denounced the terrible dangers and consequences of a society structured around the one-sided pursuit of monetary

---

110   'El centenario americano' [1889], *OC*, XIII, p. 381. In an early editorial, Whitman had also referred to those that wished to destroy Fort Greene in Brooklyn for commercial purposes as 'Sir Much-worm', Whitman [1846], p. 48.
111   Martí [1882], p. 113. 'Carta de Nueva York' [1882], *OC*, IX, p. 259. ['Es este pueblo como grande árbol: tal vez es la ley que en la raíz de los árboles grandes aniden los gusanos.']
112   'La presidencia de los Estados Unidos', [1888], *OC*, XI, p. 411. ['república corrompida por el amor predominante a la riqueza'.]
113   'El General Hancock' [1886], *OC*, XIII, p. 171. 'It can be seen that the public defect which in Mexico is called "moneyism", the unchecked desire for material wealth ... brutalizes and corrupts the Republics'. 'La religión en los Estados Unidos', [1888], *OC*, XI, pp. 425–6. ['Se ve que ese defecto público que en México comienza a llamarse "el dinerismo", el afán desmedido por las riquezas materiales ... ¡brutaliza y corrompe a las Repúblicas!'] Martí wrote as well: 'I know that a people that does not cultivate the arts of the spirit along with those of trade, fattens like a bull, and will empty itself of its decomposed insides, when its treasure is exhausted'. 'Cartas de Martí, [1885], *OC*, X, p. 184. ['Sé que el pueblo que no cultiva las artes del espíritu aparejadamente con las del comercio, engorda como un toro, y se saldrá por sus propias sienes, como un derrame de entrañas descompuestas, cuando se le agoten sus caudales'.]
114   'El problema indio en los Estados Unidos', [1886], *OC*, X, p. 375. ['Cada cual para sí. La fortuna como único objeto de la vida'.]
115   Martí [1889], p. 264; 'Vindicación de Cuba', *OC*, I, p. 237.
116   'Apuntes' [1875–1877], *OC*, XIX, p. 17. ['es la única grandeza de esa tierra']
117   'Cartas de Martí' [1883], *OC*, IX, p. 334. ['Esta ciudad grande, donde viven las gentes tan solas'.]

gain. 'It pained him sorely', Martí wrote, 'to see the country's life centered on moneymaking'. Martí quoted Phillips's warning: 'Cotton is choking you! Machines are not going to save you! Jingling of money is all one hears; there is nothing but squeaking of wheels, market dust, and clinking of dollars'. This land, he again quoted Phillips, had been 'corrupted by the sordid economy of Franklin's Poor Richard'.[118]

Whitman, as we saw, elaborated the vision of the necessary 'spiritualization' and 'compaction' of a spirit-less and fragmented world. Martí formulated a very similar notion. We must, he warned, keep the 'spirit alight in these anxious, money-grubbing times' ('tiempos ansiosos y enmonedados').[119] If men in the United States were only united by monetary interest, by the 'loving hatred' of those competing for the same prize, it was necessary, he argued, 'that they unite for something more durable'. It was necessary to give 'a common atmosphere for the isolated spirits'.[120]

Whitman too warned that size and economic power were monstrous without a 'largeness of spirit': 'The largeness of nature or the nation were monstrous without a corresponding largeness and generosity of the spirit of the citizen. Not nature nor swarming states nor streets and steamships nor prosperous business nor farms nor capital nor learning may suffice for the ideal man ... nor suffice the poet'.[121] Martí agreed that size and greatness were not the same: as indicated, already in the 1870s he lamented that size seemed to be 'the only greatness of this land'.[122] In 1889 he insisted that the United States had yet to prove it was great in terms other than mere size and 'covetousness' ('codicia').[123]

In his book of poems *Versos libres*, written in the early 1880s but not published in his lifetime, Martí used a 'broken wing' as a master metaphor for 'the world in these times':

> If you ask me for a symbol of the world
> In these times, this is it: a broken wing.

---

118 Martí [1884a], p. 65; 'Wendell Phillips', *OC*, XIII, p. 68.
119 Martí [1884], p. 152; 'Una distribución de diplomas en un colegio de los Estados Unidos', *OC*, VIII, p. 440.
120 'El problema indio en los Estados Unidos' [1886], *OC*, X, p. 375. ['Es indispensable crear a los espíritus aislados una atmósfera común'; 'que se unan por algo más durable'.]
121 'Preface', p. 6.
122 'Apuntes' [1875 7], *OC*, XIX, p. 17.
123 He wondered whether the United States would be able to fulfil 'the duties of greatness, which is to deserve it for something other than mere covetousness and size'. 'Correspondencia especial del Partido Liberal' [1889], *OC*, XII, p. 154. ['el deber de la grandeza, que es el de merecerla con algo que no sea la mera codicia y el tamaño'.]

> Gold is much worked on, the soul hardly at all –
> See my suffering: my soul lives
> As a dove trapped in a cave ...[124]

Martí's diagnosis of a fragmented and soulless social landscape yields the voice of a tortured subjectivity, cut-off from its surroundings: 'Here I am', one verse proclaims, 'alone, and torn asunder'.[125] Broken wing, the image of the broken self is recurrent:

> Broken, I return in pieces, aflame!
> I lift myself from the floor: I raise and gather
> The remains of myself ...[126]

Whitman's wish for a 'vivification' of the world suggested the presence of a deadened world, or as he puts it, of an 'unloving earth, without a throb to answer ours, / Cold earth, the place of graves'.[127] Martí, in a more anguished tone, also spoke of his situation as a living death, and of himself as a dead man that nevertheless walks on: 'And I wander on, as a corpse that walks / Mad of love, solitude, fright!'[128] His body is a walking grave: 'I have lived: I have died: and in my wandering / Tomb I live on'.[129] At its most somber, this vision turns into a death wish. Death is better than a living death: 'It is pleasing to die, horrible, to live dead'.[130] In an equally dark mood, the poem 'The Swiss Father'

---

124 'A los espacios', *oc*, XVI, p. 185.
  Si me pedís un símbolo del mundo
  En estos tiempos, vedlo: un ala rota.
  Se labra mucho el oro, el alma apenas! –
  Ved como sufro: vive el alma mía
  Cual cierva en una cueva acorralada: – .
125 Allen (ed.) 2002, 'Famous Island', p. 61. 'Isla famosa' *oc*, XVI, p. 163. ['Aquí estoy, solo estoy, despedazado']
126 'No, música tenaz', *oc*, XVI, p. 218.
  ¡Roto vuelvo en pedazos encendido!
  Me recojo del suelo: alzo y amaso
  Los restos de mí mismo; ávido y triste.
127 'Passage to India', p. 534.
128 'Hierro', *oc*, XVI, p. 143. These verses were crossed out in Martí's manuscript:
  ¡Y hecho a andar, como un muerto que camina,
  Loco de amor, de soledad, de espanto!
129 'He vivido: me he muerto', *oc*, XVI, p. 173.
  He vivido: me he muerto: y en mi andante
  Fosa sigo viviendo ...
130 'Hierro', *oc*, XVI, p. 144. ['Grato es morir, horrible, vivir muerto'.]

relates the story of a man that in Logan County, Arkansas, killed his three sons and then committed suicide. The poem praises the father, who was willing to take on the guilt for this crime in order to save his children from a meaningless life: 'From the hard burden / Of a life without faith or patria, grim / Life with no certain end or open channel'.[131] Martí's verses were not only inspired by the social landscape described in his chronicles: they were also shaped by his personal situation as an exile, separated from his wife and son, at a very frustrating moment in the efforts to build the struggle for Cuban independence. Yet they also point to the fact that, for Martí, a future, liberating 'synthesis' would require what Whitman would have called a 'vivification' of a deadened world, the 'compaction' of a fragmented social landscape, and the making whole of a shattered subjectivity.

Martí thus welcomed otherwise lamentable events which, through an unexpected interruption of a soulless and atomising life, offered a glimpse of an alternative existence. He thus described the assassination of President Garfield, and the journey of his body to its burial ground, in a manner reminiscent of Whitman's description of the transportation of Lincoln's remains in 'When Lilacs Last in the Dooryard Bloom'd': as a mass ceremony of shared, collective grief. Martí wrote: 'Just in time does this immense pain come to balance in this trading people the weakened spiritual life with commercial life, which is beneficial while kept within its natural bounds, but becomes petrifying and corrupting when it goes beyond them'.[132] (The notion of petrification reminds us of the young Whitman's image of the 'ossification of the spirit', used to describe the results of market society).[133] Similarly, Martí interpreted New York's reaction to a brutal blizzard in 1888 as proof that, after all, 'the virtues promoted by hard work suffice, in moments of difficulty, to compensate for the absence of those other virtues that have been undermined by egotism!'[134] As a result of the city's paralysis, 'isolated spirits' had found a 'shared atmosphere': 'The whole city is speaking in loud voices as if it were afraid of being alone. Those who would otherwise be jostling each other brutally are smiling today and telling each other about their mutual dangers, exchanging addresses and walking long distances besides their new friends'.[135]

---

131   Allen (ed.) 2002, 'The Swiss Father', p. 59; 'El padre suizo', *OC*, XVI, p. 150.
132   'El Presidente Garfield' [1881], *OC*, XIII, p. 206. ['A tiempo viene este dolor inmenso a igualar en este pueblo negociador, la vida espiritual enferma, y la vida mercantil, sana en su medida natural, pero, fuera de ella, petrificadora y corruptora'.]
133   Whitman [pre-1855], p. 90. Discussed in Chapter 5.
134   Martí [1888], p. 230; 'Nueva York bajo la nieve' [1888], *OC*, XI, p. 422.
135   Martí [1888], p. 230; 'Nueva York bajo la nieve' [1888], *OC*, XI, p. 422. For a discussion of this see McCarl 2006.

What vision did Martí offer of a future 'synthesis' beyond the fragmented and soulless present?[136] As he rejected a stunted and one-sided present, Martí embraced what he took to be the order, harmony and generosity of nature. Yet this cult of nature was not, for him, a repudiation of modernity: only the modern break with the past could free nature from the inherited constraints that had until then deformed it. Martí thought of his time as a mid-point between the collapse of inherited limits and the achievement of a new 'synthesis': modernity was that moment of troubled untangling of what is natural from what is artificial and imposed. Over and over, Martí retreated to this paradoxical yet, for him, central notion: modernity as the liberating dissolution of inherited dogmas and divisive doctrines, Nature as the only religion worthy of modern man, or, in other words, modernity and nature as convergent currents. This explains the appearance of nature in his work in somewhat unlikely places. Grant, at his best, was for him an exemplary leader of a modern people, yet he was also a man who had set aside 'academic', 'bookish', 'conventional' and 'imported' ideas and had instead embraced the 'new ideas that Nature suggested to him'.[137] He was a 'natural character', one of 'those who spring from Nature' as opposed to men 'cast in conventional molds'.[138] Martí said as much about Sherman, another prominent Union general: 'Sherman, a man passionately fond of justice and like Grant a product of Nature'.[139]

Such a coupling of modernity and nature is also to be found in *Leaves of Grass*: Whitman presented himself both as the poet of the modern, and of the liberation into nature. This articulation, as we saw, would have not surprised Marx. Marx explained how it is typical for capitalist modernity to think of itself as liberation of humanity into its true nature, from which it had been kept by arbitrary constraints and restrictions. Furthermore, as we see in the case of Martí, nature, as an ideal, could also be deployed to criticise capitalist modernity: the deficient present could be criticised as not having fully cleared the path for nature. Martí thus proclaimed: 'there can be no contradiction in Nature'.[140]

---

136 'This century is preparing the philosophy that will be established by the coming century. This is the century of particulars: the next one will be the century of synthesis'. 'Carta de Nueva York', [1882], *OC*, IX, p. 226. ['Este siglo prepara la filosofía que ha de establecer el siglo que viene. Este es el siglo del detalle: el que viene será el siglo de síntesis'.]
137 Martí [1885a], p. 105; 'El general Grant', *OC*, XIII, p. 104.
138 Martí [1885a], p. 80; 'El general Grant', *OC*, XIII, p. 89. ['carácter natural'; 'los que arrancan de la Naturaleza'; 'amoldados a la convención'.]
139 Martí [1885a], p. 109; 'El general Grant', *OC*, XIII, p. 107.
140 Martí [1887], p. 186; 'El poeta Walt Whitman', *OC*, XIII, p. 134.

This affirmation implied both a diagnosis and a cure: if contradictions were observable in the social realm, the problem resided in the divergence from nature, and the solution in discovering the path toward it.

This duality also shaped Martí's perspective on poetry: the present demanded a new poetry, a poetry that is both in contact with nature and thoroughly modern. In a manner reminiscent of Whitman, Martí insisted that poetry 'is more necessary to a people than industry itself, for industry provides them with a means of subsistence, while literature gives them the desire and strength of life'.[141] Material prosperity should be a means, not an end. There are needs, Martí warned, that mere commercial prosperity cannot satisfy. Art, he proclaimed, produced a deeper form of enjoyment 'than the mere possession of a fortune'.[142] If material prosperity were to become an end, he warned, humanity would find itself trapped in an incessant but unsatisfying race, incessant as it is propelled by the very same unsatisfaction it perpetuates: it is condemned to an 'always incomplete prosperity'.[143] This, again, reminds us of Whitman's description of the rich man as a 'measureless fool'.[144]

Art, Martí argued, could function as a *prefiguration* of the reconciliation of the disparate, conflicting elements of the present: 'The rhythm of poetry, the echo of music ... are ... the peaceful auguries of a future in which all will be clear'.[145] For him, the present was an unsettled period of preparation of a future synthesis. Literature should 'reveal a form of society that is closer to perfection than any now known'.[146] Martí oscillated between his lamentation that art had been denied to the United States and his praise for American authors that, according to him, offered a glimpse beyond the incongruities of the present.[147] He refers twice to an afternoon spent reading Emerson as an

---

141 Martí [1887], p. 187; 'El poeta Walt Whitman', OC, XIII, p. 135.
142 'El problema indio en los Estados Unidos', [1886], OC, X, p. 376. ['que la mera posesión de la fortuna'].
143 Without poetry, argued Martí, people 'will raise to the level of essential faculties those that should serve them as mere instruments, and will drown out with the loud noise of an *always incomplete prosperity* ('prosperidad siempre incompleta') the irremediable affliction of the soul, which only finds pleasure in the great and the beautiful'. Martí [1887], p. 187; 'El poeta Walt Whitman', OC, XIII, p. 135.
144 Whitman [1847?], p. 68.
145 'Apuntes' [1875–7], OC, XIX, p. 17. ['El ritmo de la poesía, el eco de la música ... son ... apacibles augurios de un tiempo que será todo claridad'.]
146 Martí [1887], p. 186; 'El poeta Walt Whitman', OC, XIII, p. 135.
147 'Oh, this light of the centuries has been denied to the people of North America! Size is the only greatness of this land ... never has a larger cloud of ambition fallen over a larger extension of virgin soil!' 'Apuntes' [1875–7], OC, XIX, p. 17. ['¡Ay, que esta luz de siglos ha sido negada al pueblo de América del Norte! El tamaño es la única grandeza de esa tierra. ¡Que

experience without parallel in which, as in a trance, he was able to glimpse the future ('entreví lo futuro').[148] These passages are discussed in Chapter 9, where some recent readings of Martí are critically examined.

Martí warned that the literature of the past could not have the desired impact on the present. If the spiritual void of the modern required a re-encounter with nature, it could not be filled with the poetry of the past. Martí explained that 'the literature of our time is ineffective, because it is not the expression of our times'.[149] Modern problems required modern responses. The notion was central to his endorsement of Whitman's poetic project. For Martí, Whitman's 'staggering book' constituted the grandest attempt yet to create a poetic language that was both modern and capable of relaying 'the spontaneous teaching and council of Nature'.[150]

Martí first referred in writing to Whitman in November of 1881. In 1882 he informed his readers of the existence of 'a magnificent rebellious and vigorous poet, Walt Whitman'.[151] Two years later he offered the judgment that 'There is now in the United States no poet but Walt Whitman, an admirable rebel'.[152] Three years later Martí penned his major text on Whitman. Martí's references to dozens of specific verses and images leave no doubt that he had read *Leaves of Grass* closely, including 'Song of Myself', 'A Song for Occupations', 'Salut au Monde', 'Give Me the Splendid Silent Sun', and the 'Children of Adam' and 'Calamus' clusters.[153]

---

mucho, si nunca mayor nube de ambiciones cayó sobre mayor extensión de tierra virgen!'] In an enigmatic fragment in his notebooks Martí seems to refer to a book he planned to write on five authors, four of which are American: 'My book. Emerson – Carlyle. – Motley. – the perfect Motley. Longfellow, the serene Longfellow and Walt Whitman – Adamiano'. Motley quite probably refers to American historian John Lothrop Motley. 'Fragmentos', OC, XXII, p. 116. ['Mi libro. Emerson – Carlyle. – Motley. – el perfecto Motley, Longfellow, el sereno Longfellow y Walt Whitman – Adamiano'.]

148 'Otros fragmentos' [undated], OC, XXII, p. 323; Also 'Kant y Spencer' [undated] OC, XIX, pp. 369–70.
149 'Escuela de electricidad', [1883], OC, VIII, p. 282. ['La literatura de nuestros tiempos es ineficaz, porque no es la expresión de nuestros tiempos'.]
150 Martí [1887], p. 186; 'El poeta Walt Whitman', OC, XIII, p. 135.
151 'A Bartolomé Mitre y Vedia' [1882], OC, IX, p. 18. ['grandísimo poeta rebelde y pujante, Walt Whitman'] For a list of references to Whitman in Martí's writings see: Schwarzmann and Fountain 2010.
152 'Reforma esencial en el programa de las Universidades Americanas' [1884], OC, VIII, p. 428. ['no hay ahora en los Estados Unidos más poeta ... que Walt Whitman, un rebelde admirable'.] For yet another description of Whitman as a 'rebel' see 'Libros. Notas', OC, XVIII, p. 283.
153 According to Ann Fountain, Martí's article contains at least seventy specific references to lines of *Leaves of Grass*. Schwarzmann and Fountain 2010, p. 47. Martí singled out 'When

As indicated, Martí read Whitman as both a modern poet and a man of nature: characteristics which for him (and for Whitman) were not contradictory but complementary. Informing his readers that Whitman's book had been banned, he adds: 'of course it is banned, for it is a book of nature'.[154] Men, argued Martí, 'allow themselves to be branded, like horses and bulls'.[155] They are 'molded' by fashions, schools and books and 'dislocated' by 'Universities and Latinists' until 'they no longer know each other'.[156] Against such men, Whitman stands as a man 'naked, virginal, amorous, sincere, and powerful'. When they encounter him, conventional men 'flee as if from their own consciences'.[157] But, Whitman stands serene and proud. And 'why shouldn't he take pride in himself', asks Martí, 'when he feels himself to be a living and intelligent part of Nature?'[158]

As indicated, for Martí, art could offer a glimpse beyond the present. Poetry 'announces and propagates the final, joyous concordance of apparent contradictions'.[159] While Whitman spoke of a future 'Religious Democracy', Martí described the transcendence of existing one-sidedness and isolation, prefigured in art, as the emergence of the religion that 'Humanity ... has awaited in bewilderment since it became aware of the emptiness and insufficiency of its ancient creeds'.[160] For Martí, Whitman's work announced the arrival of that 'definitive religion': 'It is not a matter of trilling rhymes and bedchamber sighs, but of the birth of an era, the dawn of the definitive religion, the renewal of mankind'.[161] Whitman, he explained, 'takes the measure of the religions without ire, but believes that the perfect religion is in Nature'.[162]

Martí insists: 'Those raised on Latin, French, and the Academy may be unable to understand this heroic grace'.[163] Embodiment of the paradoxical alliance of nature and modernity, Whitman was both the poet of nature and the specific product of the United States. 'Listen to the song of this hardworking

---

Lilacs Last in the Dooryard Bloom'd' as particularly significant: 'The mystical threnody that Whitman composed on the death of Lincoln is perhaps one of the most beautiful works of contemporary poetry'. Martí [1887], p. 185. 'El poeta Walt Whitman', *OC*, XIII, p. 134.

154   Martí [1887], p. 183; 'El poeta Walt Whitman', *OC*, XIII, p. 131.
155   Martí [1887], p. 183; 'El poeta Walt Whitman', *OC*, XIII, p. 131.
156   Martí [1887], p. 183; 'El poeta Walt Whitman', *OC*, XIII, p. 131.
157   Martí [1887], p. 183; 'El poeta Walt Whitman', *OC*, XIII, p. 131.
158   Martí [1887], p. 188; 'El poeta Walt Whitman', *OC*, XIII, p. 139.
159   Martí [1887], p. 186; 'El poeta Walt Whitman', *OC*, XIII, p. 135.
160   Martí [1887], p. 187; 'El poeta Walt Whitman', *OC*, XIII, p. 135.
161   Martí [1887], p. 192; 'El poeta Walt Whitman', *OC*, XIII, p. 140.
162   Martí [1887], p. 188; 'El poeta Walt Whitman', *OC*, XIII, p. 137.
163   Martí [1887], p. 185; 'El poeta Walt Whitman', *OC*, XIII, p. 133.

and satisfied nation', Martí invited his readers, 'listen to Walt Whitman'.[164] Whitman's poetry, he affirmed, corresponded to 'the greatest number of free men and workers the Earth has ever seen'.[165] While indicating that Whitman lived 'as man of nature', Martí insisted that his work could not be detached from the city, with its 'mosaic of occupations', its dusty streets and its 'gasping factories': 'He lives in the country, where the man of nature works the free earth ... but he does not live far from the gracious and ardent city, with its sounds of life, its mosaic of occupations, its collective epic, the dust from cart wheels, the smoke from gasping factories'.[166] Whitman's poetry was as vast as the 'mosaic of occupations' of the metropolis: 'Nothing is alien him', Martí pointed out, 'he considers everything ... He is of every cast, creed, and profession and finds justice and poetry in them all'.[167] Martí identified that multiple identity as central to Whitman's poetic voice: 'He understands all virtues, receives all rewards, works all trades, suffers from all pains ... He is the slave, the prisoner, the one who fights, the one who falls, the beggar'.[168]

Martí connected Whitman's innovations to the visible results – the 'great masses of people', the 'cities at their work', the 'tamed seas', the 'enslaved rivers', the 'mountains of merchandise', the 'towns of ships' – of a rising industrial capitalism. Whitman's quest, he claimed, was a matter 'of finding the words to echo the sound of the settlement of great masses of people, the cities at their work, the tamed seas and the enslaved rivers. Will Walt Whitman yoke consonants together and in meek couplets harness these mountains of merchandise, forests of thorns, towns of ships, combats in which millions of men fall so that right may prevail, and the Sun that rules over all and streams in limpid fire across the vast landscape?'[169] Whitman's 'apocalyptic sentences' corresponded to the needs of a modern people.[170] 'Rhyme, meter?', Martí asked. 'Oh no!', he answered: 'His rhythm lies in the linkage of his strophes, in the apparent chaos

---

164 Martí [1887], p. 187; 'El poeta Walt Whitman', *oc*, XIII, p. 136.
165 Martí [1887], p. 185; 'El poeta Walt Whitman', *oc*, XIII, p. 133.
166 Martí [1887], p. 185; 'El poeta Walt Whitman', *oc*, XIII, p. 133.
167 Martí [1887], p. 188; 'El poeta Walt Whitman', *oc*, XIII, p. 136.
168 Martí [1887], p. 191; 'El poeta Walt Whitman', *oc*, XIII, p. 139. There is perhaps an echo of Whitman in Martí's brief notes to himself about the structure of a possible book or article about 'Occupations': 'A book about: "Occupations". – Son: Let us go see how wood-engraving is done ... And a clear and detailed description. – Son: Let us go see how paper is manufactured'. 'Libros. Notas' *oc*, XVIII, p. 287. ['Un libro sobre: "Ocupaciones". – Hijo: vamos a ver como se graba en madera ... Y la descripción, clara y minuciosa. – Hijo: vamos hoy a ver cómo se fabrica el papel'.]
169 Martí [1887], p. 192; 'El poeta Walt Whitman', *oc*, XIII, p. 141.
170 Martí [1887], p. 192; 'El poeta Walt Whitman', *oc*, XIII, p. 140.

of convulsive phrases, superimposed into a skillful composition that distributes ideas into large musical groups – the natural poetic form of a people that does not build stone by stone, but with enormous blocks'.[171] In the process of molding his verse to a new epoch, Whitman tossed 'the romantic lament aside, as a useless excrescence'[172] while also mixing words 'with unheard-of audacity, placing august, almost divine words beside words thought inappropriate or indecent'.[173]

Martí thus shared Whitman's aversion to a spiritless and fragmented world, his sense of emptiness in the midst of material prosperity, his critique of one-sided cult of 'business', his desire to transcend the present, his vision of the role of art in such a transcendence, his notion of a new 'religion' mixing the experience of the modern and nature. Martí articulated his views independently of Whitman. There is no evidence that he read *Democratic Vistas* or other prose works in which Whitman explained his social views. Yet, given their shared perspective, Martí could appropriate *Leaves of Grass* for his own critical purposes while remaining faithful to Whitman's conception of his own work. He thus described *Leaves of Grass* in ways to which its author would not have objected: as a path-breaking offspring of the modern metropolis, as liberation of humanity into nature and as an antidote to the one-sidedness and isolation of the self in American civilisation.

There were, nevertheless, important differences that should not be overlooked. Martí was Cuban, not American, and he was committed to the struggle for Cuban independence. In the United States he felt himself to be an outsider, and he presented himself as such. In his push to transcend the present he reached for the resources, not only of poetic intervention, but also of political activism.[174] Both facts – his status as an outsider and his revolutionary activity –

---

171 Martí [1887], p. 192; 'El poeta Walt Whitman', OC, XIII, p. 140. Also: 'The language of Walt Whitman, entirely different from that which poets before him have used, corresponds in its strangeness and power ... to the new humanity which has congregated upon this fecund continent with such portents that in truth neither lyres nor dainty quatrains could contain them'. Martí [1887], p. 192; 'El poeta Walt Whitman', OC, XIII, p. 140.
172 Martí [1887], p. 191; 'El poeta Walt Whitman', OC, XIII, p. 139.
173 Martí [1887], p. 194; 'El poeta Walt Whitman', OC, XIII, p. 142.
174 At times, the mix of Martí's condition as an exile, his aversion to many aspects of life in New York, and his desire to rejoin the struggle for Cuban independence resulted in very bitter lines, as in the following letter to a friend: 'Everything ties me to New York, at least during several years of my life: everything ties me to this cup of poison ... [B]ut the truth is that every day, when night arrives, I feel consumed from within by venom that ... upsets my soul, and invites me to escape from myself. Every part of me is shattered. From within there comes a fire that burns me, like a fever, persistent and dry. It is death by stages. Only on the days in which I don't go out for business, or see only a few people, or I take much

differentiated him from Whitman and also shaped his response to contradictions of modernity as he perceived them, an aspect of his trajectory that we shall explore in Chapter 9.

> air now that it is spring, do I suffer less this horror of the spirit: what reins have I needed to keep the mind under control! The day in which I write that poem!' 'Cartas a Manuel Mercado' [1886], OC, XX, p. 90. ['Todo me ata a New York, por lo menos durante algunos años de mi vida: todo me ata a esta copa de veneno ... [P]ero la verdad es que todos los días, al llegar la tarde, me siento como comido en lo interior de un tósigo que ... me pone el alma a vuelcos, y me invita a salir de mí. Todo yo estallo. De adentro me viene un fuego que me quema, como un fuego de fiebre, ávido y seco. Es la muerte a retazos. Solo los días en que no bajo a negocios, o veo poca gente, o ando mucho al aire ahora que hay primavera, padezco menos de este horror de espíritu: ¡que riendas he necesitado para sujetar la mente a frenos! ¡el día que yo escriba ese poema!']

CHAPTER 7

'The Final Culmination of This Vast and Varied Republic': Whitman's Failed Transcendence of the Present

Previous chapters explored Whitman's aversion to the mutual indifference, characteristic of market relations, and to the subordination of all human pursuits to the race for 'pecuniary gain' as well as to the encroachment on free time by the demands of an increasingly strict labour discipline, typical of capitalism. Through the years, Whitman added to this a concern with the growing class polarisation generated by US capitalism in the Gilded Age. The existence of relations of exploitation in the United States had been suggested in two verses of 'Song of Myself': 'Many sweating, ploughing, thrashing, and then the chaff for payment receiving, / A few idly owning, and they the wheat continually claiming'.[1] During the 1870s and 1880s this passing reference was joined by commentaries on the conflict between capital and labour. *Democratic Vistas* thus referred, in 1871, to 'the labor question, beginning to open like a yawning gulf, rapidly widening every year'.[2]

The 'labor question' was sharply posed through the 1870s, most spectacularly during the great labour rebellion of 1877. During that tumultuous year, federal troops were mobilised to quell working-class upheavals, as the strikes of railroad workers spread from West Virginia into Maryland, rolled north as far as Buffalo and through the Mid-West and culminated in insurrections in St. Louis and Pittsburgh.[3] Whitman's 1879 text 'The Strike and Tramp Question' registered some of his conclusions in the face of the growing conflict between capital and labour. He now warned that politics had to move beyond the 'abstract question of democracy': 'Beneath the whole political world, what most presses and perplexes to-day ... is not the abstract question of democracy, but of social and economic organization, the treatment of working-people by employers, and all that goes along with it – not only the wages-payment part, but a certain spirit and principle, to vivify anew these relations'.[4] As can be seen,

---

1 'Song of Myself', p. 235.
2 Whitman [1871], p. 990.
3 For a lively description see Chapter 1 'The Great Upheaval' of Breecher 1997, pp. 13–37.
4 'The Tramp and Strike Questions' (1879), p. 1064. Whitman also wrote: 'In coincidence, and as things now exist in the States, what is more terrible, more alarming, than the total want of any

the issue, for Whitman, could not be solved through a mere wage raise: the 'spirit and principle' of the relations between working people and employers had to be 'vivified anew'. In his mind they had, therefore, acquired an objective, deadened, inhuman form.[5]

In his 1879 article, Whitman likened the recent strikes to past revolutions. Revolutions had been strikes against oppression. Recent strikes raised the issue of whether they had fully realised their emancipatory visions. The question, it now turns out, 'remains to be settled'. Whitman argued that 'The American Revolution of 1776 was simply a great strike, successful for its immediate object – but whether a real success judged by the scale of the centuries ... yet remains to be settled. The French Revolution was absolutely a strike, and a very terrible and relentless one, against ages of bad pay, unjust division of wealth-products'.[6] There is a clear indication here that strikes may be completing the work left undone by the American and French Revolutions. This was coupled with a warning that if the United States failed to avoid the emergence of the type of class polarisation that Whitman associated with Europe 'then our republican experiment, notwithstanding all its surface-successes, is at heart an unhealthy failure'.[7]

Yet, despite his concern regarding the treatment of workers and the 'yawning gulf' between classes, Whitman refused to take the side of labour against capital. It is futile to seek passages that would turn him into a socialist. An opponent of icy mutual indifference, of the one-sided pursuit of monetary profit and social polarisation, Whitman sought to abolish them while leaving private property, market relations and capitalist accumulation untouched: poetry, not social revolution, would compact a fragmented social landscape, 'comradeship' would reconcile mutually indifferent social agents. Both would, not abolish, but 'vivify' the deadened relations between capital and labour. Whitman wanted poems and personalities that 'will radiate in subtle ways ... in transactions between employers and employ'd persons, in business and wages, and sternly in the army and navy, and revolutionizing them'.[8] But this 'revolutionising' left private property, market relations and the rules of capitalist accu-

such fusion and mutuality of love, belief, and rapport of interest, between the comparatively few successful rich, and the great masses of the unsuccessful, the poor? As a mixed political and social question, is not this full of dark significance?' 'Lacks and Wants Yet' in 'Notes Left Over', p. 1070.
5 In 'Starting from Paumanok', composed in the late 1850s, Whitman had promised 'chants' he described as 'Shooting in pulses of fire ceaseless to vivify all'. 'Starting from Paumanok', p. 177.
6 'The Tramp and Strike Questions' (1879), p. 1065.
7 'The Tramp and Strike Questions' (1879), p. 1065.
8 'Poetry To-Day in America – Shakspere – The Future', p. 1015.

mulation standing.⁹ Whitman remarked in his correspondence that the United States needed a 'new breed of authors ... Hegelian, Democratic, religious'.¹⁰ He is open to the same criticism that the young Marx levelled against Hegel: he provided an ideal solution to a real problem, or, in this case, a merely poetical solution to a social problem. The song that would compact all social agents did little to abolish the social relations that pit them against each other as commodity producers or as employers and wage workers. Worse still: by providing a literary solution to a social problem (mutual indifference, the imperatives of monetary gain, class polarisation), the poet risked giving existing relations an ideal-poetical varnish, thus helping legitimise and perpetuate them. Ironically, as Erkkila, Wynn Thomas and others have suggested, Whitman's critique risked becoming a mystificatory apology for the very same social relations that generated the mutual indifference and class polarisation that he found deeply troubling.¹¹

In passages where he did mention more concrete alternatives to modern class conflicts, Whitman reverted to the vision of a small-scale agrarian economy.¹² The main thrust of his work, with its celebration of the modern, sought, as we saw, neither a return to the past nor to settle for progress in its existing forms: his work included both a celebration of modern progress and a desire to transcend its one-sidedness. Yet, unwilling to look *beyond* capitalism, he could not avoid *falling back* on the twin perspectives that Marx considered typical of the capitalist world-view: an apology of (in his case a poetically 'vivified') capitalist progress (including capitalist imperial expansion, as we shall see) and a romantic yearning for a pre-capitalist, or at least a pre-industrial, past.

As Erkkila, Sommer and others have argued, Whitman's democracy 'continued to be based on the mass participation of independent producers'.¹³ Capital-

9   As Erkkila indicates, Whitman 'never questioned the relations of private property and free enterprise'. Erkkila 1989, p. 34.
10 Quoted in Reynolds 1996, p. 481. 'Hegel's influence on Whitman's later poetry is undeniable' (p. 254).
11 Erkkila 1989, pp. 16, 76, 178. Erkkila argues that 'in his attempt to give democracy a spiritual base ... Whitman came more and more to deny the material conditions of American life' (p. 253). I would reformulate this idea: in his desire to *avoid* the need to materially transform the conditions of American life, Whitman fled into an attempt to give democracy a religious dimension. According to M. Wynn Thomas, Whitman tended to take 'the simply existent for the substantial ideal'. Thomas 1987, p. 37. The point was already suggested by Arvin in 1938. Arvin 1938, p. 69.
12 See Haddox 2004.
13 Sommer 1999, p. 45. Erkkila 1989, p. 27. Whitman embraced the criteria of progress he attributed to the Swiss political economist Sismonde de Sismondi: not 'the great wealth of a special class, but ... having the bulk of the people provided with homes or land in fee

ism was subordinating the small farmer and transforming small-town life, but Whitman clung to both as the ground for the 'perfect personalities' he wished to cultivate. The singer of the ebullient city street now yearns for town of two hundred:

> I can conceive a community ... in which ... the perfect personalities, without noise meet; say in some pleasant western settlement or town, where a couple hundred best men and women, of ordinary wordly status ... with nothing extra of genius or wealth ... I can conceive such a community organized in running order, powers judiciously delegated – farming, building, trade, courts, mails, schools, elections, all attended to; and then the rest of life, the main thing, freely branching and blossoming in each individual, and bearing golden fruit.[14]

Whitman also sought refuge in the notion of the land as the basis of a natural order, as opposed to the artificial and degraded, 'tainted', rule of the dollar, business and profit: 'I must confess I want to see the agricultural occupation of America ... permanently broaden'd. Its gains are the only ones on which God seems to smile. What others – what business, profit, wealth, without a taint? What fortune else – what dollar – does not stand for, and come from, more or less imposition, lying, unnaturalness?'[15] 'The final culmination of this vast and varied Republic', he wrote, 'will be the ... establishment of millions of comfortable city homesteads and moderate-sized farms, healthy and independent, single separate ownership, fee simple, life in them complete but cheap, within reach of all'.[16] He similarly insisted that the 'reticulation' of wealth was the basis of democracy.[17]

This vision of the prevalence of small property, secure in its access to the land, could not be further from the actual direction of capitalist progress. Whitman insisted that 'immense capital and capitalists' only counted as progress if they contributed to that 'final culmination', that is to say to the preservation of small-scale property and a fairly equal distribution of wealth: 'Exceptional wealth, splendor, countless manufactures, excess of exports, immense capital and capitalists ... artificial improvements, even books, colleges and the suf-

---

simple'. 'Who Gets The Plunder?', p. 1068. Whitman spoke of 'ten million democratic farms in the future'. 'Art Features', p. 858.
14 Whitman [1871], p. 968.
15 'Our Real Culmination', p. 1074.
16 'Our Real Culmination', p. 1074.
17 Whitman [1871], p. 950.

frage – all, in many respects ... form, more or less, a sort of anti-democratic disease and monstrosity, except as they contribute by curious indirections to that culmination'.[18] Yet, how could one realistically think that capitalist accumulation was in fact contributing 'by curious indirections' to that 'culmination'? The speculation about 'indirection' was a symptom of Whitman's unwillingness to acknowledge the many *evident* and *direct* ways in which capitalism was contributing to the very opposite result of that which he described as 'our real culmination'. As M. Wynn Thomas points out 'Somehow or other a system of untrammeled economic competition is supposed to produce a harmoniously cooperative and egalitarian social order'. That, he adds, 'is a contradiction which lies at the very heart of Whitman's convictions'.[19] In 1888, Whitman commented to his friend Horace Traubel: 'I look forward to a world of small owners'.[20] In fact, he looked *back* to a world of small owners: capitalist accumulation, while not simply eradicating small property, certainly does not tend to generalise it.

Whitman's mixed this vindication of small-scale production with a *poetic* resolution of social contradictions. In 'The Sleepers' it is sleep that 'averages' all social agents: 'I swear they are averaged now – one is no better than the other'.[21] Sleep creates an alternative social space in which master and slave are equals: 'The call of the slave is one with the master's call, and the master salutes the slave'.[22] But this solution invites an obvious objection: when the sleepers wake up, will not the averaging out and equality described here vanish? Is not this vision an illusory transcendence of conflict? As Klammer comments: 'How exactly the slave is united with the master – in fact, gains the respect of his master – is ... not clear'.[23] In the 1855 preface to *Leaves of Grass*, Whitman claims that poets would 'dissolve poverty from its need and riches from its conceit'.[24] But the means through which poetry could achieve this double objective are not specified. In 'A Song for Occupations', to take another example, the poet, referring to the rich, asks of his readers: 'Do you give in that you are any less immortal?'[25] And he adds: 'Is it you then that thought the President greater than you? / Or the rich better off than you? or the educated wiser than you?'[26] The problem,

---

18 'Our Real Culmination', p. 1074.
19 Thomas 1987, p. 77.
20 Traubel 1914, p. 315.
21 'The Sleepers', p. 549.
22 'The Sleepers', p. 550.
23 Klammer 1995, p. 155.
24 'Preface', p. 19.
25 'A Song for Occupations', p. 356.
26 'A Song for Occupations', p. 356.

of course, an impolite reader could respond, is that the rich are indeed better off than most of us and the President and those connected to him have power, and the educated enjoy privileges, from which many are excluded: references to a shared immortality sound very much like a consolation or a compensation for the inequalities that separate us on earth. Doris Sommer has thus rightly referred to Whitman's attempt to achieve a 'magical vaporization of conflict'.[27]

The 'Calamus' cluster of *Leaves of Grass*, with its vindication of comradeship, has been rightly read as an affirmation of same-sex love and as either a retreat to a personal sphere of affections beyond the reach of social conflict or, alternatively, as the enunciation of a social principle destined to transform all social relations.[28] But in both cases, as either a retreat or social model, comradeship left existing institutions and structures unaffected, as Whitman, at times, openly admitted:

> I hear it was charged against me that I sought to destroy institutions,
> But really I am neither for nor against institutions,
> ...
> Only I will establish in the Mannahatta and in every city of these states inland and seaboard,
> ...
> Without edifices or rules or trustees or any argument,
> The institution of the dear love of comrades.[29]

Thomas F. Haddox's conclusion is therefore warranted: 'even if we grant the sincerity of Whitman's radicalism ... the desire to transform conflict into mystic union ... renders effective political engagement all but impossible'.[30]

Terry Eagleton's considerations on an ethics of self-fulfillment and solidarity are useful as we attempt to specify the contours of Whitman's poetic-political project. In several works Eagleton puts forth an Aristotelian definition of happiness as 'the condition of well-being which springs from the free flourishing

---

27   Sommer 1999, p. 37.
28   Erkkila 1989, p. 153. According to Smeller, 'Calamus' oscillates between the retreat to a private world and elevation of adhesiveness to a social principle. Smeller 1998, p. 296. M. Wynn Thomas and Nicolás Magaril have also pointed out the duality in 'Calamus' as both a retreat into private comradeship, on the one hand, and a model and basis for social transformation, on the other. Magaril considers that after the Civil War Whitman's emphasis veered toward the second option. Magaril 2010, pp. 62–3, 66. See also Thomas 1987, p. 166.
29   'I hear it was charged against me', p. 281.
30   Haddox 2004, p. 7.

of one's powers and capacities'.[31] But this definition must take into account the fact that we are social animals: our self-fulfillment depends on the support of others, just as their self-fulfillment depends on our support. To develop our faculties at the expense of others is to settle for a miserable basis for self-fulfillment. Self-interest should lead us to keep others' interests at heart; just as much as they have an interest in doing the same with us: 'In damaging others, we are in the long run damaging our own fulfillment, which depends on the freedom of others to have a hand in it. And since there can be no true reciprocity except among equals, oppression and inequality are in the long run self-thwarting as well'.[32] 'The free flourishing of our faculties'[33] can only be fully realised as part of a 'common reciprocal project'.[34] That concern for others, required for our self-fulfillment as part of a reciprocal project, can be designated with the, admittedly overused, term love: 'What we have called love', argues Eagleton, 'is the way we can reconcile our search for individual fulfilment with the fact that we are social animals. For love means creating for another the space in which he might flourish, at the same time as he does this for you. The fulfilment of each becomes the ground for the fulfilment of the other'.[35]

The love referred to here is not a state of mind but an activity, a practice.[36] Nor does it refer to romantic attachment, erotic attraction or personal affection. It is what the ancients called *agape*, a love for strangers: 'This kind of activity is known as agape, or love, and has nothing to do with erotic or even affectionate feelings. The command to love is purely impersonal: the prototype of it is loving strangers, not those you desire or admire'.[37] Eagleton argues that to designate this love of strangers we 'need a term somewhere between the intensity of "love" and the rather cooler "friendship", and the fact that we lack one is probably significant'.[38] This was also Whitman's quest.

As early as 1841 the young Whitman felt the need to explain his particular use of the word love: 'By "love" ... I do not mean the sickly sentimentality which is so favorite a theme with novelists and magazine writers'.[39] Indeed, what were his word experiments with adhesiveness, comradeship, attachment, compan-

---

31 Eagleton 2007, p. 66.
32 Eagleton 2007, p. 168.
33 Eagleton 2007, p. 170.
34 Eagleton 2007, pp. 169–70.
35 Eagleton 2007, p. 168. See also Eagleton 2011, p. 86.
36 Eagleton 2007, p. 165.
37 Eagleton 2007, pp. 165, 167.
38 Eagleton 2003, p. 165.
39 Whitman [1841], p. 48.

ionship and other terms if not a search for such a third term besides friendship and 'amative love',[40] as he described it, an attempt to invent a term for the 'love of strangers' he referred to more than once?[41] His affirmations of comradeship, of fusion with the other, in 'Song of Myself', 'Starting from Paumanok', 'Crossing Brooklyn Ferry', to mention a few examples, what were they, if not the attempt to envision a new type of social bond beyond the mutual indifference of the market and the cult of the isolated individual? 'I celebrate myself, and sing myself / And what I assume you shall assume / For every atom belonging to me as good belongs to you': what do the first lines of 'Song of Myself' sing if not a 'state in which the flourishing of one individual comes about through the flourishing of others'?[42]

But, as Eagleton points out, happiness as a reciprocal project is incompatible with relations of economic exploitation. In that sense, 'happiness ... is an institutional affair: it demands the kind of social and political conditions in which you are free to exercise your creative powers'.[43] In other words, 'If the good life is one of fulfilling our natures, and if this is true of everybody, then it would take a deep-seated change to material conditions to make such fulfillment possible all round'.[44] There is then 'a politics implicit'[45] in the notion of agape or love for strangers. In the modern age, Eagleton concludes, 'this project has been known as socialism'.[46] Socialist society 'is one in which each attains his or her freedom and autonomy in and through the self-realization of others. Socialism is just whatever set of institutions it would take for it to happen'.[47]

But if there is a politics implicit in the love for strangers, it is a political conclusion that Whitman failed to draw: he stubbornly refused to link his vision of comradeship, adhesiveness, of a spiritual or 'Religious Democracy', of a poetical vivification of deadened relations, to an actual project of social or political change.[48] He ardently wished to transcend the mutual indifference, one-sided

---

40 Whitman [1871], p. 981.
41 'To You', p. 175. See also 'Song of the Open Road', pp. 301–2, and 'To a Stranger', p. 280.
42 This helps explain why, while Whitman never embraced socialism, many socialists did embrace him as a fellow thinker. Eugene Debs could thus salute a meeting of the Whitman Fellowship – organised by the poet's admirers and led by Horace Traubel, himself a socialist – with references to the 'dear love of comrades'. Debs and others thus embraced a vision of masculinity that has been described as a 'mutually dependent comradeship'. Robertson 2008, p. 255.
43 Eagleton 2007, pp. 151–2.
44 Eagleton 2003, p. 126.
45 Eagleton 2003, p. 169.
46 Eagleton 2003, p. 126.
47 Eagleton 2003, p. 170.
48 For a twenty-first century rant and analysis of the situation in the United States in the tradition of *Democratic Vistas* with a frankly anti-capitalist conclusion, see Wood 2004.

pursuit of profit, and objectified social relations that surrounded him while ignoring their connection with market competition, capitalist class relations and the imperatives of capitalist accumulation: he wished to transcend the consequences of capitalist relations without transcending capitalism.[49] Social and spiritual-aesthetic reconciliation would be attained through the mutual recognition, mediated by the poet, of social agents as part of a shared, collective, soul. As indicated, this not only made Whitman's poetic project sadly insufficient to address the evils he denounced. By almost if not completely fusing poetic enunciation and social transformation, Whitman turned, or, at least, risked turning, his protest into a justification of existing social relations.[50] His song of comradeship is thus ambiguous: the song of comradeship proposed is

49 In his monumental *Walt Whitman's America*, David Reynolds dismisses Marxism and Arvin's *Whitman* (1938) as an attempt in the 'Marxist heyday of the 1930s' to turn the poet into a socialist while having to recognise his inconsistencies (Reynolds 1996, 557). It is true that Arvin discovered an anti-capitalist undertow in Whitman's work. Yet he also documented the distance of Whitman's views from socialism, as well as his less than radical views on slavery and abolition, race and racism and the role and significance of the labour movement, among other issues. According to Arvin, Whitman always remained a 'good burgher' (p. 70) and a 'good philistine' (p. 90). He preferred to 'pick no quarrel with social arrangements as he found them'. (p. 36) Whitman, Arvin pointed out, 'wished to say Yes as sweepingly as possible, and the wish inevitably led him astray' (p. 90). Arvin 1938. To her credit, in 1989, Betsy Erkkila referred to Arvin's *Whitman* as 'still one of the best studies of the intellectual origins of Whitman's social thought' (Erkkila 1989, p. 8). Whitman's class position among craftsmen and artisans; the impact of figures such as Elias Hicks; Whitman's evolution as a Jacksonian democrat, through the Mexican War to the debates around the Wilmot Proviso; his jump to the Free Soil party and the abandonment of active party politics; his praise for loafing; his compromised views on abolition and slavery; his portrait of the Civil War from the perspective of the rank and file soldier; the creation of the 'Songs of Insurrection' cluster and its elimination a decade later; the impact of science and machinery in his worldview; his flight to spiritualism in later years; his slide from his earlier pantheism to a more traditional theism; his unwillingness to face the social contradictions of capitalist America; the attenuation of innovation in his later poetry; comradeship as a social programme linked to his vindication of same-sex love: much of what other authors have done in the area of Whitman's connection to his time and social context was mentioned or suggested by Arvin in his pioneering study, even if the fact is rarely acknowledged. This does not eliminate, of course, the limits of Arvin's work, among which his conception of homosexuality as an 'aberration' is the most prominent. A further ironic or tragic twist is the fact that in 1960 Arvin was to be arrested and penalised for the possession of 'lewd' purportedly homoerotic images.

50 The point is made eloquently by Erkkila, but is not explored or pursued as it can be. She argues that by seeking to endow an alienated reality with meaning, Whitman concluded by 'justifying' the conditions of 'dehumanization' he set out 'to challenge'. Erkkila 1989, pp. 76, 92.

'THE FINAL CULMINATION OF THIS VAST AND VARIED REPUBLIC' 145

also the song of comradeship attained. Since the one-sidedness of the present could be transcended through the work of the poet, poetic *critique* of that one-sidedness is no sooner formulated than it is overtaken by the *celebration* of a present plenitude. In *Leaves of Grass* implicit, but traceable, critique has been engulfed by a celebration of the reconciliation of the tensions it had posed.

Whitman's implicit critique of the mere race for 'products gross, or luchre' in 'Song of the Exposition' thus veered into a celebration of American capitalism as somehow propelled by a shared soul, represented by the Union. 'Think not our chant, our show, merely for the products gross or lucre – it is for thee, the soul in thee, electric, spiritual!'[51] Whitman does, as M. Wynn Thomas points out, 'a splendid cosmetic job on the unacceptable face of American free enterprise'.[52] Or, as Richard Pascal has argued, he wanted to 'transcendentalize' the profit motive, without actually abolishing it. He wanted to be both America's 'sternly watchful doomsayer' and its 'exuberant booster'.[53] But, it should be underlined that the poet, by refusing to go from the denunciation of the consequences of capitalism to that of capitalism itself, insured that in his poetic solution the 'booster' would prevail over the 'doomsayer'.

The same can be said of 'Passage to India': the poet's demand for a spiritual dimension required to complete the mere material unification of the world attained by modern industry (through canals, telegraph lines and railroads) turns into the celebration of world capitalist expansion in the 1870s and 1880s as the completion of God's or the soul's purpose, and as a voyage of the soul:

> Lo, soul, seest thou not God's purpose from the first?
> ...
> A worship new I sing,
> You captains, voyagers, explorers, yours,
> You engineers, you architects, machinists, yours,
> You, not for trade or transportation only,
> But in God's name, and for thy sake O soul.[54]

The poetic means of transcending the one-sidedness of progress in its present form thus became a means of reconciliation with it. As Rob Wilson has provocatively argued, 'Passage to India' can be read 'as literary advertisement for

---

51 'Song of the Exposition', p. 350.
52 Thomas 1987, p. 137.
53 Pascal 1989, pp. 153, 146.
54 'Passage to India', p. 532.

expansionist progress across the Pacific'.[55] The world's seas, turned into the avenues of a world market through the action of commercial and industrial capital, are poetically transformed by Whitman into the 'seas of God':

> Sail forth – steer for the deep waters only
> Reckless O soul, exploring, I with thee, and thou with me
> For we are bound where mariner has not yet dared to go,
> And we will risk the ship, ourselves and all.
> O my brave soul!
> O farther sail!
> O daring joy, but safe! are they not all the seas of God?
> O farther, farther, farther sail![56]

The spiritualisation of the imperial project is carried further in 'Prayer of Columbus', which Whitman in the final organisation of *Leaves of Grass* placed just after 'Passage to India'. Here the life and voyages of the best-known agent of the expansionist push of merchant capital in the fifteenth century is transfigured into an enterprise inspired by God, while the poet fuses his voice with that of the merchant-navigator:

> All my enterprises have been fill'd with Thee,
> My speculations, plans, begun and carried on in thoughts of Thee,
> Sailing the deep or journeying the land for Thee;
> Intentions, purports, aspirations mine, leaving results to Thee.[57]

Edward W. Said has pointed out how studies of English literature overlook how the 'literature itself makes constant references to itself as somehow participating in Europe's overseas expansion'.[58] The idea implicit in the texts

---

55 Wilson 2000, p. 531. Wilson adds, commenting on both 'Passage to India' and 'A Broadway Pageant': 'the "rondure of the world at last accomplished" looks a alot (sic) like late capitalist hegemony and the consumer-driven unity of global postmodernity' (538). I would not restrict the argument to late capitalism, nor speak of capitalism as 'consumer driven', but the general point is, I think, correct. To be fair, it should be pointed out that in 1846, as editor of the *Brooklyn Eagle*, Whitman had fiercely denounced the bloody British repression of a Sikh rebellion in India. Brasher 1970, p. 175.
56 'Passage to India', pp. 539–40. For further interesting discussion of 'Passage to India' see Loving 1982, pp. 186–8.
57 'Prayer of Columbus', pp. 540–1.
58 Said 1993, p. 14.

examined by Said is that 'outlying territories are available for use'.⁵⁹ Over and over, in a 'Passage to India', 'Prayer of Columbus', 'A Broadway Pageant', we discover, as Walter Grunzweig and others have suggested,⁶⁰ a similar feeling of participation in European or US expansion and a notion that the 'outlying territories are available for use'.⁶¹ In 'A Broadway Pageant', composed in 1860, Whitman, while celebrating the arrival of Japanese ambassadors in Manhattan, formulates a vision of a world united under US auspices and hegemony:

> I chant the new empire grander than any before, as in a vision it comes to me,
> I chant America the mistress, I chant a greater supremacy,
> I chant projected a thousand blooming cities yet in time on those groups of sea-islands,
> My sail-ships and steam-ships threading the archipelagoes,
> My stars and stripes fluttering in the wind,
> Commerce opening, the sleep of ages having done its work, races reborn, refresh'd
> Lives, works resumed – the object I know not – but the old, the Asiatic renew'd as it must be,
> Commencing from this day surrounded by the world.⁶²

Edward Whitley has contested the argument that Whitman's 'A Broadway Pageant' includes an idealisation of US imperialist tendencies. It is a weak argument in an otherwise excellent contribution. As we saw above, Whitley rightly points out that in 'Song of Myself' Whitman 'grants himself access to everything across the nation and the world'.⁶³ In 'A Broadway Pageant' he shows how 'his global vision is based on the expanding networks of international trade that converge upon New York City'.⁶⁴ Yet Whitley insists that this does not mean Whitman was idealising 'imperial Western designs'.⁶⁵ Whitman, he

---

59   Said 1993, p. 74.
60   Grunzweig 1998, p. 305.
61   Said 1993, p. 74. Said points out another imperialist tenet: the idea 'that one race deserves and has consistently earned the right to be considered the race whose main mission is to expand beyond its own domain' (Said 1993, p. 53). For an interesting discussion see Folsom 2005.
62   'A Broadway Pageant', p. 386.
63   Whitley 2006, p. 455. Whitley is debating with Rob Wilson's article quoted above.
64   Whitley 2006, p. 456.
65   Whitley 2006, p. 471.

argues, 'transforms New York City into a cosmopolitan space that partakes of Western and Eastern influences'.[66] Whitman detaches New York City from the United States and turns it into a place where 'global influences' will 'overwhelm the otherwise American character of the city'.[67] New York City becomes an 'erstwhile American space that is transformed by its communion with the world'.[68] In other words, 'Manhattan's global ties prevent New York City from being bound exclusively to any single nation-state'.[69]

The problem with this argument is that New York City and the economic forces headquartered in it are, in fact, linked to a specific nation-state, a nation-state, furthermore, that occupied an increasingly significant, if not yet dominant, role in the world capitalist economy. New York City did not float over the system of nation-states by virtue of its cosmopolitan cultural mix. It belonged to one of the rising powers within that system. Whitley asks 'whether New York's status as an international trading hub makes it the "capital and heart" of the nation ... or a node in a much larger network of global interactions'?[70] But this is a false alternative: New York City was *both* the capital of US capital, and 'a node' in a larger global network. Its growing prominence within that network was the crystallisation and condensation, not of a cosmopolitan space above and beyond national interests, but of a particular capitalist and future imperialist project. To present it as cosmopolitan space unmoored from the latter is indeed to present Wall Street as an embodiment of the universal. It is indeed to idealise US imperial projections.

As part of his argument, Whitley points out that 'A Broadway Pageant' refuses to associate the future of the United States with the frontier. Whitman identified US progress with a 'centralized trade hub rather than with a frontier outpost'.[71] Whitman, he argues, sensed that Manhattan would restructure 'global space in such a way that New York City would become the central point of any geographic region in the world'.[72] But is not this the perspective that we would expect from New York-centred industrial, financial and commercial interests? Is not this Wall Street's vision of the world? It is indeed

---

66 Whitley 2006, p. 471.
67 Whitley 2006, p. 468.
68 Whitley 2006, p. 470.
69 Whitley 2006, p. 470.
70 Whitley 2006, p. 467.
71 Whitley 2006, p. 473. The poem demonstrated 'that a city connected to the rest of the globe is a better model for defining the United States' place in the world than is a westward-moving frontier' (Whitley 2006, p. 474).
72 Whitley 2006, p. 473.

hard to avoid the conclusion that Whitman's poem puts a universal face on US international economic hegemony.[73]

It could be argued that Marx was as guilty as Whitman of uncritically embracing the imperialist project as a vehicle of progress. Did not Marx applaud the impact of British rule in India? Edward W. Said was perhaps the most influential recent scholar to endorse this view of Marx. But, as indicated in Chapter 4, this is an unwarranted simplification. Marx praised the way in which Britain was contributing to the spread of elements of modern society in Asia, but he never lost sight of the destructive means and the terrible consequences of colonial rule, or of the 'vile' motives regulating it. If he refused to idealise the pre-colonial past, neither did he merely celebrate the colonial encounter, describing it, instead, as a 'tragical couplet'. If he praised the implantation of modern industry in India, he warned that the broken lives would not be 'mended' without the intervention of working-class revolution in Britain and/or anti-colonial rebellion in India. This attitude toward the impact of British colonialism in India corresponded to Marx's general historical conception, which, in Europe, Asia and elsewhere, embraced the fruits of capitalist modernity and thus refused a romantic yearning for a pre-capitalist or pre-colonial past, while *also* refusing to take capitalist society as the definitive form of human progress. Whitman, attempting to grapple with what he considered to be the contradictions of the present, yet unable or unwilling to envision a modernist but anti-capitalist option, inevitably fell back on both romantic recuperations of the small farm and poetic idealisations of capitalist accumulation (including its imperial projections), versions of the polarity between nostalgia and apologia that Marx described as typical of thought trapped within the capitalist horizon.

To take a final example of such idealisations, in the following passage of *Democratic Vistas* Whitman combines his injunction that material progress is never complete without a spiritual-literary dimension with his celebration of both modern industry and of US hegemony. He predicted that before

> the second centennial arrives, there will be some forty to fifty great states, among them Canada and Cuba … The Pacific will be ours, and the Atlantic mainly ours. There will be daily electric communication with every part

---

73 Our analysis confirms Erkkila's judgement that Whitman's writing displays the 'baneful intermingling of idealism and imperialism that had marked and would continue to mark American history'. This is one of many examples of interesting ideas in Erkkila's path-breaking study that are presented almost in passing but not pursued systematically (Erkkila 1989, pp. 57, 113).

of the globe. What an age! What a land! Where, elsewhere, one so great? The individuality of one nation must then, as always, lead the world. Can there be any doubt who the leader ought to be? Bear in mind, though, that nothing less than the mightiest original non-subordinated SOUL has ever really, gloriously led, or ever can lead. (This Soul – its other name, in these Vistas, is LITERATURE.)[74]

The limits of Whitman's poetic and political project are evident here: his critique of the existing form of industrial progress, with its dull pursuit of profit by mutually indifferent agents, instead of leading to the demand for social transformation, concludes in an attempt to redefine US hegemony (including the annexation of Cuba) as a task of the 'Soul'. As in the texts discussed above, transcendence of the present form of progress turns into reconciliation with it. Literature and the poet come forth to spiritually and aesthetically round off the achievements of the industrialist and the navigator, all at the service of capitalist expansion.

Whitman's work can thus be read as an example of what Herbert Marcuse called the 'affirmative character of culture'. To reduce a complex argument to its kernel: Capitalism condemns most of humanity to the consequences of inequality, exploitation, subordination and social isolation. But it also constitutes 'culture' as a differentiated realm in which freedom, autonomy, beauty, goodness, and the development of our faculties – that which daily life under capitalism denies – still can be realised and enjoyed. Culture can thus act as both a standing indictment of capitalist reality (pointing out what it denies) *and* as a means of reconciliation with it (as a compensation for that denial): Marcuse referred to the second, neutralising, effect, as the 'affirmative character of culture'. By offering itself as a means, not of transcending an alienated world, but of fulfillment within it, affirmative culture 'pacifies rebellious

---

74 Whitman [1871], p. 981. The notion that one nation must always lead the world, and that the United States was destined to lead the modern world, is also found in Emerson, in a text Whitman surely read: 'In every age of the world, there has been a leading nation, one of a more generous sentiment, whose eminent citizens were willing to stand for the interests of general justice and humanity, at the risk of being called, by the men of the moment, chimerical and fantastic. Which should be that nation but these States? Which should lead that movement, if not New England? Who should lead the leaders, but the Young American?' (Emerson [1844], p. 165). Whitman would object to the privileging of New England, but not the rest. The notion was already present in some of his earlier journalistic works. He thus wrote in 1846 in the *Brooklyn Eagle*: 'The United States in twenty-five years, or less, must be the most potent nation on earth! No human means can retard this great consummation'. Quoted in Brasher 1970, p. 93.

desire'.[75] Art and literature are central elements of that ambivalent cultural realm: 'Verse makes possible what has already become impossible in prosaic reality. In poetry men can transcend all social isolation ... They overcome the factual loneliness'.[76] Culture's protest against an alienated social reality becomes a substitute for social transformation: 'Culture should ennoble the given by permeating it, rather than putting something new in its place. It thus exalts the individual without freeing him from his factual debasement ... Its realm is essentially a realm of the *soul*'.[77] One could think that these words were written with Whitman in mind. Claiming to transform reality by transforming the soul, affirmative culture becomes a school of resignation: it educates the individual in capitalist society, 'for whom the new freedom has brought a new form of bondage', so that he or she 'tolerates the unfreedom of social existence'.[78] Seeking in culture the plenitude which the rest of social life denies, protest translates into surrender: 'Affirmative culture uses the soul as a protest against reification, only to succumb to it in the end'.[79] The four elements at work in Marcuse's discussion of the dialectics of the affirmative culture – rejection of the alienation of capitalist society; culture as a richer realm of the soul and as an alternative to the former; the limits of such an opposition as it leaves the social sources of alienation intact; and its (often unintended) transformation into a means of reconciliation with the latter – read as a fitting description of the contradictions of Whitman's poetical-political project. Whitman rejects the fragmentation and one-sidedness of capitalist society. He hopes that culture and poetry will 'ennoble the given by permeating it, rather than putting something new in its place'. He fully embraces the notion that through 'poetry men can transcend all social isolation and distance'. He too protests against reification and then succumbs to it. For Marcuse, culture and works of art in capitalist society inevitably have an affirmative effect, even works that resist it. In the case of Whitman there is no resistance: he embraces it actively as part of his project of 'vivification' of the present.

Regarding this, it is useful to revisit the well-known 1968 text 'Whitman and Our Hope for Poetry' by Roy Harvey Pearce.[80] We have rehearsed ideas similar to those formulated in it. But the differences are significant. Pearce argued that one of 'Whitman's great insights ... is that ... producers were increas-

---

75   Marcuse 1969, p. 121.
76   Marcuse 1969, p. 102.
77   Marcuse 1969, p. 103.
78   Marcuse 1969, p. 121.
79   Marcuse 1969, p. 108.
80   Pearce 1969.

ingly bowed down under the weight of their products'.[81] Whitman was faced, argued Pearce, 'with the discovery that a society, a community, is greater than the sum of its individual parts; that the sum somehow generates actions and events which may destroy the parts'.[82] The poet found himself amidst a world of 'products which make possible the good life and yet, because they transcend the individual, threaten that life'.[83] Pearce concluded that Whitman 'was discovering what Marx called alienation, the alienation of the laborer from the product of his labor'.[84] Whitman thus yearned for the 'reassociation of that which had been ... disassociated: producer from product, actor from act, agent from deed'.[85]

But there is a fundamental difference between Pearce's description and Marx's concept of alienation: for Marx the dissociation of 'producer from product', of 'agent from deed', was the result of something more specific than the fact that society is greater than the sum of its component parts – which is, after all, a characteristic of *all* societies – or of the fact that products are social and transcend the individual, which, again, is a feature of all production, except that of very exceptional completely isolated producers. For Marx, the alienation of individuals from themselves and from others, and their subordination to an impersonal economic process, is the result, not of the social character of production or of the fact that society is larger than the sum of its parts, but rather of the fact that society is fragmented into *private* producers linked by the market, the movement of which becomes an objective process beyond anybody's control, a process that, in the case of *capitalist* commodity producers, also entails the subordination of the direct producers – the wage workers – to capital. Marx could thus envision a progressive reduction of alienation through the socialisation of private property and the replacement of the impersonal market with the democratic decisions of free associated individuals.[86]

Understanding alienation as a result, not of capitalism, but of the fact that society is greater than its component parts, or that the product transcends the producer, cannot allow for such a specifically anti-capitalist alternative to alienation. Sharing both Whitman's uneasiness with the present and his evasion of an anti-capitalist perspective, Pearce's essay, not surprisingly, falls back on

---

81 Pearce 1969, p. 335.
82 Pearce 1969, p. 337.
83 Pearce 1969, p. 341.
84 Pearce 1969, p. 348.
85 Pearce 1969, p. 347.
86 On progressive dealienation see Mandel 2015, Chapter 11.

Whitman's solution: the poet must become the agent of social change, or as he puts it: 'We yet expect the main things from our poets to come – as did Whitman. Our hope for poetry now lies precisely in its search for the spirit which will restore the land to productive order'.[87] Pearce's insights on the social import of Whitman's poetic project ends up reproducing his blind spots: he too wished to dissolve the consequences of capitalism without actually abolishing capitalism. Or, perhaps, he envisioned that abolition, but through poetic and spiritual means.

A similar conclusion is reached regarding Hunnicutt's otherwise unobjectionable article on Whitman, loafing and shorter working hours.[88] According to him, Whitman considered that once the satisfaction of the basic material needs had been assured, further increases in productivity should be employed to decrease working hours. Hunnicutt adds that, up to the 1920s, commentators as varied as AT&T executives, economist John Maynard Keynes, and scientist Julian Huxley, expected that increased productivity would lead to a shorter work day and that in the future the larger problem would be, not insuring material well-being, but rather determining how to employ a vastly increased leisure time. Yet, Hunnicutt reminds us that working hours have not fallen.[89] For many workers, they have increased. There is no visible tendency for productivity to translate into a shorter working day. Hunnicutt speculates on the possible reasons for this, among which he mentions 'the rise of consumerism (that people are choosing luxuries rather than leisure) and the increase of governmental support of perpetual economic growth ... so that everyone will always have a "fulltime job"'. But he concludes that 'perhaps the best explanation for the advent of work without end is the failure of belief and loss of vision that so distressed Whitman when he wrote *Democratic Vistas*'.[90] Hunnicutt's article concludes with a call to recuperate Whitman's vision of 'higher progress'.

Yet, the problem, as pointed out above, is not lack of 'belief or vision'. The root problem is capitalism. Capitalist production is production for profit. Increased profit is the objective of technical innovation under capitalism. But profit, as Marx explained, is surplus *labour*. Thus, the capitalist drive for profit leads to both constant technical innovation *and* a push to extend the working day. For Marx, 'work without end', despite fantastic advances in productivity, corresponds to the very nature of capitalism, to the fact that under capitalism the purpose of technological innovation is *not* the liberation of workers from

---

87   Pearce 1969, p. 350.
88   Hunnicutt 2008, pp. 92–109.
89   Schor 1992; Crary 2013.
90   Hunnicutt 2008, p. 105.

labour, but rather the appropriation of ever larger amounts of surplus-labour by capital. This is why the root of the problem is not lack of vision, nor can it be solved through a recuperation of it. Here again a perceptive critic fails to go beyond Whitman's limited vision: Marx's understanding of capitalism allows for a fuller exploration of the poet's contradictions.

We have linked Whitman not only to the rise of capitalism and a capitalist world market but also to the theme of equal rights and of democracy, to which he proclaimed his allegiance. If his search for an alternative to some of the consequences of capitalism was self-contradictory and self-defeating, can we conclude, nevertheless, that he was a consistent democrat? The following chapter addresses this question, which requires a further specification of Whitman's place in the conflicts and transitions of his time, and thus of the relation of our analysis to that of other scholars that have also explored this question.

CHAPTER 8

Whitman: Inconsistent Democrat, Yet More Than a Democrat

Whitman's views on labour and social class in general were hardly exceptional. As several scholars, beginning with the Marxist Newton Arvin in the 1930s, have pointed out, they corresponded to the inclinations of a specific social layer made up of artisans, craftsmen and skilled wage-workers – commonly referred to as 'mechanics' in the pre-Civil War United States.[1] Through the 1850s, in spite of the rapid spread of capitalist relations, small property owners (small farmers, shop-keepers) and independent artisans still outnumbered wage-earners in the United States.[2] Wage-earning was still widely seen as a temporary situation or condition, to be followed by some form of independent economic pursuit.[3] This expectation of social mobility toward self-employment was linked to the notion of geographical mobility: resettlement was seen as a means of social relocation as an independent producer or trader.[4] Even wage workers employed in manufacturing retained considerable control of the labour process, as machine production was only beginning its rapid advance.[5]

Himself a carpenter and a craftsman in the printing trades, Whitman adopted a perspective, as Arvin pointed out in 1938, 'neither of the patriciate ... nor of the proletariat; neither that of the magnates nor that of the workers'.[6] As such, his views were a mix of 'middle class contentedness' and 'petty bourgeois radicalism'.[7] Andrew Lawson has recently formulated a similar thesis. Whitman, he argues, belonged 'neither in the refined upper middle class nor in the rowdy working-class cultures'.[8] His perspective was thus a mixture of 'radicalism and

---

1 Newton Arvin long ago linked Whitman to the world of mechanics, 'farmers, the small merchants, the lesser professional men, and the artisans'. Arvin 1938 p. 23. Recent scholars have agreed. See for example: Thomas 2007; Erkkila 1989, p. 27; Roediger 1991, pp. 43, 45. See also Lawson 2006.
2 Foner 1998 pp. 67–8.
3 Foner 1998, p. 66.
4 Foner 1970, pp. 26–8; Foner 1998, pp. 50, 57.
5 As Charles Post, using Marx's categories, has pointed out, the formal still prevailed over the real subsumtion of labour to capital. Post 2012, p. 224.
6 Arvin 1938, p. 101. His father was also a carpenter.
7 Arvin 1938, p. 144.
8 Lawson, 2006, p. xx.

conservatism'.⁹ This, argues Lawson, corresponds to his 'continual oscillation between the fine and the coarse',¹⁰ 'the literary and the vernacular',¹¹ the 'lofty' and the 'low', the 'speculative' and the 'concrete'.¹² M. Wynn Thomas speaks of his 'forked toungue' and Erkkila of his 'streetwise poetics'.¹³

In his 1855 description of Whitman as a mixture of 'Yankee transcendentalism' and 'New York rowdyism', Charles Eliot Norton had early on linked Whitman to the city working classes. Norton registered his perplexity regarding a text that defied traditional linguistic and class frontiers, but which he was unable to dismiss as inconsequential: 'A fireman or omnibus driver, who had intelligence enough to absorb the speculations of [transcendentalism] ... and resources of expression to put them forth again in a form of his own, with sufficient self-conceit and contempt for public taste to affront all usual propriety of diction, might have written this gross yet elevated, this superficial yet profound, this preposterous yet somehow fascinating book'.¹⁴

There is a small discrepancy here, as some place Whitman somewhere between the patriciate and the proletariat, the upper-middle class and the working class, while Norton places him squarely in the working class (a fireman or omnibus driver), although with literary and intellectual pretensions above his station. In fact, to describe Whitman, above all at the time of the first edition of *Leaves of Grass*, as between classes, or as not part of the working class since he was an artisan, misses the fluidity of the class situation of the moment:¹⁵ Whitman wrote at the time that the skilled crafts were being decomposed into simpler tasks, as part of the transition to capitalist manufacture, a process at workshop level linked to the shift nationally in economic and, eventually, political power from merchant to manufacturing capital, a realignment that, in turn, opened the path to the Civil War. To more clearly place Whitman in his time we need a map of his epoch which, from the mid-1840s to the early 1890s, encompassed the transition from the mercantile republic created by the 1776 revolution to the plutocratic republic of the Gilded Age. As Betsy Erkkila pointed out in her classic study, Whitman lived through the 'capitalist trans-

---

9   Lawson 2006, p. 17.
10 Lawson 2006, p. xix.
11 Lawson 2006, p. 31.
12 Lawson 2006, p. 60.
13 Thomas 1987, p. 28; Erkkila 1989, p. 79.
14 Norton 1969, pp. 2–3. Norton similarly noted the 'writer's scorn for the wonted usages of good writing', his use of 'words usually banished from polite society' and of 'slang expressions'. The result, he argued, was 'striking' but 'laughable'.
15 Lawson, for example, speaks of him as not part of the working class since he was an 'artisan possessed of a skilled trade'. Lawson 2006, pp. xvi, xix.

formation of America'.[16] We can construct such a map thanks to the key works of researchers such as Sean Wilentz, Eric Foner, David Roediger and Charles Post, among others. We limit ourselves to the broader strokes required for our discussion, relying mostly on Post's analysis of the 'American road to capitalism'.[17]

The revolution of 1776, the revolutionary war that ensued until 1783 and the constitutional settlement of 1787, which always remained a proud point of reference for Whitman, established a republic characterised by a non-capitalist economy which included four main elements. The plantation economy based on slavery produced cash crops for export (mainly cotton by the 1840s) and tended to become self-sufficient in food production, due to the interest of the slave owners in using their labour force all through the year. It was not characterised by the imperative toward technological innovation and the introduction of labour-saving machinery, typical of capitalism, which should not be confused with incapacity to irregularly incorporate technical innovations.[18]

Independent household production was widespread both north and south. Normally, independent farmers, after providing for their needs, sold part of their crop, but were not forced to do so in order to retain access to the land. Such was the case because (and as long as) land was available either cheap or free, legally or not (through squatting, the occupation of lands without title or legal claim), while debt, rent, tax or mortgage burdens, if present, were light or could be paid in kind. Such producers were not subject to market competition which would coerce and discipline them to increase productivity, innovate and specialise according to land types.[19]

Artisan and small craft production provided goods that farmers did not manufacture. Free from the dictates of market dependence, artisans and farmers operated within a web of trade and craft regulations and mutual help customs, which some historians have labelled a 'collective individualism'.[20]

Finally, merchant capital, its biggest concentrations located in the largest cities, and, above all, the largest ports, derived its profits from connecting these social and productive sectors with each other and with external markets. The expansion of slave production, given its slow-changing technological basis,

---

16   Erkkila, p. 11.
17   Besides Post 2012, we rely on Wilentz 2004; Foner 1970, 1980 and 1990; Hugins, 1960; Taylor 1968, Mandel, B. 1955.
18   Post 2012, Chapter 3.
19   Post 2012, Chapter 2. In the case of the United States, the recurrent demographic crises normal in such economies were avoided thanks to the availability of new land for settlement (via the previous removal indigenous inhabitants).
20   Wilentz 2004, p. 102; Post 2012, Chapter 2.

implied its territorial expansion. Merchant capital had no conflict with this, since its profits were derived from buying and selling goods, not from their elaboration. It was relatively indifferent to the social relations under which they were produced, as long as they could be bought and sold at a profit. Merchant capital could thus coexist profitably with the expansion of the southern slave plantation economy. New York was a major centre of merchant capital, closely and lucratively linked to the cotton trade and the expansion of the slave economy to the south. The city was also the location of many and diverse artisan and craft activities.[21]

Needless to say, the frontiers between historical periods are jagged: forms of market-dependent farming as well as the first elements of capitalist manufacturing were already present by the 1790s, but they had not attained the importance they later acquired.

What historians have called bi-sectional politics, or bi-sectional parties, best corresponded to this socio-economic configuration. Competing parties were dominated by sectors of both northern merchant capital and the southern planters and sought the support of farmers and artisans in all regions. Such politics depended on the systematic avoidance of slavery as a federal or national issue: parties officially presented themselves as neither for nor against slavery, and tried to avoid polarisation around this question. Abolitionism was anathema to this type of politics, as it tended and sought to provoke precisely such a polarisation. For merchant capital and its representatives it was a disruptive element and they sought to convince artisans and farmers that it was irrelevant to their situation. This policy required considerable manoeuvring as some issues, such as the question of runaway slaves (a problem posed by one of the many forms of active slave resistance against their masters) and the organisation of new territories tended to bring up the question of slavery at a federal and not only state level.[22]

But the merchant republic was not static. Under the pressure of merchant capital (including land speculators and banks) and of the state, which curtailed access to land and enforced tax and debt collection, farmers progressively became market-dependent: increasingly they had to sell in order to pay taxes, operating or mortgage debts or, in some cases, rents, or risk losing access to the land. They were now subject to market discipline which forced them, under threat of ruin and dispossession, to reduce costs, innovate and specialise according to soil type. The North East, including New York, was in the vanguard

---

21   For artisans in the mercantile city see Wilentz 2004, Chapter 1.
22   Post 2012, Chapter 5.

of this transition to market-dependent agriculture: it had been largely completed by the 1840s, while it was still spreading in the Ohio Valley and the Great Plains from 1840 to 1860.[23]

A similar process occurred in craft and artisan production, under the pressure of commercial and credit capital: masters and journeymen increasingly differentiated into manufacturing capitalists and wage-workers. In other cases, merchants opted to establish manufacturing operations. Either way, capitalist manufacturing made its appearance and found a growing internal market in the increasingly market-dependent agricultural sector: it processed the materials generated by an expanding market-subordinated agriculture and provided it with tools and consumer goods. A dynamic agro-industrial complex thus stood at the axis of the American road to capitalism.[24]

New York was again in the vanguard of this process, if not as part of the agro-industrial complex (although it included important sugar-refining operations, for example). By the time Whitman arrived there it was undergoing a process of 'metropolitan industrialisation'. Crafts were being subdivided and 'sweated': subdivided to adapt them to the new division of labour in factories; 'sweated' as specific tasks were put out to labourers working at home or in smaller workshops. Between 1825 and 1850, according to Wilentz, New York became a 'manufacturing city'.[25]

By the 1840s a tipping point was attained: manufacturing capital progressively gained its financial independence from merchant capital. As it became an autonomous force, increasingly conscious of its needs and interests, it began to shift the pre-existing terrain of US politics, typical of the mercantile republic. In contrast to merchant capital, manufacturing capital was not indifferent to the expansion of slave production: manufacturing capital sought expanding markets and zones for investment which the territorial extension of slavery would have blocked. Bi-sectional politics, based on the co-existence of merchant capital and the expansion of slave production, became increasingly impossible as the question of slavery now moved to the centre of the national political debate. The exodus from the Democratic Party after the Mexican War of many opponents of the extension of slavery, the formation of the Free Soil Party in

---

23 According to Post, small farmer and artisan resistance to merchants, land speculators and tax collectors was most radically expressed in Shay's Rebellion of 1786. These events helped convince merchants and planters of the need to create a stronger state capable of enforcing property titles, creditor's rights and debt and tax payments. This was attained through the constitutional reorganisation of 1787. Post 2012, Chapter 4.
24 See also Taylor 1968.
25 Wilentz 2004, Chapter 3.

1848 by former Democrats and former Whigs and other currents, the founding of the Republican Party in 1854, the split of the Democratic Party in 1860 were all steps in this reorientation of US politics along the lines of the conflict between a newly consolidated northern capitalism and the slave plantation economy in the South. The clash over the organisation of the new territories to the West (including those acquired through the war with Mexico) was the first moment of this intensified conflict that would only be resolved through the Civil War. Slaves were not passive observers: the crisis over the Fugitive Slave Law of 1850 and its legal and constitutional ramifications, for example, was the result of their constant search for emancipation through escape from their masters, a process recently revisited by Eric Foner.[26] The defeat of the slave owners' rebellion by the Union armies, in turn, insured the rapid expansion of industrial capitalism after 1865, with its unprecedented concentrations of capital, while also posing the problem of the economic remaking of the South and the future condition of the former masters and the former slaves.

Whitman was largely a product of the pre-Civil War 'artisan republicanism', the world of craftsmen proud of their personal skills but increasingly confronted by the capitalist reorganisation of production.[27] He sought, as Sean Wilentz puts it, to 'poetize the soul of the artisan republic'.[28]

He may have drawn some of his views from an earlier time: from the vanishing world of the non-market dependent world of small household agricultural producers and the artisans linked to them. This could serve as the basis for his appreciation for 'loafing', present in many passages of *Leaves of Grass*: a world not ruled by the capitalist market imperatives of constant innovation, incessant expansion and relentless measurement and intensification of labour. Commodity exchange combined with freedom from market compulsion could sustain practices and attitudes that mixed 'independence and community'.[29] Trade as an option but not as an obligation to retain access to the land allowed the survival of 'kinship and communal bonds of mutual obligation'.[30] Whitman's vision of a 'loafer kingdom' or of small communities of two hundred settlers enjoying ample free time thus clung to the options that household producers lost as they became commodity producers subordinated to market discipline. His 'indolence' and 'laziness' and his desire to mix 'personal wealth

---

26 Foner 2015.
27 Erkkila 1989, p. 27. She describes him as a product of the working-class culture of Brooklyn and New York. Erkkila 1989, p. 69.
28 Wilentz 2004, p. 389.
29 Post 2012, pp. 51–7; Erkkila 1989, p. 95.
30 Post 2012, p. 57.

and commonwealth'[31] were rooted in that non-capitalist form of commodity production, which the ongoing economic transition was demolishing.

It was from this social vantage point of artisan and skilled-craft republicanism that Whitman, far beyond the 1840s, denounced both large concentrations of moneyed wealth and the corruption of government he associated with it, while never questioning market relations or the private monopoly of land or means of production as such.

But to limit our characterisation to this would give the impression that Whitman was a consistent plebian democrat, defender of workers and small producers, as he liked to portray himself, if not a consistent critic of capitalism, which, after all, he never claimed to be. Yet his inconsistencies as a democrat were equally striking. The social location we have associated him with – that of pre-Civil War mechanics, artisans and craftsmen – allowed for, not one, but a whole range of views on each of the key conflicts we have outlined, such as slavery and abolition, the situation of fugitive slaves, the settlement of the West, the conduct and aims of the Civil War and the situation of freedpeople after the war. Artisan republicanism was compatible, for example, with a principled opposition to slavery and support for the extension of full citizenship to African Americans. The passages in *Leaves of Grass* where Whitman identified with escaped slaves and in which he portrayed blacks as self-confident, autonomous agents, clearly suggest such sympathy for emancipation. But white artisan republicanism also proved compatible with an accommodating attitude toward slavery – as long as it remained contained in the South, for example – and with the adoption of racist standards excluding non-whites from full citizenship, a perspective congruent with the bi-sectional politics of merchant capital before the Civil War. As Davis Roediger has pointed out, contempt for *slavery* among white workers could easily coexist with contempt for *slaves* and contempt for slaves with contempt for *blacks* in general. Workers could assert their rights as freemen, both against employers who would, if allowed, reduce and degrade them to the status of slaves, and against blacks, who, it seemed to some, allowed themselves to be thus reduced and degraded. Blacks were not only slaves but 'slavish'. Working-class pride could be mobilised against the employers *and* against blacks. 'White revolutionary pride', Roediger argues, 'could thus open the way for republican racism'.[32]

Opposition to the extension of slavery, or to slavery itself, on such grounds did not imply a vindication of equal rights for blacks, but rather a desire for

---

31   Erkkila 1989, p. 95.
32   Roediger 1991, p. 35.

the least possible contact with them, or, if possible, for their removal from the United States. Regarding this, it must be admitted that, as Arvin pointed out long ago and others have documented since, Whitman's interventions, taken as a whole, leaned in the direction of the more conservative orientation we have just summarised. According to Wilentz, Whitman wanted to 'poetize the soul of the artisan republic'. Roediger reminds us that in the United States the formation of the working class went hand in hand with a 'sense of whiteness'.[33] If we put both assertions together it is less surprising that Whitman's writing is haunted by a 'sense of whiteness', although there are, as we have indicated, countercurrents.[34] Luke Mancuso has argued, on the contrary, that Whitman's post-bellum work registers a commitment to racial equality. While ably argued, this claim is unconvincing. It will be addressed below.

Of course, Whitman was no mere reflection of his context; he was also an active participant in it. As Roediger warns, it is a mistake to think that racism was simply imposed on the nascent working class by its exploiters: the former had a hand in producing it.[35] Whitman, as editor and journalist (and often as poet), identified himself and hailed his readers as 'workingmen': to that extent he exemplified how the pre-bellum working-class public sphere actively produced a 'sense of whiteness'. He did not passively receive it, he helped construct it.

He began his political evolution in the 1840s as a Jacksonian Democrat.[36] The Democratic Party, led by slave owners in the South and merchants in the North, needed and vied for the support of small farmers and workers everywhere.[37] Whitman was, until 1847, an active member, as journalist, editor and

---

33   Roediger 1991, p. 8.
34   In passing, Roediger suggests Whitman's link to this perspective. Roediger 1991, p. 44.
35   Roediger 1991, p. 9.
36   Whitman's father was evidently politically inclined, as the names of Walt's brothers indicate: Andrew Jackson, George Washington and Thomas Jefferson. Erkkila 1989, p. 14.
37   For an illuminating discussion see two unjustly forgotten texts by Harry Braverman issued under the pseudonym Harry Frankel, 'The Jacksonian Period' and 'Three Conceptions of Jacksonianism' originally published in 1946 and 1947 respectively and reissued in Frankel 1976. Following Post 2012, it would be necessary to revise his notion of planter control of the federal government for that of merchant capital connected with planter interests, but many points remain valid. After breaking with the Democratic Party in 1847, Whitman denounced the latter's subservience to the slave-owning interest in the 1850 poem 'Song for Certain Congressmen' (1076):
We are docile dough-faces,
They knead us with the fist
They, the dashing southern lords,
We labor as they list

party activist, of the northern wing of the Jacksonian coalition.[38] His articles mixed attacks on privileged corporations with faith in American industry, vindications of labour as the backbone of the republic with briefs in defence of free trade, rejection of slavery and the slave trade with opposition to abolitionist agitation.

Erkkila, in her classic study, tends to conflate Whitman's opposition to slavery and the extension of slavery with an abolitionist position. But Whitman himself rejected such an association. He was repelled by slavery and opposed it openly.[39] But, while yearning for abolition, he was willing to postpone it to an indefinite future, if slavery was confined to the existing slave states and if the federal government was not deployed to enforce it. He was, as he wrote in an 1847 editorial of the *Brooklyn Eagle*, for 'limiting slavery to where it already exists'.[40] Slavery, he argued, 'shall be allowed to spread no further'.[41] He sharply differentiated this from the 'wicked wrong, of "abolitionist" interference with slavery in the Southern States'.[42] With that, he underlined, 'we have nothing to do'.[43]

Pursuing that formula, during the 1850s Whitman opposed *federal* government intervention to defend slave-owning interests, as in the case of the Fugitive Slave Law of 1850, which empowered Federal authorities to return escaped slaves to their owners. But he argued that northern *state* governments had to return escaped slaves to their masters all the same.[44] Thus, as M. Wynn Thomas has pointed out, barely a year after expressing his sympathy for runaway slaves in the first edition of *Leaves of Grass*, Whitman endorsed their return to their masters.[45]

'A Boston Ballad', Whitman's poetic intervention in this debate, evidenced his concern, not so much with the plight of the runaway slaves, but rather with the, from his perspective, illegitimate intrusion of federal power in state juris-

---

        For them we speak – or hold our tongues,

        For them we turn and twist ...

38   The description of Whitman's evolution that follows largely abides by the fairly similar accounts by Arvin, Allen, Erkkila, Kaplan, Klammer, Wynn Thomas and Reynolds among other critics and biographers.

39   Whitman [1846c], pp. 187–91.

40   Whitman [1847], p. 212.

41   Whitman [1847e], p. 219.

42   Whitman [1847a], p. 202.

43   Whitman [1847a], p. 202.

44   'The Eighteenth Presidency!', p. 1320.

45   Thomas 2007, p. 75. Arvin referred to this as Whitman's 'rather inglorious record in the days of Abolitionism'. Arvin 1938, p. 33.

diction: while actions of the President's marshal in Boston are portrayed as a return to monarchical despotism and a betrayal and reversal of the American Revolution, the question of slavery and the resistance of the runaways to it goes unmentioned.[46]

Nor can 'Boston Ballad' be seen as Whitman's equivalent of William Lloyd Garrison's burning of the Constitution as a document compatible with slavery.[47] Garrison rejected the federal constitution because he accepted no compromise with slavery. Whitman rejected federal intervention but conceded that state governments had to return the captured runaway slaves to their owners.

Besides a brief mention of John Brown, and what can be read as an implicit reference to the Underground Railroad in one of the passages referred to above (where he mentions sheltering a slave 'before he recuperated and pass'd north'),[48] Whitman – exuberant, irrepressible poet of democracy and freedom – signally left us no song to abolitionism, the first of his great missing poems, as we shall see.[49]

He was, furthermore, not above the occasional idealisation of the slave South, which was to leave its trace in *Leaves of Grass*, as in the following verses of 'Our Old Feulliage' published in 1860 (under a different title):

> There are the negroes at work in good health, the ground in all the directions is cover'd with pine straw,
> In Tennessee and Kentucky slaves busy in the coalings, at the forge, by the furnace blaze, or at the corn-schucking,
> In Virginia, the planter's son returning after a long absence, joyfully welcom'd and kiss'd by the aged mulatto nurse[50]

---

46   'A Boston Ballad', pp. 404–6.
47   Buinicki 2011, p. 85.
48   'Song of Myself', p. 197. The reference to John Brown is in 'Year of Meteors', first included in the 1865 edition of *Leaves of Grass*, p. 380. Brown's execution is mentioned along the visit of an English prince, the arrival of the steamer *Great Eastern*, the completion of a census and the passing of a meteor.
49   For further discussion of slavery in some of the preparatory materials for *Leaves of Grass*, see Higgins 2002. Higgins points out that 'Whitman mentions slavery only three times in the notebook, none of which shows much humanitarian concern for the slaves' (p. 61). He adds: 'What is remarkable about each of these passages is their matter-of-fact acceptance of slavery. Speaking "indifferently" to "Sambo" in the sugar fields is a far cry from expressing any real concern over the fate and condition of African American slaves' (p. 61). Klammer 1995, p. 159. 'Our Old Feulliage', p. 320.
50   'Our Old Feulliage', p. 320.

M. Wynn Thomas has pointed out that the draft versions of this poem included descriptions of the harsher aspects of slavery. But Whitman excluded them from the published text. This reinforces, Thomas argues, the impression that Whitman on the brink of the Civil War, still sought a conciliatory tone toward the slave South, in spite of his dislike of slavery.[51] Erkkila thus went too far when she argued that 'At the same time that Karl Marx was making his revolutionary critique of Western capitalism, Whitman began mounting his own attack on American capitalism from the viewpoint of the laboring class'.[52] Marx would have considered an accommodating attitude toward slavery as incompatible with the 'viewpoint of the laboring class'. Furthermore, while young Jacksonian Whitman did attack corporations as corrupt and monopolistic, his attachment to a market-based individualism made his sympathy with labour stop short of supporting either unions or legislation limiting the length of the working day, not to speak of 'mounting an attack on American capitalism'.[53] For him, the alternative to monopolies and privileges was free trade, which he felt was beneficial to both workers and their employers. He extended this judgement to unions: while he at times supported the struggle for higher wages, he also argued that unions tended to become an unwarranted interference in the normal functioning of the market, with negative results. In 1846, as editor of the *Brooklyn Eagle*, Whitman warned that 'organized associations, to "regulate" the prices of labor, are the most fallacious things in the world'.[54] He added that '[t]here is not, to our knowledge one single instance of their having met with permanent success', and he added: 'They are, moreover, when proceeding beyond a certain limit, contrary to that clear, high, immutable truth, the freer and more without restrictions you leave trade and prices to regulate themselves, the better for all parties'.[55] The young editor clearly sympathised with the plight of badly paid workers, but he considered that an 'awakened public opinion' was the only means of improving their situation.[56] As Arvin pointed out in 1938, 'it is evident that his doctrines were at war ... with his sympathies'.[57] Or, as Lawson puts it, 'Whitman's laissez-faire faith' frustrated

---

51   Thomas 1994, pp. 139–41.
52   Erkkila 1989, p. 37.
53   Arvin 1938, pp. 235, 242.
54   'Illy paid labor in Brooklyn' (26 March 1846), quoted in Brasher 1970, p. 130. See also Brasher 1960.
55   'Illy paid labor in Brooklyn' (26 March 1846), quoted in Brasher 1970, p. 130. These comments were made in relation to a March – May 1846 strike at the construction firm Voorhis, Stranahan and Company, which was building the Atlantic Dock and Basin in Brooklyn.
56   Whitman [1847b], p. 151. Discussed in Brasher 1970, p. 134.
57   Arvin 1938, p. 123.

'his sympathies with the working class of his own city'.[58] Nor was Whitman, as M. Wynn Thomas has pointed out, beyond blaming the unemployed for their poverty and favouring cuts in the aid to the poor to force them to seek employment.[59] Whitman never freed himself from the contradiction of his rejection of many consequences of capitalist relations and his unwillingness to reconsider the vision of a self-regulating market as 'better for all parties'.

Whitman broke with Jacksonian Democracy precisely over the issue on which, for him, there could be no compromise (and which would eventually split the Democratic Party): not slavery, but the *extension* of slavery. At first, Whitman was a strident supporter of the US invasion of Mexico in 1846.[60] But he broke with the Democratic Party when it failed to support the Wilmot proviso, which sought to exclude slavery from the newly acquired territories. The West, Whitman insisted, must be set apart for the settlement of free labourers. This conviction pushed him out of the Democratic Party and pulled him into Free Soil party in 1848.

Interestingly, one passage from Whitman's editorials of the time, calling on American workers to oppose the extension of slavery, reads as an anticipation of the catalogues of occupations in *Leaves of Grass*. Whitman insisted that all mechanics needed to speak with one voice. With that objective in mind, he called

> upon every mechanic of the North, East, and West – upon the carpenter, in his rolled up sleeves, the mason with his trowel, the stonecutter with brawny chest, the blacksmith with his sooty face, the brown fisted shipbuilder, whose clinking strokes rattle so merrily in our dock yards – upon shoemakers, and cartmen, and drivers, and paviers, and porters, and millwrights, and furriers, and ropemakers, and butchers, and machinists, and tinmen, and tailors and hatters, and coach and cabinet makers – upon the honest sawyer and mortar-mixer too, whose sinews are their own.[61]

But for Whitman, the burning issue remained not the reality of slavery in the South, but the possibility of slavery in the West; not slavery as it affected four million slaves, but slavery, as he put it in 1856, 'in its relation to the whites'.[62] For him, as he had explained during the debate over the Wilmot proviso, the fun-

---

58   Lawson 2006, p. 88.
59   He formulated such a position in 1858. Thomas 1987, pp. 158–9.
60   Arvin describes his nationalism at the time as of the 'headiest sort'. Arvin 1938, p. 27.
61   Whitman [1847], p. 210.
62   'The Eighteenth Presidency!', p. 1311. The point is discussed by Klammer 1995, pp. 36–8.

damental confrontation posed by slavery was, not the conflict between slaves and their masters, but rather the conflict between the 'grand body of white workingmen, the millions of mechanics, farmers, and operatives', on the one hand, and 'the few thousand rich, "polished", aristocratic owners of slaves at the South'.[63] Western lands, he proclaimed, rightfully belonged to working people, not 350,000 'masters of slaves'.[64]

The concern with slavery 'in its relation to the whites' was compatible, of course, with a racist conception that sought to save the West, not for free labour in general, but for free *white* labour, a perspective present in at least some of Whitman's texts. Whitman proposed keeping the Oregon territory for white settlers, while favouring the relocation of free blacks outside the United States, an alternative to their incorporation as citizens favoured by many at the time, including future president Abraham Lincoln.[65] As Kenneth Price has pointed out, this perspective lurks between the lines in one of Whitman's best-known passages in 'I Sing the Body Electric', which at first strikes the reader as unproblematic in its proclamation of the human worth and cultural potential of African-Americans. Yet, as Price points out, the poet envisions the latter, not as future fellow citizens, but as the founders of separate, parallel republics:[66] 'In him the start of populous states and rich republics'.[67]

Whitman's break with the Democratic Party and his participation in the 'free soil' campaign roughly coincided with his shift from politics to poetry, which led to the publication of *Leaves of Grass* in 1855. Jerome Loving has suggested the most convincing explanation for this reorientation: it was the logic of Whitman's growing disenchantment with American politics that pushed him into a poetic project as a means of achieving national unification and coherence. Poetry would succeed where politics had failed. Or as Erkkila puts it, poetry became a way of pursuing politics by other means.[68]

But the terms and means of that coherence are problematical. Ed Folsom has discussed one of Whitman's preparatory notebooks for 'Song of Myself', specifically the place where verses clearly prefiguring the finished work first appear. There Whitman writes 'I am the poet of slaves and of the masters of

---

63 Whitman [1847], p. 208.
64 'The Eighteenth Presidency!', p. 1316. M. Wynn Thomas points out and discusses this in Thomas 1994, p. 138.
65 Erkkila 1989, pp. 47, 150–1; Klammer 1995, pp. 39, 64–5, 161; Arvin 1938, p. 42; Reynolds 1996, p. 372.
66 Price 2004, p. 19.
67 'I Sing the Body Electric', p. 256.
68 Loving 1982, pp. 67–74.

slaves'. Later he adds: 'Entering both so that both shall understand me alike'. Folsom argues that Whitman wanted both the slave and the slave owner to identify with the same 'I' at which point slavery would end. The slave owner needed to discover the slave 'within himself' and the 'slave needs to see the master within himself'.[69] Mutual identification of master and slave may very well have been Whitman's notion or intuition. But did it envision the abolition of slavery, as Folsom argues? Was it not rather an attempt to imagine an understanding between slave and slave owner in spite of the persistence of slavery, an attempt to dissipate the hate, resentments, fears and antagonisms of slavery without embracing the need to combat slavery actively, not unlike the way he rejected the consequences of capitalism without rejecting capitalism? He thus stood with the slave and the slave owner, the worker and the capitalist. He had learned, as Folsom points out, to 'absorb dichotomies'. But this is another way of saying that he refused to take sides. It was not his version of abolition, but a substitute for it. It was an evasion of the fundamental conflict of the time.

Whitman's views on abolition, slavery and the West spilled over into his vision of the war as an attempt to preserve the Union: against the treachery of the 'masters of slaves' he sang not only of the mobilisation of Union armies but also of the bravery and dedication to their cause of Confederate soldiers, in textual anticipation of what he hoped would be a rapid post-war reconciliation of painfully estranged brothers. (Implicitly *white* brothers, as we discuss below.) He thus insisted, for example, that 'The grand soldiers are not comprised in those of one side'.[70] He similarly told the tale of 'Two Brothers, One South, One North', in which he foregrounded, not the conflict opposing North and South, or freedom and slavery, but the shared, admirable, commitment of the two brothers to their respective sides, as well as the vision of their reunion at the moment of their sacrifice: 'In the same battle both were hit … both badly wounded, and both brought together here after a separation of four years. Each died for his cause'.[71]

In this tale of union, division and reunion, the story of emancipation of four million slaves becomes an almost invisible footnote: Whitman, who broached just about all aspects, large or small, public or intimate, of his time and of the war in particular, produced no significant poem on arguably the greatest single

---

69   Folsom 2014, p. 9.
70   Whitman [1882], p. 720.
71   Whitman [1882], p. 771. See the mention of the 'fiery patriotism' of the armies of 'both sides' in the Civil War. 'Our Eminent Visitors, Past, Present and Future', pp. 1137–8. For similar point see Erkkila 1989, p. 208.

step forward for freedom in his lifetime.[72] 'Drum-Taps', his collection of Civil War poems, signally fails to mention both emancipation and the participation of blacks in the Union armies. What may count as his poem on emancipation, 'Ethiopia Saluting the Colors', is a brief, disappointing text. In it, Whitman chooses to invent an inarticulate, 'hardly-human' figure, which the poetic voice approaches with more puzzlement than sympathy: 'Who are you dusky woman, so ancient hardly human?' Later the poem returns to this question: 'What is it fateful woman, so blear, hardly human?'[73] As Erkkila points out, 'Ethiopia' remains 'the figure of another country, an exotic alien figure'.[74]

Several passages give testimony to Whitman's startling failure to register the drama of both emancipation and of the subsequent incorporation of two hundred thousand black soldiers and sailors into the Union army and navy, an initial, if ultimately frustrated, step toward black enfranchisement. In the note entitled 'Paying the 1st U.S.C.T.', the poet offered his observations during a payday of black troops in July 1863.[75] Whitman is almost surprised at the attractive appearance of the group before him: 'Certes, we cannot find fault with the appearance of this crowd – negroes though they be. They are manly enough, bright enough, look as if they had the soldier-stuff in them, look hardy, patient, many of them real handsome young fellows'.[76] He is satisfied that 'thoroughly African physiognomies' are scarce and that, despite their presence, no face is 'utterly revolting': 'Occasionally, but not often, there are some thoroughly African physiognomies, very black in color, large, protruding lips, low-forehead, etc. But I have to say that I do not see one utterly revolting face'.[77] But then, Whitman reports, there is 'some trouble': 'One company, by the rigid rules of official computation, gets only 23 cents each man. The company (K) is indig-

---

72 Gay Wilson Allen, author of a classic biography of Whitman, underlined the fact that, for the poet, the preservation of the Union and not abolition remained the paramount issue of the war. Allen 1955, p. 325.

73 As Kaplan puts it '"Ethiopia" had ... served the flag but was "Ethiopia" still'. Kaplan 2003, p. 292. For a discussion of this poem see Magaril 2010, pp. 56–7. Referring to the woman in the poem, Buinicki has written that 'The coming of the troops inspires action on her part'. But it is hard to see any action on her part, besides standing and responding to the soldier's question. It is true that the mention of Ethiopia indicates that the history of the United States is connected to Africa. But is it not also a symptom of the incapacity of seeing blacks as part of the American polity and society? Buinicki 2011, p. 108.

74 Erkkila 1989, p. 241.

75 'November Boughs', p. 1181. U.S.C.T. refers to United States Colored Troops. According to Kaplan, during July 1863 some friends invited Whitman to observe black troops as they collected their pay in Analostan Island, off Georgetown. Kaplan 2003, p. 291.

76 'November Boughs', p. 1182.

77 'November Boughs', p. 1183.

nant, and after two or three are paid, the refusal to take the paltry sum is universal, and the company marches off to quarters unpaid. Another company (I) gets only 70 cents. The sullen, lowering, disappointed look is general. Half refuse it in this case'.[78] And that is all he has to say about this incident: the affirmation of personal dignity implicit in this act of individual and collective protest by black soldiers, most of which were surely penniless, at least some of which were former slaves, quite simply escapes him, or at least, fails to make it into his testimony. This blindness is not repaired by a final positive if qualified comment that an observer has to be 'well pleas'd' with the black troops or at least 'the beginning of them'.[79]

Whitman's distance from abolitionism before 1860 and his relegation of emancipation to the margins of his narrative of the war, translated into little concern for the situation of freedpeople after the war. It is striking to discover that *Specimen Days*, as close to a book of memoirs as Whitman ever wrote, leaps from the end of the war in 1865 straight to 1876, with no consideration of the tumultuous intervening years.[80] Yet, that decade witnessed the mighty clash between the planters' attempt to salvage as much of the old racial and oligarchic order as they could and the opposite radical push to remake the South through federal protection of freedpeople, the adoption of new constitutional provisions, the enactment of civil rights legislation, and the subsequent promulgation of black suffrage, which in turn enabled the election of blacks to state government and congressional posts. The more audacious among the radical Republicans, such as Thaddeus Stevens, wished to combine these measures with land redistribution as means of turning propertyless freedpeople, painfully vulnerable to the impositions of their former masters, into independent small farmers, while breaking the backbone of the economic and political power of the planter class. By the early 1870s, this democratic agenda was in retreat, as the planters launched the backlash that soon annulled black suffrage, revoked civil rights legislation or allowed it to expire, made constitutional guarantees inoperative, and institutionalised new forms of racial domination, amidst the emergence and consolidation of new relations of semi-capitalist exploitation of agricultural labour (variations of sharecropping).[81] All of the issues posed over the brief but intense life of Reconstruction – suffrage, citizenship, individual freedom, free speech, and land distribution – spoke directly to Whitman's often-expressed concerns and con-

---

78   'November Boughs', p. 1183.
79   'November Boughs', p. 1183.
80   Erkkila points this out in passing. Erkkila 1989, p. 295.
81   The commanding work on Reconstruction is Foner 1988.

victions. Yet they amount to an empty gap in his memoirs.[82] Beyond that text, we know that Whitman entered this period supporting President Andrew Johnson, a proponent of rapid reconciliation with the defeated Confederacy, against his radical opponents in Congress, and concluded it with favourable commentaries on Rutherford B. Hayes, whose recognition as President-elect after the deadlocked election of 1876 was assured through a compromise that included the dismantling of the remaining traces of federal responsibility for Reconstruction.[83] Meanwhile, in 1872, his opposition to black suffrage during the debates surrounding the Fifteenth amendment to the Constitution provoked a break with William Douglas O'Connor, until then a friend and a foremost ally against his critics (creator of the designation 'the good gray poet' in 1866).[84]

Whitman has been praised for looking at the war from the perspective of the common soldier, the rank-and-file participant. Betsy Erkkila has argued that he was more interested in the 'character' shown by the 'American people' during the war than the 'issues that provoked the war'.[85] But, as Cristanne Miller has explained in her discussion of how Whitman reworked 'Drum-Taps', keeping slavery largely out of sight turned the war into an inexplicable 'aberration'.[86] It put aside the issue that most concerned slaves and blacks in general, as well as consistent democrats. Combined with that absence, the 'fraternal mourning for the South's and North's equally "divine" dead'[87] led to a vision of reconciliation unconcerned with the need for a democratic agenda regarding freedpeople and blacks in general.[88] Unconcerned with slavery, the interest in the 'character' shown by the 'American people' both 'North and South' would thus seem to refer to white people, a notion underlined by the absence of blacks in Whitman's war poems.

Abolition, Emancipation, Reconstruction: it is hard to avoid the conclusion that the poet of democracy missed the encounter with *all* the main democratic

---

82 Nor does Whitman address these events in *Democratic Vistas*, his major political text. See on this Henkel 2010. Freeburg has also pointed out that Whitman ignored the fundamental issues raised by the debates around Reconstruction. Freeburg 2014, pp. 88–90.

83 Arvin 1938, p. 71; Erkkila 1989, p. 245; Reynolds 1996, p. 560. Praise of Hayes in Whitman [1882], pp. 869–70.

84 Lott 1998, p. 477; Arvin 1938, p. 71. For Whitman's relation with O'Connor see Robertson 2008.

85 Erkkila 1989, p. 208.

86 Miller 2009, p. 183.

87 Miller 2009, p. 184.

88 Miller 2009, p. 184.

battles of his time and place. To this we must add Whitman's many remarks favourable to white supremacy in the South. Reynolds cites several examples: 'I shall not like to see the nigger in the saddle', proclaimed Whitman, '–it seems unnatural'.[89] In 1890, he remarked: 'If I lived South I should side with the Southern whites'.[90] Envisioning an all-white world, he explained in 1888 that the 'nigger like the Injun, will be eliminated: it is the law of races, history, whatnot: always so far inexorable – always to be'.[91] In an undated text, unearthed by Kenneth Price, Whitman affirms that 'the south will yet come up'. Regarding blacks Whitman envisioned three options: they 'could filter through'; they could 'gradually eliminate and disappear, which is most likely', or they could develop 'all the attributes of a leading and dominant race, (which I do not think likely)'.[92]

Ed Folsom has argued that Whitman's long lost article in the *New York Times* on Lincoln's second inauguration (rediscovered in 1980) presents an image of a renewed, egalitarian, democratic and multi-racial nation through its portrait of the racially-mixed crowds in the mud-covered streets of Washington D.C. This may well be a return to the empathy shown with the slave and the admiration and respect for the black dray driver expressed in 'Song of Myself' ten years earlier.[93] But as Folsom himself indicates, the vision was all too brief: a year later Whitman described black crowds in the same streets in unequivocally derogatory terms, while also opposing the election, thanks in large part to the support of black voters, of Sayles Jenks Bowen, a partisan of radical Reconstruction, as mayor of Washington D.C.[94]

Perhaps Whitman's clearest statement on Reconstruction is his brief text 'Results South – Now and Hence' published in 1876. There Whitman rejects slavery as one of the 'sins' of southern whites, but portrays Reconstruction as a period of 'black domination' and as a 'horror' visited on whites (evidently the third-person pronoun and 'South' in the text refers to southern whites exclusively), a situation, he argued, acceptable perhaps as atonement for their 'sins', but not as a permanent arrangement:

---

89 Reynolds 1996, p. 471. Original in Traubel 1982, p. 323.
90 Reynolds 1996, p. 493. Originally in Traubel 1992, p. 158.
91 Traubel 1915b, p. 283. For a commentary on this and/or similar texts see: Reynolds 1996, p. 472. Also Sill 1990.
92 Price 1985, p. 205.
93 Folsom 2014, pp. 24–5. The article by Whitman was published in the *New York Times*, 12 March 1865. See Bandy 1985.
94 Whitman's racist comments on the black crowds in 1868 were first discussed by Arvin and Erkkila. Arvin 1938, p. 32; Erkkila 1989, pp. 240–1.

The utter change and overthrow of their whole social, and the greatest coloring feature of their political institutions – a horror and dismay, as of limitless sea and fire, sweeping over them ... – the black domination, but little above beasts, – viewed as temporary, deserved punishment for their slavery and Secession sins, may perhaps be admissible; but as a permamency of course is not to be considered for a moment.[95]

White supremacy would return to the South. Far from the project of Reconstruction, here Whitman's views were closer to the vision of Redemption, as the restoration of white rule in the South was to be called by its proponents. For Whitman, at least in this text, the problem was neither slavery nor the legacy of slavery but rather the former slaves. Whitman asked: 'Did the vast mass of blacks in Slavery in the United States, present a terrible and deeply complicated problem through the just ending century? But how if the mass of the blacks in freedom ... should present a yet more terrible and more deeply complicated problem?'[96] The conclusion bears repetition: for Whitman free blacks could pose a 'more terrible' problem than slavery. Regarding such passages, one can only conclude that Roediger's judgment of white working-class perspectives applies to Whitman: 'Plebian goals could degenerate for understandable though tragic reasons, from Republican hatred of slavery to a republican disdain for slaves and for free Blacks, and then to a mere racial pettiness that robbed republicanism of any remaining grandeur'.[97]

Thus, Whitman's trajectory was quite contradictory. Actively attached to the new world created by nascent modern industry, he was nonetheless troubled by key features of the all-pervasive pursuit of profit. But the form he gave his critique of a fragmented, deadened and polarised social universe threatened to transform his work into an apology of the very same structures whose consequences he derided. Furthermore, while he considered himself a poet of democracy and freedom, he nonetheless failed to embrace the actual and more urgent democratic struggles around him.

Simply put, Whitman's democratic principles were less than universal, as they faltered as soon as it became a matter of extending them, or extending them fully and unconditionally, to non-whites.[98] Of course, this could confirm

---

95 Whitman 1876, p. 66. This text discussed by Erkkila 1989, p. 241.
96 Whitman 1876, p. 66.
97 Roediger, p. 60.
98 Reynolds has presented Whitman's views on African-Americans as describing an arc from 'fairly conservative', to 'quite progressive' to 'deepened conservatism' after the war. Reynolds, p. 125.

Whitman's place – if not that of the first *Leaves of Grass*, where his inconsistencies are, if not absent, at least present in their more muted form – as a representative of US democracy: after all, is not the previous sentence an accurate description of the course of democracy in the United States through most of its history?

In a sense, Whitman has been given both too little and too much credit. Too little credit: Whitman was not simply a poet of American democracy or a complacent singer of democracy in general, understood as basic democratic freedoms, space for individual initiative and elected government. Going beyond mere celebration, Whitman questioned the dire consequences of the atomisation of the social fabric, the commodification of all human activities and the resulting alienation of individuals from themselves and from others. He yearned for a form of 'compaction' and comradeship that 'business' civilisation had not and could not produce. Yet, Whitman has also been given too much credit: Whitman, poet of democracy, signally failed to grapple with some, indeed the key democratic issues of his time. An inconsistent democrat, yet more than a democrat: Whitman's legacy cannot be cleansed of such unresolved tensions.

Luke Mancuso has argued that Whitman's poetic work during Reconstruction signals a commitment to the 'weaving of the ex-slaves into the national household'.[99] Boiled down to its key argument, Mancuso's thesis can be summarised as follows. Both the Civil War – with the forceful assertion of the indissolubility of the Union – and Reconstruction – through the intrusion of Federal authority to protect the rights of blacks in the former Confederacy – constituted an expansion of federal power over older notions of state rights and sovereignty. The Union now took precedence over its component parts. Whitman's texts of the Reconstruction era, argues Mancuso, indicate a similar shift away from an attachment to state rights and local loyalties toward an emphasis on national unity. As the poet proclaims: 'I will not make poems with reference to parts, / But I will make poems, songs, thoughts, with reference to ensemble'.[100]

This intensified emphasis on Union and National integration over state sovereignties, argues Mancuso, should be read as an embrace of Radical Reconstruction, that is to say, of the attempt to remake the South through federal intervention: Whitman was the 'federal poet' doing a 'cultural work' akin to the

---

99 Mancuso 1997, pp. 2, 3. Two recent studies have praised Mancuso's study without commenting on it in detail: Wilson 2014a; Buinicki 2011.
100 'Starting from Paumanok', p. 183.

legislative efforts of Radical Republicans. Yet, Mancuso admits that this 'cultural work', in contrast to the work of Radical Republicans, was carried out undercover, as Whitman now opted to 'camouflage' his views: 'After the war, Whitman had begun to camouflage his representations of blacks, but I suggest that behind his furtiveness lay the ongoing cultural work of weaving ex slaves into the national household'.[101] We are therefore asked to consider Whitman's emphasis on national union as a coded endorsement for black enfranchisement. But this takes as proven precisely what must be demonstrated. After all, there is no doubt that Whitman was the poet of the Union and of American nationality. What is not clear is his vision of blacks within that Union, and, more specifically, his views on the debates and battles around Reconstruction. One cannot simply assume that his commitment to Union and Nationality was tantamount to an endorsement of Reconstruction. Yet this is precisely the assumption that Mancuso makes, as he reads specific calls for racial equality and concrete endorsements for Reconstruction into Whitman's general affirmations of national union, while also finding a racial dimension in passages that hardly warrant such an interpretation.

Consider his discussion of the poem 'The City Dead-House'. Whitman's moving text describes the body of a dead prostitute: 'Her corpse they deposit unclaim'd, it lies on the damp brick pavement'. Mancuso considers that Whitman's vision of the prostitute should be read as a coded endorsement of black citizenship: 'Both blacks and prostitutes were disenfranchised citizens, beyond the boundaries of white respectability, but Whitman's poetic reconstruction of them placed them at the heart of the Republican polity'.[102] But in this poem there is no sign of a 'poetic reconstruction' of blacks, much less of their relocation to the 'heart of the Republican polity': this racial dimension has been engrafted into a text that makes no mention of it, remarkable as it otherwise may be.

Mancuso considers the ship in the poem 'Aboard at a Ship's Helm' to be an allegory of the 'Ship of State'. In the poem, the ship avoids disaster, thanks to a warning bell, and the skill of its steersman. Mancuso reads the poem as a warning that only by 'engaging in an egalitarian revision of its social relations' could the Union 'avoid another cataclysm'.[103] Elsewhere, he quotes Whitman's famous inscription: 'One's self I sing, a simple separate person, / Yet utter the word Democratic, the word En-masse'. According to him, in this passage 'sep-

---

101 Mancuso 1997, p. 3.
102 Mancuso 1997, p. 35.
103 Mancuso 1997, p. 35. Mancuso offers a similar reading of the ship that appears in 'Passage to India', p. 97.

arate person' stands for 'state sovereignty', while 'En masse' refers to 'national citizenship': he reads it as an endorsement of federal intervention in defence of democratic rights.[104] Yet, even if we grant that the ship in 'Aboard at a Ship's Helm' is an allegory of the 'Ship of State', it is not at all evident that its avoidance of disaster refers to 'an egalitarian revision of its social relations'. Similarly, even if we were to grant that the 'separate person' and 'En masse' stand, respectively, for state's rights and national citizenship, this can hardly be taken as an indication of Whitman's views on black citizenship in general, or the specific measures formulated within the framework of Radical Reconstruction.

Mancuso reads Whitman's description of the 'well-trained', 'lean and sinewy' athlete in 'The Runner' as a warning that 'Without such athletic vigilance, the ever-present danger to the Union lay in its static attachment to a moribund past'.[105] He argues that Death in 'When Lilacs Last in the Dooryard Bloom'd' stands for 'the death of historical continuity with the antebellum tolerance of the slavocracy'.[106] Referring to these passages in an otherwise favourable review, Klammer argues that Mancuso 'strains the credibility of certain readings'.[107] But this judgment is equally true of the other passages offered by Mancuso to support his thesis.

More generally, the notion of 'camouflage' poses an interesting question: if Whitman wished to intervene in the debate over the rights of blacks, and if he was as committed to the incorporation of freedpeople as equal citizens as Mancuso claims he was, why would he choose to 'camouflage' his views, why would he opt to discursively bury them in such a way that only an elaborate textual analysis could unearth them (and then only as tentative extrapolations)? Why would Whitman, willing to explore sexual taboos deemed obscene by public opinion, choose to 'camouflage' his views on an issue on which *many* commentators at the time were taking a clear, public and forceful stance?[108] On balance, we must conclude that regarding this question Whitman did not articulate a consistent yet 'camouflaged' position but rather clung to what, at best, amounted to an ambiguous and evasive attitude.

Like Mancuso, Martin T. Buinicki has explored Whitman's work on *Leaves of Grass* in the epoch of Reconstruction. His contribution is interesting, but

---

104 Mancuso 1997, p. 22.
105 Mancuso 1997, p. 35.
106 Mancuso 1997, p. 25.
107 Klammer 1997, pp. 40, 43.
108 As Erkkila and others remind us, Whitman wrote boldly about masturbation, repressed sexual desire, sexual organs, the sexual act, female eroticism and homosexual attraction. Erkkila 1989, p. 78.

contradictory: its specific claims would invalidate some of his conclusions. Buinicki speaks of the 'poet's work of reconstruction'. This work, according to him, included the preparation of the 1871 edition of *Leaves of Grass* and the work of reorganisation leading to the 1881–2 edition. In 1871, Whitman created the cluster entitled 'Songs of Insurrection'. It included texts that reaffirmed the right and the duty to resist oppression ('O latent right of insurrection! O quenchless, indispensable fire' as he proclaims in 'Still Though the One I Sing') as well as the text entitled 'Walt Whitman's Caution' in this edition ('To the States' in later editions):

> To The States or any one of them, or any city of The States, *Resist much, obey little*,
> Once unquestioning obedience, once fully enslaved,
> Once fully enslaved, no nation, state, city of this earth, ever afterward resumes its liberty.[109]

In the 1871 edition, 'Songs of Insurrection' was placed several clusters after 'Drum Taps', the cluster dedicated to the Civil War, and very close to the end of the book (only followed by the poem 'To You' and the cluster 'Songs of Parting'). The placing, if read as part of a narrative, would seem to indicate that the Civil War still had left much work to be done to attain the greatness that Whitman predicted for the United States, including, perhaps, more resisting, disobeying and appealing to the 'latent right of insurrection'. This edition, it should be remembered, coincided with Whitman's harsh criticisms of many aspects of American society in *Democratic Vistas*.

All of this, Buinicki explains, was reconstructed by Whitman for the 1881–2 edition. The 'Songs of Insurrection' cluster disappeared.[110] Its components were scattered and placed before 'Drum Taps' and leading to it. 'Drum Taps' now occupied the centre of the book, preceded by the cluster entitled 'By the Roadside' (including some of the former components of 'Songs of Insurrection') which incorporated the poet's doubts, fears and worries, to be resolved by the experience of the war. In this fashion, Buinicki argues, Whitman achieved 'narrative progression' from doubt and uncertainty to unity and reaffirmation forged by the war, as recorded in 'Drum Taps'.[111] Whitman created a 'poetic story'

---

109 'To the States', p. 172.
110 Arvin had already commented on the appearance and disappearance of 'Songs of Insurrection'. Arvin 1938, pp. 138–9.
111 Buinicki 2011, p. 96.

in which the Civil War 'will rally the country and the poet … restore their unity of purpose, and put them both, back on the march'. Whitman thus constructed what Buinicki calls a 'poetic and national Reconstruction narrative'.[112]

But there is an evident discrepancy here: 'Unity of purpose' was one thing that the war did not bring about. Quite the opposite: it issued into a tremendous decade-long clash over the future of the South and the situation of the former masters and slaves. Yet Whitman's 'reconstruction narrative' invites no consideration of the problems, experiences and tasks posed by the outcome of the war, neither of the extension of civil rights, the exercise of new freedoms, nor the enfranchisement of the former slaves, not to speak of land redistribution. Simply put: Whitman's 'national Reconstruction narrative' neglects actual Reconstruction. If Whitman's 'poetic story' portrayed the war as 'rallying' the nation and putting it 'back on the march', it failed to indicate which of the contrary orientations it should follow. It exhibits the same void as *Specimen Days*. Or rather, through its silences it implicitly endorsed a 'unity of purpose', a 'national' reunion, at the expense of radical Reconstruction. Whitman's 'poetic story' culminating in the war, as ably described by Buinicki, corresponds, not to Reconstruction, but to its opposite: either disregard for the legacy of slavery (which Reconstruction sought to address) or worse, the reversal and entombment of the latter, in the name of national unity and reconciliation. The 'sense of whiteness', to use Roediger's term, persists, as the 'poetic story' suggests a reconciliation through the recognition of the bravery and fortitude displayed during the war, both 'North and South', combined with the unspoken erasure of Reconstruction from memory or programme: the bravery exhibited both North and South tends to become *white* bravery, North and South. If Whitman was not the poet of Redemption (even if in some texts, such as 'Results South', quoted above, he came close to endorsing it), neither was he the poet of Reconstruction.

Critics do not overlook the fact that Whitman's vision of reconciliation left fundamental issues unanswered, due to sympathies for segregation or Southern reaction. Those we have mentioned (Mancuso, Buinicki) and others discussed below (Erkkila, Folsom) are quite aware of the injustices involved and explicitly reject them. Rather they are inadvertently pushed, betrayed we could say, to ignore this by the frequent adoption in texts about Whitman of the generalised, common-sense vision of the war as a sectional conflict. Within that dialectic of North and South (or Union and Secession, Federal and Confederate, Blue and Grey), the war becomes a moment of division, a 'fratricidal' tragedy,

---

112 Buinicki 2011, p. 108.

to be lamented, while reunion, unity and reconciliation in turn become the legitimate post-war agenda. Whitman is seen then as generously contributing to that reconciliation.

But this narrative sidelines the fact that reconciliation could take many forms, that post-war reconciliation as it actually evolved after 1876 was one of several options and that it was, furthermore, a reconciliation built on the brutal suppression of African-American and, more generally, of radical or consistently democratic aspirations.

The narrative of division-war-reunion and its twin, the talk of sectional healing and reconciliation, suppress the fundamental fact that each section, North and South, was internally divided and harboured different, antagonistic, interests. The post-bellum South, in particular, included the planters and the ex-slaves, with opposing interests and agendas. One could not be reconciled with one without antagonising the other. There could be no commitment to black democratic aspirations without provoking the bitter and hostile reaction of the economically and racially dominant sectors in the South. To heal the fracture with Southern white propertied classes required suppressing the black struggle for civil rights, political incorporation and economic empowerment. Simply put, there could be no reconciliation with *both* ex-slaves and southern reaction, just as there could not be an alliance with both slaves and masters before emancipation. We cannot be satisfied then with the notion that Whitman, or anyone else for that matter, favoured reconciliation but must inquire: which?[113]

The lure of the talk of reconciliation trips texts that otherwise recognise Whitman's less than admirable views on race after the war. For example, in an

---

113 There is an old-fashioned Marxist lesson in this: we need a class perspective on the 'sectional' conflict, if only to prevent these blind spots. A point well-made long ago by Harry Braverman, writing under the name Harry Frankel. Frankel 1976. The problem also arises in the discussion of the period *before* the Civil War. Folsom thus writes that in 1855 the United States was 'five years away from discovering how fully the forces of division and violence would overcome the fading hopes of unity and absorption of differences' (Folsom 2014, p. 8). But one wonders what in 1855 could the 'hopes of unity and absorption' of differences entail? Hope of accommodation with, or tolerance of, slavery, to avoid the division and violence of a war? Abolition of the violence inherent to the slave regime? But how could this be attained without division and violence? Talk of unity, division and reconciliation is inadequate to understand the conflicts tearing American society apart during this period. Erkkila similarly refers to the division in the 1850s of the Democratic Party 'which had formerly been a force for union, encompassing a diversity of sectional interests in its ranks' (Erkkila 1989, pp. 146–7). But the Democratic Party was not simply a 'force for union', but rather the union of planter and mercantile interests, built on the perpetuation of slavery. Its breakup was not the collapse of 'unity', but part of the polarisation that eventually led to the demise of slavery.

unguarded moment Betsy Erkkila, whose extraordinary book we have drawn upon many times, comments that by 1868 Whitman '[l]ike many in the country ... hoped for a retreat from the more radical premises of Republican reconstruction and a restoration of balance through the election of Ulysses S. Grant'.[114] 'Balance', of course, has a very positive, conciliatory ring. Readers may take this as a benign, magnanimous stance. Nevertheless, at that point the 'more radical premise' of Reconstruction was the conviction that the absence or premature removal of federal power from the South would lead to perpetuation of white rule in its starkest forms. Seeking 'balance' on this issue, the touchiest for southern ruling sectors, implied accommodation with an unreconstructed South, including the structuring of new forms of racial oppression, as the rapid adoption of Black Codes by the early unreconstructed southern state governments demonstrated. Such a 'balance' meant a renunciation of the democratic agenda of Reconstruction. This may very well have been the policy of 'many' in the country, although certainly not of many African-Americans. It may have been also the position of most white Americans (although in 1868 this is less clear), but this only means that Whitman was among those favouring policies that abandoned a truly democratic agenda in the South and not among those pushing for it.

Similarly, when critics speak in general and rather abstractly of Whitman being interested 'not just in his own healing, but that of his countrymen',[115] or of Whitman writing 'as the nation was reconstructing itself politically and healing from the war',[116] or of an 'an audience hungry for reconciliation',[117] or of his notion that the war created 'unity of purpose', the commendable ring of such terms (healing, reconciliation, unity of purpose, balance) must be tempered by some fundamental questions: Unity for which purpose? Were the reconciliation and the healing referred to premised on the fight against racial oppression or, rather, on the avoidance of conflict or compromise with its promoters?[118]

---

114 Erkkila 1989, p. 245.
115 Martin G. Murray quoted in Buinicki 2011, p. 145.
116 Folsom and Price 2005, p. xiv.
117 Buinicki 2011, p. 11.
118 When Buinicki states that by the late-1870s the 'public imagination' was moving from the 'contentious' debates of Reconstruction to the commemoration of the war the impression we get is that of progress from divisive conflict to reconciliation. But we need to ask if the African-American 'public imagination' was content with commemorating the war and leaving behind the debates about Reconstruction. Almost certainly not. In which case, it would be more accurate to speak about *white* public imagination, or part of it, and of the retreat, in terms of the struggle for democracy, that this passage from 'debate' to 'commemoration' implied. Buinicki 2011, p. 77.

In conclusion, there is no reason to revise Cristanne Miller's, Thomas F. Haddox's and Scott Henkel's argument that Whitman ignored the plight of the ex-slaves while embracing a vision of unity and reconciliation that turned its back on Reconstruction. As Haddox has argued: 'One searches in vain for any intimation that the post-Civil War Union, however alarming its situation, is anything but a single family, rapidly forgetting its recent fratricidal struggle'.[119] To this we can add a fact pointed out by Erkkila and underlined by Ed Folsom: in his reconstruction of *Leaves of Grass* for the 1881–2 edition, Whitman eliminated the so-called 'Lucifer' passage, in which a slave, confident in his strength, vows revenge against his master. Whitman thus erased, as Folsom points out, 'one of the greatest passages in American poetry about a black slave gaining a voice' and he silenced 'that voice for over seventy-five years, until readers began once again reading earlier versions of the poem'.[120]

Here we can also return to Folsom's notion of a 'ghost-black speaker' in Whitman, which he extends to the poem 'Reconciliation' written near the end of the war. As we pointed out, Folsom ably argues that in some passages, such as the episode of the injured fireman in 'Song of Myself', Whitman does not write *about* blacks but rather constructs a black voice through which he speaks: references to the whiteness of the faces around him are indications of this imagined black subjectivity, not of white racist pride. Folsom extends this notion to 'Reconciliation' which speaks from the perspective of a soldier kissing the white face of his dead enemy.

> For my enemy is dead – a man as divine as myself is dead;
> I look where he lies, white-faced and still, in the coffin – I draw near;
> I bend down, and touch lightly with my lips the white face in the
>   coffin.[121]

The overemphasis on the whiteness of the face, argues Folsom, is a symptom that it marks a defining difference with the speaker: the voice insisting on the whiteness of his dead enemy corresponds to Whitman's 'ghost-black speaker'. Our interest here is not to determine whether this reading is correct or not, but rather to consider the consequences of both options. If incorrect, the poem would stand as another example of the vision and desire for white reconcili-

---

119 Haddox 2004, p. 8. Henkel similarly argues: 'Such unproblematized reconciliation can take place only through erasure of the memory of slavery, of the presence of freed and terrorized blacks in the South' (Henkel 2010, p. 186).
120 Folsom 2014, p. 11. Erkkila 1989, p. 291.
121 'Reconciliation', p. 453.

ation, of Union and Confederate, Blue and Gray reconciliation that excludes African-Americans. If correct, it stands as a call for reconciliation of blacks with white America *without* addressing any of the then very visible pressing issues of white oppression in the post-bellum South: for the poet the end of the war and the sacrifices it had imposed were sufficient ground for reconciliation, as they were not for the white and black proponents of Radical Reconstruction.[122] Furthermore, as read by Folsom, the poem, in 1865, would seem to seek and act of reconciliation and a recognition of a shared 'divine' nature, not from the white, but from the black soldier. But this hardly subverts the bitter legacy of white oppression or the reality of white racism. The problem of white racism is not addressed. For that to happen, the demand for recognition had to be addressed to the oppressor, not the oppressed; racist whites, not blacks; the former 'masters of slaves' not the former slaves. Consider the extraordinary potential change in meaning due to a simple reorientation of the gesture described in 'Reconciliation': a kiss by a white veteran, North or South, on the cheek of a black dead soldier. That would be the image of a radical, interracial reconciliation and reconstruction. The fact that it was not formulated and could not be formulated without generating tremendous rejection and resistance is a further indication that there was no reconciliation without conflict and that the reconciliation that was enacted in the poem and beyond was built on the silencing of the aspirations of freedpeople and of Radical Reconstruction.

José Martí was fascinated and troubled by the capitalist metropolis. He hailed the work of Whitman as part of the aesthetic dimension necessary to an otherwise one-sided modernity. Whitman embraced the modern while wishing to transcend what he took to be its limits and contradictions. Martí did likewise. The following chapter explores the logic and reach of Martí's alternative to the existing forms of modernity and progress.[123]

---

122   Rapid reconciliation with 'my enemy' would have required: the end of Federal military rule in the South; amnesty of all participants in the rebellion; rapid restoration of the former states; respect for slave owners' landed property and delegation of matters regarding suffrage to the states (which would have led to the disenfranchisement of blacks), for example. This was the program of some of the political currents seeking rapid reconciliation with the defeated South in 1868. Du Bois 1979, p. 375.

123   As Arvin points out, even in the days of Kansas civil war, Whitman was still arguing that slavery had 'redeeming points'. Arvin 1938, p. 35.

CHAPTER 9

A 'Damaged and Alien Civilization': Martí's Search for an Alternative Modernity

Martí's aversion to what he took to be the asphyxiating one-sidedness and desolate fragmentation of American society and his vision of an increasingly corrupt republic was not formulated as a vague impression. Between 1881 and 1894, he analysed the more spectacular features of American society during a decade of financial panics, industrial crisis and sharpened, massive and often violent class conflict. Martí described the functioning of US political machines: democratic ideals were one thing, the actual operation of city, state and federal governments was quite another. He was equally interested in the spread of financial speculation and the resulting banking crashes. Beginning in 1882, he took note of the rise of a new wave of labour militancy, linked to the growth of the Knights of Labor. Some of Martí's longest texts on the United States deal with the 'Haymarket affair' of 1886. He wrote sympathetic reports of the rise of the United Labor Party in New York City, and of Henry George's near victory as its candidate for mayor in 1887. Although it is not essential for our discussion, it can be argued that the events of 1886–7 – the Haymarket riot, the execution of four anarchist leaders – marked a turning point. Before then, Martí had more often than not combined his description of the ills of American society with the conviction that it would bring forth the means to heal itself: machine politics would be dismantled by the forces of reform; financial speculation would not survive the inevitable day of reckoning, even if the nation underwent a period of general hardship; the rise of a pragmatic labour movement made a peaceful solution to the tensions between labour and capital possible, while the consolidation of large fortunes would be reversed before the crystallisation of a new privileged dominant caste. After 1886 Martí's views hardened. By 1894 he considered that the 'problems of humanity', rather than being resolved, were 'being reproduced' in the United States'.[1] None of this weakened his commitment to a modern Latin America, or modernity, as some authors have suggested, but it propelled him to the conclusion that it would have to be a *different* modernity. As in the case of Whitman, the question arises as to whether the means he proposed fit the ambitious objective he had embraced.

---

1 Martí [1894], p. 330; 'La verdad sobre los Estados Unidos', OC, XXVIII, p. 292.

As early as 1881 Martí allotted dozens of pages to describe New York City politics. He spared no scorn in his description of political bosses and machines.[2] While confident they were being undermined by reform efforts, he warned that the economic forces that fostered political corruption could survive in other fields: 'Tyranny, defeated in politics, reappears in commerce. This industrial country has an industrial tyrant'.[3] Financial speculation was a particularly dangerous aspect of the activities of these 'commercial' or 'industrial tyrants': 'To this is added a commercial vice ... the swelling of values above their real level, produced by ... speculation'.[4] In 1888 he described Wall Street trading as a form of robbery and of gambling: 'In the stock exchanges, where does business end and robbery start? Or is robbery everything and there is no business? How is the gambling in the stock exchange different from any other gambling?'[5] Through such speculative schemes a few magnates endangered the well being of the whole nation, since the former inevitably collapsed: 'In time, real value imposes itself, almost always in a sudden and violent form, and all the false order ... built on hollow values, falls to the ground'. An honest man, Martí concluded, 'cannot gamble on the ruin of a country'.[6]

Beginning in 1882, Martí reported the emergence of a new social agent, at the other end of the social spectrum: 'We are at the height of a struggle between capitalists and workers'.[7] According to him, the reasons for the conflict were simple. His description betrayed his sympathies for one of the embattled forces: 'The worker demands a wage that enables him to eat and clothe him-

---

2 For example: 'The despicable boss; head of the party; who fixes the elections, bends them, takes advantage of them, gives them to his friends, denies them to his enemies, sells them to his adversaries; who demands money from his employees so that he can conduct the elections that will keep them their jobs; who, by pressing the button of the spring that moves the political machine, at his will, puts the wheels in motion, or stops them, or breaks them; who imposes the candidates on the party'. 'Carta de Nueva York', [1881], *OC*, IX, pp. 97–8.
3 'Cartas de Martí', [1884], *OC*, X, p. 85. ['La tiranía acorralada en lo político, reaparece en lo comercial. Este país industrial tiene un tirano industrial'.]
4 'El problema industrial en los Estados Unidos' [1885], *OC*, X, p. 303. ['A esto se junta un vicio mercantil ... y este es la hinchazón de los valores por sobre su importancia real, producida por ... la especulación'.]
5 'Un día en Nueva York' [1888], *OC*, XII, pp. 69–70. ['¿dónde acaba el negocio en las bolsas, y empieza el robo? ¿o todo es robo, y no hay negocio? ... ¿Qué más es el azar de la bolsa, que cualquier otro azar?']
6 'El problema industrial en los Estados Unidos', [1885], *OC*, X, pp. 303–4. ['El valor real a la larga se impone, casi siempre de un modo súbito y violento, y todo el orden falso ... edificado sobre estos valores huecos, viene a tierra ...; un hombre honrado ... no puede jugar a la ruina de un país'.]
7 Martí [1882b], p. 243; 'Carta de los Estados Unidos', *OC*, IX, p. 322.

self. The capitalist denies it to him'.[8] The movement was neither improvised nor chaotic: 'these uprisings are no longer isolated cases ... There is no longer a city without as many associations as trade unions. The workers have gathered into a colossal association known as the Knights of Labor'.[9] Martí sought to convey both the vastness of the movement and the crystallisation of opposed social forces:

> All at once strikes break out among the millworkers of Chicago, the miners of Cumberland, the embankment workers of Omaha, the blacksmiths of Pittsburgh, the spinners of Lawrence. In Pittsburgh, the blood of two guards is spilled. In Omaha, an unemployed blacksmith dies from a bayonet wound ... The funeral seemed like a truce in a war. Two thousand silent men say much. The soldiers stood in line, their cartridges prepared, their hands ready, their bayonets fixed. And thus they stand; that is how they now eye each other, workers and soldiers, face to face.[10]

Martí underlined a new feature of the conflict. In the past, employers had played workers of different nationalities against each other. But class solidarity now deprived the employers of that weapon: 'This marks a great event in the struggle. Formerly ... the employers would approach the Italians, who were willing to work for a low wage. But now, since the Italians are resisting because they realise that if better working conditions are achieved for others, they will be achieved for themselves, the employers will have to yield to the just demands of the employed'.[11]

As early as 1882 Martí concluded that the relation between capital and labour (those who sell labour and 'those who trade in it') was the 'colossal problem' ('el colosal problema') of the modern world. The United States would be the 'colossal theatre' in which the 'tremendous social battle' ('batalla social tremenda') that would settle it would be fought.

---

8   Martí [1882b], p. 243; 'Carta de los Estados Unidos', *OC*, IX, p. 322.
9   Martí [1882b], p. 244; 'Carta de los Estados Unidos', *OC*, IX, p. 323.
10 'Carta de Nueva York' [1882], *OC*, IX, pp. 280–1. ['A un tiempo estallan huelgas entre los molineros de Chicago, los mineros de Cumberland, los terraplaneros de Omaha, los herreros de Pittsburg, las hilanderas de Lawrence. En Pittsburg, corre la sangre de dos guardianes. En Omaha, muere con una bayoneta en el costado, el herrero sin empleo ... Parecía el entierro tregua de campaña. Dicen mucho, dos mil hombres silenciosos. Y de pie en las filas, estaban los soldados, preparado el cartucho, atenta la mano, calada la bayoneta. Y así quedan; así se ven ahora faz a faz, trabajadores y soldados'.]
11 Martí [1882b], p. 246; 'Carta de los Estados Unidos', *OC*, IX, p. 324.

It is in this land, even if it seems like a premature prophecy, that the new laws that will rule the relations between the men that labour and those that trade with that labour will be decided. In this colossal theatre the colossal problem will come to an end. Here, where the workers are strong, the workers will fight and win ... In other lands racial and political battles are fought. In this land the tremendous social battle will be fought.[12]

'The struggle', Martí assured his readers, 'will be such that it will move and stir up the universe'.[13]

Five years later Martí reaffirmed his conviction that 'all the problems that interest and confuse mankind' were to be posed 'and be resolved in the United States'.[14] According to Martí, workers were forced to organise in order to resist those that derived their wealth from their labour.[15] Big capital did not

12 'Carta de Nueva York' [1882], *OC*, IX, p. 278. ['En esta tierra se han de decidir, aunque parezca prematura profecía, las leyes nuevas que han de gobernar al hombre que hace la labor y al que con ella mercada. En este colosal teatro llegará a su fin el colosal problema. Aquí, donde los trabajadores son fuertes, lucharán y vencerán los trabajadores ... En otras tierras se libran peleas de raza y batallas políticas. Y en esta se librará la batalla social tremenda'.]
13 'The battle will be such that it will move and stir up the Universe. That which is brewing is the new laws. This is everywhere an epoch of realignment and restructuring. The last century threw out the elements of the old life, with sinister and vigorous anger. Hindered in its path by the ruins ... this century, which is a time of particulars and preparation, is accumulating the lasting elements of the new life' (Martí [1882b], p. 247); 'Carta de los Estados Unidos' [1882], *OC*, IX, p. 325. ['El combate será tal que conmueva y renueva el Universo. Estas que hierven, son las leyes nuevas. Esta es en todas partes época de reenquiciamiento y de remolde. El siglo pasado aventó, con ira siniestra y pujante, los elementos de la vida vieja. Estorbado en su paso por las ruinas ... este siglo, que es de detalle y preparación, acumula los elementos durables de la vida nueva'.] The United States would be the main stage of the general transition he had a described a few months earlier: 'This century is preparing the philosophy that will be established by the coming century. This is the century of particulars: the next one will be the century of synthesis'. 'Carta de Nueva York' [1882], *OC*, IX, p. 226. ['Este siglo prepara la filosofía que ha de establecer el siglo que viene. Este es el siglo del detalle: el que viene será el siglo de síntesis'.]
14 Martí [1887b], p. 278; 'El cisma de los católicos en Nueva York', *OC*, XI, p. 144. ['Tal parece que en los Estados Unidos han de plantearse y resolverse todos los problemas que interesan y confunden al linaje humano'.]
15 'The rapid and visible concentration of public wealth, of lands, of means of communication, of enterprises, by a wealthy caste that legislates and rules, has provoked the rapid concentration of workers that only through their coming together tightly in a formidable league ... can successfully claim their rights against ... those that derive all their wealth from the products of the labour of those they mistreat' (Martí 1980, 'Correspondencia particular del *Partido Liberal*', [1886], p. 20). ['La concentración rápida y visible de la riqueza pública, de tierras, de vías de comunicación, de empresas, en una casta acaud-

only amass economic power but used it to control Congress and most elected officials.[16]

Yet, at least until 1886, Martí seemed confident that the conflict would find a peaceful solution: there were no fixed upper or lower classes in America. Capitalists were often former workers. The doctrines of European socialism had little chance of taking root in America. A moderate, specifically American, labour movement, exemplified by the leadership of the Knights of Labor, and a peaceful reform movement, such as the one inspired by the ideas of Henry George, would gradually attain the desired social reforms. American labour organisations, he argued, 'are powerful, because they arise directly from their problems. It is not European socialism transplanted. It's not even the birth of an American socialism. Here there is no caste to defeat ... Those buried in a bronze coffin ate in a tin plate'.[17] Martí trusted that a century of

---

alada que legisla y gobierna, ha provocado la concentración rápida de los trabajadores, quienes solo apretándose en liga formidable ... pueden oponer con éxito sus derechos a ... los que derivan toda su riqueza de los productos del trabajo que maltratan'.] 'This epoch', he argued, had created new 'nobles' and a new type of 'aristocracy': 'large corporations' (Martí 1980, 'Correspondencia particular del *Partido Liberal*' [1886], p. 36). Modern conditions had generated a 'feudalism in land and industry' (Martí 1980, 'Correspondencia particular del *Partido Liberal*' [1886] p. 70). ['un nuevo feudalismo en la tierra y en la industria'.]

16 Martí 1980, 'Correspondencia particular del Partido Liberal' [1886], pp. 21, 34, 35. In an 1885 chronicle singled out by Laura Lomas, Martí constructed a stark contrast between the splendour of New York City, on the one hand, and the toil, poverty and repression suffered by miners in the Monongahela River valley, the source of the coal that kept New York in motion, on the other. In Martí's words: 'Who, after seeing these luxuries ... these commercial palaces ... who after seeing the streets of New York ... would believe, that in the Monongahela, where they extract the coal, thousands of hungry and anguished miners live barely better than insects without ... bread ... or clothing for their children, with no more than wooden benches for furniture and no refuge but houses made of planks from boxes? Who ... would suspect that there ... where the miners bring out the coal that moves it [the city], and sustains it, armed men, with no fear of law or judge ... gather and fall upon a town and kill the men and set in on fire'. 'Placeres y problemas de septiembre', [1885], *oc*, X, pp. 298–9. ['¿Quién que viera estos lujos ... estos palacios mercantiles ... quien que viera estas calles de Nueva York ... creería que, poco más que insectos, viven en hambre y angustia, allá ... en el Monongahela, de donde sacan el carbón, millares de mineros, que no tienen ... pan ... ni vestidos para sus hijos, ni más muebles que bancos de madera, ni más asilo que casas hechas de tablas de cajones? ¿quién ... sospecharía que allá ... donde los mineros sacan de la tierra el carbón que la mueve, y la sustenta, los hombres, sin miedo a la ley ni juez que se les oponga, ... se congregan armados, caen sobre un pueblo vivo y matan a sus hombres y le ponen fuego?'] Lomas discusses this text in Lomas 2008, p. 165.

17 'El problema industrial en los Estados Unidos' [1885], *oc*, X, p. 308. ['Son poderosas, porque

'republican habits' would enable the American people to adopt the necessary reforms without the need of bloody revolutions.[18]

In 1886 Martí was quick to relay the news of a new strike wave.[19] The railroads, and with them the economies of several states, had been paralysed: 'Trains do not move. Merchandise piles up in enormous quantities. Day after day the strike grows. Goods are not shipped out, imports do not arrive on schedule ... A railroad system brought to a halt ... is like a glutted aorta. So it has been for two weeks in Missouri and Kansas'.[20] Martí underlined the role of the Knights of Labor, the size of the movement and the solidarity bringing together workers from different regions and crafts:

> Entire states are striking, entire work regions comprising two or three states. From local chapter to local chapter ... the Order of the Knights of Labor has been spreading from its birthplace in Philadelphia throughout the republic: first in the factories of the East, then in larger cities, then in the railroad centers of the West, and finally among the farmers and miners of the Pacific Coast states. What a few strong-willed tailors began twenty years ago ... is today a technical association ... by means of which, if a Texas railroad company should dismiss one of its workers without cause, the blacksmiths of Pittsburgh, the shoe factories of New England, the cigar makers of New York would be prepared to send their share of assistance to the Texas railroad strike until the worker in question has been returned to his post.[21]

---

nacen directamente de sus propios problemas. No es el socialismo europeo que se trasplanta. No es siquiera un socialismo americano que nace. Acá no hay una casta que vencer ... Los que reposan en ataúd de bronce comieron en tina de lata'.]

18   Martí 1980, 'Correspondencia particular del *Partido Liberal*' [1886], pp. 21, 23.
19   'La revolución del trabajo', [1886], *oc*, x, p. 394.
20   Martí [1886], p. 255; 'Las huelgas en los Estados Unidos', *oc*, x, p. 404.
21   Martí [1886], pp. 253–4; 'Las huelgas en los Estados Unidos', *oc*, x, p. 403. ['Hoy, todo es huelga, huelga formidable. Estados enteros hay en huelga; regiones enteras de trabajo, que abarcan dos o tres Estados. De asamblea en asamblea, o sea de gremio en gremio, ha ido extendiéndose la orden de los Caballeros del Trabajo desde su cuna en Filadelfia, por toda la República, en las manufacturas del Este primero, luego en las grandes ciudades, después en los ferrocarriles que van al Oeste, al fin entre los campesinos y mineros de los Estados del Pacífico. Lo que empezaron ... hace veinte años unos cuantos sastres de brava voluntad, es hoy ... vastísima masonería, por medio de la cual, si en un ferrocarril de Tejas despiden a un obrero sin razón, ya están los herreros de Pittsburg, los zapateros de la Nueva Inglaterra, los cigarreros de New York disponiéndose a ayudar con su cuota a la huelga de los ferrocarrileros de Tejas, hasta que el obrero despedido sin justicia sea vuelto a su puesto'.]

Martí reaffirmed his conviction that the labour question was a central issue of the times. Characteristically, it was posed in the United States 'as everything presents itself here ... suddenly and on a colossal scale'.[22] He emphasised the role of the Knights of Labor in part because he admired the moderate views of its leaders. He wrote admiringly of Uriah Stephens, founder of the order and of Terence Powdery, its leader through the 1880s.[23] His 1883 report of a New York activity marking the death of Karl Marx was shaped by this orientation. He described Marx as a fighter for justice, but chided him for nurturing class hatreds. European workers that brought their Old World doctrines and resentments to the United States were doing a disservice to American labour, despite their admirable dedication to a just cause.[24]

Martí's initial reaction to the May 1886 events in Chicago's Haymarket Square was coloured by this perspective. He described it as a horrific plot organised by cowardly agitators. The tragedy resulted from the attempt to transplant European doctrines to America. Yet, by November 1887, when he chronicled the execution of four anarchist leaders, his views had undergone a radical transformation.[25] He now argued that anarchist violence, regrettable as it may be, was a natural response to intolerable exploitation. The anarchists 'were violent incendiaries', yes. But Martí now hastened to add: 'From hell they come: what language would they speak but the language of hell'.[26] With a startling formula he conveyed his vision of an expanding economy marked by a growing social polarisation: the Chicago anarchists 'reason like cornered animals. All that grows seems to them to be growing against them'.[27] Perhaps they were

---

22 'The century has rotten walls ... The workers, hammer in hand, when not Winchester in arm, have begun to detect the cracks and to turn them into wide doors, through which they may come to enjoy in peace, even if stained by their own or another's blood, a new state in which labor will be paid at a price sufficient to keep the home above misery and to provide for old age ... In the United States the problem presents itself, as everything presents itself here, as this country gives it: colossally and suddenly' (Martí [1886a], p. 261); 'Las grandes huelgas en Estados Unidos' [1886], *oc*, x, p. 411. ['El siglo tiene las paredes carcomidas ... Los trabajadores, martillo en mano, cuando no Winchester al hombro, han comenzado ya a palpar las hendiduras, y a convertir en puertas anchas los agujeros, por donde entren a gozar en paz, aunque se les manchen los vestidos de la sangre propia, o ajena, de un estado nuevo en que el trabajo sea remunerado a un precio suficiente para sustentar la casa sin miseria y amparar la vejez ... En los Estados Unidos se presenta el problema, como acá se presenta todo, y como lo da el país: colosal y súbito'.]
23 Martí 1980, 'Correspondencia particular del *Partido Liberal*', [1886], p. 27.
24 Martí [1883a], pp. 130–3; 'Carta de Martí', *oc*, ix, pp. 388–9.
25 On Martí and the Haymarket events see Christopher Conway's excellent study: Conway 2004. See also Mestas 1993; Schnirmajer 2005.
26 Martí [1887a], p. 200; 'Un drama terrible', *oc*, xi, p. 338.
27 Martí [1887a], p. 200; 'Un drama terrible', *oc*, xi, p. 337. ['Todo lo que va creciendo les parece que crece contra ellos'.]

'madmen', but they were 'compassionate madmen'.²⁸ Martí summarised their views: 'From a wondrous, peaceful village, the republic was transformed into a monarchy in disguise'.²⁹ The conclusion could not be clearer: 'America, then, is the same as Europe!'³⁰ Martí summarised the ideas of the anarchist leaders and seemed to endorse them: 'This republic, in its excessive worship of wealth, has fallen ... into the inequality, injustice, and violence of monarchies'.³¹ If America had become a 'monarchy in disguise', the anarchists had been faithful to the Declaration of Independence, which enjoined them to rebel. According to Martí, 'since it was clear that they were living beneath an abject despotism, what else could they do but their duty, as set forth in the Declaration of Independence, and overthrow it to replace it with a free alliance of communities that exchange equivalent products among themselves, govern themselves ... by mutual agreement, and educate themselves by scientific methods without distinction of race, creed, or gender?'³² The points included in Martí's explanation are not generalities but an accurate summary of the specific programme adopted by the International Working People's Association, an anarchist network founded in 1881.³³ He was evidently familiar with it.

Through 1887 and 1888, as he rethought his initial reaction to the Haymarket events, Martí chronicled the turbulences provoked by other insurgent movements, including the rise of the United Labor Party in New York, Henry George's near-win as its candidate for mayor, and the split within the Catholic Church between priests supporting George and their ecclesiastical superiors.³⁴ As José Ballón has shown, Martí owned and studied a copy of the 1887 edition of *Contemporary Socialism* by John Rae, a general overview of the socialist currents of the time, an indication of his interest in this topic.³⁵ The 'popular republic', Martí wrote in 1888, was becoming a 'republic of classes'.³⁶ He now argued that 'political liberty' was a precious achievement, but the growth of economic

---

28 Martí [1887a], p. 205; 'Un drama terrible', *OC*, XI, p. 342. ['locos de piedad']
29 Martí [1887a], p. 197; 'Un drama terrible', *OC*, XI, p. 335.
30 Martí [1887a], p. 200; 'Un drama terrible', *OC*, XI, p. 338.
31 Martí [1887a], p. 197; 'Un drama terrible', *OC*, XI, p. 335.
32 Martí [1887a], p. 205; 'Un drama terrible', *OC*, XI, p. 342.
33 The programme is summarised in Breecher 1997, p. 46. The programme, adopted in 1883, was written among others by two of the Chicago martyrs, Albert Parsons and August Spies. Roediger and Foner 1989, p. 136.
34 Martí mentions the Grangers in 'Narraciones fantásticas' [1888], *OC*, XIII, p. 344. See Conway 2004, p. 45.
35 Ballón 1988, pp. 55–77. The book was first published in 1884 by Charles Scribner's and Sons.
36 'La religión en los Estados Unidos' [1888], *OC*, XI, p. 425. ['la República popular se va trocando en una República de clases'.]

inequality in the United States demonstrated that it was not sufficient to attain a just society. There was a fundamental problem in a system which allowed industrial advances to become the source of vast inequalities. Political liberty fell short of its mission if it did not become a means for the peaceful realisation of social and economic equality. This was the lesson that the experience of the United States had made clear:[37]

> When it was understood that the most useful inventions, put to work in unlimited numbers in the freest country on earth, produce in a few years the same poverty, the same inequality, the same accumulation of wealth and hate, the same upheavals and risks as in the nations with despotic governments ... when it was ... seen that the marvels of machinery, the richness of the soil, the size of the population, public education, religious tolerance and political liberty, combined with the widest and most virile system imagined by men, create a feudalism in land and industry, with all the elements of a social war, *then it became clear* that political liberty is not enough to make men happy and that there is an essential flaw in the system ... which allows the unlimited accumulation of wealth of a public character in a few hands, [and] deprives the working majority of the health, fortune and rest necessary to lead a life.[38]

Eric Foner has summarised some of the dominant ideological justifications of Gilded Age capitalism in the United States: the market as the most efficient organiser of resources and best distributor of rewards according to personal merit and effort; marked inequality as an indicator of the inevitable ascendance of the fittest and ablest; poverty as a problem resulting from individual irresponsibility, to be addressed, not through union action or government inter-

---

37 Martí 1980, 'Correspondencia particular del *Partido Liberal*' [1886], pp. 68, 75.
38 Martí 1980, 'Correspondencia particular del *Partido Liberal*' [1886], p. 70. Our emphasis. ['Cuando se palpó que los inventos más útiles, puestos en ejercicio con abundancia ilimitada en el país más libre de la tierra, reproducen en pocos años la misma penuria, la misma desigualdad, las mismas acumulaciones de riqueza y de odio, los mismos sobresaltos y riesgos que en los pueblos de gobierno despótico ... cuando se observó definitivamente que la maravilla de la mecánica, la exuberancia del suelo, la masa de la población, la enseñanza pública, la tolerancia religiosa y la libertad política, combinadas con el sistema más amplio y viril imaginado por los hombres, crean un nuevo feudalismo en la tierra y en la industria, con todos los elementos de una guerra social, entonces se vió que la libertad política no basta a hacer a los hombres felices y que hay un vicio de esencia en el sistema ... que permite la acumulación ilimitada en unas cuantas manos de la riqueza de carácter público, priva a la mayoría trabajadora de las condiciones de salud, fortuna y sosiego indispensables para sobrellevar la vida'.]

vention, but personal effort. Martí's views, while not frankly anti-capitalist, evidently ran in a very different direction.[39] If, as Foner argues, this was the epoch of 'Liberty of Contract and its Discontents', Martí was certainly among the latter.[40]

Interestingly, the year defined by the Haymarket affair (1886–7), during which Martí sharply altered his views on the main social tendencies within the United States, was described equally by Friedrich Engels, Marx's lifelong collaborator, as a crucial moment in the class struggle in North America. Obviously unknown to each other, Engels in London and Martí in New York coincided in their identification of the same events and organisations as particularly significant, while the evolution of Martí's ideas on the main tendencies of American society corresponded to Engels's description of the ideological impact of those tumultuous events. Writing in January of 1887, Engels, as if describing some of Martí's ideas until then, remarked that 'In February 1885, American public opinion was almost unanimous on this one point: that there was no working class, in the European sense of the word, in America; that consequently no class struggle between workmen and capitalists, such as tore European society to pieces, was possible in the American republic; and that, therefore, Socialism was a thing of foreign importation which could never take root on American soil'.[41] But this had been followed, Engels explained, by a wave of strikes culminating with the 1886 battles over the 8-hour day, a movement which, he argued, had shaken 'American society to its very foundations'.[42] According Engels, the Order of the Knights of Labor was the tendency 'most typical of the present

---

39 Martí had read de Tocqueville and perhaps saw his own observations as confirmation of the latter's warning that the growing differentiation between capital and labour could lead to the rise of a new aristocracy and was thus the gravest future danger to democracy. In a chapter entitled 'How an aristocracy may emerge from industry', de Tocqueville had argued that '[a]s the principle of the division of labor is applied … the worker becomes weaker, more limited and more dependent'. He added that 'at the very moment that industrial science constantly lowers the standing of the workers, it raises that of the bosses'. He concluded that 'a natural impulse appears to be prompting the emergence of an aristocracy from the very heart of democracy'. He still hoped that the tendencies toward a wide distribution of property would prevail, but warned that 'this is the direction in which the friends of democracy should constantly fix their anxious gaze; for if ever aristocracy and the permanent inequality of social conditions were to infiltrate the world again, it is predictable that this is the door by which they would enter' (Tocqueville 2003, pp. 646–8). In a way, he was arguing that the development of capitalism would be the greatest threat to democracy.
40 Foner 1998, pp. 120–2.
41 Engels 1973, p. 16.
42 Engels 1973, p. 19.

state of the movement, as it is undoubtedly by far the strongest'.[43] Yet, he added, the creation of a United Labor Party, and its campaigns in New York and other cities, demonstrated how quickly the American labour movement was moving forward. Vast sections of the working class, he commented, had become 'conscious of the fact, that they formed a new and distinct class of American society; a class of ... more or less hereditary wage-workers, proletarians. And with true American instinct this consciousness led them at once to take the next step towards their deliverance: the formation of a political working-men's party, with a platform of its own, and with the conquest of the Capitol and the White House for its goal'.[44] Engels's remarks cannot but remind us of Martí's evolution. As Engels argued regarding public opinion in the United States, in mid-1886 Martí was still insisting on the artificiality of European notions of class conflict in an American soil allegedly open to economic betterment through individual effort, while denouncing the Haymarket 'agitators' as murderers. Yet, by late 1887 he had abandoned such views and had embraced much of labour's critique of a Republic that had become a class society not unlike Europe. Meanwhile, he enthusiastically reported the initiatives of the United Labor Party and Henry George's campaign as the dawn of a new age. While the Cuban revolutionary in New York never became a socialist, the coincidences between his diagnoses and emphases and those of the German expatriate socialist in London are undeniable and striking.

Martí's doubts regarding the United States would only grow with the passage of time. In 1889, in his 'Vindication of Cuba', he insisted that Cubans 'admire this nation, the greatest ever built by liberty, but they dislike the evil conditions that, like worms in the heart, have begun in this mighty republic their work of destruction'.[45] By the time he wrote his essay 'The Truth about the United States' in 1892, he referred to the latter as a 'greedy, authoritarian republic'[46] and spoke of the 'crude, unequal, and decadent character of the United States'.[47] He now categorically affirmed that '[r]ather than being resolved, the problems of humanity are being reproduced here'.[48]

While chronicling the evolution of class war in the United States, Martí was also concerned with the drift of racial conflict. In 1891 he warned that the dominant sectors in the United States 'believe in the inferiority of the Negro race, which they enslaved yesterday and torment today, and of the Indian, whom

---

43   Engels 1973, p. 21.
44   Engels 1973, p. 17.
45   Martí [1889], pp. 263–4; 'Vindicación de Cuba', OC, I, p. 237.
46   Martí [1894], p. 332; 'La verdad sobre los Estados Unidos', OC, XXVIII, p. 293.
47   Martí [1894], p. 333; 'La verdad sobre los Estados Unidos', OC, XXVIII, p. 294.
48   Martí [1894], p. 330; 'La verdad sobre los Estados Unidos', OC, XXVIII, p. 292.

they are exterminating'.[49] Regarding these issues, his views had shifted over the years. Through the mid-1880s he referred admiringly to what he took to be an ongoing reconciliation between North and South. Abolition had removed the issue that divided them in the past. The North could tolerate a now harmless cult of the heroes of the Confederacy. He even chided the Republicans for keeping alive the memory of slavery in order to manipulate black voters. He ignored the ongoing dismantling of the democratic achievements of Reconstruction. Yet, an 1887 chronicle registers Martí's sombre forebodings regarding this issue. In the first part of his chronicle he admiringly describes President Cleveland's decision to return to the South some of the Confederate flags captured during the war. He also describes the reconciliation of Confederate and Union veterans, during a commemoration of the Battle of Gettysburg.[50] Yet after presenting such a positive image of tolerance and graciousness built on mutual recognition of valour and common respect for the fallen, Martí turned to recent events in which black communities had been the victims of deadly attack by white armed groups and of removal at the request of white neighbours. An attack, Martí explained, had been led by the mayor of Oak Ridge (a hamlet near New Orleans). Such official complicity insured that the crime would go unpunished and that it would not be the last of its kind.[51] Regarding the removal of a northern black community so that white neighbors would not have to witness their miserable living conditions, Martí considered it ironic that the consequences of the oppression to which blacks had been 'criminally' subjected were thus used to perpetuate it. Blacks were entitled to 'reparation' for past wrongs. Instead, the consequences of those wrongs were turned against them.[52] The second part of Martí's chronicle thus grates painfully with the preceding description of Cleveland's magnanimity toward the defeated South, and the image of 'grey' and 'blue' reconciliation. The chronicle concluded omin-

---

49   Martí [1891], p. 306; 'La conferencia monetaria de las repúblicas de América', *OC*, VI, p. 160.
50   'Cleveland. El incidente de las banderas', [1887], *OC*, XI, p. 233. See Montero 2002.
51   'Who will punish the mayor, if he is the law? For another hunt he is perhaps cleaning the rifle'. 'Cleveland. El incidente de las banderas', [1887], *OC*, XI, p. 238. ['¿Al alcalde quién lo castigará, si él es la ley? Para otra cacería estará limpiando el rifle'.]
52   'They are owed reparation for the offense, of course they are owed; and instead of lifting them from the misery into which they were thrown, thus removing their unattractive and miserable appearance, they take advantage of that appearance that they criminally gave them to refuse them a human treatment'. 'Cleveland. El incidente de las banderas', [1887], *OC*, XI, pp. 237–8 ['¡Se les debe, por supuesto que se les debe, reparación por la ofensa; y en vez de levantarlos de la miseria a que se les echó, para quitarles su apariencia antipática y mísera, válense de esta apariencia que criminalmente les dieron para rehusarles el trato con el hombre!']

ously (and prophetically): 'It is the dawn of a formidable problem'.[53] In contrast to Whitman's statement on the situation in the South in 1876, the problem for Martí was not 'the blacks' but rather the way they were treated by a society dominated by whites and the lack of 'reparation' for their situation.[54]

In 1892 Martí returned to this topic through a chronicle of a lynching in Texarkana, Arkansas. Martí obtained the information for this article from the New York press, a source that was often racist and favourable to the brutal assertion of white rule. This is part of the *New York Times* report of the lynching of Edward Coy:

> Texarkana, Ark., Feb. 21 – The crime, the long pursuit, final capture, and awful death of Edward Coy, the negro who met his end at the stake at the hands of an outraged and infuriated populace yesterday, continues [to be?] the all-absorbing topic on the streets today. A number of citizens deprecate the manner of punishment, but their number is insignificant compared with the great majority which lends its unqualified endorsement to the deed, insisting and proclaiming loudly that no punishment conceivable was too severe to inflict upon a man whose crime was so shocking and brutal as the deed of Coy.
>
> It is also agreed that a terrible death, such as fire alone can inflict, is the only means through which other negroes of like disposition are to be deterred from the commission of like crimes. The rope has but little terror for the negro, but he has a terrible dread of fire, and when it becomes known that death at the stake is the certain fate of criminals such as Coy was known to be, it is believed fewer cases of this kind will be perpetrated.[55]

As indicated, Martí took his information from this and similar reports. But his controlled yet intense description of the event left a markedly different impression:

---

53   'Cleveland. El incidente de las banderas', [1887], *OC*, XI, p. 238. ['Es el albor de un problema formidable'.] Regarding Whitman's vision of sectional reconciliation, Scott Henkel has argued that 'Such unproblematized reconciliation can take place only through erasure of the memory of slavery, of the presence of freed and terrorized blacks in the South'. As can be appreciated, Martí's text moved in the opposite direction: his portrait of racist terror could not but problematise the preceding portrait of Cleveland's magnanimity toward the South and the image of North-South reconciliation during the Gettysburg commemoration (Henkel 2010, p. 186).
54   Whitman 1876, p. 66. See our discussion in Chapter 8.
55   'She called for the torch', *New York Times*, 22 February 1892.

'Here he comes! Here he comes!' It's the black man who is coming out of the stable tightly bound: one man pushes him, another hits him in the face. He goes on walking, steady on his feet: 'I offered Mrs. Jewell no offense! You're going to kill me, but I offered her no offense'. 'We're going to kill you, Coy, you dog, kill you like the dog you are ...' And they take him up the street surrounded by rifles, ... along with the crowd of men and women, five thousand souls in all ... And the bound black man comes along at a trot ... and behind him, as he trots along, the five thousand souls come running. Coy was trussed against the tree trunk with iron hoops. They threw buckets of petroleum over his head until his clothing was drenched ... The ladies waved their handkerchiefs, the men waved their hats. Mrs. Jewell reached the tree, lit a match, twice touched the lit match to the jacket of the black man, who did not speak, and the black man went up in flames, in the presence of five thousand souls.[56]

Martí is horrified by that which the *New York Times* correspondent attempted to justify. Martí's views on the situation of Native Americans also shifted over the years. While sympathetic to the plight of a displaced people, he favoured the attempts to incorporate the 'Indian' to capitalist civilisation through the institution of private landed property within their communities. Nevertheless, there are texts in which he presented an admiring portrait of communal property. Describing the social order of the Cherokees, he wrote in 1885:

> All the land belongs in common to the tribe; which does not exclude property, or the right to pass it on according to the laws of the tribe; since the land is of he who works it, but only ... as long as he works it, for as soon as the owner of the land ceases to work it, it returns to the commons ... And with the land returning to the commons as soon as the owner does not work it, the possession of land by only one hand, and all that follows from it, is blocked. The country of the Cherokees has seventy thousand inhabitants: there is not one beggar.[57]

---

56 Martí [1892], p. 313; Martí 1980, 'Carta de José Martí' [1892], pp. 187–8.
57 'Cartas de Martí', [1885], OC, X, pp. 273–4. ['Toda la tierra pertenece en común a la tribu; lo que no excluye la propiedad, ni el derecho de traspasarla según las leyes de la tribu; pues la tierra es del que la cultiva, eso sí, mientras la trabaje, porque en cuanto el propietario de la tierra no la trabaje vuelve al común ... Y con que la tierra vuelva al común tan pronto como su propietario no la cultiva, se estorba que una misma mano llegue a poseer mucha tierra, y cuanto viene de eso. Setenta mil habitantes tiene el país de los cheroqueses: no hay ni un mendigo'.] In at least one text Martí presented his vision of a future egalitarian society as a return, under modern conditions, to the equality characteristic of 'primitive'

Other texts suggested that state policies toward the 'Indian' led to a tragic result: the destruction of their communities, first through their separation from their lands, then through their concentration in designated territories and finally through their fall into idleness and alcoholism and their growing dependence on relief from the state that had driven them to their lamentable condition. In 1889 Martí summarised a speech by Sioux leader Red Cloud:

> The Great Father sends me word to sell him my lands, and if I refuse, it will be like water in a pond where big fish eat up the little fish. It will do me no good to fence my land, for the white men will leap over the fence and take my land away. The Great Father has deceived me as if I were a child, has robbed me as if I were a child. I do not want to sign any more treaties, for the Great Father will then order his soldiers to take away from me what the treaty told me was mine.[58]

Martí adds: 'all had to sign because they were forced to do so at gunpoint. The white colonisers have been closing in on Sioux territory for twenty years, the way a snake tightens its coils around the vanquished prey and are already fencing some of their borders, waiting for the command to enter'.[59]

In 1889 Martí turned his chronicle of a mad rush of settlers into land opened for private claims in Oklahoma into a compressed replay of US history: in a few hours a new settlement reenacts the displacement of the Native Americans, the installation of private property, the creation of an elected government, the rising power of the banks, the spread of land speculation and political corruption, and the disregard for nature and for human life.[60] But the United States had not only revealed itself as a very flawed model of modernity. Actively engaged in the struggle against Spanish colonial rule in Cuba and Puerto Rico, Martí increasingly saw the United Sates as a threat to the independence of the Antilles. The United States was turning into a 'Caesarian and invading' ('cesárea e invasora') republic.[61] Referring to Francis Cutting, a promoter of US intervention in Mexico, Martí proclaimed: 'We love the country of Lincoln as

---

cultures: 'All the yearning of civilization is to return to the simplicity and the justice of the primitive organization and to ... reestablish the pure and fair patriarchal societies' (Martí 1980, 'Correspondencia particular del Partido Liberal' [1886], p. 73). ['Todo el anhelo de la civilización está en volver a la sencillez y la justicia de los repartimientos primitivos ... y restablecer las relaciones puras y justas de las sociedades patriarcales'.]

58 Martí [1889a], p. 227; 'Cartas norteamericanas', OC, XII, pp. 291–2.
59 Martí [1889a], pp. 227–28; 'Cartas norteamericanas', OC, XII, p. 292.
60 'Como se hace un pueblo nuevo en los Estados Unidos' [1889], OC, XII, pp. 203–12.
61 'En los Estados Unidos' [1889], OC, XII, p. 135. See Hidalgo Paz 1988.

much as we fear the country of Cutting'.[62] It remained to be seen whether the United States, 'a people born of freedom, rises to increase it, or to oppress it',[63] whether it would be able to fulfill 'the duty of greatness, which is to deserve it for something other than mere covetousness and size'.[64]

Martí's shifting attitude toward Republican leader and Secretary of State James Blaine encapsulated his evolving perspective on the United States. In 1881, Martí described him as 'this brilliant man, capable of healthy, audacious and glorious politics, and a friend of the America of the South'.[65] By 1889 he saw him as an example of political corruption and demagoguery and of US imperial ambitions.[66] Referring to the commercial treaties and the Pan American Conference of 1889 promoted by Blaine, Martí argued that Spanish America, after saving itself 'from the tyranny of Spain', now needed 'to declare its second independence'.[67] Latin America, as he put it in 1894, had to resist a 'damaged and alien civilization ('dañada y ajena')'.[68]

Martí's worst fears hit home when the depression of the early 1890s prompted a nativist reaction against Cubans in Florida, a key base of support for his revolutionary efforts. Cubans in the United States risked sharing the fate of the 'zorros of California or the last *tejanos*',[69] that is to say, of the Mexicans who had found themselves in a submerged social space after their territories had been annexed by the United States. Martí asked rhetorically: 'Why, O Spanish tyranny, did we fly from you only to find all your horrors in an American republic? Why did we trust and love this inhuman and ungrateful land?'[70] He concluded: 'We have no other friend ... than ourselves ... Cubans: to Cuba!'

Separated from Cuba, Martí was increasingly estranged from what he felt was a one-sided civilisation. He was, as Jesús David Saldívar has pointed out, a double exile.[71] In his 1881 text on Coney Island, he portrayed himself as an exile

---

62   Martí [1889], p. 264; 'Vindicación de Cuba', *OC*, I, p. 237.
63   'Correspondencia especial del Partido Liberal' [1889], *OC*, XII, p. 154. ['pueblo hijo de la libertad, se levanta para aumentarla, o para oprimirla'.]
64   'Correspondencia especial del Partido Liberal' [1889], *OC*, XII, p. 154. ['el deber de la grandeza, que es el de merecerla con algo que no sea la mera codicia y el tamaño'.]
65   'Noticias de los Estados Unidos', [1881], *OC*, IX, p. 41. ['Este brillante hombre, capaz de una política sana, intrépida y gloriosa, y amigo de la América del Sur'.]
66   See Martí [1889b], pp. 338–67; 'Congreso Internacional de Washington', *OC*, VI, pp. 46–63.
67   Martí [1889b], p. 340; 'Congreso internacional de Washington', *OC*, VI, p. 46. ['De la tiranía de España supo salvarse la America española; y ahora ... urge decir, porque es la verdad, que ha llegado para la América española la hora de declarar su segunda independencia'.]
68   Martí [1894], p. 331; 'La verdad sobre los Estados Unidos', *OC*, XXVIII, p. 292.
69   Martí [1894a], p. 325; '¡A Cuba!', *OC*, III, p. 51.
70   Martí [1894a], p. 328; '¡A Cuba!', *OC*, III, p. 54.
71   Jesus David Saldívar, 'Introduction' to Ramos 2001, p. xxiv.

from his homeland and also from a 'superior spiritual world'. Away from Cuba and a stranger in a land 'devoid of spirit' he turned the concern for the 'spirit' into a marker of his Hispano-American identity. 'It is well known', he wrote, 'that a sad melancholy steals over the men of our Hispanoamerican peoples who live here ... Nostalgia for a superior spiritual world invades and afflicts them ... because this land is devoid of spirit'.[72] Thus, Cuban patriotism was for him both an affirmation of Cuban independence *and* a desire for a different kind of civilisation. But, if Martí wished to return to Cuba, and if he was 'nostalgic' for a 'superior spiritual world', he did not envision a return to the past. If he distanced himself from the US model, he did so in the name of an alternative modernity. For him, the United States was an experiment, a sketch, a colossal, but nevertheless transitory, incomplete, 'damaged' draft of a future modern 'synthesis'. Cuban independence was, for him, neither a mere battle for political separation, nor a rejection of modernity. It was the vehicle for an alternative modernity, beyond the problems that, far from being solved, as he had once thought, were being reproduced in the United States.

In an influential and in many ways admirable study, Julio Ramos has presented Martí's texts on the United States as participants in the founding of an autonomous modern intellectual sphere. Modernity, he argues, is characterised by the formation of an intellectual-artistic sphere consciously differentiated from the economic and political realms. The demarcation of this modern intellectual identity, he adds, is largely brought about through its self-definition as the opposite of what it rejected as a degraded mass commercial culture and, more specifically, through its construction of the city as a space of cultural degradation. According to Ramos, 'self-representation as a response to the fragmentary and "antiesthetic" movement of the modern city' was a 'driving impulse behind fin de siècle literature – and a legitimizing mechanism for literature's virtual autonomy'.[73] This autonomous sphere marks its frontiers and legitimises itself through a discourse of resistance against a threatening cultural crisis that must be constantly averted. As Ramos succinctly puts it: the 'critique of modernization made the modernization of critique possible'.[74] Thus, the modern intellectual thinks of himself or herself as the articulator of a fuller culture against the 'turbulent world of the street'.[75] For Ramos, Martí is

---

72   Martí [1881], p. 92; 'Coney Island' (1881), *oc*, IX, p. 126.
73   Ramos 2001, p. 189. As Susana Rotker puts it, writers, displaced from political power or marginalised by the market, 'began to take their identity from that very displacement'. Rotker 2000, p. 16.
74   Ramos 2001, p. 227. It was 'a paradoxical mode of becoming specialized, to be sure', p. 232.
75   Ramos 2001, p. 244.

an example of this. 'In Martí', he says, the city is linked 'to the representation of disaster, of catastrophe, as a distinctive metaphor for modernity'.[76] For Martí, the 'urban order' is 'profoundly inorganic'.[77] It unleashes a 'dispersing movement',[78] a 'destructuring impulse, the annulment of harmony'.[79] The city 'overruns boundaries, formal limits – forever displacing and configuring them'.[80] It creates 'a fluid and unstable world',[81] 'an ineluctably fragmented world'.[82] Martí, Ramos points out, 'would not deliver himself to the deterritorialized flows' of the city.[83] He wished to 'contain' the 'threat of heterogeneity, tied to the urban flow'.[84] It is thus appropriate to speak of Martí's 'resistance to modernization'.[85]

Ramos quotes a passage of Martí's chronicle of Coney Island: 'With great bursts of laughter others applaud the skill of someone who has succeeded in bouncing a ball off the nose of an unfortunate man of color, who, in exchange for a paltry day's wage, stands day and night with his head poking out through a piece of cloth, dodging the pitches with ridiculous movements and extravagant grimaces'.[86] For Ramos this passage can be read as part of the legitimisation of the artist as the guardian of culture: 'The figure of the abused black performer, who ironically lives by the aggression of the crowd, is by no means coincidental: for Martí, the market subjects the artist to an intense degradation that is matched by the transformation of the signs of tradition ... into strange amusements'.[87] Thus, according to Ramos, Martí affirmed a Latin American identity against US culture and also against the culture of the modern city. He thus did so while claiming a privileged role for intellectuals within that national project.[88]

---

76   Ramos 2001, p. 118.
77   Ramos 2001, p. 204.
78   Ramos 2001, p. 194.
79   Ramos 2001, p. 203.
80   Ramos 2001, p. 191.
81   Ramos 2001, p. 172.
82   Ramos 2001, p. 172.
83   Ramos 2001, p. 204.
84   Ramos 2001, p. 210.
85   Ramos 1988, pp. 133–43. Ramos speaks of Martí's 'resistance to modernization' ['resistencia a la modernización'], p. 140.
86   Martí [1881], p. 93; 'Coney Island', OC, IX, p. 127.
87   Ramos 2001, p. 221.
88   Susan Antebi has developed a similar perspective. According to her, Martí denounced the 'exploitation and cruelty' of the Coney Island freak-shows. Yet, according to her, Martí does so as a 'distanced, culturally privileged, and disembodied observer'. Martí's description of the freak-shows is thus read as part of a process through which he constructs 'the US urban masses as his own monstrous other'. Defining 'himself against the Coney Island

This argument is not so much wrong as one-sided. To be sure, there was a conservative side to Martí's reaction to the modern city. This is nowhere more evident than in his views on US women, a perspective informed by a conservative ideal of womanhood as a domestic buttress for the worldly pursuits reserved for men. In his first text on the United States, he warned that US women led a 'virile existence':[89] 'Their fast going up and down stairs, up and down the streets, the resolute, well-defined object of their actions, their too virile existence, deprive them of the calm beauty, the antique grace, the exquisite sensitiveness which make of women those superior beings'.[90] In the United States one could observe a 'toughening of the feminine soul'.[91] At times, Martí admitted that this was a necessary evil, but it was an evil nonetheless. Women, he wrote, 'must become thick-skinned' and learn to 'save themselves from the wolf of poverty and the wolves of life', that is to say, from unscrupulous men 'moved by appetite'.[92] The city emerges as a scenario of predatory men and 'thick-skinned women' or, as he put it in his poem 'Love in the City': 'The city is a cage of dead doves/And avid hunters!'[93] It was, Martí argued, better for the 'female soul' to be toughened than 'debased'. 'Yet', he concluded, 'how painful it is to see how the habits of a virile life gradually change these beauteous flowers into flowers of stone! What will become of men on the day when they can no longer rest their heads on a warm, female bosom?'[94]

Over and over, Martí returns to this domestic ideal. He wrote an admiring portrait of engineer Washington Roebling, who led the completion of the construction of the Brooklyn Bridge after the death of his father John Roebling. Martí's description of the younger Roebling's wife's direct involvement in the project, after her ailing husband was confined to his residence, concluded with a similar declaration: 'But none of her feats with noble metals gains her more admiration than having strengthened the soul – in a weakened body – of her husband. To build: that is the task of man: – To console, which is to give

---

scene', Martí constructs 'an elite, disembodied Spanish American self, in opposition both to the freaks on the platform, and to the unruly, apparently gullible masses consuming the show'. Antebi 2005. We discuss these views below.

89   Martí [1883a], p. 135; 'Carta de Martí', OC, IX, p. 392. ['vida viril'.]
90   Martí [1880], p. 37. 'Impresiones de América II', OC, XIX, p. 116.
91   Martí [1883a], p. 135; 'Carta de Martí', OC, IX, p. 392.
92   Martí [1883a], p. 135; 'Carta de Martí', OC, IX, p. 392.
93   Allen (ed.) 2002, 'Love in the City', p. 63; 'Amor de ciudad grande', OC, XVI, p. 170. In a similar vein he affirms in 'Bosque de rosas': 'Esa es la lidia humana: ¡la tremenda/Batalla de los cascos y los lirios!' 'Bosque de rosas', en Martí 1982, p. 169. This poem does not appear in OC.
94   Martí [1883a], p. 136; 'Carta de Martí', OC, IX, p. 392.

strength to build: therein resides the great labor of women'.⁹⁵ That dichotomy – men construct, women console – reappears in his comparison of the women involved in reform movements and the wife of President Cleveland: 'But none of these ladies attracts the affection bestowed everywhere on the young wife of the President, who, to the ungrateful task of working like a man, prefers the more useful and difficult one of consoling him'.⁹⁶ Similarly, as Ramos has pointed out, Martí's description of Coney Island includes his troubled portrait of women promenading without their husbands or children, passages that present the amusement park as a landscape of lost affections and broken families.⁹⁷ 'The city', as one verse in the poem 'Love in the City' declares, 'appalls me'.⁹⁸ This is undoubtedly Martí at his most conservative.⁹⁹

But there are other dimensions to Martí's reaction to the modern city. For him modernity was also the 'time of broken fences',¹⁰⁰ a time in which 'genius is moving from the individual to the collectivity', in which the 'traits of the privileged are being diluted and expanded to the masses'.¹⁰¹ Martí felt he had to assimilate, and convoked others to assimilate, 'the modern, multiple life, in all its forms'.¹⁰² New York was an agglomeration of solitary pursuits, but it was also a new Babel where cultures were joined and not scattered. The elevated train

---

95   'Dos damas norteamericanas', [1883], *OC*, XIII, p. 252. ['Pero de estas hazañas en metales nobles ninguna le vale más pro que la de haber mantenido a buen temple en su trémulo cuerpo, el alma de su esposo egregio. Construir: he ahí la gran labor del hombre: – consolar, que es dar fuerzas para construir: he ahí la gran labor de las mujeres'.]
96   'Sobre los Estados Unidos' [1887], *OC*, XI, p. 135. ['Pero ninguna de estas damas despierta el cariño mostrado en todas partes a la joven esposa del Presidente, que a la faena ingrata de trabajar como el hombre, prefiere la más útil y difícil de consolarlo'.]
97   Ramos 2001, p. 195.
98   Allen (ed.) 2002, 'Love in the City', p. 65; 'Amor de ciudad grande', *OC*, XVI, p. 172. ['Me espanta la ciudad'.]
99   Many other examples could be offered. See for example: 'Carta de Nueva York' [1882], *OC*, IX, p. 248; 'Sobre los Estados Unidos' [1887], *OC*, XI, p. 135 and 'Las ferias campestres' [1887], *OC*, XI, pp. 310–11. To be fair it must be pointed out that Martí also saw the 'feminine spirit' as the source of the artistic sensibility, essential to a balanced national culture: his criticism of the demise of the feminine spirit was both a conservative affirmation of a traditional stereotype and part of his attack on a one-sided commercial culture. Martí thus asked: 'Does the absence of the feminine spirit, source of artistic sensibility and complement to national identity, harden and corrupt the heart of this astonishing people? Only time will tell'. Martí [1881], p. 89; 'Coney Island' [1881], *OC*, IX, p. 123. ['si la ausencia del espíritu femenil, origen del sentido artístico y complemento del ser nacional, endurece y corrompe el corazón de ese pueblo pasmoso, eso lo dirán los tiempos'.]
100 Martí [1882a], p. 45; 'El Poema del Niágara', *OC*, VII, p. 226.
101 Martí [1882a], p. 47; 'El Poema del Niágara', *OC*, VII, p. 228.
102 'Cartas de Martí', [1885], *OC*, X, p. 235. ['La moderna vida múltiple, en todas sus formas'.]

A 'DAMAGED AND ALIEN CIVILIZATION'   203

was an ugly excrescence of the modern city – to be replaced by the equally modern subway. Coney Island was devoid of 'spirit', but the Brooklyn Bridge was 'the steel hyphen between ... two words of the New Gospel'. American factories were hellish but they also taught workers to treat the extraordinary as commonplace. If New York politics were corrupt, it was still the 'monumental' place where 'the new world' ('el mundo nuevo') was being created.[103] Martí wrote of composing

103   'Cartas de Martí', p. 19 enero 1883, *oc*, IX, p. 350. ['ciudad monumental ... donde, como en cimientos dignos de él, se asienta ... ¡el mundo nuevo!'] Or consider Martí's description of the Palace of Industry of the Paris exposition of 1889. The sight of the achievements of modern industry moves Martí into a vision of human brotherhood. Here machines do not provoke fear, but a heightened, joyous awareness of human potentialities: 'We have to go see the greatest marvel, the audacity of which softens the heart, and makes one feel like embracing all men and calling them brothers ... Let us enter through the gate of the Palace of Industry ... Through a corridor that makes us think of grand things one reaches the stair leading to the balcony ... one lifts the eyes: and one sees ... a steel hall in which two-thousand horses could easily move ... And it is all covered by machines that turn, crush, hiss, that throw light, that cross the air silently, that move trembling underneath the earth! The main machines are placed in four rows in the middle. Their power comes from a red oven. It comes through belts ... The wheels of the belts hang from pillars placed in four rows. Around them, linked together, are placed all the machines of the world, those that make steel-dust, those that sharpen needles. Women in red aprons work the Dutch gilt paper. A cylinder that reminds us of an elephant is cutting envelopes. A mortar separates the grain of wheat from the husk. Over there the metals that make up the printer's letters are fused, there paper is made from cloth or wood, here the presses print the newspaper ... A machine brings air to the tunnel of a mine, so that the miners are not asphyxiated. Another crushes the cane, and gives a cascade of honey. Tears come to the eyes, while seeing the machines from the balcony! ... At night a man presses a button, and an electric sky hanging from the roof showers light over the machines'. 'La exposición de París' [1889], *oc*, XVIII, p. 426. We could say of this passage what Leo Marx pointed out regarding Whitman's 'Passage to India': it is penetrated by 'a sense of buoyant power that arises from the sight of the machine's motion across the landscape'. Leo Marx 2000, p. 223. ['Tenemos que ir a ver la maravilla mayor, y el atrevimiento que ablanda el corazón, y hace sentir como deseo de abrazar a los hombres y de llamarlos hermanos ... Entremos por el pórtico del Palacio de las Industrias ... Por un corredor que hace pensar en cosas grandes, se va a la escalera que va al balcón ... se alzan los ojos: y se ve ... una sala de hierro en que podrían moverse a la vez dos mil caballos ... ¡Y toda está cubierta de máquinas, que dan vueltas, que aplastan, que silban, que echan luz, que atraviesan el aire calladas, que corren temblando por debajo de la tierra! En cuatro hileras están en el centro las máquinas mayores. De un horno rojo les viene la fuerza. Viene por correas ... De cuatro filas de postes cuelgan las ruedas de las correas. Alrededor, unidas, están todas las máquinas del mundo, las que hacen polvo de acero, las que afilan las agujas. Unas mujeres de delantal colorado trabajan el papel holandés. Un cilindro, que parece un elefante que se mueve, está cortando sobres. Un mortero separa el grano de trigo de la cáscara ... Allí se funden los metales con que se hacen las letras de imprimir, allí se hace el papel de tela o de madera, allí la prensa imprime el diario ... Una máquina echa aire en el pozo de una mina, para que no

an Ode to the modern city, of which he considered New York to be 'the best type': 'Ode. – To the city. Modern city, so that it lasts. To gather, as in pieces of marble, so that they endure, the marvels characteristic of a city of our times. New York, the best type. Through the arches of the bridge, hissing locomotives. Factories. Masses. The Mills building'.[104] His sketch includes all the distinctive features of the modern metropolis – bridge, locomotive, factory, masses, skyscraper – which he described as 'marvels'. Martí embraced nature as an ideal. But for him this was not in contradiction with modernity: a Natural equilibrium could only be attained through the removal of limiting traditions and institutions. But in Ramos's reading Martí's ambivalence regarding the modern metropolis more often than not becomes a flat rejection of it.[105]

Consider, furthermore, Martí's description of the 'unfortunate man of colour' in Coney Island. Ramos argues that in this passage Martí identifies with the 'unfortunate' performer, turning his situation into a metaphor of his own condition as an artist in a degraded mass commercial culture. But the metaphor, it seems to us, works precisely because the 'unfortunate man of colour', while *not* an intellectual, is nonetheless a reified victim of a commercial leisure and entertainment industry. Startlingly, Martí's image of the 'unfortunate man of colour' is a reminder of the crucial aspect the city that his postmodern critic forgets: the modern city is the site, not only of heterogeneity, dispersion and fluidity, as Ramos would have it, but *also* of oppression and exploitation.[106]

---

se ahoguen los mineros. Otra aplasta la caña, y echa un chorro de miel. ¡Pues da ganas de llorar, el ver las máquinas desde el balcón! ... De noche, un hombre toca un botón ... y por sobre las máquinas ... derrama la claridad, colgado de la bóveda, el cielo eléctrico'.]

104 'Otros fragmentos', *OC*, XXII, p. 306. ['Oda. – A la ciudad. Ciudad moderna, para que quede. Reunir, como en trozos de mármol, que duren, las maravillas características de una ciudad de estos tiempos. New York, el mejor tipo. Por entre los arcos del puente, locomotoras silbantes. Fábricas. Masas. El edificio de Mills'.] The Mills building was a modern 10-floor office building located in Broad Street at the Northeast Corner of Exchange Place. It made a considerable impression on Martí, who also refers to it in '¿Cuál es el objeto de la torre?' [1883], *OC*, IX, p. 474.

105 These elitist views are closer to the ideas of Uruguayan author José Enrique Rodó. Yet, as Magaril has correctly underlined, Rodó's and Martí's views should not be conflated. Both Martí and Rodó had profound misgivings regarding US mass culture, but the latter's elitism led him to admire Poe and Emerson as individual geniuses within a mediocre culture. He could hardly embrace Whitman's 'word en-masse'. Martí, by way of contrast, did embrace Whitman's democratic, all-encompassing chant, while praising the 'decentralization of intelligence' and the fact that 'man is losing out to men', that 'the traits of the privileged are being diluted and expanded to the masses', as he wrote in his introduction to Pérez Bonalde's poem. Magaril 2010, pp. 36–39.

106 Lomas makes a similar point. Lomas 2008, p. 139.

In other words, Ramos's vision of modernity, of city life, mass culture and the urban crowd, embraces the iconoclastic, ever-changing, aspect of modern capitalism, its tendency to undermine inherited forms, hierarchies and models. But it lacks Marx's (and to some extent even Martí's) twin notion of capitalism as a system of exploitation. To put it otherwise: while describing Martí's averse reaction to the city, Ramos relies on an idealised, one-sided vision of the latter as a reign of heterogeneity, fluidity, openness and dispersion. Against that one-sided background, cleansed of the consequences of capitalist exploitation and of the resistance it provokes, Martí's uneasiness with the modern metropolis cannot but appear as a flight from the (idyllically conceived) fluidity of the city street, the city crowd and of a rising mass culture.

Once we restore the contradictions – the exploitative nature and the social polarisations – of capitalism to our analysis, our understanding of Martí's reaction to it is enriched. The modern city is the site, not only of a new mass culture, or of 'fluidity', but *also* of capitalist exploitation. It is the site, not only of the intellectual's response to the former, but also of working-class resistance to the latter, the site, not only of the city crowd, but of the militant labour march. Consequently, it also can be the site of complex, sometimes contradictory, combinations of conservative intellectual resistance to the city, yes, *and* of radical rejection of exploitation and of sympathy with the resistance in the streets, as well. In Martí we find not only the former but also the latter. Martí thus celebrated aspects of the modern city (as in his text on the Brooklyn Bridge, among many examples) and was troubled by others (as in his text on Coney Island or his conservative commentaries on women and family life), while also sympathising with working-class resistance to capitalist exploitation.[107]

---

107   Even regarding mass entertainment Martí harboured a mixed perspective, as shown by his description of P.T. Barnum, certainly not a representative of genteel culture, as 'a man of genius who has invested everything in fairs and circuses' ['hombre de genio que lo ha puesto todo en casas de fieras y circos']. Martí added: 'He who discovers means to attract and distract others, is a benefactor of humanity'. ['El que descubre medios de atraer y distraer a los demás – es un benefactor de los hombres'.] 'Un mastodonte' [1883], OC, VIII, p. 409. Lomas 2008, p. 96. Martí's denunciation of class oppression and identification with its victims is not absent, even if it is rarer and less explicit, from his *Versos libres*. See the following passage from the poem 'Estrofa nueva':
Un obrero tiznado, una enfermiza
Mujer, de faz enjuta y dedos gruesos:
Otra que al dar al sol los entumidos
Miembros en el taller, como una egipcia
Voluptuosa y feliz, la saya burda
En las manos recoge y canta y danza:
Un niño que sin miedo a la ventisca,

The complex combination of anguish, celebration, hope and protest that characterised Martí's reaction to the modern city can be traced in one of his texts on Henry George's campaign for mayor of New York City in 1887. Martí begins the chronicle with an indictment: 'Cities are rotting'. He immediately identifies the source of the rot: economic inequality separating the wealthy from the impoverished mass.[108] Yet the same conditions that had brought about this lamentable situation also brought forth the means for correcting it. Henry George's campaign for mayor was no mere local initiative. It signalled, Martí assured his readers, 'the birth, on a biblical scale, of a new human era'.[109] Martí could thus also celebrate the present: 'Great are our times; great is the joy of living in them'.[110]

Idealising the modern city frames Martí as a conservative elitist observer, which he was not, although there were conservative angles to his perspective. In a way, he had a more accurate conception of the modern city and a more radical attitude towards it than some of his critics: he did not idealise it, nor

> Como el soldado con el arma al hombro,
> Va con sus libros a la escuela: el denso
> Rebaño de hombres que en silencio triste
> Sale a la aurora y con la noche vuelve,
> Del pan del día en la difícil busca, –
> Cual la luz a Memnón, mueven mi lira

Consider his description of a heat wave and its impact on the city's poor: 'Summer in New York is not hateful for the heat ... but for the way in which it tortures the unhappy people that only have the roofs of their houses as a park ... or the freshness of the floor tiles ... From the roofs of the tenement houses, which are the majority in the poor neighborhoods, hang clusters of legs ... From one chimney to the next, searching for cooler bricks to recline upon, exhausted workers pass ... their hair, ruffled, their mouths, fallen; the women, bloodless, tired from their domestic routines, which are deadly in the summer: their cheeks are caves; their eyes, embers or prayers; if their breast can be seen it does not concern them; they barely have enough strength to quiet the cry of the gaunt creature that is dying on their lap'. 'Por la bahía de Nueva York' [1888], *OC*, XII, p. 23.

108 'The cities are rotting; their inhabitants group themselves in hardened castes ... in the home of freedom itself, palaces with golden balconies are accumulating on one side ... and on the other ... the sickly and deformed children of the workers'. Martí 1980, 'Correspondencia particular del *Partido Liberal*' [1886] p. 64. ['Se pudren las ciudades; se agrupan sus habitantes en castas endurecidas ... en la morada misma de la libertad se amontonan de un lado los palacios con balcones de oro ... y de otro ... los hijos enclenques y deformes de los trabajadores'.]

109 Martí 1980, 'Correspondencia particular del *Partido Liberal*' [1886], p. 66. ['el nacimiento, con tamaños bíblicos, de una nueva era humana'.]

110 Martí 1980, 'Correspondencia particular del *Partido Liberal*' [1886], p. 66. ['Grandes son nuestros tiempos; es grande el gozo de vivir en ellos'.]

did he simply want to yield to its 'fluidity' and 'heterogeneity', but sought to transform it, if not subvert it. There were aspects of it that appalled him, but he also discerned liberating forces within it. To put it provocatively: the more notable problem here is not Martí's but his critic's blind spot to the contradictory realities of the *capitalist* metropolis.[111]

As further evidence for a reading of Martí as an elitist observer which she shares with Ramos, Susan Antebi quotes a passage of Martí's text on the Brooklyn Bridge: 'And the creators of this bridge, and those who maintain it, and those who cross it seem – but for the excessive love of wealth that gnaws at their intestines like a worm – men carved out of granite, like the bridge itself'. According to Antebi, 'While the phrase seems to oppose the impenetrable granite of the bridge to the horrifying intestinal flesh-as-worm, the juxtaposition at once creates a jarring link between the bridge and the gnawing worm. The intestinal worm ... invades the imagery of the sentence, paradoxically transforming granite to flesh, and flesh to bridge'. According to Antebi, Martí's horror at the worm extends to the bridge and the crowd. But such a reading ignores Martí's argument: he is repelled, not by the bridge or the crowds that move through it, but by the 'excessive love of wealth'. He is appalled, not by the material achievements of modernity such as the bridge, but by the power of money within it. He does not reject a worm-like crowd: he wishes to rescue the crowd from a worm-like subordination to monetary ambitions. Modernity is not the same as the excessive pursuit of wealth: Martí wishes to extricate the former from the latter, as from a flaw that could undermine its achievements. To transform the bridge or the crowd into extensions of the worm is to flatten Martí's critique of some salient aspects of capitalist modernity into an elitist rejection of it.[112]

As pointed out before, Martí repeatedly uses the image of the 'worm' to refer to precisely the same phenomena he associates it with in this passage. Thus, in his 1889 'Vindication of Cuba' Martí writes that Cubans 'admire this nation ... but they dislike the evil conditions that, like worms in the heart, have begun in this mighty republic their work of destruction ... They cannot

---

111   For a more balanced view of Martí's attitude, similar to the one presented here, see Reyes 2015.
112   I would formulate a similar objection to Antebi's reading of Martí's articles on Coney Island, mentioned in footnote 88: it unjustifiably flattens Martí's rejection of the cruelty, exploitation and brutality of many aspects of capitalist mass culture into an elite rejection of the urban masses. The argument that justifies the slippage from the former to the latter appears to me as dubious as the alleged mutation of granite to worm-infested flesh in Antebi's reading of Martí's text on the Brooklyn Bridge. Antebi 2005.

honestly believe that excessive individualism, reverence for wealth ... are preparing the United States to be the typical nation of liberty'.[113]

Ramos's does not entirely disregard the question of the specifically *capitalist* nature of modernity and of Martí's reaction to it. He mentions in passing that his thesis does not 'invalidate Martí's powerful critique of the reification of daily life in capitalist society'.[114] But he does not integrate this insight into his reading of Martí. Of course, a reading which takes the specifically *capitalist* nature of modernity as a central fact, formulated, furthermore, from the standpoint of a radical questioning of *capitalist* mass commercial culture, runs contrary to two key tenets of much postmodern criticism: first, the suspicion that all critiques of mass commercial culture are elitist claims to cultural privilege by an enlightened minority; secondly, the aversion to a radical opposition to capitalism, as one of the grand narratives of emancipation that lean toward or even inevitably lead to an authoritarian synthesis. This postmodern or post-Marxist common sense, which haunts Ramos's text, this anxiety with any criticism of mass culture or capitalism, not to speak of a socialist 'synthesis', as potentially elitist or authoritarian, favoured, if it did not ensure, that the mentions of Martí's reaction to capitalist exploitation and alienation remained passing references. The result is a flattened vision of modernity, cleansed of its capitalist nature, and, consequently, a one-sided reading of Martí, blind to key aspects of his response to it.

Ramos argues that 'Martí's discourse is asserted over and against capitalist modernity'.[115] This is an ambiguous formulation: this description could apply to both a conservative opponents of modernity (landowning classes, aristocratic castes or the Catholic hierarchy, for example) and to modern opponents of capitalism. Marx, for example, was certainly opposed to 'capitalist modernity', not because he was anti-modern but because he was anti-capitalist. As he positioned himself 'over and against capitalist modernity', did Martí envision a renunciation of modernity or an alternative modernity? At times, as in the passage quoted above, Ramos's answer is ambiguous. More often than not his reading turns Martí into an opponent of modernity *tout court*.

Recognising that Martí, as we have argued, was more of an alter-modernist than an anti-modernist, does not leave him off the hook, so to speak. It exposes him rather to a different critical question, which does not arise from Ramos's approach, namely: how would a Cuban republic solve the problems that,

---

113 Martí [1889], pp. 263–264; 'Vindicación de Cuba', *OC*, I, p. 237.
114 Ramos 2001, p. 222.
115 Ramos 2001, p. 206.

according to him, were being reproduced in the United States? Martí's answer was vague, to say the least. It amounted to a programme not too different from Whitman's: the vision of an equalisation of fortunes through the widespread distribution of landed property, and a harmonisation of the opposed claims of labour and capital.[116] Thus, even if Martí, unlike Whitman, combined his exaltation of the poet with political activism, his patriotic project was vulnerable to the same critique as Whitman: it is not possible to transcend the consequences of capitalism (the fragmentation, the lack of a 'shared atmosphere',[117] the 'glacial metallisation', the growing social polarisation) without transcending capitalism itself.

Martí was aware of Latin America's lag in political and economic development. Through his chronicles he sought to hasten the modernisation of the southern republics. But his observation of US life nurtured his misgivings regarding its status as a model. Martí's logic parallels that of the young Marx, even if they reached different conclusions. The young Marx argued in 1843 that Germany had not yet achieved the 'political emancipation' that Britain, France and the United States had attained to some degree (the United States more so than the others) through their revolutions. Germany was *'below the level of history'.*[118] But backwardness has its advantages: through the critique of the reality of the advanced nations, Germans could discover that 'political emancipation' did not amount to complete 'human emancipation'. Backward Germany, the young Marx concluded, had to aspire, not only to catch-up with, but to transcend the 'political emancipation' already attained by modern nations. There was, in other words, an alternative modernity beyond existing modernity. It is at this point in the young Marx's argument that the proletariat first appears in his texts as the agent of 'human emancipation', in Germany and elsewhere: it emerges as the leader of the process that Trotsky would later describe as permanent revolution, the combination, in the young Marx's terms, in backward Germany of political and human emancipation.[119]

---

116   In 1884, in a review of a text by Herbert Spencer, Martí had broached the question of socialism. Social reforms, according to Spencer, Martí explained, would lead to socialism and to the enslavement of all by the state. Martí argued that social reform would remove the causes of social discontent and thus make radical upheavals unlikely. While Martí's views shifted over the years, it seems that he never went beyond this left but reformist orientation, as far as the transcending of capitalism was concerned. 'Herbert Spencer' y 'La futura esclavitud' [1884], *OC*, XV, pp. 387–92.

117   'El problema indio en Estados Unidos' [1886], *OC*, X, p. 375. ['Es indispensable crear a los espíritus aislados una atmósfera común'.]

118   Marx [1843–4], p. 246.

119   Marx [1843–4], p. 256.

Like Marx regarding Germany in 1843, Martí was conscious of Latin America's backwardness if compared to the United States. And his experience of North American modernity led him to conclude, as the young Marx had done regarding Germany, that Latin America had to aspire to transcend the US model of modernity through a fuller, truly human, less one-sided, synthesis. Here the roads diverged. For Martí, the agent of that future synthesis would be a free-farmer agriculture and progressive labour legislation within a republican patriotic project. For Marx, it required workers' self-organisation leading to expropriation of capital and to the collective ownership of that which under capitalism 'grows against them', to use Martí's words.[120]

Troubled by the consequences of capitalist progress but unwilling to question its basic structures, Whitman mixed the vision of small farming communities with a poetic idealisation of the present. Martí, while more openly pro-labour, also sympathised with land redistribution. Nor did he always avoid the tendency to idealise the present. This is evident in passages where he seeks to humanise what otherwise seemed as the impersonal, 'glacial', 'metallised', nature of capitalist progress. Contemplating the achievements of modern industry, Martí trusted that they could never become completely divorced from their producers. Referring to the Brooklyn Bridge, he thus wrote 'that any organism invented by man ... is bound to bear a resemblance to man'.[121] Describing the demolition of the islet of Flood Rock in the East River, he pointed out how the explosive mechanism was set off by the hand of a small girl: even the more potentially destructive forces unleashed by progress could be brought under the control of the, from his perspective, most delicate hand.[122] Speaking of an exposition of railroad equipment in Chicago, Martí wrote of the identification of operative and machine: 'Machinists come to love their machines, to know them, and caress them ... [M]an ... infuses soul into everything he touches. The machine sometimes seems like a wife to the machinist. And the visitors of the Exposition seemed as children of those old

---

120   Martí [1887a], p. 200; 'Un drama terrible', *OC*, XI, p. 337. Of course, six decades later Cuban revolutionaries that considered themselves inheritors of Martí did carry out a combined democratic, anti-imperialist and anti-capitalist revolution.

121   Quoted in English in Susana Rotker, *The American Chronicles of José Martí*, p. 94. ['por ser ley, que anuncia ... que todo organismo que invente el hombre ... esté dispuesto a semejanza del hombre'. 'El Puente de Brooklyn' [1883], *OC*, IX, p. 428 (This passage is not included in the translation by Esther Allen).

122   In another passage, Martí describes the Eiffel Tower as a triumph of modern industry and then, in passing, adds a detail that seeks to reconcile it with nature: 'Atop the cupola, a small bird has made its nest'. 'La exposición de París' [1889], *OC*, XVIII, p. 414. ['En lo alto de la cúpula, ha hecho su nido una golondrina'.]

locomotives, judging by the tenderness with which they looked at them'.[123] It was typical of Martí to fall back on a vision of the family as a world of personal affections, and to adopt a frankly male perspective. The fact does not turn Martí into an outright conservative or elitist thinker, given the other aspects of his work, such as his opposition to the aristocratic privileges of the past and the social inequalities of the present, his defence of modern mass democracy and his sympathy for the demands of labour. Furthermore, it should be underlined that in passages such as this, Martí, far from rejecting the machine, sought to reconcile himself with it. Yet, in the pursuit of that reconciliation, Martí, not unlike Whitman in 'Song of the Exposition', 'Passage to India', 'Year of the Modern' and other texts, also came close to idealising the present. Contrary to his description, the dynamics of the human organism, the rules of affection, however conceived, are *not* the laws that control the relations between producer, machine or product under capitalism. Under capitalism, all social agents find themselves under the rule of impersonal forces, as the result of which their interactions are turned into an autonomous power: the human hand, delicate or not, does not orient the machine of economic development.

Unlike Ramos, Laura Lomas has underlined Martí's identification with oppressed and exploited sectors within the United States, a welcome contrast to the reading of Martí as a privileged, elitist observer of the modern city. But her polemical thrust is directed primarily against certain interpretations of Martí's relations to American authors and, above all, his relation with Emerson and Whitman. Regarding this, she argues against the tendency to simply assimilate Martí with Whitman and Emerson: such a reading turns Martí into their passive disciple, subtly confirming a feeling of imperial intellectual superiority, while cleansing Martí's texts of their bristling hostility toward many aspects of American society and culture.[124] Against this reassuring normalisation of Martí into a mere follower of Emerson and an uncritical admirer of Whitman, Lomas rightly points out how Martí was far more critical than either author of the forms of oppression and exploitation suffered by Indians, Blacks, Mexicans and workers in the United States.[125]

---

123 'La Exposición de material de ferrocarriles de Chicago' [1883], OC, VIII, p. 357. ['Los maquinistas llegan a amar a sus máquinas, y a conocerlas, y a acariciarlas ... [E]l hombre, siempre y por sobre todo bueno, infunde alma en cuanto toca. Esposa llega a parecer a veces al maquinista su máquina. E hijos de aquellas locomotoras viejas y despedazadas parecían los visitantes de la Exposición, por el cariño con que las miraban'.]
124 Lomas 2008, p. 64.
125 Lomas refers to 'Prohibition of Colored Persons' (May 1858), an unsigned editorial of the *Brooklyn Daily Times* written by Whitman.

But Lomas pushes this argument farther than the evidence warrants. She claims that critics have missed the hidden ironic core of Martí's texts on Emerson and Whitman. Thus, according to Lomas, 'Martí's critique of ... [Whitman's] rhetoric outweighs his admiration'.[126] He sought 'to expose the pretense of liberty that increasingly posed a threat to Martí's America'.[127] He wished to 'draw out Whitman's investment in a national political project that has betrayed American principles of equality and self-government'.[128] For Martí, agues Lomas, Whitman dressed 'an expansionist agenda ... in meretricious images of freedom and democracy'.[129]

The exhibits offered to defend this thesis are weak. The point, it should be underlined, is *not* whether Martí was more critical of oppression within the United Sates or of American expansionism, than Emerson or Whitman. Of that there can be little doubt. The problem to be addressed is Martí's attitude toward Emerson and Whitman: did he read them, as Lomas argues, as representatives of the more objectionable tendencies within American society, or did he, on the contrary, differentiate these authors from those tendencies, as examples of what he found admirable in the United States?

To support her thesis, Lomas examines two passages in which Martí described his experience reading Emerson. Martí writes: 'I have walked enough through life, and tasted its varied offerings. Well, the greatest pleasure, the only absolutely pure pleasure I have enjoyed to this day was that of the afternoon in which, from my bare room, I saw the city lying before me, and I discerned the future, thinking of Emerson'.[130] In a second passage Martí writes: 'The imperfection of this existence is evidenced in the fact that in all of it there are only a few moments of absolute bliss, pure bliss, which are those of full renunciation, of confusion of man with nature. (Emerson. The Emerson afternoon: when man loses the sense of self, and is transfused in the world)'.[131]

---

126   Lomas 2008, p. 182. Lomas refers to the 'mock-congratulatory aspects' missed by critics. (p. 178). There *are* moments of mock or ironic praise in Martí's writings, such as his hyperbolic description of Buffalo Bill as a man who can stop one bullet with another. 'William F. Cody "Buffalo Bill"' [1884], OC, XIII, p. 281.
127   Lomas 2008, p. 181.
128   Lomas 2008, p. 178.
129   Lomas 2008, p. 206.
130   'Otros fragmentos' [undated], OC, XXII, p. 323. ['Ya he andado bastante por la vida, y probado sus varios manjares. Pues el placer más grande, el único placer absolutamente puro que hasta hoy he gozado fue el de aquella tarde en que desde mi cuarto medio desnudo vi la ciudad postrada, y entreví lo futuro pensando en Emerson'.]
131   'Kant y Spencer' [undated], OC, XIX, pp. 369–70. ['Lo imperfecto de esta existencia se conoce con que en toda ella apenas hay unos cuantos momentos de dicha absoluta, dicha

Lomas argues: 'In giving this event the name "evening of Emerson", Martí underscores the evanescence of Emerson's explanatory power. Martí defines a post-Emersonian pivot from which he sees the city lying before him and senses what the future may bring'.[132] But Martí's emphasis is not only on the evanescence of the moment, but rather on the extraordinary intensity and significance of the experience, despite its brevity. Martí was here close to an idea formulated by Emerson in 'The Over-soul': 'There is a difference between one and another hour of life in their authority and subsequent effect. Our faith comes in moments; our vice is habitual. Yet there is depth in such brief moments which constrains us to ascribe more reality to them than to all other experiences'.[133] Martí was more critical of the United States than Emerson, but it is hard to read the quoted passage as anything but a declaration of deeply felt affinity with him. There is, furthermore, a third passage in which Martí's mentions 'the Emerson afternoon': a note in which Martí lists what he describes as the 'supreme moments' of his life, 'the hours that truly count'. The passage also speaks to Martí's closeness with Emerson: 'Emerson afternoon' is first on the list.[134] Martí also wrote a superlatively admiring portrait of Emerson at the time of his death in 1882, a text devoid of anything resembling an ironic detachment from its subject.[135]

A similar conclusion is reached regarding Lomas's comments on Martí and Whitman. Lomas mentions a passage in which Martí argues that Whitman's 'artistry' is 'hidden' and in which he compares the poet to a rider who always maintains his horses under control, while giving the contrary impression: 'he uses his artistry, which is entirely hidden, to reproduce the elements of his picture in the same disorder he observed them in nature'. At times, his 'mind does wander ... but then, as if he had only let the reins go slack for a moment without letting go of them, he suddenly gathers them in and steadies the team of bucking horses with a horsebreaker's fist'.[136] For Martí, argues Lomas, Whitman's ability to hide his artistry 'exemplifies the tactics of imperial modernity hidden within the rhetorical flourishes of democracy'.[137] Martí exposed Whitman's

---

pura, que son los de pleno desinterés, los de confusión del hombre con la Naturaleza. (Emerson. La tarde de Emerson: Cuando pierde el hombre el sentido de sí, y se transfunde en el mundo.)']

132 Lomas 2008, p. 141.
133 Emerson [1841], p. 134.
134 'Libros' [undated], OC, XVIII, p. 288.
135 'Emerson' [1882], OC, XIII, pp. 15–30. Martí singled out the essay 'Nature' (1836) as his favourite among Emerson's writings.
136 Martí [1887], p. 193. 'El poeta Walt Whitman', OC, XIII, p. 141.
137 Lomas 2008, p. 178.

devious art of maintaining control, while creating the illusion of freedom, 'of achieving and maintaining a position of power without acknowledging the historical use of force in its achievement'.[138] The reader will seek in vain for any indication in the text inviting such a reading. The point, again, is not Martí's anti-imperialism, nor Whitman's expansionist inclinations. The point is whether Martí read Whitman as representative of that expansionism. Nothing in the text supports such an interpretation.

Martí described how Whitman 'With a single gesture ... tosses the romantic lament aside, as a useless excrescence'.[139] Whitman, according to him, did not use ornamented language to hide vapid thoughts: 'he is not one of those who send an impoverished thought tripping and dragging along beneath the ostentatious opulence of its regal garments'.[140] Martí is praising Whitman for pushing aside romantic clichés and empty word-play. Lomas reads these formulations as a denunciation by Martí of Whitman's attitude toward Latin American culture as an 'impoverished thought' or as a 'useless excrescence' to be tossed aside – an interpretation that is nowhere suggested by Martí's text.[141] Martí certainly thought that many North Americans had a disdainful attitude toward Latin America. But there is no indication that the quoted passages attribute such views to Whitman. In them he does not attribute a disdain for Latin American culture to Whitman, rather he praises him for his poetic audacity. Consider, to conclude, Martí's reference to Whitman as a man who has escaped social convention and is, therefore, a deeply unsettling figure to those still trapped by it:

> Like the pudding in its mould, man is formed by the book or forceful teacher that happened to come his way, or by the fashions of his time; schools, be they philosophical, religious, or literary, only straitjacket men as the livery does the lackey; men allow themselves to be branded, like horses and bulls, and go about proudly displaying their brands so that when they find themselves before a man who is naked, virginal, amorous, sincere, and powerful ... when they find themselves before so sinewy and angelical a father as Walt Whitman, they flee as if from their own

---

138   Lomas 2008, p. 185.
139   Martí [1887], p. 191; 'El poeta Walt Whitman', *OC*, XIII, p. 139. ['De un solo bote echa a un lado, como excrecencia inútil, la lamentación romántica'.]
140   Martí [1887], p. 193; 'El poeta Walt Whitman', *OC*, XIII, p. 141. ['No es él, no, de los que echan a andar un pensamiento pordiosero, que va tropezando y arrastrando bajo la opulencia visible de sus vestiduras regias'.]
141   Lomas 2008, p. 182.

consciences and balk at recognizing the true nature of their dimmed, housebound, gimcrack species in his fragrant and superior humanity.[142]

According to Lomas 'Martí locates himself amongst those who flee their conscience, who balk at recognizing their condition, and who are branded. Whitman, by contrast, occupies the position of an influential, authoritative master'.[143] Martí is the 'branded man',[144] while 'Whitman the master brands the foreheads of doll-like, easily molded inferiors'.[145] Martí thus allegedly portrays Whitman as defining 'a hierarchical relationship between superior and inferior *species*'.[146] Yet in Martí's text Whitman does not brand other men as inferiors: *society* brands men with its traditions and ready-made molds. Whitman is not an enslaving master but an example of liberation. Everything in Martí's text suggests that he did not identify with the 'branded' men, but rather admired Whitman, the poet who escaped convention, a token of a 'fragrant and superior humanity', as he described him. Consistent with this, Martí repeatedly described Whitman, admiringly, as a rebel.[147] In a rarely mentioned note to himself he recorded his desire to write a book about the 'rebel poets': 'My book. The rebel poets: Oscar Wilde – Giuseppe Carducci – Guerra Junqueiro – Walt Whitman'.[148] We find the same call for liberation from inherited moulds in Martí's 'Preface' to Pérez Bonalde's poem, discussed above:

---

142 Martí [1887], p. 183; 'El poeta Walt Whitman', *oc*, XIII, p. 131. ['Como el budín sobre la budinera, el hombre queda amoldado sobre el libro o maestro enérgico con que le puso en contacto el azar o la moda de su tiempo: las escuelas filosóficas, religiosas o literarias, encogollan a los hombres, como al lacayo la librea; los hombres se dejan marcar, como los caballos y los toros, y van por el mundo ostentando su hierro; de modo que, cuando se ven delante del hombre desnudo, virginal, amoroso, sincero, potente – del hombre que camina que ama, que pelea, que rema –, del hombre que, sin dejarse cegar por la desdicha, lee la promesa de final ventura en el equilibrio y la gracia del mundo; cuando se ven frente al hombre padre, nervudo y angélico Walt Whitman, huyen como de su propia conciencia y se resisten a reconocer en esta humanidad fragante y superior el tipo verdadero de su especie, descolorida, encasacada, amuñecada'.]
143 Lomas 2008, p. 204.
144 Lomas 2008, p. 205.
145 Lomas 2008, p. 209.
146 Lomas 2008, p. 205.
147 See the two passages mentioned above: 'A Bartolomé Mitre y Vedia' [1882], *oc*, IX, p. 18 and 'Reforma esencial en el programa de las Universidades Americanas' [1884], *oc*, VIII, p. 428.
148 'Libros. Notas' *oc*, XVIII, p. 283. ['Mi libro. Los poetas rebeldes: Oscar Wilde – Giuseppe Carducci – Guerra Junqueiro – Walt Whitman'.]

> We come into life like wax, and chance pours us into prefabricated molds. Established conventions deform true existence ... To safeguard human free will and leave human spirits in their own seductive form, to refrain from marring virgin natures by imposing the prejudices of others upon them ... – this is the only way to populate the earth with the vigorous and creative generation it needs ... It is urgent that men be returned to themselves and extricated from the bad government of convention that suffocates or poisons their sentiments ... He who obstructs, in any way, the free, direct, and spontaneous employment of the magnificent faculties of man is guilty of betraying nature.[149]

Lomas is right in warning against assimilating Martí's conceptions with Emerson's and Whitman's. She is equally right in contrasting their inconsistencies regarding the opposition to oppression within the United States, on the one hand, with Martí's clearer identification with the oppressed, on the other. From this she mistakenly concludes that Martí associated Emerson and Whitman with the forms of oppression and expansionism he opposed. But whatever *we* may think of Whitman, for Martí he was fully on the side of democracy, of liberation from convention and of nature. To argue that Martí resisted Whitman as a slave plots against his master is to misrepresent his views as their opposite.

To summarise: Martí's attitude toward the United States and the rising capitalist metropolis as exemplified by New York was complex and nuanced, even contradictory, a fact which has made it particularly vulnerable to one-sided readings. Martí was both attracted and repelled by life in the United States, and his critique of it had both progressive (anti-imperialist, anti-racist, pro-labour) and conservative (for example, sexist) dimensions. Most students of his texts have underplayed his fascination with modern life as he experienced it in New York, while emphasising either his more anti-imperialist or conservative rejection of it. Such is the case both of authors who only refer to an anti-imperialist Martí (Lomas, for example), on the one hand, and of those who speak of an elitist chronicler of modern life (such as Ramos), on the other.

---

149 Martí [1882a], pp. 49–50; 'Poema del Niágara', *OC*, VII, pp. 230–1. ['Se viene a la vida como cera, y el azar nos vacía en moldes prehechos. Las convenciones creadas deforman la existencia verdadera ... [D]ejar a los espíritus su seductora forma propia; no deslucir con la imposición de ajenos prejuicios las naturalezas vírgenes ... ¡He ahí el único modo de poblar la tierra de la generación vigorosa y creadora que le falta! ... Urge devolver los hombres a sí mismos; urge sacarlos del mal gobierno de la convención que sofoca o envenena sus sentimientos ... ¡Reo es de traición a la naturaleza el que impide, en una vía u otra, y en cualquiera vía, el libre uso, la aplicación directa y el espontáneo empleo de las facultades magníficas del hombre!']

A recent study by Cuban scholar Marlene Vázquez Pérez typically emphasises Martí's anti-imperialist critique of US culture and society, while largely ignoring his fascination with it and downplaying the more conservative angles of that critique.[150] As in the case of Ramos, the picture that emerges is not wrong but one-sided. Here we have attempted to honour the contrasting, even contradictory dimensions of Martí's conceptions.

Martí was both fascinated and repelled by the United States. By the time he wrote 'The Truth about the United States' his aversion to American society had gained the upper hand, yet he never became a socialist. The work of C.L.R. James, a fellow Caribbean revolutionary, provides an interesting contrast: a socialist thinker, James's texts of the late 1940s and early 1950s register his appreciation for what he took to be the emancipatory forces gathering within the United States. Chapter 10 examines his attempt at an overall interpretation of his subject, including the place of Whitman within it.

150   Vázquez Pérez 2010.

CHAPTER 10

C.L.R. James's *Notes on American Civilization*, or the Song of the C.I.O.

Cyril Lionel Robert James was born in 1901 in Trinidad, at the time a colony of Great Britain. A gifted son of working people, he attended Queen's Royal College, the colony's elite secondary educational institution. After graduating and through the 1920s, the young James began making a name for himself as a cricket journalist. He was equally interested in literature, and by 1928 completed the manuscript of a novel, *Minty Alley*. By then he was also involved in the growing movement for West Indian self-government, which had emerged in the aftermath of the First World War, under the leadership of Arthur Andrew Cipriani. In 1932 James moved to Great Britain. During that year he published *The Life of Captain Cipriani* and helped his friend, and Trinidad cricket star, Learie Constantine, write his autobiography: two endeavours that reflected his twin interests in cricket and politics. Sympathetic to labour's demands in the midst of the Great Depression, James joined the Labour Party while also hoping it would come around to supporting West Indian self-government. By 1933 he was earning a living as a reporter for the *Manchester Guardian*. His political education was advancing apace. In 1932 he encountered the recently published English translation of Trotsky's *History of the Russian Revolution*. Trotsky's text, which combined a narrative of the events of 1917 with comparative excursions on the English, French and 1848 revolutions, had a lasting impact on him. Trotsky's combination of theory and concrete analysis, of historical exploration and discussion of contemporary political questions, his nuanced presentation of the role and intersection of economic relations, the state, classes, parties and individuals in a complex historical situation convinced him of the superiority of Marxism as a means of historical analysis and of political intervention. By 1933 Trotsky was in exile as the main leader of the Russian Revolution that had taken up the struggle against the growing bureaucratisation of the Soviet state. He was the best known architect of the International Left Opposition, an attempt to construct a revolutionary anti-Stalinist current, committed to the struggle against both capitalism and the bureaucratic regime in the Soviet Union. In 1934 James joined the British Trotskyist organisation, which at that point operated as a tendency within the Independent Labour Party, a left split from the Labour Party. In 1937 he published *World Revolution 1917–1936. The Rise and Fall of the Communist International*, one of the earlier attempts at a comprehensive critical, Marxist, anti-Stalinist appraisal of the evolution of the Communist movement from its birth in the wake of the Russian revolution through its remaking under the impact of the process of bureaucratisation in the Soviet Union. In 1938 he published what many consider his masterpiece: *The Black Jacobins: Toussaint L'Ouverture and the San Domingo Revolution*. James's book told the history of the interaction of the French and Haitian revolutions, of the rise of Napoleon in the metropolis and his clash with the defiant Haitian masses, determined to defend the freedom they had conquered, a process leading to the birth of Haiti as an independent state. James wrote admiringly, but not uncritically, of L'Ouverture, calling the reader's attention toward both the past and what he considered to be the imminent upsurge of anti-colonial struggles around the world. It was an achievement worthy of James's model, Trotsky's *History of the Russian Revolution*. In 1938, the United States section of the Trotskyist current, the Socialist Workers Party, organised a lecture tour for James. He accepted the invitation for what should have been a brief sojourn in America. Illegally overstaying his visa, James remained in the United States for fifteen years, until he was deported in 1953. In the United States, James joined the SWP and in 1939 travelled to Mexico to participate in conversations with Trotsky regarding the struggles of blacks in the United States. By 1940, the SWP split over the analysis of and attitude toward the Soviet state. James sided with those that now objected to Trotsky's description of the Soviet Union as a worker's state, which had to be defended against outside intervention, in spite of its monstrous bureaucratic deformation. James joined the new Workers Party within which he led his own current. In 1947 James and his current returned to the SWP, but left it again in 1951 to create an independent organisation. Around this time James wrote two significant works: *Notes on American Civilization*, a manuscript that remained unpublished in his lifetime and *Mariners, Renegades and Castaways: The Story of Herman Melville and the World We Live In*, published in 1952 and written while he was confined in Ellis Island awaiting the outcome of his deportation proceedings. What follows focuses on these works, which constitute an attempt at a global interpretation of American society. They include his extensive considerations on Whitman.

In a manner reminiscent of Whitman's description of inner expansion ('what widens within you, Walt Whitman?') and of Martí's feeling of inner growth while contemplating modern engineering achievements ('as if mountain peaks were rising within our minds'),[1] James wrote of the 'sense of expansion' provoked by his first journey across the United States: 'I remember my first

---

1 Martí [1883] p. 143; 'El puente de Brooklyn', OC, IX, p. 425.

journey from Chicago to Los Angeles, by train, – the apparently endless miles, hour after hour, all day and all night and the next morning the same again, until the evening. I experienced a sense of expansion which has permanently altered my attitude to the world'.[2] José Martí was both fascinated and repelled by the United States. He considered Whitman part of what was most admirable in America, and part of what it needed most: the search for a new art, fit for modern times. Yet, what was admirable in the United States was not, on balance, sufficient for Martí: by the early 1890s his aversion had overruled whatever attraction he felt toward it. James, arriving in the United States in 1940, also was both repelled and fascinated by it. But in his case it was the second feeling that prevailed. James's combination of Marxist politics and frank admiration for the United States rested on a third key element of his outlook: his trust in the revolutionary potential of the American working class.

James is often presented as a prophet of anti-colonial revolution. Donald E. Pease argues, for example, that James came to doubt 'that world revolution would originate in the metropolitan countries of Europe rather than in the underdeveloped peripheries'.[3] It is, of course, true that James was an advocate of the combination of anti-colonial and socialist struggles. Yet he was neither the first nor the only activist to embrace such a perspective. The notion that socialist revolution could first arise in the periphery and not in the centres of world capitalism was the central idea of Trotsky's concept of permanent revolution, first formulated in 1906, regarding the prospects of revolution in Tsarist Russia, and later extended by its author to the colonial and semi-colonial world in the aftermath of the Chinese revolution of 1926–7.[4]

As Timothy Brennan has rightly pointed out, what was distinctive and rather unique in James, compared to other anti-colonial thinkers, was, on the contrary, his trust in the revolutionary impulse of the *metropolitan* and, above all, the American working class.[5] His manuscript, *Notes on American Civilization*, sought to understand, explain and cultivate that impulse. In the process he constructed his vision of the United States in the nineteenth century through the examination of three figures who he considered particularly significant: Walt Whitman, Herman Melville and Wendell Phillips. As we shall see, in contrast to Martí, James had few positive things to say about Whitman. Yet, it can be argued that despite this, his intellectual project was in many ways reminiscent of Whitman's. But, as the subtitle of his work on Melville indicates, James's glance at

---

2 James 2001, p. 159.
3 Pease 2001, p. viii.
4 Trotsky 1978. For an introduction to Trotsky see Mandel 1979 and 1995.
5 Brennan 1997, p. 233.

the past was shaped by his concern with his present. Thus, before considering his interpretations of Whitman, Melville and Phillips, we will first examine the vision of the tensions and potentials of American society in the late 1940s that framed them.

In his 1949–50 *Notes* James proposed to discuss the 'essential conflict' between 'liberty, freedom, pursuit of happiness, free individuality', which he took to be real, active forces in US history, and 'the economic and social realities of present-day America'.[6] For him, there was a 'fundamental conflict' between the feeling of potential mastery over the means and objects of human labour and the feeling of impotence instilled by the hierarchical organisation of production: 'There is on the one hand the need, the desire, created ... by the whole mighty mechanism of American industry, to work, to learn, to master the machine, to cooperate with others ... to organize the plant as only workers know how. And on the other hand, the endless frustration of being merely a cog in a great machine, a piece of production as is a bolt of steel'.[7]

James described how the industrial relations studies 'painted a picture of a working force in deep but baffled hostility with the conditions of labor as they existed in contemporary industry'.[8] Hostile to the conditions imposed on it, but still baffled by them – these terms roughly summarised James's vision of the US working class.

There was, according to James, a deep contradiction – a potentially explosive contradiction – at the very centre of American society. Pushing in one direction was the American aspiration to personal self-fulfillment and development combined with the sense of human potential engendered by modern productive forces – in other words, the legacy and results of American democratic struggles combined with the achievements of American industry. Against this stood the limits of an authoritarian productive order, that is to say, the economic and social subordination of labour to capital and the material subordination of labour to the machine, owned and deployed by capital against it:

> Upon a people bursting with energy, untroubled by feudal remains or a feudal past, soaked to the marrow in a tradition of individual freedom, individual security, free association ... upon this people ... has been imposed a mechanized way of life at work, mechanized forms of living, a mechanized totality which from morning till night, week after week, day after day, crushed the very individuality which tradition and the

---

6   James 1993, p. 31.
7   James 1993, p. 167.
8   James 1993, p. 107.

abundance of mass-produced goods encourages. The average American is baffled by it, has always been. He cannot grasp the process by which genuine democracy escapes him.[9]

There was then a contradiction at the very centre of the 'modern mechanized collectivized world' between the 'building up on the one hand of all sorts of possibilities and vistas for the individual personality, and on the other its confinement of the personality to a narrow routinized existence'.[10] The United States was the land of freedom, but 'freedom has been lost in modern industrial production'.[11]

This contrast between 'possibilities' and 'confinement' did not only characterise the situation of the wage-earner. James approached the problem from the perspective, not only of class, but of gender. Women in the United States, he wrote, were 'the freest, the most advanced, with the greatest opportunities for self-development in the world'.[12] 'But', he added, more often than not 'the girl who has gone to college or otherwise had the opportunity to develop her abilities ... is suddenly transformed into a wife, dependent upon her husband, dropping behind in the race, where formerly she had gone side by side with him through high school and college or in the early stages of a business career'.[13] Women, he explained, want to 'establish themselves as individual human beings with rights to independence and self-development'.[14] But, for women, that 'self-development comes to a halt'[15] as 'all the needs for free self-expression which her upbringing and social education have fostered' are now confined to 'two rooms, kitchen and bath'.[16] Women at home and workers in the factories thus found themselves in an analogous situation: 'The final result is a permanent underlying bitterness and sense of frustration. It is the direct counterpart of the sense of hopelessness and frustration felt by the masses of workers in modern industrial production'.[17]

According to James, just as women wanted to 'establish themselves as individual human beings with rights to independence and self-development',[18]

---

9   James 1993, pp. 116–17.
10 James 1993, p. 147.
11 James 1993, p. 107.
12 James 1993, p. 212.
13 James 1993, p. 213.
14 James 1993, p. 222.
15 James 1993, p. 220.
16 James 1993, p. 220.
17 James 1993, p. 215.
18 James 1993, p. 222.

workers 'want to manage and arrange the work they are doing without any interference or supervision by anybody'.[19] Workers and women wished to take control of their own lives. James based this appreciation on a more tangible reality than the conclusions of industrial relations experts. He was writing at the high point in the rise of the Congress of Industrial Organizations, the C.I.O., in the wake of a decade and a half of mass labour battles, which had brought unionisation into the hitherto open-shop centres of US industry (auto, steel, rubber, electric appliances). The three general strikes of 1934 (Minneapolis, Toledo and San Francisco) had been followed by the sit-down strikes of 1936–7 against General Motors, among other employers, the victory over Ford in 1940, the coal miners' strikes and wildcats (brief, unauthorised strikes) in other industries during the war, leading to the massive strike wave of 1946–7. While most labour leaders had pledged there would be no strikes during the war, there were in fact more than 14,000 strikes involving around 6,700,000 workers between Pearl Harbor and V-J Day, more than in any comparable period in the past. Many were conducted over, not wages or benefits, but shop-floor issues, i.e., over the definition in practice of what employers took to be their 'right to manage'.[20] During the 1946 strike wave 4.6 million workers went on strike at one point or another.[21] As Breecher points out, and as James thought at the time, 'The potential capacity of the workers to paralyze not just one company or industry but the entire country was demonstrated'.[22] By then, the labour movement had reached an unprecedented visibility and weight in American life.

For James, the C.I.O. embodied far more than the aspiration for better wages, benefits and working conditions. It embodied the potential for a radical transformation of American society: 'The first and most fundamental illusion to be shattered is that the C.I.O. was formed as an instrument of "collective bargaining", to negotiate about wages, ... to help in redistribution of income, etc'.[23] The C.I.O. reflected a desire to challenge the despotism of management in the shop floor: 'It was no instrument for collective bargaining and getting out the vote for the Democratic Party. It was the first attempt of a section of the American workers to change the system ... into something which would solve what they considered to be their rights, their interests and their human needs'.[24]

---

19   James 1993, p. 166.
20   Breecher 1997, pp. 243–4.
21   Breecher 1997, pp. 237–48; Preis 1978, pp. 147–83.
22   Breecher 1997, p. 248.
23   James 1993, p. 172.
24   James 1993, p. 173.

James's *Notes* closely followed Marx's vision of capitalism as both a form of exploitation and as a liberating force, as both a limiting structure and as the creator of both the material conditions for human liberation and of the social agents capable of undertaking it, as well as Marx's vision of the United States 'as the most modern form of existence of bourgeois society'.[25] Nowhere, argued James, had capitalism developed human ingenuity or led people beyond inherited social and cultural forms, nowhere had it instilled on a whole culture a sense of its power to reshape itself and its environment, more fully than in the United States. Yet workers lived that process, not as their liberation and growing mastery over their own lives, but rather as their subordination to an economic apparatus and to forces beyond their control, as the frustration, in the midst of an unprecedented productive potential, of their deeply felt desire for self-development and self-determination. As Martí had put it in 1887, while explaining the actions and ideas of the Haymarket martyrs: 'All that grows seems to them to be growing against them'.[26] That tension, James argued, would be the source of the future American revolution, as a self-organised working-class seized the productive system it had created and placed it at the service of the development of all.

But the radical evolution of the C.I.O. was by no means assured. According to James, the C.I.O. in 1950 stood at a crossroads: it could be reduced to an agent for collective bargaining, as employers and management experts hoped, or it could develop as the expression of a desire for deeper social change. Walter Reuther, President of the United Auto Workers, represented the first option.[27] The second option, argued James, was best represented not by radical left groups, not even by a figure linked to the socialist left, but rather by John L. Lewis, president of the United Mine Workers. Lewis, a key figure in the split of the old American Federation of Labor and the birth the C.I.O. in the mid- and-late 1930s, and the leader of the wartime coal miners' strikes in defiance of the rest of organised labour's no-strike pledge, was for James the individual that, along with Franklyn D. Roosevelt, and despite his 'immense limitations', had 'had the most powerful impact materially and otherwise upon his fellow Americans'.[28]

What was the source of Lewis's decisive role in American society between 1935 and 1950? 'The source of Lewis's power', argued James, 'is very simple.

---

25 Marx 1993, p. 104.
26 Martí [1887a], p. 200; 'Un drama terrible', *OC*, XI, p. 337.
27 James 2001, pp. 189.
28 James 1993, pp. 268–9.

He follows the miners and the miners alone. Follows them? Yes, *follows them*.[29] While not a radical, Lewis was attuned to the rebellious mood of the rank-and-file miners and of other workers. He did not initiate the more defiant mobilisations, but he embraced and led them if he sensed a growing mass support behind them. In 1935, following the mass strikes of 1934, he had split from the A.F.L. and led the creation of the C.I.O.; during the war, as unrest grew in the mines, he had defied the wartime no-strike pledge and resisted the onslaught of the Roosevelt administration and its allies, including the Communist Party and Communist-led unions. He was, argued James, the only labour leader willing to take effective action to oppose the restrictive Taft-Hartley labour relations act of 1947.

While the future of the C.I.O. was still an open question, James was confident that its rise and consolidation demonstrated that the American people felt a 'great unfinished desire', not only for high wages and shorter hours, but also, and more fundamentally, 'for ... free association, for common social ends. It is the only means', he added, 'whereby the powerful and self-destroying individualism can find fulfillment'.[30] James's celebratory vision of the prospects for social change in the United States makes his *Notes* a veritable Song of the C.I.O. He forcefully argued against authors who spoke of a decline or decadence of American civilisation, justified with references to the alleged intellectual or cultural shallowness of the American public. Responding to a comparison of contemporary America to ancient Rome by Max Lerner, Jr., James protested:

> The great mass of the Romans were in the days of the decline slaves, backward agriculturalists, or a city mob. The splendid peasants and artisans of the early city-state were gone. Now look at the people in America today who work. Forget for a moment the rulers, the owners, the enormously wealthy, and the great body ... attached to these. Take the industrial workers, the unorganized workers, the farmers, the clerical assistants, the small functionaries, the vast majority of the nation ... When or where was there ever such a powerful body of men and women, when and where was there such 'inner strength' in a nation? It is not their weakness that is ruining civilization.[31]

James's defence of the American majorities went further: his incorporation of the situation of women into his vision of the labour movement and of social-

---

29 James 1993, p. 269.
30 James 1993, p. 209.
31 James 1993, p. 264.

ism was matched by his pioneering interest in American mass and commercial culture. James considered that most products of the latter – magazines, comics, detective fiction, thrillers and gangster movies, radio shows and soap operas – as well as the cult of film stars and sports heroes, constituted a diversion, manipulation and neutralisation of the aspirations of the American people. But he insisted that they could not be that without *also* being an expression, however distorted, of those aspirations. The promise and impulse for liberation could also be read within the often-dismissed superficiality of mass commercial culture. Within it one could find 'the clearest ideological expression of the sentiments and deepest feelings of the American people and a great window into the future of America and the modern world'.[32] Referring to some of the chapters of his *Notes*, which we examine below, James argued that

> Melville left no serious descendants. In the chapters devoted to contemporary America, the place given to Whitman and Melville is given to the modern film, the radio and the comic strip, to Charles Chaplin, Rita Hayworth, Sam Spade, Louis Armstrong, Dick Tracy and Gasoline Alley. I propose to show that here is not mere shoddiness, vulgarity, entertainment. On the contrary. Here, after the writers of the middle of the nineteenth century, are the first genuine contributions of the United States to the art of the future and an international art of the modern world.[33]

Turning to Hollywood, James argued that from the contradiction in the 'modern mechanized world' between 'the possibilities ... for the individual personality' and its 'confinement' within narrow and hierarchical limits, there arose the 'need to realize the thwarted possibilities or certain parts of them through some symbolic personality'.[34] The Hollywood gangster was such a 'symbolic personality' that neutralised but also expressed 'the deepest feeling of the American people': 'He is the persistent symbol of the national past ... the past in which energy, determination, bravery were certain to get a man somewhere in the line of opportunity'.[35] Workers and women, aspiring 'to self-development as human personalities',[36] but deprived of it, could find an 'esthetic compensation' in 'the contemplation of free individuals who go out into the world and settle their problem by free activity and individualistic methods. Gangsters get

---

32   James 1993, pp. 119, 225.
33   James 1993, p. 35.
34   James 1993, p. 147.
35   James 1993, p. 127.
36   James 1993, p. 222.

what they want ... then are killed. In the end "crime does not pay" but for an hour and a half ... [the movies] have given to many millions a sense of active living'.[37] The 'esthetic compensation' was both a diversion *and* expression of that drive for 'active living'. The popularity of Chaplin's tramp was another example: '*The tramp was an individual.* He defied the growing mechanization and socialization. He was an individual to the point of *extreme idiosyncrasy*'.[38] The star system was not a mere imposition on a deluded public: 'If the great body of the public did not need stars, there would be no stars'.[39] The public sees 'in them examples of that free individuality which is the dominant need of the vast mass today'.[40] James probed the fascination with the 'private and public existence' of Rita Hayworth, for example, as a sign and a symptom of a desire to 'revolt against the general conditions'[41] of the present. 'Not only in their artistic', he added, 'but in their public lives these stars are the real aristocracy of the country and they perform one essential function of any genuine aristocracy. They fill a psychological need of the vast masses of people who live limited lives'.[42]

But, of course, the fascination with the stars both reflected a desire for a fuller life and helped neutralise it within the confines of the existing social system. Similarly, gangster films 'overcome that reality without touching fundamental relations ... It finally ends in becoming an iron barrier to the very needs it sought to satisfy, if even partially'.[43] But there was a further, graver danger: identification with the star could be replaced with identification with an authoritarian leader. The star-system carried the symptoms of both labour's revolt and of fascism.[44]

Combined with revolt from below, the means of modern popular culture would enable a reintegration of politics, art and daily life – a recuperation, on an unprecedented scale, of the role of the dramatist in Greek antiquity, as James understood it.[45] Aeschylus and other playwrights had been 'the intellectual leaders of the people'. Their art had been 'inextricably tied to the realities of the day'.[46] Now, with modern media, argued James, 'we have in our hands,

---

37   James 1993, p. 127.
38   James 1993, p. 133.
39   James 1993, p. 142.
40   James 1993, p. 146.
41   James 1993, p. 142.
42   James 1993, p. 146.
43   James 1993, p. 222.
44   James 1993, p. 161.
45   James 1993, pp. 151, 156.
46   James 1993, p. 156.

the means' through which 'in an infinitely more complex manner, great drama will be written, about the great problems which confront men today, by men conscious of the mass audience as Aeschylus was conscious, with an audience ready to participate to the full'.[47] If Aristophanes were to reappear in the present, James imagined, he would not be interested in the limited audience of the theatre. Instead,

> he would write for the films to which 95 million people go every week. He would arrange for a great film festival for the coming July 4 ... Then in the presence of the Chief Executive, the Judiciary, Congress ... in one theater in Washington, the whole population on the same day at the same time would see his film. It would have in it slapstick, a great deal of plain indecency, but ... the film would contain the most unbridled blows at American democracy, calling things by their names and naming names as well.[48]

It was the subversive potential of such an experiment, not the public's alleged shallowness, which prevented anything resembling it from being attempted: the public 'would understand it all too well. That is why such things are not written for the film'.[49] Such was the potential for an 'artistic comprehensive integration of modern life'[50] that film, radio and comic strips both revealed *and* neutralised. James registered his hope and a warning: 'When the modern film, comic strip and radio can take up capital and labor, housing, the union question, religion, the Negro question, Russian communism and dramatize them with the freedom of sixth-and fifth-century Greece, we would open just such possibilities as Aeschylus saw when he added extra characters to the leader of the chorus. Until then gangster films and Rita Hayworth'.[51]

James formulated a harsh indictment on American intellectuals: eagerly reading and writing books about Lenin or Stalin, they failed to detect the significance of John L. Lewis and of his impact on American life; intensely engaged in the study of Kafka and Dostoyevsky, they disdained the products of American mass culture. Yet it was in Lewis's U.M.W., in spite of its leader's lack

---

47   James 1993, p. 155.
48   James 1993, p. 157.
49   James 1993, p. 158.
50   James 1993, p. 150.
51   James 1993, p. 158. As Bill Schwarz has argued 'Over half a century ago this expansive sense of the locations of politics – in the home, at the movies, within one's own innermost reveries – was radically daring to an extent which, today, may be difficult to appreciate'. Schwarz 2005, p. 24.

of socialist consciousness, and in gangster movies, comic strips and the like, that the auguries of the coming American revolution – a revolution, as all true revolutions, from below – could be read.[52]

James's attitude toward intellectuals cannot be divorced from his conception of the rise of the bureaucracy, as a distinct social agent in the modern world, a perspective which informed his analysis of the welfare state, the politics of the trade union leaderships, of the Soviet Union, and of fascism (and of Melville, as we shall see). For James, intellectuals were key participants in the world-wide emergence of a *new* independent social force, *besides* labour and capital: the impulse toward the bureaucratic-totalitarian response to the crisis of capitalism. James argued that in the context of the turmoil following the World Wars 'new social types' emerged 'in Europe and the world'.[53] Hit by the devastations and irrationalities of capitalist civilisation, managers, technicians, 'administrators, executives, organizers, labour leaders, intellectuals'[54] were turning against the market and the capitalist system. But the alternative to capitalism that *they* envisaged was *not* a workers' democracy but rather a disciplining and reordering of society from above, a project that was *neither* capitalist (or, at least not capitalist in its classical form) nor socialist: 'Nobody ... thought that in the managers, the superintendents, the executives, the administrators would arise such loathing and bitterness against the society of free enterprise, the market and democracy'.[55] Such was the common basis, argued James, of modern totalitarianism in its fascist and Stalinist versions. The exhaustion of the Russian Revolution had brought forth 'the same social type as the Nazis'.[56] Against capitalist instability, chaos and crisis, some embraced the banner of the 'master race', others the conception of the 'master plan'.[57] The outcome of the Second World War had increased the power of attraction of the latter relative to the former: 'in every type of country', argued James, 'have arisen tens of thousands of educated men, organizers, administrators, intellectuals, labor leaders, nationalist leaders, who are ready to do in their own country exactly what the Communists are doing in Russia'.[58] This is why, concluded James, the 'totalitarian madness' 'spreads irresistibly'.[59]

---

52 James 1993, p. 269.
53 James 1993, p. 245.
54 James 2001, pp. 9, 14.
55 James 2001, pp. 9, 14.
56 James 2001, pp. 14, 39.
57 James 2001, p. 120.
58 James 2001, p. 14.
59 James 2001, p. 14.

It is *this* particular conception of the bureaucracy, and not the opposition to bureaucratic rule as such, that differentiated James's perspective from Trotsky's. It is a mistake to argue that upon arriving in the United States, James 'admonished Trotsky for his failure to criticize the Soviet Union's bureaucratization'.[60] In fact, Trotsky had campaigned against the bureaucratisation of the Soviet state at least since 1923 and had denounced each step in the process of Stalinisation. The differences between James and Trotsky and other members of the SWP concerned, *not* the need to combat bureaucratisation, but rather the conception of the *nature* of the bureaucracy as a social agent. For Trotsky, the bureaucracy was a privileged layer nestled in the organisations (parties, unions, states) created by labour in the struggle against capital. For James the bureaucracy constituted an independent *class* opposed to both capital and the working class. For Trotsky there was only one anti-capitalist force: the labour movement, hindered by the bureaucratic, including the Stalinist, formations within it. For James there existed, not one, but *two* parallel anti-capitalist forces: labour's emancipatory project and the bureaucratic totalitarian response to the crisis of capitalism. For Trotsky, Stalinism in the Soviet Unions and the Communist Parties elsewhere were bureaucratic formations *within* the Soviet state and the labour movement, but they did not represent a separate class. For James the Communist Parties were the bearers of an anti-capitalist but not socialist impulse.[61] Unrelated as it may seem to it, James's stance on this issue

---

60   Pease 2001, pp. x–ix.
61   James would later argue that the bureaucracy constitutes a new form of state capitalism. The disagreements between Trotsky and James did *not* revolve around the need to struggle against bureaucratic rule, the importance of the anti-colonial struggles, the need to combine the national liberation and socialist struggles in the colonial and semi-colonial world, the centrality of blacks in the struggle for socialism in the United States or the importance of the cultural dimension of the anti-capitalist struggle. Their major differences revolved around the nature of the Soviet state and of other labour (party, union) bureaucracies and around the notion of a vanguard party. Trotsky's theory clung to the classical Marxist view of labour and capital as the fundamental classes of modern societies. Both classes could generate bureaucratic layers and structures, but the latter did not constitute new bureaucratic classes or embryos or strands of a new bureaucratic class. Working-class organisations, such as trade unions or labour parties, could undergo a process of bureaucratisation if their leaders monopolised decisions, detached themselves from the control of the rank and file, perpetuated themselves in their posts, and accumulated material privileges. Yet, such bureaucratic formations constituted a parasitic or privileged layer *within* the labour movement, not an independent bureaucratic class. Trotsky extended this conception to the analysis of the Soviet state: the bureaucracy was not a new dominant class, but rather a privileged layer living off (and thus deforming and undermining) structures organically linked to the working class, in this case a nationalised and planned economy, required to undertake the transition from a capitalist to a socialist economy. Thus, in spite of its

guided his reading of nineteenth century US culture, including his views on the three figures he placed at the centre of his analysis: Whitman, Melville and Wendell Phillips.

Speaking of Whitman and Melville, James wrote that 'it is in the writings of these two men that both the past of America and the indications of the future were given'.[62] Referring to Whitman he affirmed that he 'cannot ever be ignored in any consideration of the American people'.[63]

---

hideous bureaucratic deformation, the Soviet Union, given its nationalised and planned economy, remained a 'workers' state'. Socialists had to battle against the bureaucracy, but they were also bound to defend the achievements of the revolution – expropriation of the capitalist class, creation of a nationalised, planned economy – that the bureaucracy had undermined but had not yet reversed. Consistent with this analysis, Trotsky insisted that New Deal, fascist and labour bureaucratic layers did not constitute strands of a nascent 'bureaucratic class'. New Deal, corporate or fascist bureaucrats were organically linked to the capitalist class. Labour, Socialist and Communist parties, in spite of their bureaucratic nature were still formations, however deformed, of the workers' movement. Trotsky argued, furthermore, that bureaucratisation was a danger, but not the inevitable outcome of party and other labour organisations: ever vigilant against bureaucratic tendencies, revolutionaries should not abandon the effort to organise revolutionary parties. Revolutionaries, argued Trotsky, should propose a united front of all working class organisations – reformist, socialist, communist – against the danger of fascism, for example. In contrast to Trotsky's concept of the struggle of two fundamental classes – capital and labour – each equipped or burdened with their bureaucratic formations, James and his co-thinkers, at least at this stage in the late 1940s, considered that modern politics was a three-way confrontation between capital, labour and the 'new social types' turning against *both* capital and labour. These new social types embodied the tendency toward a bureaucratic society, or, perhaps, a new form of bureaucratic or state capitalism. While Trotsky insisted that socialists had to both oppose Stalin's regime *and* defend the Soviet Union against its capitalist enemies, James concluded that socialists had no business defending the new class domination that had emerged in the Soviet Union. Instead of siding with the Soviet state or proposing pacts with Communist parties, socialists must form a separate, radical current, opposed to the rule of capital and to the exaltation of the 'master plan'. James and his co-thinkers eventually came to the conclusion that bureaucratic manipulation flowed inevitably from the notion of a revolutionary party: revolutionaries committed to the antibureaucratic perspective could not seek to organise such parties without defeating their own purposes. Many admirers and students of James's work tend to dismiss his Trotskyism as a straitjacket from which he was thankfully able to escape. In spite of our admiration for James, we do not think that his break with Trotskyism was an unalloyed progress. For the record it is perhaps appropriate to indicate that we consider James's theory of the bureaucracy and of the Soviet state far inferior to Trotsky's in terms of explanatory power of the evolution of world politics, within and without the Soviet Union, after 1950. On the issue of the Soviet bureaucracy see Trotsky 1942 and 1977. Also Mandel 1992.

62   James 1993, p. 31.
63   James 1993, p. 222.

Whitman, according to James, had expressed both 'American individualistic passion and the craving to mingle with all *his* fellow-men'.[64] Whitman 'is an isolated individual. But he craves *free association* with his fellows'.[65] His catalogues of persons and occupations, argued James, corresponded to this desire to 'bridge the gap' separating him from others.[66] There are in *Leaves of Grass*, James explained, 'scores of such passages enumerating things; and enumerating people. Here is a man desperately striving to make contact with his fellow men at their daily work and play. He mentions hundreds of them, trying to show that he knows what they do, whether they are thieves, prostitutes, Negroes, bakers, cooks, workers, he is one of them'.[67] Yet Whitman's enumerations, instead of 'bridging the gap', only enlarged the list of isolated individuals: no matter how exhaustive, the enumeration could not alter the *relationship* between the listed fragments. There was in Whitman's poetry a sharp, painful contrast between the 'greatness of the effort and the poverty of the result':[68] his extensive catalogues did not bring him any closer to the sense of community he sought. Attempting to 'bridge the gap' by adding elements to his catalogues, Whitman failed to engage the deeper problem that had to be tackled, if that 'gap' was to be superseded, namely, the need to transform the reified connections that exist between social agents in a society premised on private property, regulated by market competition and ruled by the imperatives of capitalist accumulation.

Much in Whitman's poetry, argued James, hinged on his attempt to avoid the realities of class division, polarisation and conflict in America.[69] Whitman proclaimed in 'Song of the Open Road': 'My call is the call of battle – I nourish rebellion'. James commented: 'He nourished nothing of the kind. He shared to the full his countrymen's delusive belief, based on America's early history, that America in its mere existence was a rebellion'.[70] But America had long ceased being a rebellion: American democracy was now under the control of big capital, which could hardly be described as a rebellious force. Unwilling to recognise the gravity of the social contradictions within the republic, Whitman's writing, argued James, combined the 'visionary ideals of individual freedom and concrete subordination to the reality of the prevailing regime'.[71]

---

64 James 1993, p. 58.
65 James 1993, p. 55.
66 James 1993, p. 58.
67 James 1993, p. 57.
68 James 1993, p. 58.
69 James 1993, pp. 60, 63.
70 James 1993, pp. 64–5.
71 James 1993, p. 59.

There was a way out for Whitman, argued James: not ignoring, but recognising the growing polarisation of American society and placing himself on the side of labour. Capitalism compels wage workers to do what all social agents, according to its rules, must do: seek the highest possible price for the commodity they sell. Yet, workers are powerless if they confront capital as individuals. To pursue their individual self-interest, wage earners are compelled to sustain their demands *collectively*. For wage workers, solidarity is not an empty slogan, but the means necessary to further their individual interests. Thus, out of the egotistical logic of the market there emerges a social agent whose interests demand an opposite logic of unity, association and solidarity. That particular class bears the seeds of a radical reorganisation of all social relations. Integration of a fragmented social whole required identification, not with *all* classes or social agents, in the manner of Whitman's catalogues, but rather with the *particular* force capable of reshaping and remaking that whole. The road to fraternity ran through the interests, not of all classes as Whitman imagined, but of a *specific* class. Only an active working class mobilised for its self-emancipation could embody and deploy the type of solidarity and comradeship that Whitman valued and sought. Yet Whitman, the poet of the Union never became the poet of unions. He systematically evaded taking sides in the sharpened class struggles of the time. To side with labour was to be against capital and he wished to be with all. Attempting to be with all he found himself isolated: 'one who is one with everybody is one with nobody. Whitman', James explained, 'is alone, he has no sense of belonging to any section of society, no class to which he belongs, no class which he is against'.[72] Having closed off his way to the labour movement he condemned himself to his lengthy, yet inescapably incomplete catalogues.[73]

---

72 James 1993, p. 58. As M. Wynn Thomas would argue much later, he wished to 'manufacture a persona professedly independent of class position' (Thomas 2007, p. 76). Whitman recognises his passivity in 'I Sit and Look Out': 'I sit and look out upon all the sorrows of the world, and upon all oppression and shame, / .... / I observe the slights and degradation cast by arrogant persons upon laborers, the poor, and upon negroes, and the like; / All these – all the meanness and agony without end I sitting look out upon,/See, hear, and am silent' (p. 232).

73 As Eagleton puts it, the search for a more harmonious society requires, not the renunciation by the oppressed of their class interests, but the opposite: 'What Marx finds in the present is a deadly clash of interests. But whereas a utopian thinker might exhort us to rise above these conflicts in the name of love and fellowship, Marx himself takes a very different line. He does indeed believe in love and fellowship, but he does not think they will be achieved by some phoney harmony. The exploited and dispossessed are not to abandon their interests, which is just what their masters want them to do, but to press them all the way through. Only then might a society beyond self-interest finally emerge' (Eagleton

James based his argument on *Leaves of Grass*. He did not mention Horace Traubel's record of his conversations with Whitman between 1888 and 1892 (the first three volumes were available in 1950), many passages of which confirm his thesis. Traubel reports how Whitman affirmed: 'in the bottom meanings of *Leaves of Grass* – there is plenty of room for all. And I, for my part, not only include anarchists, socialists, whatnot, but Queens, aristocrats'.[74] Hoping to include 'anarchists' and 'aristocrats', as James was to argue, Whitman barred his way to any systematic consideration of what he called 'the present system'. Traubel, an admirer of Whitman and a socialist, reports how his interlocutor often came close to questioning significant aspects of capitalist society, yet refused to draw the logical conclusions of his own reflections. Whitman commented: 'Every day we read long accounts of people without work – thousands of them. There's something rotten in Denmark: what is it? ... There's something rotten in America too'.[75] To this, Traubel, referring to past conversations, answered: 'Walt, you don't want me to talk of the labor question: you've got it right there: you are talking of it yourself!'[76] Whitman responded in turn: 'There's certainly something crooked: some snarl: will we ever know what it is?' Traubel insisted 'I have told you what it is'. Whitman continues his evasive action: 'I know you have: but what is it?' Traubel comments on the exchange: 'That's the sort of evasive way he drops into when he's dodging discussion'.[77] At times Whitman denounced a central feature of US capitalism, but immediately retreated into passivity or the conviction that change would eventually come without the need for a movement to bring it about. 'Horace', he commented, 'we are all under the thumb of the millionaires: ours is a millionaire government'.[78] But then he adds: 'the millionaires must have their innings, too: that is a phase we are going through – can't skip'.[79] Traubel asked if he meant that millionaires would not always rule, to which Whitman answered: 'The people, who are now

---

2011, p. 78). Whitman's vision of union, compaction, adhesiveness, companionship tended toward the false harmony described by Eagleton and favoured the nullification by the oppressed of their interests, 'which is just what their masters want them to do'. What starts as a protest against capitalism concludes as a reconciliation with it.

74   Traubel 1964, p. 227.
75   Traubel 1953, p. 393. Whitman similarly commented: 'What you told me of these banks, these vast structures, these movings of money in great masses, implies a menace with which we may have serious trouble later on – may produce crises in which our democracy itself will treble in the balance'. Traubel 1953, p. 470.
76   Traubel 1953, p. 393.
77   Traubel 1953, p. 393.
78   Traubel 1953, p. 231.
79   Traubel 1953, p. 231.

asleep, will yet wake up'.⁸⁰ Traubel complained that when others said as much Whitman dismissed them as 'doctrinaires and partisans'.⁸¹ Whitman admitted that he was inconsistent, but went no further.

In another exchange Whitman praised Andrew Carnegie for making the largest contribution to a fund in his honour. Traubel pointed out that Carnegie 'has more money than all the rest put together'. Whitman reportedly responded: 'Damn your logical brain'.⁸² Traubel added: 'I don't think his generosity ... makes up for his greed as towards the people from whom he derives all his money'. This seemed to be a consideration that Whitman preferred to avoid: 'There's your logical faculty buzzing again: you're unbearable when you get going on that tack'. But he added: 'Though when you put it that way Horace, I acknowledge that you shake me a little'.⁸³

Over and over Whitman criticised an aspect of the present, and then attempted to convince himself that all was right after all: 'We seem to have entered an age, an atmosphere, of trusts, banks, stocks, capital – overwhelming mass of it – but I am not clear what it all means: not at all clear'.⁸⁴ He added: 'it baffles me to declare what it all means'.⁸⁵ Then he adds: 'and yet it is all right: we must believe it is all right'.⁸⁶ He 'wishes well to all reformers'⁸⁷ such as Henry George, but would join no movement to transform the 'present system': 'I know of no school in this, our day, – not Gladstone's, Henry George's, any other, – who, offers anything adequate – anything that would land us at the goal, any more than the present system'.⁸⁸ The world, he argued, must be accepted 'as it is'. To Traubel's argument that his support for land distribution was similar to George's programme, he responded: 'No – no – no Horace! I am not to be entrapped ... I am a great contender for the world as it is – the ill along with the good'.⁸⁹ Against anarchist and socialists, he insisted that 'the world anyhow is as good as it can be'.⁹⁰

---

80   Traubel 1953, p. 231.
81   Traubel 1953, p. 231.
82   Traubel 1953, p. 153.
83   Traubel 1953, p. 154.
84   Traubel 1953, p. 470.
85   Traubel 1953, p. 470.
86   Traubel 1953, p. 470. As Arvin pointed out in 1938, like the more conservative Hegelians, Whitman tended 'to believe that the real is in fact the rational'. Arvin 1938, pp. 90–1.
87   Traubel 1964, p. 509.
88   Traubel 1964, p. 509.
89   Traubel 1964, p. 276.
90   Traubel 1964, pp. 22–3. In another exchange, Traubel attempts to move Whitman toward the notion of collective property. Whitman acquiesces, but seems to do so as an attempt to appease his interlocutor. Traubel describes the exchange, opened by Whitman: '"I look

Not wishing to take sides with one class against another, Whitman, argued James, 'tried to prove that, contrary to Europe, in America all men were equal, that all men were knitted together by a common bond of Democracy ... He developed special poetical methods of his own to overcome the potent fact that men were not equal, and as time went on, he adopted every shibboleth of the time to maintain ... his fantastic thesis'.[91] James thus anticipated Doris Sommer's argument that, for Whitman, class division was 'unspeakable' and that his attempt to erase it poetically made his work politically 'available to everyone, left and right'.[92]

Whitman's song of democracy and of the individual, his praise of the body, argued James, was compatible with the official Cold War discourse of the American ruling sectors and with the seductions of capitalist advertising. 'Today in the "cold war"', James argued, 'the picture of America which is being presented to the world by the rulers of America is Whitman's picture. Free individuals, free enterprise, science, industry, Democracy – that is the Voice of America'.[93] Similarly, he added, 'The very attempt to represent these as ideals for the whole world is no more than an extension of Whitman's Salut au Monde and Passage to India. His "body beautiful" and "body electric" ... are the reservoir from which advertisers of foods, toothpaste, vitamins, deodorants draw an unending

---

forward to a world of small owners." I put in: "Or maybe no owners at all". He asked: "What do you mean by that? ... Do you mean ... owning things in common?" I nodded ... He said: "I don't know: I haven't thought it out: it *sounds* best: could it be best? could it be made to work?"' To Traubel's demand of his opinion Whitman responds: '"You've got me on the witness stand: you're like a lawyer." ... Then he acquiesced: "I have to believe it: if I don't believe that I couldn't believe anything."' Traubel 1914, p. 315.

91 James 1993, p. 56. Arvin had already pointed out how Whitman proved incapable of writing poems about mill workers, sweated labour, strikes and lock-outs since they would puncture his desired vision of a socially harmonious America. Arvin 1938, p. 245.

92 Sommer 1999, pp. 48, 37, 38. Indeed, he anticipated what the more prescient students of Whitman's work were to argue in later years. M. Wynn Thomas has argued that Whitman wished to 'manufacture a persona professedly independent of class position'. He hoped to poetically dissolve 'social conflict' and the difference between workers and owners. M. Wynn Thomas, 'United States and States United', p. 76. According to Haddox, Whitman's 'refusal to recognize intractable conflicts manifests itself in' his 'lists and catalogues, in which a potentially endless proliferation of objects nevertheless coheres into a single visionary whole' (Haddox 2004, p. 2). We feel that this overstates the 'coherence' attained by Whitman's vision. Lawson points out that Whitman invented a poetic language adequate to his shifting space between classes. But he adds: 'The invention comes at a high price, however – the price of social and political isolation'. Lawson, 2006, p. 104. All of these insights already appear in James's *Notes* drafted in 1950.

93 James 1993, p. 60.

source of inspirations by which to cheat and corrupt the American people'.[94] James would have not been surprised by the 2009 commercials for Levis jeans, prepared by the Wieden+Kennedy advertising agency, which centrally incorporated portions of Whitman's poems 'Pioneers! O Pioneers!' and 'America'.

Referring to *Democratic Vistas*, Scott Henkel has recently lamented how '[i]n our historical moment ... Whitman's essay has been appropriated by writers like George Will to put a bright façade on the atrocity of the current Iraq occupation'.[95] Thomas F. Haddox has similarly argued that the fact that 'conservative commentator David Brooks has recently published a defense of *Democratic Vistas*, in which he holds up Whitman's jeremiad as a riposte to snobbish critics who love to "say something stupid about America", only confirms how easily the text can be made to serve a complacency that refuses to be unduly troubled by even the most blatant departures from a democratic ideal'.[96] C.L.R. James would have found these appreciations neither strange nor surprising. He could justifiably take them as confirmations of a diagnosis he had formulated more than sixty-five years ago.

Nor would James have been surprised by the tone and content of Harold Bloom's 2005 introduction to *Leaves of Grass*. There Bloom describes *Leaves of Grass* as 'the American Torah',[97] as 'the secular Scripture of the United States of America'.[98] Whitman is 'the American Christ',[99] and the critic seeks 'his Blessing'.[100] American political possibilities are confined within the limits set by Whitman: 'If we still have democratic vistas, they are those he sketched in his 1871 prose work of that title'.[101] This uncritical celebration of Whitman turns into an affirmation of American dominance beyond its frontiers. Bloom proclaims that Whitman 'is the greatest artist this nation has brought forth, but such judgment needs to be taken further. No comparable figure in the arts has emerged from the last four centuries in the Americas: North, Central, South, or the Caribbean'.[102] Whitman, author of the 'secular scripture of the United States' is the 'greatest writer engendered by the New World, whether in Amer-

---

94 James 1993, p. 60.
95 Henkel 2010, p. 102. See George Will, 'Iraqi Democratic Vistas'. 7 September 2003. http://townhall.com/columnists/GeorgeWill/2003/09/07/iraqi_democratic_vistas.
96 Haddox 2004, p. 16.
97 Bloom 2005, p. xxxiv.
98 Bloom 2005, p. vii.
99 Bloom 2005, p. xxxiii.
100 Bloom 2005, pp. xxi, xxvii.
101 Bloom 2005, p. xxxiii. For a discussion of why *Democratic Vistas* does not suffice for a democratic project see Henkel 2010, pp. 101–26.
102 Bloom 2005 p. xi.

ican English, Spanish, Portuguese, or French'.[103] Literature becomes global or at least continental competition in which the US entry emerges triumphant. It is a sad outcome to see Whitman become the means for such nationalist boasting and imperial bluster.[104] But James would have argued that this is not the case of a dominant culture illegitimately appropriating the work of an artist for its own hegemonic purposes: Whitman's own attempt to be with all, his refusal to take sides in the class struggle, had invited such an appropriation of his work.

This is a large part of Whitman's tragedy: generously trying to be with all, he refused to take tides, considering it a limitation, and thus ended up isolated, ineffectual and, it could be argued, betraying himself. Wishing to be with both slave and master, as we saw above, wishing to prevent national division, he rejected abolitionism, thus compromising with slavery (whose abolition he was willing to postpone indefinitely), which he despised. Desiring to reconcile North and South, Union and Confederacy after the war, he rejected Reconstruction, thus betraying the radical democracy he professed (although here the racism imbibed from his milieu also had a role). Aspiring to embrace both labour and its employers, he accommodated to the rule of capital, while resenting many of its consequences. Ed Folsom argues that Whitman's desire, present in his earliest notebooks, to be with slave and slave owner, indicated that the poet had learned to 'absorb dichotomies'.[105] But his admirable desire for inclusivity, James argued in 1950, blinded him to the fact that there are dichotomies that need to be abolished, and can only be abolished by taking sides: with the slave against the slave owner, with labour against capital. Such is the taking of sides that also liberates us from isolation and opens the path to a truly inclusive society. There can be no poetic escape from this choice, a futile enterprise in which, James argued, Whitman lost his way.

David S. Reynolds's exhaustive exploration of Whitman's relation with his cultural context would also confirm James's general appreciation. As he grew older Whitman was increasingly recognised as a significant figure, a process that would seemingly correspond to his desire to be 'absorbed' by his coun-

---

103 Bloom 2005, p. xvi.
104 Harold Bloom has complained that Whitman's 'political involvements are much overemphasized at our bad moment in criticism, when everything has been politicized'. Bloom 1994, p. 492. To 'politicize' the humanities is to recognise that they are not a disinterested field above class and social struggles. It is to see that they too are the site of the affirmation of, and resistance to, forms of domination and oppression. To see this is to understand that we cannot escape politics: our choice is not whether to read politically but rather *which* politics we embrace. The call for an apolitical reading, such as Bloom's, is itself a political position.
105 Folsom 2014, p. 9.

try: 'But had America absorbed him?', asks Reynolds. 'Fancy fetes', he responds, 'the Wall Whitman cigar, and money from Andrew Carnegie were hardly what he had in mind when he had envisaged being absorbed by his country'.[106] Unknowingly echoing an idea James had suggested in 1950, Reynolds adds that Whitman's attitude to his own commodification was ambiguous: 'Walt Whitman as capitalist commodity? The poet often put up lip-service resistance to his own commodification. But he let it happen, in some cases with enthusiasm'.[107]

Yet, as Doris Sommer argues, and James would have agreed, Whitman was not only available for the right. According to James, a radical deepening of democracy in the United States, based on an insurgent labour movement, such as he hoped to see in the near future, could not afford to ignore Whitman's poetic revolution. In fact, despite his critical distance, there is much in James's *Notes* that is closer to Whitman's approach than he admitted. Besides the 'sense of expansion' afforded by the display of modern productive forces over a vast continent, James shared with Whitman an admiration for American technical ingenuity; an appreciation for the American notion of individual self-development and the active, self-directed pursuit of happiness; a suspicion of those claiming to speak for the people (as in Whitman's suspicion of elected officials and his vision of 'Rulers strictly' drawn from 'the masses', or, more specifically, the mass of 'qualified mechanics');[108] a respect for mass popular culture and the vision of a future integration of art and politics; trust in the transformative potential of such an integration (James's appreciation of the yet unused potential of the modern mass media and Whitman's notion that without 'that ultimate vivification – which the poet or other artists alone can give – reality would seem incomplete');[109] and a faith in the ultimately demo-

---

106   Reynolds 1996, p. 5.
107   Reynolds 1996, p. 546. Reynolds points out that Whitman became 'financially and ideologically entangled with capitalists' (p. 546). The point was made by Arvin in 1938. It is interesting that James makes almost no reference to Arvin's study, an attempt to elaborate a Marxist reading of Whitman. James's reticence was perhaps linked to the fact that Arvin was at the time connected to the Communist Party, a current of socialism quite different from his.
108   'Rulers Strictly Out of the Masses', p. 1070. For a discussion of the notion of grassroots democracy in *Democratic Vistas*, see Henkel 2010.
109   'A Backward Glance o'er Travel'd Roads', p. 659. Referring to the American people, Whitman predicted in 'By Blue Ontario's Shore' that in the future 'Their Presidents shall not be their common referee so much as their poets shall'. James commented that 'The ancient Greeks ... looked upon their great writers as second to none in the state'. James 2001, p. 115. C.L.R. James quotes a passage by Auden comparing antiquity with the present regarding the problem of specialisation: 'Yes I can see all the works of a great civilization; but why

cratic and egalitarian possibilities inherent in mass production. Furthermore, some of Whitman's poems function at several levels: as love poems, as a vindication of same-sex love, and as a vision of comradeship as a connection beyond the rules of the market. Running ahead of his time, yet also harking back to Whitman, James suggested the need to explore the search for intimate contact between men, always haunted by the fear of proscribed homosexuality, as part of a consideration of the tensions of American society, and, in particular the need to study 'what has been called "comradeship" among the men' in the army during both world wars.[110]

For James, Whitman had expressed the vitality of American individualism and a frustrated yearning for community. Unwilling to acknowledge the growing polarisation of American society, Whitman's writing had become an evasion of the contradictions emerging around it, with dire political and poetical consequences. Herman Melville, on the other hand, according to James, had looked more deeply into the tensions building up within the United States: peering beyond his time, he had prefigured the rise of modern totalitarianism. James read Melville as a partial anticipation of his own analysis of mid-twentieth-century world politics as a three-way battle between capital, labour, and the bureaucratic-authoritarian response to the crisis of capitalism.[111]

The key to James's interpretation was his understanding of Captain Ahab's character in *Moby Dick*, and his relation to both the capitalist owners of the *Pequod* and its crew. Ahab was as contemptuous of the commercial interests, profits and property rights of the owners of the *Pequod* as of the crew he cajoled or manipulated into the pursuit of the white whale.[112] Ahab, James points out, 'consigns the rights of owners to perdition', he is 'utterly contemptuous' of their property and their profits.[113] Melville, argued James, thus brilliantly anticipated how the crisis of capitalism would generate an anti-capitalist yet undemocratic and totalitarian response. The pursuit of the white whale, at the expense of *both* crew and capitalists was a prefiguration of the fascist pursuit of the 'master race' and of the Stalinist cult of the 'master plan'. Ahab was an exploration of how, through the emergence of new social types, 'the society of free individual-

---

I cannot meet any civilized persons? I only encounter specialists, artists who know nothing of science, scientists who know nothing of art, philosophers who have no interest in God, priests who are unconcerned with politics, politicians who know only other politicians' (James 1993, p. 153). This cannot but remind us of Whitman's concern for the lack of well-rounded 'Personalities' in the midst of material progress.

110   James 1993, p. 224.
111   For further debates around James's work on Melville see Cain 1995; Pease 2000; Keith 2009.
112   James 2001, pp. 5, 6, 88.
113   James 2001, pp. 6, 88.

ism would give birth to totalitarianism'.[114] Ahab was a brilliant anticipation of the 'totalitarian type', of the 'modern totalitarian dictator' that would step into world politics with the shock of the world war, the exhaustion of the Russian Revolution and the general crisis of capitalism.[115] He embodied the reaction of managers, supervisors, administrators, labour bureaucrats, technicians and intellectuals to that crisis. Faced with a 'violent catastrophe that ruins them and convinces them that the life they have been living is intolerable', argued James, they 'are going to seek a new theory of society and a program of action, and on the basis of this theory and this program, they are going to act. This is what happens to Ahab when a whale bites off his leg'.[116]

Yet, while Melville understood and portrayed how Ahab was leading the *Pequod* to destruction, he had little faith in the crew, as a collective agent capable of resisting his iron will and his manipulative skills. His topic was not only how 'the society of free individualism would give birth to totalitarianism',[117] but also how it would 'be unable to defend itself against it'.[118] Regarding this, Melville also offered, argued James, an anticipated study of the 'modern young intellectual'. Ishmael, his narrator, 'wavers constantly between totalitarianism and the crew'.[119] Like many intellectuals sympathetic to labour and attracted to the orbit of the Communist parties, Ishmael harboured a sincere sympathy for the crew but had little trust in it. He feared Ahab, but was fascinated by him.[120] Ishmael's dilemma thus anticipated the choice facing contemporary intellectuals between the worship of the fascist, Stalinist or even welfare state or leader, on the one hand, and seeking a connection with the insurgent forces from below visible in the more radical moments of the labour movement in the United States and other countries, on the other.[121]

For James, nineteenth-century America had produced a brilliant example of such a connection: not Whitman's celebration of the self and his frustrated yearning for community, nor Melville's pessimism, despite its merits, regarding the authoritarian currents within American society, but Wendell Phillips's radical abolitionism.[122] Phillips and his co-thinkers, through their identification

---

114 James 2001, p. 54.
115 James 2001, pp. 9, 15; James 1993, p. 76.
116 James 2001, p. 11.
117 James 2001, p. 54.
118 James 2001, p. 54.
119 James 2001, p. 40.
120 James 2001, p. 42.
121 James 2001, p. 42.
122 Richard Hofstadter, writing in 1948, commented that 'the historical reputation of Wendell Phillips stands very low'. Hofstadter disagreed and so did James. Hofstadter 1948.

with slave resistance and through their collaboration with free blacks, former slaves and the Underground Railroad were able to find 'what both Whitman and Melville had failed to find'.[123] They were able to become the 'expression of precise social forces'[124] struggling for their own emancipation. Slave revolts, the Underground Railroads (networks supporting and aiding runaway slaves), the civil war in Kansas, the raid at Harper's Ferry, the formation of the Republican Party had been the analogues in the nineteenth century of the rise of the C.I.O. in the twentieth. Within that current, Phillips had developed the most consistent perspective pushing for a revolutionary war to end slavery and to destroy the social order based on it. In that context he showed 'the same breadth of view, the revolutionary conception of democracy, and political ruthlessness which are associated with what is loosely called Bolshevism'.[125] It was, James wrote, 'perhaps the highest peak reached by the United States intellectuals in the foreshadowing of the future'.[126] Here James crossed paths with José Martí: the Cuban writer and revolutionary, as we saw above, had drawn a similarly admiring portrait of Phillips, both as an abolitionist and as a critic of the reduction of American culture to market values and monetary ambitions.[127]

James summarised his vision of Whitman, Melville and Phillips and the radical abolitionists: '(1) Whitman: a singer of loneliness and Democracy with a capital D. (2) Melville: prophet of destruction. (3) Abolitionism: advocates of mass revolution'.[128]

If Melville had anticipated the threat of the totalitarian dictator, the radical abolitionists had prefigured the rise of modern socialism from below.[129]

James wrote this at a time when he believed 'The signs of an accumulating social explosion are everywhere'.[130] A new type of abolitionism was in the making: 'the great masses become abolitionist now; themselves to wipe away the conditions of their own slavery. These cannot be abolished by anybody else'.[131] James's expectations, formulated in the aftermath of the great strike-wave of 1946–7 and at a time when the future evolution of the C.I.O. still seemed undecided, were not unfounded. But, as in the case of other revolutionaries who nurtured similar hopes, they were to be frustrated: US capitalism was now

---

123 James 1993, p. 87.
124 James 1993, p. 85.
125 James 1993, pp. 96, 226.
126 James 1993, p. 92.
127 Martí [1884a]; 'Wendell Phillips', OC, XIII, pp. 55–70.
128 James 1993, pp. 97–8.
129 James 1993, p. 87.
130 James 1993, p. 274.
131 James 1993, p. 276.

poised for its post-war expansion, during which an increasingly bureaucratised labour movement would be neutralised within the limits of the routine contract negotiation of wages and other benefits. This was the domestication of the C.I.O. into a mere collective bargaining agent that James had railed against through his contrast of Walter Reuther and John L. Lewis. But the course of American labour in the 1950s and 1960s was to follow the path of Reuther's U.A.W. and not of the more militant moments of Lewis's U.M.W., or, to be fair, of the early years of the U.A.W. itself.[132] James himself was in 1950 near the end of his fifteen year sojourn in the United States. By the time he wrote his essay on Melville he was confined in Ellis Island, waiting for the result of his appeal of a deportation order. Indeed, *Mariners*, which he mailed to all the members of the US Senate, was part of his plea against that order. This fact evidently, and understandably, had an impact on the elaboration of the text, and, above all, on its 'Postscript', which has provoked some bitter exchanges.

According to Paul Buhle, in the 'Postcript' James came close to sliding into the rhetoric of plain anti-communism and into less than admirable special pleading of his case in the context of a generalised repression of all the left. Donald E. Pease has objected, arguing that James's opposition to Stalinism should not be confused with any complicity with Cold War anti-communism. Yet there are some undeniable and troubling ambiguities in the 'Postscript'.

The problems, we argue, stem from two factors: a mechanical application by James of his theory of the nature of Stalinism as expression of a new bureaucratic class and the attempt to accomplish two divergent, political and legal, objectives with the same text. In the 'Postscript' James extends the discussion of *Moby Dick* as an anticipation of the totalitarian-bureaucratic, Fascist or Stalinist, threat, through a chronicle of his experience in Ellis Island. The axis of the story is his relationship with a fellow prisoner, referred to as M, a member of the Communist Party. James relates how M consistently acted 'with the deepest conviction as the defender ... of the people on Ellis Island against the cruelties and inhumanities of the administration'.[133] M looked after the sick, the elderly, the young, and people with mental disabilities.[134] In all cases he was a 'defender of elementary human decency'.[135] As a result of this, he developed an 'astonishing influence' over his fellow prisoners.[136] M was not the only member

---

132 For a discussion of the evolution of the US labour movement in this period see Davis 1986; Moody 1988.
133 James 2001, pp. 127–8.
134 James 2001, pp. 128–30.
135 James 2001, p. 132.
136 James 2001, p. 150.

of the Communist Party awaiting deportation. James wrote that their attitude toward him was 'not only correct, but genuinely friendly'.[137] They warned him of possible dangers and even smuggled in food for him, when his health began to deteriorate.[138] After this James announces his conclusion: 'You need a long and well-based experience of Communism and Communists to know that M in reality was a man as mad as Ahab ... that if it suited his purpose ... he would subject both officers and the men he championed to a tyranny worse than anything they could conceive of'.[139] Referring to M's behavior, James affirms: 'I, who have spent many years studying Communism, knew very well what it symbolized'.[140] Earlier in the text, James had pointed out that in Ellis Island he had learned much about 'world communism' and 'what modern civilization is up against'.[141]

James provides no evidence for the notion that M is 'a man as mad as Ahab', besides the fact that he belonged to the Communist Party. This, as indicated, is an extremely mechanical application of James's theory of the Soviet state and of bureaucratic rule, whatever one may think of that theory as such. James's text implicitly follows this logic: 1) the Soviet state is the vehicle of a new form of class domination (James would soon redefine this as a new form of capitalist domination); 2) thus, *all* Communist parties, around the world are also the vehicles of that form of class domination; 3) thus, all *individual* members and militants of those parties, such as M, are bearers and representatives of bureaucratic domination. Leaving aside the question of whether the Soviet state represented a new form of class rule, accepting this thesis need not lead to conclusions 2 or 3. Yet only following the mechanical reasoning summarised above could one conclude, on the basis of the evidence provided by James (membership in the Communist party) that M's 'human decency' hid a man 'as mad as Ahab'.

In his response to Buhle, Donald E. Pease has argued that '*Pace* Buhle, James's insistence on the distinction between his politics and M's has not disallowed him solidarity with M's opposition to capitalism'.[142] But a close reading of James's text demonstrates that this is not the case. James considers M a man as 'mad as Ahab'. For James, the Communist party is *not* a bureaucratic formation *within* the labour movement. For him, M is *not* a fellow if misguided social-

---

137 James 2001, p. 133.
138 James 2001, pp. 133, 136.
139 James 2001, p. 132.
140 James 2001, p. 150.
141 James 2001, p. 128.
142 Pease 2001, p. xxv.

ist, but the representative of an opposing social class: there is a class divide between him and M. For James, as he explained in his *Notes*, Communists 'are fully conscious men of the centralized bureaucratized totalitarian solution to the fundamental problems of the day'.[143] As Pease correctly argues, James's 'insistence on the distinction between his politics and M's' may not, and did not, annul James's anti-capitalism. But contrary to Pease's argument, James harboured no solidarity with M, since he considered his anti-capitalism to be fundamentally different from his own: a totalitarian, bureaucratic project that was equally anti-capitalist and anti-labour, not unlike the mad Ahab stood against the owners of the *Pequod* and its crew.

The position suggested by Pease (independent socialist position and differentiation from M's Stalinist policies, yet willingness to stand together against capitalist repression) describes, not James's position in the 'Postscript', but the position of the 'orthodox' Trotskyist current from which he had detached himself and which the students of his work generally hold in low regard. For the SWP, for example, the Soviet bureaucracy was not a new dominant class; the Communist party of the United States and the parties in other countries were not the representatives, or a strand, of a nascent bureaucratic class. They were a current (along with other trade union and political bureaucracies) within the labour movement. Its individual members could range from vicious party hacks to sincere activists attracted, for example, by the prestige of the Russian revolution. Such was the 'orthodox' Trotskyist position, and such, as indicated, was *not* James position in 1950–2.

If James reduction of M to a man 'as mad as Ahab' is unconvincing, there is a further, more troubling, aspect of his 'Postscript'. The text was written while James was fighting deportation. Through his chronicle of Ellis Island, James seemed to be arguing that he should not be deported since he, as his attitude toward M and the Communists demonstrated, was frankly, consciously and militantly anti-totalitarian. It is hard to believe that James thought that such an affirmation of anti-totalitarianism and anti-Stalinism would make his anti-capitalism and socialism somehow palatable to US immigration officials, judges or members of Congress. Yet one cannot avoid the conclusion that this was part of the logic behind the 'Postscript'. James, to put it bluntly, was *not* being dishonest or unprincipled, but he *was* attempting to accomplish two very different tasks with the same text, and the results were less than brilliant.

On the one hand, he addressed his American readers, inviting them to fight against the totalitarian threat (prefigured in the character of Ahab) through a

---

143 James 1993, p. 249.

struggle against capitalism and for a democratic socialism. On the other, he addressed US officials and legislators (he mailed his text to all members of the US Senate, as indicated), alerting them that he was an opponent of totalitarianism, wise to the tricks of even the more attractive Communists, such as M. He similarly explained that 'I prefer to see B gangster pictures than the latest examples of cinema art'[144] and he added: 'I know the petty imitators of things European in literature and politics, as far removed from the lives of people of the United States as the Left Bank in Paris. I have seen and have heard ... American intellectuals apologizing for their "Coca-cola civilization". Though their ancestry may go back for three hundred years, they are greater enemies of the American people than I am'.[145] Such statements served a similar, somewhat contradictory, double function. They partook of his appreciation for what he took to be the anti-capitalist dimension of mass commercial culture (film, radio, detective fiction, comics, and television) and conveyed his critique of the leftist intellectuals that disdained it while combining their elitism with support of the Soviet bureaucracy or its US representatives. At the same time, they attempted to demonstrate that he was, after all, a good, movie-going, Coca Cola-drinking American, immune to Parisian fashions.

James sought to, but in the end he could not have it both ways: turning anti-totalitarianism and American-ness into a plea against deportation, as he attempted to do, would have required a clear renunciation of his socialist perspective (which he did not formulate), while an affirmation of socialism (to which he remained faithful) made any plea against deportation on the grounds of anti-totalitarianism or American-ness disingenuous. The message was garbled. It could only confuse many fellow radicals (and future readers), while not deceiving his enemies: an object of confusion and bitter exchange even among his admirers, the 'Postcript' did little to prevent his deportation in 1953.

James had much to say regarding what he saw as the limits of Whitman's social and artistic vision. Yet he did not deny his achievement. According to him: 'The genuine passion of the isolated Whitman to get into contact with his fellow-men ... produced another great stage in the development of the poetic language'.[146] Whitman's verse, he argued, 'can express, as he expressed, the most intimate personal feelings', but it could also be 'a chant, a chant to

---

144 James 2001, p. 159.
145 James 2001, p. 159.
146 James 1993, p. 66.

be sung by millions of men'. It could be both 'subtle and intricate beyond the elaborate verse-forms that preceded it' and a 'popular' means of expression. James predicted that 'If some day all men will be educated and feel the need of expression in verse, some such form as Whitman used will be the medium'.[147]

Recent considerations on James and Whitman by Chistopher Freeburg and Ivy G. Wilson merit some commentary. Freeburg argues that 'C.L.R. James found himself possessed by Whitman's "craving to mingle with all his fellow men", his rejection of standardized poetic forms, and his refusal to put the modern world in individual terms'. He similarly writes of 'James's adoration of Whitman's democratic idealism' and of his praise 'for Whitman's verse'. Freeburg makes these comments while contrasting James with other authors that criticised the poet for not rejecting racism.[148] But this amounts to a misrepresentation of James's perspective. Terms such as 'possessed', 'adoration' and even 'praise', if isolated from other aspects of James's assessment, give the impression that he was an uncritically enthusiastic reader of Whitman. In fact, as we have seen, James was deeply critical of Whitman's poetic project, which he certainly considered a political failure, open to its utilisation by the apologists of capitalism and of US imperialism at a later stage.

Ivy G. Wilson offers a longer but rather baffling commentary on James's approach to Whitman. According to Wilson: 'In his phase as a Marxist-Leninist, James ... shies away from deep reflections of race in "Notes on American Civilization"'.[149] This statement suggests that Marxism excludes an interest on race or racism, an untenable notion methodologically, since nothing in the theory provides for such an exclusion, or historically, given the many Marxists, or authors influenced by Marxism, that have addressed these issues. It also ignores the fact that James wrote abundantly on race and racism precisely as a Marxist: his classic *The Black Jacobins* and his many articles on black struggles in the United States in the 1930s and 1940s were all Marxist texts.[150] His conversations with Trotsky in 1939 attest to the interest of these two Marxists on the question of race.[151] If anything, James's career is testimony to the combination of Marxism with an interest in race, racism and anti-racism. Plus, it should be

---

147 James 1993, pp. 66–7.
148 Freeburg 2014, pp. 82–3.
149 Wilson 2014b, p. 105.
150 James 1996.
151 Trotsky 1994. A co-thinker of Trotsky and James at the time, Max Shachtman, also wrote a Marxist exploration of the race question in the United States. See Shachtman 2003.

pointed out that the *Notes* include a ten-page section entitled 'The Negroes in the United States': if this issue was not James's main focus in this text, neither was it entirely absent.[152]

Wilson argues that instead of questions of race, James was interested in the relationship between 'individualism' and 'collectivism'. In his reading, that polarity determined the terms of James's approach to Whitman and Melville. According to Wilson, James was interested in 'the particular US dialectic of individualism and collectivism that masked itself under the banner of liberal democracy'.[153] He similarly states that for James, Whitman 'prefigured much of the crisis of modern world-systems where polities were trying to negotiate the relationship between individualism and collectivism, or what Whitman called "en masse"'.[154] But in this discussion the nature of what Wilson calls the 'dialectic of individualism and collectivism' is never explained. Is collectivism crushing the individual? Is the individual seeking a collective connection? From this all too abstract perspective, Wilson concludes that James's main objection to Whitman was his failure to affirm true individuality. James, he argues, felt that when 'blacks or anyone else, for the most part, are listed in *Leaves of Grass*, they are virtually undistinguishable from one another'.[155] James, Wilson explains, compared this to Melville: 'representations of individualism' in *Moby Dick*, as opposed to *Leaves of Grass*, are 'authentic and true in so far as they depict the *Pequod*'s crew as characters possessed of body and soul'. By way of contrast, in *Leaves of Grass*, 'individualism falls flat' as the poet relies on 'vapid catalogs' and a list of 'types often bereft of interiority'.[156] But, as we have seen, for James the failure of Whitman did not reside in his failure to affirm individuality but rather in his incapacity to establish the connection he yearned for with others and his lack of understanding that such a connection required, not avoiding, but taking sides in the class struggles of his time.

According to Wilson, James saw Whitman as trying to 'reconcile a faith in individualism while maintaining a commitment to the masses'.[157] It would seem that the masses threatened to overwhelm his individuality, which the poet tried to rescue without breaking with the former. We have argued that, for James, Whitman's problem was the opposite: that of an individual seeking connection with the masses, and failing. The catalogues were a failure not due

---

152 James 1993, pp. 200–11.
153 Wilson 2014b, p. 105.
154 Wilson 2014a, p. xii.
155 Wilson, 2014b, p. 119.
156 Wilson, 2014b, p. 119.
157 Wilson 2014b, p. 119.

to their lack of individuality, but to their incapacity to connect: the list, no matter how long and inclusive, could not alter the separation between the poet and the items listed.

Regarding James's reading of Melville, Wilson correctly argues that 'James is able to see that individualism exponentially centralized will ... lead to the kind of dictatorship and totalitarianism embodied by Ahab'.[158] Yet, it must be said that for James the totalitarianism prefigured by Ahab is not the result of the centralisation of individualism, but rather of the response of certain social classes and groups to the crisis of capitalism, the catastrophes of war and the contradictions of revolutions in situations of scarcity and isolation. But in Wilson's discussion of James, capitalism, capitalist organisation of production, its limits on human potentialities, the struggle between capital and labour, the different response to capitalist crisis by middle-class sectors, and thus fascism and Stalinism, evaporate into an abstract dialectic of individualism and collectivism, which does not do justice to the nuances of James's overall analysis and leads to a misreading of his critique of Whitman: James's critique of Whitman's incapacity to break out of his isolation becomes a rejection of his failure to affirm the individual.

While James wrote his *Notes* in Manhattan in or around 1950, Pedro Mir, a Dominican poet living in Cuba to escape the reach of the Trujillo dictatorship, was at work on a long poem. It was eventually published under the title *Countersong to Walt Whitman (Contracanto a Walt Whitman)* in 1952, the year before James published his work on Melville. James had predicted that in the future Whitman's verse would be mined for the means to express 'the most intimate personal feelings' and the aspiration for social change involving 'millions of men'.[159] As if responding to James's call, Mir appropriated some aspects of Whitman's verse, reconstructed it, and placed it at the service of a frankly anti-capitalist and anti-imperialist perspective that was neither nationalist nor simply anti-American.

---

158 Wilson 2014b, p. 119.
159 James 1993, pp. 66–7.

CHAPTER 11

'Now Has Come the Hour of the Countersong': Pedro Mir and Walt Whitman

A discussion of Pedro Mir's *Countersong to Walt Whitman* is a fitting conclusion to this volume. The poem, within a broad Marxist framework, broaches issues posed by Martí and James: the contradictions of American civilisation, the place of Whitman's work within them, the possible solution to the former and Whitman's potential role in it.

Pedro Mir was born in San Pedro de Macorís in the Dominican Republic in 1913. His father, a technician in a sugar-mill, was Cuban. His mother was Puerto Rican. In the late 1920s Mir was sent to Santo Domingo, capital of the republic, to pursue his education. Mir began writing, although not publishing, poems in the early 1930s. In 1937, well-known intellectual (and future president) Juan Bosch published some of his poems along with a praiseful introduction. Mir graduated from law-school in 1941. During the Second World War he moved in circles discreetly opposed to the Trujillo dictatorship. Under the impact of the civil war in Spain, the arrival in Santo Domingo of Spanish republican refugees, and the prestige gained by Communist parties in the struggle against fascism, Mir moved to the left. If not a member, he was certainly close to the pro-Moscow Communist left, a current quite different from James's anti-Stalinist Marxism. In 1947 Mir moved to Cuba where he renewed his contact with fellow exile Juan Bosch, who helped him publish his first major poem, 'Hay un país en el mundo', in 1949. Soon after this Mir began working on a new long poem, *Countersong to Walt Whitman*. Seeking a publisher he went to Mexico and then to Guatemala, at the time under Jacobo Arbenz's government and, along with Bolivia, one of the focal points of the Latin American left, where his poem was published in 1952. Mir participated in writers' congresses in Austria and Rumania in the early 1950s, activities which confirm his contact with the Communist movement at the time. Yet it would be a mistake to reduce his work to Stalinist pamphleteering.[1]

---

[1] Mir was by no means the only Latin American author to grapple with Whitman. Besides Martí, Nicaraguan Rubén Darío, Argentinean Jorge Luis Borges and Chilean Pablo Neruda, to mention three stellar figures, wrote texts inspired by Whitman. See Alegría 1954 and Magaril 2010. Also Raab 2001 and Bloom 1994, pp. 463–92.

Mir is rarely mentioned in discussions of Whitman's impact outside the United States and is never discussed at length.[2] Here we explore six aspects of Mir's *Countersong*. His poem is, among other things:

1. A portrait of capitalism as both destructive and liberating, and a vision of its future transcendence by the very same forces created by it.
2. A vision of the course of American civilisation, of some of its contradictions and tensions, from the colonial era to the Cold War.
3. A consideration of the role and place of Whitman in US history and the attitude of a future revolutionary transformation toward him.
4. An affirmation of Caribbean and Latin American self-determination against US imperial power.
5. A deconstruction of the simplistic opposition of Latin America and the United States, revealing the internal tensions within each and the potential solidarities across their borders.
6. An appropriation and transformation of Whitman's poetic language and the tone of 'Song of Myself', an homage which was nevertheless not a servile imitation.

Countersong has 18 sections: an introduction in which the poet describes himself and proclaims his intention of telling us who Walt Whitman is (an objective restated in Section 3) is followed by 17 numbered sections that in chronological order deal with:

1. North America before the advent of private property, market relations and individualism (Sections 1 and 2).
2. The formation of a new type of individual consciousness and the sudden eruption of that new subjectivity through the American Revolution (Sections 4 and 5).
3. The material expansion, the diversity of labours and the cultivation of the individual within the new republic, including passing references to the defence of the Union in the Civil War and its protagonists (Sections 6, 7 and 8).
4. The place and role of Whitman within that historical process (Section 8 and 9).

---

2   Fernando Alegría mentions him in passing in 'Whitman in Spain and Latin America', his contribution to the 1995 collection *Walt Whitman and the World* edited by Gay Allen Wilson and Ed Folsom (p. 82). He also mentioned him briefly in his earlier *Walt Whitman en Hispanoamérica*. Mir is not among the twenty-six poets listed by Ed Folsom and Kenneth M. Price as examples of Whitman's influence on writers beyond the United States in their *Re-scripting Walt Whitman: An Introduction to his Life and Work*. Ivy G. Wilson, like many others, refers to the more prominent examples of Lorca and Neruda, but ignores Mir. Alegría 1995; Wilson, 2014; Folsom and Price, 2005, p. x.

5. The rise and consolidation of capitalism and its impact on the individual, transformed from an acting subject into an object acted upon by money and capital as an alien impersonal power (Sections 10 and 11).
6. The external projection of that internal dynamic: US imperial expansion and its internal counterpart in Latin America, with the consolidation of despotic personalities, bending all to their individual will (Sections 12 and 13).
7. The impact of this radical inversion within American civilisation on the meaning and reception of Whitman's work (Section 14).
8. The coming collective response to the market, capitalist, imperialist and dictatorial domination, which Mir's poem boldly announces (Section 15 and 16).
9. The recuperation of Whitman's legacy and of market and capitalist individualism in the process transcending and transforming them (Section 17).

This division can be simplified into three parts dealing with:
1. The rise of the American republic and the flowering of market individualism (Sections 1–9).
2. The subordination of the republic and the individual to the power of capital (Sections 10–14).
3. The collective overthrow of the rule of capital and the recuperation of a redefined individualism (Sections 15–17).[3]

The turning points of Mir's narrative are the American Revolution, the rise of big capital after the Civil War and the future abolition of capitalist rule. In his poem, three stages in the evolution of Whitman's relation to the larger culture correspond to this periodisation: the mutual identification of Whitman and his people; Whitman's separation and alienation from the people and his appropriation by the oppressors; and the recuperation of Whitman by the people.

A brief note regarding some problems is in order, before we attempt to demonstrate that the preceding summary actually corresponds to Mir's text. Most readers are probably not familiar with Mir's *Countersong*. To break it up, as we must do, into separate pieces, does no justice to the rhythm, flow and cumulative impact of the text taken as a unit. We can only hope that readers take this discussion as an invitation to examine Mir's whole text as it was meant to be read.[4] The only existing translation of Mir's poem into English, by Jonathan Cohen and Donald D. Walsh, has many accomplished moments, but

---

3 For a discussion of the subdivisions of Mir's poem see Santiago Pedrosa 1980. Also the thesis by the same author: Santiago Pedrosa 1979.
4 Mir 2009 contains his major works.

it also offers some solutions that can be misleading, sometimes seriously so. To translate, for example, 'insospechada' as 'trusting' is to give the impression that the original is close to the meaning of 'unsuspecting', when, in fact, it means unexpected (or unsuspected). To translate 'nosotros' (we), deployed by Mir as a refrain close to the end of the poem, as 'we the people', is to engraft on the word a specific historical and political association with the US Constitution that the text does not warrant. Worst of all, translating 'los indios y las indias' ('Indian men and Indian women') as 'Indian braves and squaws' incorporates a racist and derogatory term which is not in the original. In some cases what could be considered a better, if not ideal, word or formulation has been included within brackets.[5]

Mir's poem opens with a very Whitmanian affirmation of the individual self, and more specifically of a located self and a bearer of many voices: a self that 'contains multitudes', that is itself 'a kosmos', not unlike the poetical voice it addresses:

> I,
>   a son of the Caribbean,
> Antillean to be exact.
> The raw product of a simple
> Puerto Rican girl
>   and a Cuban worker,
> born precisely, and poor,
> on Quisqueyan soil.
> Overflowing with voices,
> full of eyes
> wide open throughout the islands,
> I have come to speak to Walt Whitman,
> a kosmos,
>   of Manhattan the son.[6]

It would not be surprising, the poem continues, if nobody knew who this Caribbean 'I' is. But it would be distressing if people had forgotten who Walt Whitman was:

---

5   The study by Santiago Pedrosa includes a detailed discussion of many formal aspects of Mir's text. Santiago Pedrosa 1979.
6   Santiago Pedrosa has pointed out that Mir, in an introductory note, incorrectly stated that Whitman's 'Song of Myself' *begins* with the lines 'I, a kosmos, of Manhattan the son'.

> Nobody had better ask me
> who Walt Whitman is.
> I would go sob on his white beard.

The poem then announces its objective:

> And yet,
> I am going to say again who Walt Whitman is,
> a kosmos,
>   of Manhattan the son.

Immediately suggesting that an explanation of Whitman cannot be divorced from a wider historical process, the first section begins with a description of the American wilderness before the imposition of private property: 'There once was a virgin wilderness. [a pure territory] / Trees and land without deeds or fences'. Mir chose to ignore the existence of Native American peoples. Thus, in this section the absence of private property ('of deeds and fences') results in the image of a continent devoid of human presence. The section seeks to convey a sense of vastness not unlike the feeling of expansion referred to by James when describing his first trip across North America. But a new force, that of market possessive individualism ('the word mine') was about to be unleashed:

> All that was missing was for the word
>   mine
> to go deep inside the caverns and caves
> and fall into the furrow and kiss the North
> Star. And for every man
>   to carry on his chest,
> under his arm, in his eyes and on his shoulders,
> his abundant I,
>   his permanence
> in himself,
> and to spill it out on that wild and savage [unrestrained] land.

The 'I' that could unleash 'the word mine' was already present, but still hindered by the limits imposed by British rule:

> Outside was the firm system of the Law.
> There was the zealous
>   rule of conduct.

> The Cotton Law, the Dream Law,
> the English Law, hard and definite.
> And scarcely
> a short-lived I appeared between two eyelids,
> the observance of the Law was casting its light.
> And then,
> everyone suppressed their disparaged I

Here the poem reaches its first turning point: the 'leap' provoked by the American Revolution and the arrival of the word 'Democracy':

> All of a sudden
> the most inconspicuous I
> found his hidden reward.
> Freedom of Work. Freedom of Conscience.
> Freedom of Speech. The Open Road. [Freedom of the Road]
> Freedom to set out, to plan ahead and to dream.
> Freedom to fail, to love and to name.[7]

In his *Notes on American Civilization*, written at roughly the same time, C.L.R. James had similarly argued that 'uninhibited individualism' had been the 'the ideal in 1776', an ideal that could not be ignored, if the tensions of American Civilisation were to be understood.[8] This was a freedom available to all, making each individual a sovereign over his own person ('of the sweet assembly held in my heart') and linking all as equals:

> In all the land
> the great door of opportunity opened
> and the whole world had access to the word
>   mine.

In his *Notes*, C.L.R. James similarly referred to this initial period of the American republic as a 'unique' historical example of the 'ideal conditions of bourgeois individualism': 'No one is very rich, no one is very poor. Opportunity is open

---

7 Santiago Pedrosa points out how in passages such as these, Mir's text exhibits several Whitmanian traits such as the repetition of key words, phrases and structures, including the use of the anaphora. Unfortunately the pages of the thesis by Santiago Pedrosa are not numbered. He discusses the 'Countersong' in Chapter IV. Santiago Pedrosa 1979.
8 James 1993, p. 46.

to all. Thus in actual living conditions America is unique. The social conditions embody the *ideal* conditions of bourgeois individualism'.[9] In that initial stage in which 'the word mine' was available to all, in which property was widely distributed, human activity unleashed a vigorous economic and material expansion:

> Men went onward with their destiny
> that was robust and manly,
> 			sweaty. They piloted boats
> and days. On the way they fought with Indian braves
> and squaws. [Indian men and women][10] At night they told their tales
>   and spoke
> of towns. Out on the breeze they hung their shirts
> and roads. In the valleys they put their stagecoaches
> and towns. Out on the breeze they hung their shirts
> and the odor of their chests from swinging the axe
> ...
> That land kept growing upwards
> and downwards.
> 		Skyscrapers
> 				and mines
> kept leaving the earth's surface,
> 				united together and far apart.
> The strongest ones, the brightest ones, the ones
> most capable of blazing a trail, went onward.
> Others stayed behind. But the march
> went on with no rest, no looking back.

This world was still open to transformation through individual initiative. General progress and the growth of the individual still advanced hand in hand:

> I the cowboy and I the adventurer
> and I the pioneer and I the gold panner
> ...
> and I the preacher with my baritone voice
> and I the maiden who have my face
> and I the prostitute who have my figure

---

9   James 1993, p. 40.
10   The Spanish original reads: 'los indios y las indias'.

and I the merchant, captain of my silver
and I
    the human being
in pursuit of fortune for myself, above me,
behind me.

Mir's chronicle of this initial epoch in US history concludes with a reference to the Civil War and the rise of leaders (presumably Lincoln, Grant and others) that he, like Whitman and Martí, portrayed as still connected to the labouring classes:

The Yankee clipper
began to sail the wild seas,
on land steel structures were erected,
poems and codes and marble statues were inscribed
and that nation obtained its fierce battles
and its glorious dates and its perfect heroes
who still had on their lips
            the fragrance
and the sap
    of the sweet-smelling land with which they made
        their bread, their journey and their gear ...

Whitman was, for Mir, the poet of that new subjectivity, rooted in a fairly equal distribution of property, freedom of movement and initiative within a web of interconnected labours, or, as Marx puts it, of a 'totality of real kinds of labour, of which no single one is ... predominant'.[11] Thus, Whitman said 'I':

and the fisherman understood himself in his slicker
and the hunter heard himself in the midst of his gunshot
and the woodcutter recognized himself in his axe
and the farmer in his freshly sown field and the gold
panner in his yellow reflection on the water
and the maiden in her future town
           growing and maturing
under her skirt
and the prostitute in her fountain of gaiety

---

11   Marx 1993, p. 104.

and the miner of darkness in his steps beneath his
   homeland ...
...
And all the people saw themselves
when they heard the word
                    I
and all the people heard themselves in your song
when they heard the word
               I, Walt Whitman, a kosmos,
               of Manhattan the son ... !

As Santiago Pedrosa has pointed out, at this point in the poem Mir uses three metaphors (a pool, a garden, a guitar) to describe the poet's relation to his people: he is the 'crystal-clear pool / where a people discover their perfect / likeness'; 'a deep garden / where all men recognize themselves / through language' and 'the chord of a boundless guitar / where the fingers of the people play/their ... innumerable song'. In Section 10 we come upon the second major historical shift: the transformation of the market economy into a power unto itself, the emergence of a 'cold' impersonal 'I' as an objective process, as a thing endowed with a will of its own, the power that will now shape the lives of all social agents. This is what Martí had described as the process of 'glacial metallization' and the *Manifesto* had referred to as immersion in 'the ice-cold water of egotistical calculation':

Nobody knew on what disheveled night,
a cold visage, of some low spineless creature,
appeared on a coin. What shriveled up likeness
suddenly turned into a loud, round piece of metal.
What dry face was seen passing from hand to hand.
What dry mouth suddenly said
                    I
and began to fit in, to fulfill itself and to multiply
on all the coins.
On coins made of gold, of copper, of nickel,
on coins made of hands, of veins of virgins,
of farmers and shepherds, of goatherds and masons.
Nobody knew who was the first one to be let loose.
But one morning he was seen acquiring the dawn.
But one morning he was seen buying the conscience.

The images of 'a shrivelled up likeness' and of a 'cold visage' echo with Whitman's description of the living dead with 'dimes in their eyes' in 'Song of Myself' and of people 'cadaverous as a corpse' in an early editorial.[12] But the subordination of all to the objective rules of the market, to an impersonal 'I', was coupled with the subordination of the dispossessed majority to the power of capital. A historical epoch that had begun with the access of all to 'the word mine' now led to the exclusion of most from it and to the emptying of their selves:

> And from the depths of the rivers, from the ravines, from the pith
> of the underbrush, from the ridges of the mountain ranges,
> passing through torrents of sweat and blood,
> the Banks, the Trusts, the monopolies, the Corporations
> all sprang up ... And, when nobody knew it,
> the face of the little girl and the heart
> of the adventurer and the cavorting of the cowboy and the longings
> of the pioneer ended up there ... and that whole immense land
> began to circulate through the vaults of the Banks, the books
> of the Corporations, the offices of the skyscrapers,
> the calculating machines ...
>   And then, finally:
> one morning he was seen acquiring the great door of opportunity
> and since then nobody has had access to the word mine
> and since then nobody has understood the word I.

In an otherwise clear discussion, Pedrosa mistakenly identifies Whitman's 'I' as described by Mir, as rooted in *capitalist* property. This is one-sided. In Mir's poem capitalism at first propitiates the type of individual agency celebrated by Whitman, but its subsequente evolution – the growing concentration of capital – crushes it. The following section underlines the loss, the annulment of that 'I':

> Go through the furniture and automobile plants, the docks,
> the mines, the apartment houses, the celestial elevators,
> the brothels, the instruments of artists;
> ...
> No use.
> You will not find the pure sound of the word

---

12   Whitman [pre-1855], p. 90. Discussed in Chapter 5.

I.

...
You will not find
        ever again
                the flawless sound
of the word
    I.

The 'word I' has now been monopolised. There is only one 'I', ruling over the rest. It resides in Wall Street, a synecdoche for finance capital:

Now,
    listen to me carefully:
if any of you wants to find again
the old word
    I
go to the street paved with gold [the street of gold], go to Wall Street.

In his *Notes*, C.L.R. James presented a similar historical sequence. 1776 had proclaimed the principle of an 'uninhibited individualism'. Until 1861, American society, 'with all its defects', had actually corresponded to that principle to a degree unmatched by other societies on the road to capitalism.[13] But the 1870s marked the rise of a 'new individualism', the individualism of the 'captains of industry', of the 'great corporations'.[14] It was the rise of this 'new individualism', the 'absolute opposite',[15] according to James, of its predecessor, that Mir's poem described as the appearance of an 'I' that deprived all others of 'the word mine'. Referring to this period, Eric Foner has pointed out how the consolidation of capitalist corporations in the Gilded Age transformed the rhetoric of individual freedom, which had originated in a fairly egalitarian society of small producers before the Civil War, into a justification of the unfettered control of capital *over* the producers.[16] Of course, Marx had long before described how the transition to capitalist production implied the emergence of a form of private property that excluded most social agents from it.[17] It is *capitalism*, not socialism, which deprives most people of private property over the means of production. Such is

---

13   James 1993, pp. 46, 104.
14   James 1993, p. 102.
15   James 1993, p. 103.
16   Foner 1970, p. 38.
17   'Private property ... based ... on the fusing together of the ... individual with the conditions

the process described by James as the emergence of a 'new individualism', and by Mir as the emergence of the new 'I' that deprives others of 'the word mine'. The individual now becomes a dependent variable: capital becomes the active force in society. The power of capital hollows out the democratic promise of individual fulfillment and self-determination. Or as Marx had put it: 'It is not individuals who are set free by free competition; it is, rather, capital which is set free'.[18]

But the power of Wall Street reaches beyond the United States. The republic now becomes an empire. 'Bring me the Antilles', the new imperialist 'I' commands:

> And in the midst of a silent aroma
> here comes the island of Santo Domingo.
'Bring me Central America'.
> And in the midst of a frightening aroma
> here comes Nicaragua silenced.
'Bring me South America'.
> And in the midst of a gloomy aroma
> here comes Venezuela limping.
> And in the midst of a heavenly ruin
> here comes Colombia falling.
> here comes Ecuador falling.
> here comes Brazil falling.
> here comes Puerto Rico falling.
> In the midst of a salty mass
> here comes Chile falling ...
> They all come. Here they come falling.

Cuba brings her grief wrapped in a shudder of masquerades [carnivals].
   Mexico brings her rancor wrapped in a single border glance.
   And Haiti, and Uruguay and Paraguay, they come falling.

Thus emerges a second 'harsh' and 'modern' 'I', besides the one that resides in Wall Street: the will of the Latin American dictators. After advising us to visit Wall Street to observe the new form of the word 'I', the poem continues:

---

of his labour, is supplanted by capitalist private property, which rests on the exploitation of alien, but formally free labour' (Marx 1977, p. 928).

18   Marx 1993, p. 650.

> If you want to find the harsh modern sound
> of the word
> > I
> > > go to Santo Domingo.
> Pass through Nicaragua. Ask around in Honduras.
> Listen to Perú, to Bolivia, to Argentina.
> Everywhere you will run into a high-sounding captain
> > > > > > > > an I.
> A shining leader,
> > > an I, a kosmos.
> A God-sent man,
> > > an I, a kosmos, son of his homeland.

Whitman's affirmation of his individuality and of its amplitude ('a kosmos, of Manhattan the son') becomes the oppressive force of the dictator's will. Excluded from 'the word mine', subordinated to the impersonal 'I' of the market, to the concentrated 'I' of the corporations and banks, to the imperial 'I' of Wall Street and to the authoritarian 'I' of dictators, the dispossessed can no longer recognise themselves in Whitman's song:

> You,
> > who in the middle of the night said,
> > > I, Walt Whitman, a kosmos
> > > > of Manhattan the son
> and an entire people discovered themselves in your tongue
> and all rushed full tilt into building their house,
> today,
> > when they have lost their house,
> ...
> today ...
> today the people do not recognize you
> > > > > tattered Walt Whitman,
> because your sign is locked up in the vaults of the Banks,
> because your voice is on islands guarded by reefs of
> > > bayonets and daggers

Here the poem reaches its third and final reversal: 'now has come the hour of the countersong'. The countersong, presented through a typically Whitmanian catalogue, is structured around a new word. Not the word 'I', but the word we:

> And now
> it is no longer the word
> 					I
> the accomplished word
> the password to begin the world.
> And now
> now it is the word
> 					we.
> And now,
> now has come the hour of the countersong.
> > We the railroad workers,
> > we the students,
> > we the miners,
> > we the peasants,
>
> ...
>
> > We the white-skinned,
> > the black-skinned, the yellow-skinned,
> > the Indians, the copper-skinned,
> > the Moors and dark-skinned,
> > the red-skinned and olive-skinned,
> > the blonds and platinum blonds,
> > united by work,
> > by misery, by silence

But the *Countersong* was not a repudiation of Whitman, nor was the affirmation of Latin American self-determination an expression of unqualified anti-Americanism. The *Countersong* was to be a *recuperation* of Whitman. The *Countersong*, the 'song of ourselves', was the 'justification' that Whitman had demanded from future poets. Against those 'who came to isolate him from his people, / to separate him from his blood and his land', the poem proclaims while quoting Whitman's 'Poets to Come':

> No, Walt Whitman, here are the poets of today
> aroused to justify you!
> 'Poets to come! ... Arouse! for you must
> 		justify me'.
> Here we are, Walt Whitman, to justify you.

To justify Whitman is to join the American people in the struggle against their rulers. Raising his voice against US capitalism and imperialism, the 'son of the Caribbean' movingly embraces Whitman as its 'constant companion' from Manhattan:

> Here we are
> saving your hills of Vermont,
> your woods of Maine, the sap and fragrance of your land,
> your spurred rowdies, your smiling maidens,
> your country boys walking to creeks.
> Saving them, Walt Whitman, from the tycoons
> who take your language for the language of war.
> No, Walt Whitman, here are the poets of today,
> the workers of today, the pioneers of today, the peasants of today,
> firm and roused to justify you!
> O Walt Whitman of aroused beard!
> Here we are without beards,
> without arms, without ears,
> without any strength in our lips,
> spied on,
> red and persecuted,
> full of eyes
> wide open throughout the islands,
> full of courage, of knots of pride
> untied through all the nations,
> with your sign and your language, Walt Whitman,
> here we are
> standing up
> to justify you
> of Manhattan our constant companion!

Mir's text has been described as animated by a desire to annul the individual self in a collective entity (the people, the mass, the workers), an objective defeated by the very same act of poetic enunciation, which is inescapably individual.[19] This is mistaken on at least two counts. Far from celebrating the annulment of individual subjectivity, Mir's poem denounces that annulment: this is

---

19   His call to transcend Whitman's 'I' would thus correspond to his desire to demonstrate the triumph of the collective over the individual. Matos Moquete 2007, p. 214; José Manuel Batista adopts a similar perspective in Batista 2009, pp. 235, 255.

one of the accusations levelled in the poem *against* capitalism. It is capitalism which deprives the majority from access to 'the word mine'. It is capitalism that hollows out the subjectivity of most individuals, which are now subordinated to the will of others (capital, imperialism, dictators). It follows, secondly, that, far from desiring the annulment of the individual self, the poem imagines the transformation of workers, reduced to objects and excluded from 'the word mine' by capital, into active social agents. It wishes to rejoin the producers with the means of production and with their products, from which they are separated under capitalism. But workers cannot assert their individual interest against capital through individual action. As wage-slaves they can only respond to the concentrated power of capital, they can only pursue their individual interests through *collective* action: the 'we' invoked at the end of the poem. Nor can they become the proprietors of modern means of production – of factories, railroads or ships – except as collective owners. Far from annulling their individuality, collective action would be the means of liberating it from its subjugation by capital and of its subordination to the impersonal rules of the market. The 'we' at the end of the poem is not meant to annul the very definite 'I' that speaks from the very first line of the text. Mir's point, a classically Marxist point, is that the individual cannot hope to flourish on its own: to do so, it must join others in a collective anti-capitalist project. That socialist project, as evoked by Mir's poem, does not turn its back on Whitman, poet of the individual self. As we have seen, *Countersong* is *both* a response to and a justification of Whitman. It claims him as its 'constant companion' from Manhattan, while also affirming that a new 'song of *ourselves*' is necessary, if the 'Song of Myself' is to be rescued from its appropriation by capital: socialism is necessary if the possibilities of individual self-development first revealed, then blocked and betrayed by capitalism, are to be realised.[20]

Mir's embrace of Whitman attests, furthermore, to the non-nationalist character of his affirmation of Latin American self-determination. The *Countersong*'s anti-imperialism does not affirm an untouched Latin American culture cleansed of North American influences: it is constructed through the encounter and active mixing with Whitman's verse. As Edward W. Said argued: 'Throughout the exchange between Europeans and their "others" … the one

---

20 Batista has argued that Mir associates Whitman with US imperialism. Yet it is evident that that the opposite is the case. Mir, far from rejecting, embraces Whitman as his 'companion'. He does attack his appropriation by imperialism, from which he wishes to rescue him. Batista's triple dislike for Mir's politics, his notion that anti-imperialism always amounts to crass anti-Americanism and that socialism means the obliteration of the individual results in a consistent misreading of Mir's poem. Batista 2009.

idea that has scarcely varied is that there is an "us" and a "them", each quite settled, clear, unassailable, self-evident'. Said adds: 'We are still the inheritors of that style by which one is defined by the nation, which in turn derives its authority from a supposedly unbroken tradition'. Against this, Said insists that there are no pure identities or traditions, and that anti-imperialism should have other foundations than the simplistic opposition between 'us' and 'them': 'I have no patience with the position that "we" should only or mainly be concerned with what is "ours"'.[21] Mir would have no quarrel with Said: in *Countersong* his formulation of an anti-imperialist vision embraces Whitman as 'our constant companion from Manhattan'. Yet contrary to what Said's misreading of Marx would lead one to expect, Mir's political conception was rooted in a Marxist internationalist perspective, opposed to imperial and colonial rule, yet also committed to the solidarity of oppressed classes *across* national frontiers and identities, a commitment that, in turn, requires a critical distance from nationalist ideologies incompatible with it. If Mir could anticipate Said it is because an important strand of Marxism long before had formulated a similar critique of nationalism.

On the basis of the discussion in previous chapters, it should be evident that Mir's *Countersong* tended to save Whitman from some of his ambiguities. According to Mir, an impeacheably democratic Whitman was illegitimately captured by the discourse of capital, from which the poets of the future, linked to an insurgent working-class and poor peasantry, would rescue him. C.L.R. James, as we have seen, insisted that Whitman, as a result of his refusal to take sides in the social conflicts of his time, had prepared the ground for his future appropriation by the ideologists of American hegemony. Furthermore, Mir's construction of a pristinely democratic Whitman depends on a parallel idealisation of the American past. As Christopher Conway has pointed out, Mir's *Countersong* hardly mentions the situation of Native Americans (ignoring their presence before the spread of capitalist society over North America, and their displacement and destruction as result of that process) and the importance of slavery before the Civil War and of racial oppression since then.[22] Mir's denunciation of US capitalism thus hinges, at least in part, on an idealised vision of the American past, and, above all, of the American West. In what amounts to 'a remythologizing of the American West',[23] Mir's *Countersong*

---

21   Said 1993, p. xxv.
22   Conway 1998, p. 169. Nor does Mir consider the situation of the population of the territories taken from Mexico in the 1840s or the unequal legal situation of women until at least the 1920s.
23   Conway 1998, p. 170.

associates 'cowboys, pioneers, and farmers ... with innocence destroyed'.[24] The West is thus portrayed as 'a lost Eden'.[25] Mir's poem thus 'promotes a classless, agrarian and ultimately ahistorical vision of the Anglo-American past'.[26] Conway's argument is irrefutable. We would add that the image of the cowboy and the vision of the West connected to it are far more present in Mir's *Countersong* than in *Leaves of Grass*. One cannot avoid the notion that Mir's representations drew more than he would have admitted from the typical images of the Hollywood western or, at least, was centred on a few poems such as 'Pioneers!, O Pioneers!'. Yet Mir's poetic narrative still captured key tensions, ironies and contradictions of capitalist civilisation in the United States which can be summarised in a series of tense pairings: celebration of the independent producer/growing exclusion of most people from productive property; pursuit of personal independence and self-development/subordination of most individuals as wage-labourers; promise of democratic rule/the reality of massive corporate power; self-image as a democratic power/support for dictatorial regimes. C.L.R. James, as indicated, would have agreed that Mir had idealised Whitman. Yet, he also felt, like Mir, that there was a contradiction between the promise of American individualism, between the American 'pursuit of happiness' and the outcome of American capitalist development. This was the contradiction around which he built his *Notes on American Civilization* and around which Mir constructed his *Countersong*. To which we can add another twist: James would have not been surprised if, as we have suggested, the sources of Mir's vision included the Hollywood western. As we saw, James considered that these elements of US mass culture were no less marked by the contradictions of 'American civilization', as compensation, and thus tacit acknowledgement, of its broken promises. James predicted that future poets seeking to combine personal, intimate expression with a popular chant could very well turn toward Whitman, in spite of his limitations. On that too, Mir and James, Caribbean exiles writing at roughly the same time but independently of each other, also seem to have been in agreement.

In a commentary on the reception of Whitman's work in Latin America, Enrico Mario Santí formulated several claims that bear reconsideration in the light of this discussion of *Countersong*. Santí considers that the story of Whitman's reception in Latin America is 'a narrative of Error' characterised by the 'disparity between what Whitman actually was and wrote and what

---

24 Conway 1998, p. 168.
25 Conway 1998, p. 169.
26 Conway 1998, p. 169.

they [Latin American authors] imagined he was and wrote'.[27] Rubén Darío's invocation of Whitman's verse in his 'Ode to Roosevelt', written in 1907 in response to the rise of the United States as the preeminent continental power, is, for, Santí, an early example of this 'narrative of Error', of the disparity between the 'actual' Whitman and what others imagined him to be: 'despite the blank verse Darío adopted as a Whitman password in his ode, what his persona expressed in that particular poem was not so much Whitman's proverbial eroticism or democratic chant as a turgid anti-imperialist speech echoing Old Testament prophecy'.[28] For Santí this suppression of the 'actual' through the creation of an 'imagined' Whitman is inherent to any attempt to appeal to him or his work against US imperialism: 'Such an erratic relationship, in turn, depends on a political paradox: it wishes to borrow Whitman's mask from North America as the rhetorical shield of Latin America *against* North American imperialism. Whitman thus became rhetorically useful and even politically expedient, but that expediency was no less subject to bad faith'.[29] There is in Latin American 'Whitmanism' a large dosage of self-deception: a dialogue, not with the 'actual', but rather with an imagined Whitman. The negative consequences of this wish 'to borrow Whitman's mask ... *against* North American imperialism' are compounded as the Whitman cult is turned into a vehicle for the realisation of the poet's 'totalising ambition': the creation of a poem or a series of poems that would somehow encompass all of Latin America's natural, historical, social and cultural reality, thus constructing a desired unity out of its fragments. The results, according to Santí, are bad imitations of Whitman and thus derivative and unoriginal works. Santí suggests this, rather than clearly affirming it, above all through his (at least in this article) invariably negative references to Pablo Neruda's *Canto general*, which he considers an example of the adoption by a Latin American author of the imagined Whitman model. Santí generalises further and considers that the Whitman cult is a specific case of a wider Latin American cultural paradox: 'being an American Self through the language of the European Other – the Whitman model in particular may yet turn out to be the most dramatic instance of that general cultural paradox'.[30] In other words, seeking a Latin American self through Whitman or donning Whitman's mask can only reproduce the alienation of the self while misrepresenting and thus

---

27 Santí 1990, p. 161.
28 Santí 1990, p. 161.
29 Santí 1990, p. 161.
30 Santí 1990, pp. 161–2.

avoiding a true dialogue with the other. Against this, Santí praises Jorge Luis Borges's manner of dealing with the Whitman cult and with the underlying paradox.

Two texts on Whitman ('Nota sobre Walt Whitman', 1947; 'Camden, 1892', 1964) and his story 'El Aleph', according to Santí, embody Borges's alternative to Neruda's *Canto general*: a refusal to imitate Whitman's verse and a renunciation to a totalising ambition, and the elaboration, through that double refusal, of a truly autonomous voice, capable of a real dialogue with the actual Whitman. Referring to 'El Aleph', Santí writes: 'Its lesson runs along proverbial Borgesian lines: at no time do we reach the Other more than when we decide to be ourselves. Thus imitating Whitman in literature bears the same error as imitating our peers in real life: we thereby succeed not in being the Other but in alienating ourselves, becoming a mere abstraction'.[31] As this 'lesson ... along Borgesian lines' unfolds, the problem of imperialism, and of the need to confront it, vanishes: this seems to be an unstated aspect of Borges's 'lesson', as articulated by Santí.

There are two problems with Santí's argument: his avoidance of the contradictions of American society, and his incapacity to envisage the relation between the United States and Latin America, in terms other than the interaction or oppositions of *national* cultures, identities, or entities. Once we consider the contradictions of American capitalism and allow for other collective subjects besides national cultures, Santí's judgments seem less convincing. Consider the possibility that the rise of corporations and capitalist monopolies and/or the imposition of US colonial or semi-colonial rule in the Caribbean and Central America do contradict some past practices and promises of American democracy, however flawed (racially limited for example) they may have been. In that case, to invoke US democratic traditions against American imperialism is a perfectly legitimate gesture, rooted, not in a misunderstanding, but rather in an accurate appreciation of the contradictions and tensions *within* American society. Consider, furthermore, the possibility that Whitman's work was, at least in part, connected to the democratic currents weakened, threatened or revoked by the consolidation of big capital and its imperial projection: in that case, contrary to Santí's argument, to invoke Whitman, or part of Whitman's work, against US imperialism need not be an act of bad faith, self-deception or misrepresentation.[32]

---

31 Santí 1990, p. 174. Harold Bloom reiterates the argument in *The Western Canon*. Bloom 1994, pp. 480–1.
32 It is not difficult to demonstrate that the rise of big business and of the United States as a colonial and interventionist power after the Spanish-American War, with its imme-

We have seen how Whitman's poetry, despite all ambiguities, celebrates a plebian and democratic nation of comrades equally empowered to develop their individual selves, a vision hardly compatible with the rise of capitalist production and big business. To invoke Whitman's voice against the rise of big business is not to join a 'narrative of Error'. It is witness to a fairly accurate understanding of the contradictions, inversions and ironies of the evolution of capitalism and its attendant ideologies in general and in the United States in particular, and of the fact that Whitman's writing, without in any way denying its erotic dimension, can also be read against that economic, social and political background. These are, as we have seen, the underlying assumptions of Mir's *Countersong*.[33]

Consider, furthermore, the possibility that modern collective agents and/or subjectivities need not be reduced to *national* identities or cultures, i.e. the possibility that there may exist *class* forces and political movements capable of forging solidarities and identifications not along but *across* national identities and discourses. From the perspective of a commitment to working-class or anti-capitalist struggles conceived as an inherently international project, for a Latin American socialist, such as Mir, to identify with American workers is not an act of self-alienation, or of turning oneself into an abstraction, but rather an attempt to redefine one's loyalties, to construct a new collective affiliation, in other than national or strictly national terms. If Whitman's writing was at least in part the expression of some of the US components that could go into such an international democratic/anti-imperialist/anti-capitalist current, reworking his form of expression need not yield an impoverished replica or block the formulation of an autonomous voice. This is a further, equally reasonable assumption of Mir's *Countersong*.[34]

---

diate consequences (colonial rule over the Philippines and Puerto Rico, semi-colonial control and intervention in Cuba, the Dominican Republic, Haiti and Central America) was denounced and resisted *within* the United States as a violation of democratic and republican principles that the critics associated with the American political tradition. For a discussion regarding Puerto Rico, see Bernabe 1996.

33   Such borrowings of Whitman are not a thing of the past. Witness the declarations of Puerto Rican poet Martín Espada: 'There are so many things to take away from *Leaves of Grass* 150 years later, one of which is obviously that Whitman is a poet of faith. His faith, however, is not faith in God: it's faith in democracy, and it's faith in poetry, and the power of poetry to change people and change the world. We need that kind of faith right now at a time when democracy is being challenged by those who claim to uphold it, who make war in the name of democracy, when in fact it's a war of profit'. Carvalho 2008, p. 25.

34   Indeed, as Edward Whitley has pointed out, in 1937 future Whitman biographer Gay Wilson Allen had argued that, despite Whitman's intentions, the American people had not made his work their own: Whitman had been appropriated instead by democratic

This is not to say that in the process of appropriating Whitman there can be no disparities between the 'actual' and the 'imagined' Whitman. It is not even an argument that Mir's *Countersong* always avoided such misreadings. Mir certainly ignored, or was unaware of some of the expansionist or proto-imperialist connotations of some passages of *Leaves of Grass*. The point is that such misreadings are not inherent to the attempt to embrace Whitman or aspects of his verse against the rise of big capital or of US imperialism, nor should that attempt be considered a symptom of self-alienation, or of the Latin American paradox of searching a self through the language of the European Other. Nor does it necessarily lead to a derivative result or degraded imitation. If Santí refers to the lesson of Borges's settling of accounts with Whitman, we can speak of the alternative lesson of Mir's *Countersong*: we can, and should, think of ourselves as part of an international 'we' of the dispossessed, while also vindicating, indeed, in order to fully vindicate, our individual selves; we can, and should work for Latin American self-determination against US imperialism, while also embracing all that is admirable in 'American civilization', to use James's term. To borrow Mir's formulation: We have comrades in Manhattan.

The expansion of American capitalism, the rise of American democracy, the emergence of modern individual subjectivity, Whitman's role in that process, the alienating dynamics of a market and capitalist economy, the imperial consequences of capitalist development and the enlistment of Whitman into that project, the possibility of a socialist transcendence of the capitalist present, the forging of a new type of universal solidarity through the struggles of the dispossessed: as this chapter has attempted to demonstrate, all of these elements are to be found in Pedro Mir's *Countersong* in a concentrated and particularly intense form, as the Dominican poet sought a dialogue with Whitman and adapted his verse to his own historical vision. To summarise Mir's *Countersong* is therefore 'a backward glance o'er travel'd roads', to borrow the title of Whitman's epilogue to *Leaves of Grass*.

To conclude: Pedro Mir and C.L.R. James read Whitman against the background of the contradictions of capitalist modernity, contradictions which are present in *Leaves of Grass* and in José Martí's chronicles of North American life in the 1880s. Whitman and his three Caribbean interlocutors fervently embraced the promise of a new world issued by North American democracy and industry, but recoiled from its alienating dimension. Whitman sought a poetical solution, which left him stranded between an apology of capitalism

---

and proletarian forces *outside* the United States. More than a US national poet, he was an international proletarian poet. Allen 1937, pp. 48–52. See also Whitley 2006, p. 469.

('vivified' and 'spiritualised' by art) and an impotent nostalgia for the small town and farm (the antimony between boosterism and nostalgia which Marx considered typical of bourgeois thought), and which also failed to address the problem slavery and its legacy. He became a celebrator of US imperial ambitions. Martí rejected the present as an unfinished world, a troubled moment of transition, preceding a future synthesis: the United States, he concluded by the late 1880s, was not the model for such a synthesis. His solution was to envisage Cuban independence (and a 'second independence' for Latin America) as the vehicle for an alternative modernity: an anti-imperialist if not frankly anti-capitalist solution, which claimed Whitman as the singer of the liberating dimension of modern life opposed to the sinister aspects of American society (its social fragmentation, class polarisation and one-sided pursuit of material wealth). James and Mir were, of course, Marxists, who openly rejected capitalism, while embracing its liberating achievements, thus refusing to choose between the apologia of capitalist progress and the nostalgia for the past (the dilemma that Whitman was unable or unwilling to escape), even if Mir's *Countersong* did idealise the early stages of the American republic and its westward expansion. They read Whitman differently: James as part of the dominant discourse of American capitalism, Mir as a poet of the people captured by capital. They agreed that the liberation of the individual required mass collective action, and even James considered that the poetry of that upheaval would have to engage with Whitman's songs, which is what, independently of him, Mir did in his *Countersong to Walt Whitman*.

We are not strangers to this conversation. We are immersed in it, willingly or not. The world created by capital; the promise of liberation through science and technology; the end of local isolation and barriers; the transformation of that liberating potential into the reality of exploitation and subjection to a tyrannical world market and the subordination of all human activity to the pursuit of monetary gain; the impossibility of returning to the past and the need to reject the notion that with 'this emptiness', as Marx put it in 1857, 'history has come to a standstill': what are these, if not the coordinates of our situation at the start of the twenty-first century? The *Communist Manifesto* proclaimed that workers have only their chains to lose and a world to win. The outlook today is bleaker. The abolition of capitalism is now required to stop the drift toward ecological catastrophe. But the task is unchanged: to bring forth the present-day abolitionists, the collective agent envisoned by James in his comments on the C.I.O., the international anti-capitalist 'we' invoked by Mir in his *Countersong*. Not only losing our chains, but not losing most of our world hinges on it.

References

Achcar, Gilbert 2013, *Marxism, Orientalism, Cosmopolitanism*, New York: Haymarket.
Ahmad, Aijaz 1992, *In Theory. Classes, Nations, Literatures*, London: Verso.
Alegría, Fernando 1954, *Walt Whitman en Hispano América*, México: Colección Studium.
Alegría, Fernando 1995, 'Whitman in Spain and Latin America', in Gay Allen Wilson and Ed Folsom (eds.), *Walt Whitman and the World*, Iowa: University of Iowa Press.
Allen, Esther (ed.) 2002, *José Martí Selected Writings*, New York: Penguin.
Allen, Gay Wilson 1937, 'Walt Whitman – Nationalist or Proletarian?' *English Journal*, 26: 48–52
Allen, Gay Wilson 1955, *The Solitary Singer. A Critical Biography of Walt Whitman*, New York: Macmillan Company.
Antebi, Susan 2005, 'Caliban and Coney Island: Spanish American Narratives of Corporeal Difference and Performance', *Disability Studies Quarterly*, 25, 4. Available at http://dsq-sds.org/article/view/615/792 (last visit 28 November 2017).
Arvin, Newton 1938, *Whitman*, New York: Russell and Russell.
Ballón, José 1988, 'José Martí en Nueva York: Dos hitos de su lectura cultural', in Colectivo de autores 1988.
Bandy, W.T. 1985, 'An unknown "Washington Letter" by Walt Whitman', *Walt Whitman Quarterly Review*, 2, 3: 23–7.
Batista, José Manuel 2009, 'Ni cósmico, ni democrático: el "Contracanto a Walt Whitman" de Pedro Mir', *Symposium*, 62, 4: 235–57.
Bernabe, Rafael 1996, *Respuestas al colonialismo en la política puertorriqueña, 1899–1929*, Rio Piedras: Huracán.
Bernabe, Rafael 2002, *La maldición de Pedreira: aspectos de la crítica romántico-cultural de la modernidad en Puerto Rico*, Río Piedras: Huracán.
Bloom, Harold 1994, *The Western Canon. The Books and School of the Ages*, New York: Harcourt Brace.
Bloom, Harold 2005, 'Introduction and Celebration', *Walt Whitman's Leaves of Grass. The First (1855) Edition*, New York: Penguin.
Brasher, Thomas L. 1960, 'Organized Labor versus Whitman's "Immutable Truth"', *Walt Whitman Review*, 6, 4: 63–6.
Brasher, Thomas L. 1970, *Whitman as Editor of the Brooklyn Eagle*, Detroit: Wayne State University Press.
Brecher, Jeremy 1997 [1972], *Strike!*, Cambridge, Mass: South End Press.
Brennan, Timothy 1997, *At Home in the World. Cosmopolitanism Now*, Cambridge: Harvard University Press.
Bucke, Richard Maurice 1970 [1883], *Walt Whitman*, New York-London: Johnson Reprint Corporation.

Buhle, Paul 1988, *C.L.R. James. The Artist as Revolutionary*, London: Verso.

Buinicki, Martin T. 2008, '"Average-Representing Grant": Whitman's General', *Walt Whitman Quarterly Review*, 26, 2: 69–91.

Buinicki, Martin T. 2011, *Walt Whitman's Reconstruction: Poetry and Publishing Between Memory and History*, Iowa City: Iowa University Press.

Cain, William E. 1995, 'The Triumph of the Will and the Failure of Resistance: C.L.R. James's Readings of *Moby Dick* and *Othello*', in *C.L.R. James: His Intellectual Legacies*, edited by Selwyn R. Cudjoe, William E. Cain, Amherst: University of Massachusetts Press.

Carpenter, Frederick 1934, *Ralph Waldo Emerson. Representative Selections*, New York, American Book Company.

Carvalho, Edward 2008, 'A Branch on the Tree of Whitman: Martín Espada Talks about *Leaves of Grass*', *Walt Whitman Quarterly Review*, 26, 1: 23–34.

Chaffin, J. Thomas 1977, 'Give Me Faces and Streets: Walt Whitman and the City', *Walt Whitman Review*, 23: 109–20.

Colectivo de autores 1988, *José Martí y los Estados Unidos*, La Habana: Centro de Estudios Martianos.

Collier, Michael 2005, 'On Whitman's "To a Locomotive in Winter"', *Virginia Quarterly Review*, 81, 2: 202–5.

Conant, William C. 1883, 'The Brooklyn Bridge', *Harper's New Monthly Magazine*, 66: 396, 925–46.

Conway, Christopher 1998, 'Of Subjects and Cowboys: Frontier and History in Pedro Mir's "Countersong to Walt Whitman"', *Walt Whitman Quarterly Review*, 15, 4: 161–71.

Conway, Christopher 2004, 'The Limits of Analogy: José Martí and the Haymarket Martyrs', A *Contracorriente: A Journal of Social History and Literature in Latin America*, 2, 1: 33–56.

Crary, Jonathan 2013, *Late Capitalism and the Ends of Sleep*, London: Verso.

Crawley, Thomas E. 1970, *The Structure of Leaves of Grass*, Austin: University of Texas Press.

Cronkhite, G. Ferris 1954, 'Walt Whitman and the Locomotive', *American Quarterly*, 6, 2: 164–72.

Cruz, Mary 1988, 'Una de las más sorprendentes creaciones martianas: "El poeta Walt Whitman"', *Anuario del Centro de Estudios Martianos*, 11: 130–9.

Cutler, Ed 1998, 'Passage to Modernity: *Leaves of Grass* and the 1853 Crystal Palace Exhibition in New York', *Walt Whitman Quarterly Review*, 16, 2: 65–89.

Davis, Mike 1986, *Prisoners of the American Dream. Politics and Economy in the History of the US Working Class*, London: Verso.

Díaz Quiñones, Arcadio 2006, 'José Martí (1853–1895): la guerra desde las nubes', in *Sobre los principios. Los intelectuales caribeños y la tradición*, Bernal: Universidad Nacional de Quilmes.

Dickstein, Morris 1991-2, 'The City as Text: New York and the American Writer', *TriQuarterly*, 83: 183–204.
Doudna, Martin K. 1977, 'The Atlantic Cable in Whitman's "Passage to India"', *Walt Whitman Review*, 23: 1, 50–2.
Du Bois, W.E.B. 1979 [1934], *Black Reconstruction in America 1860–1880*, New York: Atheneum.
Eagleton, Terry 2003, *After Theory*, New York: Basic Books.
Eagleton, Terry 2007, *The Meaning of Life*, New York: Oxford University Press.
Eagleton, Terry 2011, *Why Marx Was Right*, New Haven and London: Yale University Press.
Emerson, Ralph Waldo [1837], 'The American Scholar', in Carpenter 1934.
Emerson, Ralph Waldo [1841], 'The Over-Soul', in Carpenter 1934.
Emerson, Ralph Waldo [1844], 'The Young American', in Carpenter 1934.
Engels, Friederich 1973 [1887], 'Preface to the American Edition' in *The Condition of the Working Class in England*, Moscow: Progress Publishers.
Erkkila, Betsy 1989, *Whitman the Political Poet*, New York-Oxford: Oxford University Press.
Erkkila, Betsy 2007, 'Whitman, Marx, and the American 1848', *Leaves of Grass: The Sesquicentennial Essays*, edited by Susan Belasco, Ed Folsom, and Kenneth M. Price, Lincoln, Nebraska: University of Nebraska Press, 35–61.
Folsom, Ed (ed.) 1994, *Walt Whitman: The Centennial Essays*, Iowa City: University of Iowa Press.
Folsom, Ed 2005, 'What a Filthy Presidentiad!', *Virginia Quarterly Review*, 81, 2: 96–113.
Folsom, Ed and Kenneth M. Price 2005, *Re-scripting Walt Whitman: An Introduction to his Life and Work*, Malden, MA: Blackwell.
Folsom, Ed 2014, 'Erasing Race. The Lost Black Presence in Whitman's Manuscripts' in Wilson 2014.
Foner, Eric 1970, *Free Soil, Free Labor, Free Men. The Ideology of the Republican Party before the Civil War*, London: Oxford University Press.
Foner, Eric 1980, *Politics and Ideology in the Age of the Civil War*, Oxford: Oxford University Press.
Foner, Eric 1988, *Reconstruction: America's Unfinished Revolution*, New York: Harper and Row.
Foner, Eric 1990, 'Blacks and the US Constitution, 1789–1989', *New Left Review* 183.
Foner, Eric 1998, *The Story of American Freedom*, New York: W.W. Norton.
Foner, Eric 2015, *Gateway to Freedom. The Hidden History of the Underground Railroad*, New York: W.W. Norton.
Foner, Phillip S. (ed.) 1975, José Martí *Inside the Monster. Writings on the United States and American Imperialism*, translated by Elinor Randall, Luis A. Baralt, Juan de Onís, Rosalyn Held Foner, New York: Monthly Review.

Foster, John Bellamy 2000, *Marx's Ecology: Materialism and Nature*, New York: Monthly Review Press.

Foster, John Bellamy 2009, *The Ecological Revolution. Making Peace with the Planet*, New York: Monthly Review Press.

Frankel, Harry (pseudonym of Harry Braverman) 1976 [1946], 'The Jacksonian Period', in *America's Revolutionary Heritage. Marxist Essays*, edited by George Novack, New York: Pathfinder Press.

Frankel, Harry (pseudonym of Harry Braverman) 1976 [1947], 'Three Conceptions of Jacksonianism', in *America's Revolutionary Heritage. Marxist Essays*, edited by George Novack, New York: Pathfinder Press.

Frassinelli, Pier Paolo 2009, 'Repositioning C.L.R. James', *Journal of Postcolonial Writing*, 45, 1: 91–6.

Frau, Juan 2002, 'Una traducción polémica: León Felipe ante la obra de Whitman y Shakespeare', *Hermeneus. Revista de Traducción e Interpretación*, 4, 33–70.

Freeburg, Christopher 2014, 'Walt Whitman, James Weldon Johnson and the Violent Paradox of American Progress' in Wilson 2014.

Friend, Robert 1973, 'The Quest for Rondure: A Comparison of Two Passages to India', *Hebrew University Studies in Literature*, 1, 1: 76–85.

Geffen, Arthur 1984, 'Silence and Denial: Walt Whitman and the Brooklyn Bridge', *Walt Whitman Review*, 1, 4: 1–11.

Golden, Arthur 1973, 'Passage to Less than India: Structure and Meaning in Whitman's "Passage to India"', *PMLA*, 88: 1095–1103.

Gohdes, Clarence 1959, 'Nationalism and Cosmopolitanism in Whitman's Leaves of Grass', *Walt Whitman Review*, 5, 1: 3–7.

González, Aníbal 1983, *La crónica modernista hispanoamericana*, Madrid: José Porrúa Turranzas.

Grossman, Jay 1990, '"The Evangel-Poem of Comrades and of Love": Revising Whitman's Republicanism', *American Transcendental Quarterly*, 4, 3: 201–18.

Grunzweig, Walter 1998, 'Imperialism', in *Walt Whitman. An Encyclopedia*, edited by J.R. LeMaster, Donald D. Kummings, New York-London: Garland Publishing.

Haddox, Thomas F. 2004, 'Whitman's End of History: "As I sat Alone by Blue Ontario's Shore", *Democratic Vistas*, and the Postbellum Politics of Nostalgia', *Walt Whitman Quarterly Review*, 22, 1: 1–22.

Henkel, Scott 2010, 'Leaves of Grassroots Politics: Whitman, Carlyle, and the Imagination of *Democratic Vistas*', *Walt Whitman Quarterly Review* 27, 3: 101–26.

Herreshoff, David 1967, *American Disciples of Marx: from the Age of Jackson to the Progressive Era*, Detroit: Wayne State University.

Hidalgo Paz, Ibrahím 1988, 'Pueblo y gobierno estadounidenses en la política martiana (1892–1895)', in Colectivo de autores 1988.

Higgins, Andrew C. 2002, 'Wage Slavery and the Composition of *Leaves of Grass*: The 'Talbot Wilson' Notebook', *Walt Whitman Quarterly Review* 20, 2: 53–77.

Hoare, Quentin (ed.) 1975, *Karl Marx. Early Writings*, New York: Vintage.

Hofstadter, Richard 1948, 'Wendell Phillips: the Patrician as Agitator', in *The American Political Tradition*, New York, Alfred A. Knopf.

Holloway, Emory (ed.) 1932, *The Uncollected Poetry and Prose of Walt Whitman*, 2 Vols., New York: Peter Smith.

Hugins, Walter 1960, *Jacksonian Democracy and the Working Class*, Stanford: Stanford University Press.

Hunnicutt, Benjamin Kline 2008, 'Walt Whitman's 'Higher Progress' and Shorter Work Hours', *Walt Whitman Quarterly Review*, 26, 2: 92–109.

James, C.L.R. 1993 [1949–50], *American Civilization*, edited by Anna Grimshaw and Keith Hart, Cambridge, Mass: Blackwell.

James, C.L.R. 1996, *On the 'Negro Question'*, edited by Scott McLemee, Jackson: University Press of Mississippi.

James, C.L.R. 2001 [1953], *Mariners, Renegades and Castaways. The Story of Herman Melville and the World We Live In*, Hanover, NH: University Press of New England.

Kaplan, Justin 1989, 'The Biographer's Problem', *The Mickle Street Review*, 11: 80–8.

Kaplan, Justin (ed.) 1982, *Walt Whitman. Complete Poetry and Collected Prose*, New York: The Library of America.

Kaplan, Justin 2003 [1980], *Walt Whitman. A Life*, New York: Harper Collins-Perennial Classics.

Keith, Joseph 2009, 'At the Formal Limits: C.L.R. James, *Moby Dick* and the Politics of the Novel', *Interventions: International Journal of Postcolonial Studies*, 11, 3: 352–66.

Klammer, Martin 1995, *Slavery and the Emergence of 'Leaves of Grass'*, University Park: Pennsylvania State University Press.

Klammer, Martin 1997, 'Review of Mancuso, *The Strange War Revolving*', *Walt Whitman Quarterly Review*, 15, 1: 40–4.

Larsen, Neil, and Ronald W. Sousa 1983, 'From Whitman (to Marinetti) to Alvaro Campos: A Case Study in Materialist Approaches to Literary Influence', *Ideologies and Literature*, IV (Second Cycle), 17, 94–115.

Laurie, Bruce 1997 [1989], *Artisans into Workers. Labor in Nineteenth-Century America*, Urbana and Chicago: University of Illinois Press.

Lawson, Andrew 2006, *Walt Whitman and the Class Struggle*, Iowa City: University of Iowa Press.

Ledbetter, James (ed.) 2007, *Dispatches for the New York Tribune: Selected Journalism of Karl Marx*, London: Penguin.

Leonard, James S. 1980, 'The Achievement of Rondure in "Passage to India"', *Walt Whitman Review*, 26, 4: 129–38.

Lomas, Laura 2008, *Translating Empire: José Martí, Migrant Latino Subjects, and American Modernities*, Durham, NC: Duke University Press.

Lott, Deshae E. 1998, 'O'Connor, William Douglas (1832–1889)', in *Walt Whitman. An*

Encyclopedia, edited by J.R. LeMaster, Donald D. Kummings, New York-London: Garland Publishing.
Loving, Jerome 1982, *Emerson, Whitman and the American Muse*, Chapel Hill and London: University of North Carolina Press.
Lowy, Michael 1993, *On Changing the World. Political Philosophy from Karl Marx to Walter Benjamin*, Atlantic Highlands, N.J.-London: Humanities Press.
Lowy, Michael and Robert Sayre 2001, *Romanticism Against the Tide of Modernity*, translated by Catherine Porter, Durham-London: Duke University Press.
Lowy, Michael 2015, *Ecosocialism: A Radical Alternative to Capitalist Catastrophe*, Chicago: Haymarket.
McCarl, Clayton 2006, 'La ciudad a la deriva: Nueva York en las obras de Walt Whitman y José Martí', *LL Journal*, 1, 1: 98–107.
Magaril, Nicolás 2010, 'Poetas del futuro. Recepciones de Walt Whitman en el mundo de habla hispana', Masters thesis, Universidad Nacional Autónoma de México.
Mancuso, Luke 1997, *The Strange War Revolving. Walt Whitman, Reconstruction, and the Emergence of Black Citizenship, 1865–1876*, Columbia, SC: Camden House.
Mandel, Bernard 1955, *Labor Free and Slave. Workingmen and the Anti-Slavery Movement in the United States*, New York: Associated Authors.
Mandel, Ernest 1977 [1962], *Marxist Economic Theory*, translated by Brian Pearce, London: Merlin.
Mandel, Ernest 1979, *Trotsky. A Study in the Dynamic of his Thought*, London: New Left Books.
Mandel, Ernest 1992, *Money and Power. A Marxist Theory of Bureaucracy*, London: Verso.
Mandel, Ernest 1995, *Trotsky as Alternative*, translated by Gus Fagan, London: Verso.
Mandel, Ernest 2015 [1967], *The Formation of the Economic Thought of Karl Marx*, translated by Brian Pearce, London: Verso.
Marcuse, Herbert 1969 [1937], 'The Affirmative Character of Culture', in *Negations. Essays in Critical Theory*, translated by Jeremy Shapiro, Boston: Beacon.
Martí, José [1871], 'From Notebook 1', in Esther Allen (ed.) 2002.
Martí, José [1880], 'Impressions of America (By a Very Fresh Spaniard)', in Allen (ed.) 2002.
Martí, José [1881], 'Coney Island', in Allen (ed.) 2002.
Martí, José [1882], 'Prizefight', in Allen (ed.) 2002.
Martí, José [1882a], 'Prologue to Juan Antonio Pérez Bonalde's Poem of Niagara', in Allen (ed.) 2002.
Martí, José [1882b], 'Knights of Labor Strike', in Foner (ed.) 1975.
Martí, José [1883], 'The Brooklyn Bridge', in Allen (ed.) 2002.
Martí, José [1883a], 'Tributes to Karl Marx, Who Has Died', in Allen (ed.) 2002.
Martí, José [1884], 'Graduation Day', in Allen (ed.) 2002.
Martí, José [1884a] 'Wendell Phillips', in Foner (ed.) 1975.

Martí, José [1885], 'The World's Biggest Explosion', in Allen (ed.) 2002.
Martí, José [1885a] 'General Grant', in Foner (ed.) 1975.
Martí, José [1886] 'An Epidemic of Strikes', in Foner (ed.) 1975.
Martí, José [1886a] 'The Labor Problem in the United States', in Foner (ed.) 1975.
Martí, José [1887], 'The Poet Walt Whitman', in Allen (ed.) 2002.
Martí, José [1887a], 'Class War in Chicago: A Terrible Drama', in Allen (ed.) 2002.
Martí, José [1887b] 'The Schism of the Catholics in New York', in Foner (ed.) 1975.
Martí, José [1888], 'New York Under Snow', in Allen (ed.) 2002.
Martí, José [1889], 'A Vindication Cuba', in Allen (ed.) 2002.
Martí, José [1889a] 'Indians and Negroes', in Foner (ed.) 1975.
Martí, José [1889b] 'The Washington Pan-American Congress', in Foner (ed.) 1975.
Martí, José [1891], 'The Monetary Conference of the American Republics', in Allen (ed.) 2002.
Martí, José [1892], 'A Town Sets a Black Man on Fire', in Allen (ed.) 2002.
Martí, José [1894], 'The Truth About the United States', in Allen (ed.) 2002.
Martí, José [1894a], 'To Cuba', in Esther Allen (ed.) 2002.
Martí, José 1963–73, *Obras Completas*, La Habana: Editorial Nacional de Cuba.
Martí, José 1980, *Nuevas cartas de Nueva York*, Ernesto Mejía Sánchez (ed.), México, Siglo XXI.
Martí, José 1982, *Ismaelillo. Versos libres. Versos sencillos*, Iván Schulman (ed.), Madrid: Cátedra.
Mataix, Remedios 1999, 'Amor y temor de ciudad grande: Notas sobre la poética urbana de José Martí' in *Escrituras de la Ciudad*, José Carlos Rovira (ed.), Madrid: Palas Atenea, 75–91.
Marx, Leo 2000 [1964], *The Machine in the Garden. Technology and the Pastoral Ideal in America*, London: Oxford.
Marx, Karl [1843–4], 'A Contribution to the Critique of Hegel's Philosophy of Right. Introduction', in Hoare 1975.
Marx, Karl [1844], 'Economic and Philosophical Manuscripts', in Hoare 1975.
Marx, Karl and Frederick Engels [1845], *The German Ideology*, in Marx and Engels 1976, Vol. 5.
Marx, Karl and Friedrich Engels [1848], *Manifesto of the Communist Party*, in Marx and Engels 1976, Vol. 6.
Marx, Karl [1853], 'The British Rule in India' in Ledbetter (ed.) 2007.
Marx, Karl [1853a], 'The Future Results of British Rule in India', in Ledbetter (ed.) 2007.
Marx, Karl [1858], 'History of the Opium Trade (I)', in Ledbetter (ed.) 2007.
Marx, Karl and Frederick Engels 1976, *Collected Works*, New York: International Publishers, Vols. 5, 6.
Marx, Karl 1977 [1867], *Capital. A Critique of Political Economy*, Vol. 1, translated by Ben Fowkes, New York: Vintage.

Marx, Karl 1981 [1895], *Capital. A Critique of Political Economy*, Vol. 3, translated by David Fernbach.

Marx, Karl 1993 [1857–8], *Grundrisse. Foundations of the Critique of Political Economy (Rough Draft)*, translated by Martin Nicolaus, London: Penguin.

Mason, John B. 1973, 'Walt Whitman's Catalogues: Rhetorical Means for Two Journeys in "Song of Myself"', *American Literature*, 45, 1: 34–49.

Matos Moquete, Manuel 2007, 'Poética política en la poesía de Pedro Mir', in *Aproximaciones a la literatura dominicana (1930–1980)*, edited by Rei Berroa, Santo Domingo: Colección del Banco Central de la República Domnicana-Departamento Cultural.

Matthiessen, F.O. 1941, *American Renaissance: Art and Expression in the Age of Emerson and Whitman*, London-New York: Oxford University Press.

Mestas, Juan E. 1993, *El pensamiento social de José Martí: Ideología y cuestión obrera*, Madrid, Pliegos.

Miller, Cristanne 2009, 'Drum-Taps: Revisions and Reconciliation', *Walt Whitman Quarterly Review*, 26, 4: 171–96.

Miller, Edwin Haviland (ed.) 1969, *A Century of Whitman Criticism*, Bloomington-London: Indiana University Press.

Mir, Pedro 1993 [1952], *Countersong to Walt Whitman & Other Poems*, translated by Jonathan Cohen and Donald D. Walsh., Washington, D.C.: Azul Editions.

Mir, Pedro 2009 [1952], 'Contracanto a Walt Whitman' in *Poemas*, Miguel Angel García (ed.), Madrid: La Discreta.

Moody, Kim 1988, *An Injury to All: The Decline of American Unionism*, London: Verso.

Molloy, Sylvia 1996, 'His America, Our America: José Martí Reads Whitman', in *Breaking Bounds. Whitman and American Cultural Studies*, edited by Betsy Erkkila, Jay Grossman, New York-Oxford: Oxford University Press.

Montero, Oscar 2002, 'Racism in the Republic: Martí and the Legacy of the U.S. Civil War', *Ciberletras*, 7.

Myers, Henry Alonzo 1934, 'Whitman's Conception of the Spiritual Democracy, 1855–56', *American Literature*, 6, 3: 239–53.

Norton, Charles Eliot 1969 [1855], 'Review of *Leaves of Grass*', in *A Century of Whitman Criticism*, edited by Edwin Haviland Miller, Bloomington-London: Indiana University Press.

Pannapacker, William 2006, 'Lawson, Andrew. *Walt Whitman and the Class Struggle* [review]', *Walt Whitman Quarterly Review*, 24, 1: 37–41.

Parker, Simon 1999, 'Unrhymed Modernity: New York City, the Popular Newspaper Page, and the Forms of Whitman's Poetry', *Walt Whitman Quarterly Review*, 16, 3: 161–71.

Pascal, Richard 1989, '"Dimes on the Eyes": Walt Whitman and the Pursuit of Wealth in America', *Nineteenth-Century Literature*, 44, 2: 141–172.

Pearce, Roy Harvey 1969, 'Whitman and Our Hope for Poetry', in *Historicism Once More. Problems and Occasions for the American Scholar*, Princeton: Princeton University Press.

Pease, Donald E. 1993, 'Walt Whitman's Revisionary Democracy', *The Columbia History of American Poetry*, edited by Jay Parini and Brett C. Millier, New York: Columbia University Press, 148–71.
Pease, Donald E. 1998, 'José Martí, Alexis de Tocqueville, and the Politics of Displacement. José Martí's "Our America"', in *From National to Hemispheric Cultural Studies*, edited by Jeffrey Belnap and Raúl Fernández, Durham, NC: Duke University Press.
Pease, Donald E. 2001, 'C.L.R. James's *Mariners, Renegades and Castaways* and the World We Live In', in James 2001.
Pease, Donald E. 2000, 'Doing Justice to C.L.R. James's *Mariners, Renegades, and Castaways*', *Boundary 2: An International Journal of Literature and Culture*, 27, 2: 1–19.
Pease, Donald E. 2011, 'C.L.R. James's *Moby-Dick*: The Narrative Testimony of the Non-Survivor', *Leviathan. A Journal of Melville Studies*, 13, 1: 34–44.
Post, Charles 2012, *The American Road to Capitalism. Studies in the Class-Structure, Economic Development and Political Conflict, 1620–1877*, Chicago: Haymarket Books.
Preis, Art 1978 [1964], *Labor's Giant Step. Twenty Years of the CIO*, New York: Pathfinder Press.
Price, Kenneth M. 1985, 'Whitman's Solutions to "The Problem of the Blacks"', *Resources for American Literary Study*, 15, 2: 205–8.
Price, Kenneth M. 2004, *To Walt Whitman, America*, Chapel Hill: University of North Carolina Press.
Raab, Josef 2001, 'El gran viejo: Walt Whitman in Latin America', *CLCWeb: Comparative Literature and Culture: A WWWeb Journal*, 3.2.
Ramos, Julio 1988, 'Trópicos de la fundación: poesía y nacionalidad en José Martí', in Colectivo de autores 1988.
Ramos, Julio 2001, *Divergent Modernities: Culture and Politics in Nineteenth-Century Latin America*, translated by John D. Blanco, Durham: Duke University Press.
Reyes, Jessika 2015, '"Los tiempos están revueltos; los hombres están despiertos": problemas de la modernidad en *Escenas Norteamericanas* de José Martí', Ph.D. Thesis, Centro de Estudios Avanzados de Puerto Rico y el Caribe.
Reynolds, David S. 1996, *Walt Whitman's America. A Cultural Biography*, New York: Vintage.
Reynolds, David S. 2005, *Walt Whitman*, Oxford University Press, 2005.
Reynolds, David S. 2010, '"Affection Shall Solve Every One of the Problems of Freedom": Calamus Love and the Antebellum Political Crisis', *Huntington Library Quarterly: Studies in English and American History and Literature*, 73, 4: 629–42.
Robertson, Michael 2008, *Worshipping Walt. The Whitman Disciples*, Princeton: Princeton University Press.
Rodgers, Cleveland and John Black (eds.) 1920, *The Gathering of the Forces*, 2 vols., New York: G.P. Putnam's Sons.

Rodríguez, Pedro Pablo 1988, '"Definir, avisar, poner en guardia ..." visión martiana de Estados Unidos en *La América*', in Colectivo de autores.

Roediger, David R. and Philip S. Foner 1989, *Our Own Time. A History of American Labor and the Working Day*, London: Verso.

Roediger, David R. 1991, *The Wages of Whiteness. Race and the Making of the American Working Class*, London: Verso.

Rotker, Susana 2000, *The American Chronicles of José Martí: Journalism and Modernity in Spanish America*, translated by Jennifer French and Katherine Semler, Hanover, NH: University Press of New England.

Rubin, Joseph Jay, and Charles H. Brown (eds.) 1950, *Walt Whitman of the New York Aurora. Editor at Twenty-Two*, State College, Pennsylvania: Bald Eagle Press.

Sanborn, Frank B. 1897, 'Reminiscent of Whitman' [1897], *The Conservator*, 8, 3: 37–40.

Said, Edward W. 1993, *Culture and Imperialism*, New York: Alfred E. Knopf.

Santí, Enrico Mario 1990, 'The Accidental Tourist: Walt Whitman in Latin America', in *Do the Americas Have a Common Literature?*, edited by Gustavo Pérez Firmat, London and Durham: Duke University Press.

Santiago Pedrosa, José 1980, '"El Canto de mi mismo", de Walt Whitman y el "Contracanto" de Pedro Mir', *Mairena*, II, 5: 5–14.

Santiago Pedrosa, José 1979, 'Viaje a la muchedumbre de Pedro Mir: hay un poeta en el mundo', Masters Thesis-Departamento de Estudios Hispánicos-Universidad de Puerto Rico-Río Piedras.

Schmidgall, Gary (ed.) 2006, *Conserving Walt Whitman's Fame. Selections from Horace Traubel's Conservator, 1890–1919*, University of Iowa Press.

Schnirmajer, Ariela Erica 2005, 'José Martí ante la cuestión obrera: Acerca de las batallas del sujeto moderno', *Decimonónica: Journal of Nineteenth Century Hispanic Cultural Production*, 2, 1: 55–68.

Schor, Juliet B. 1992, *The Overworked American. The Unexpected Decline of Leisure*, New York: Basic Books.

Schulman, Iván A. 1997, 'Narrando la nación moderna', *José Martí: Historia y literatura ante el fin del siglo XIX*, edited by Carmen Alemany, Ramiro Muñoz, and José Carlos Rovira, Alicante, Spain: Universidad de Alicante with Casa de las Américas, 51–73.

Schwarz, Bill 2005, 'C.L.R. James's American Civilization', *Atlantic Studies: Literary, Cultural, and Historical Perspectives*, 2, 1: 15–43.

Schwarzmann, Georg M. and Anne Fountain 2010, *The Influence of Emerson and Whitman on the Cuban Poet José Martí: Themes of Immigration, Colonialism, and Independence*, Lewiston, NY: Mellen.

Shachtman, Max 2003 [1933], *Race and Revolution*, edited by Christopher Phelps, London: Verso.

Shulman, Robert 1982, '"Song of Myself": Whitman's Individualism and Market Society America', *Lamar Journal of the Humanities*, 8, 2: 18–25.

Sill, Geoffrey 1990, 'Whitman on 'The Black Question': A New Manuscript', *Walt Whitman Quarterly Review*, 8, 2: 69–75.

Smeller, Carl 1998, 'I Saw In Louisiana a Live-Oak Growing' (1860), in *Walt Whitman. An Encyclopedia*, J.R. LeMaster, Donald D. Kummings, (eds.), New York-London: Garland Publishing.

Smith, Tony 1993, *Dialectical Social Theory and its Critics. From Hegel to Analytical Marxism to Postmodernism*, Albany: State University of New York Press.

Sommer, Doris 1999, *Proceed with Caution, When Engaged by Minority Writing in the Americas*, Cambridge, Mass: Harvard University Press.

Spann, Edward K. 1972, *Ideas and Politics. New York Intellectuals and Liberal Democracy, 1820–1880*, Albany: SUNY Press.

Spann, Edward K. 1981, *The New Metropolis. New York City, 1840–1857*, New York: Columbia University Press.

Stacy, Jason 2008, *Walt Whitman's Multitudes: Labor Reform and Persona in Whitman's Journalism and the First Leaves of Grass, 1840–1855*, New York: Peter Lang.

Taylor, George Rogers 1968 [1951], *The Transportation Revolution, 1815–1860*, New York: Harper and Row.

Tanuro, Daniel 2013, *Green Capitalism: Why it Can't Work*, translated by Jane Ennis, London: Merlin.

Thomas, M. Wynn 1982, 'Walt Whitman and Mannahatta-New York', *American Quarterly*, 34, 4: 362–78.

Thomas, M. Wynn 1987, *The Lunar Light of Whitman's Poetry*, Cambridge: Harvard University Press.

Thomas, M. Wynn 1994, 'Whitman and the Dreams of Labor', in Folsom (ed.) 1994.

Thomas, M. Wynn 2009, 'Stacy, Jason. *Walt Whitman's Multitudes: Labor Reform and Persona in Whitman's Journalism and the First Leaves of Grass, 1840–1855*. [review]', *Walt Whitman Quarterly Review*, 26, 3: 158–60.

Thomas, M. Wynn 2007, 'United States and States United: Whitman's National Vision in 1855', in Folsom (ed.) 2007.

Tocqueville, Alexis de 2003 [1835, 1840], *Democracy in America*, translated by Gerald E. Bevan, London: Penguin.

Trachtenberg, Alan 1994, 'The Politics of Labor and the Poet's Work: A Reading of "A Song for Occupations"', in Ed Folsom (ed.) 1994.

Traubel, Horace L. 1914, *With Walt Whitman in Camden*, Vol. III, New York: Mitchell Kennerley.

Traubel, Horace L. 1915a, *With Walt Whitman in Camden* Vol. I, New York: Mitchell Kennerley.

Traubel, Horace L. 1915b, *With Walt Whitman in Camden*, Vol. II, New York: Mitchell Kennerley.

Traubel, Horace L. 1953, *With Walt Whitman in Camden*, Vol. IV, edited by Sculley Bradley, Philadelphia: University of Pennsylvania Press.

Traubel, Horace L. 1964, *With Walt Whitman in Camden*, Vol. v, edited by Gertrude Traubel, Carbondale, Illinois: Southern Illinois University Press.
Traubel, Horace L. 1982, *With Walt Whitman in Camden*, vi, edited by Gertrude Traubel and William White, Carbondale: Southern Illinois University Press.
Traubel, Horace L. 1992, *With Walt Whitman in Camden*, vii, edited by Jeanne Chapman and Robert MacIsaac, Carbondale: Southern Illinois University Press.
Trotsky, Leon 1942, *In Defense of Marxism*, New York: Pioneer Publishers.
Trotsky, Leon 1977 [1937], *The Revolution Betrayed. What is the Soviet Union and Where is it Going?*, translated by Max Eastman, New York: Pathfinder.
Trotsky, Leon 1978 [1930, 1906], *The Permanent Revolution and Results and Prospects*, translated by John G. Wright and Brian Pearce, New York: Pathfinder.
Trotsky, Leon 1994 [1967], *On Black Nationalism and Self-Determination*, edited by George Breitman, New York: Pathfinder.
Tyree, J.M. 2006, 'Thoreau, Walt Whitman, and the Matter of New York', *New England Review*, 27, 1: 61–75.
Vázquez Pérez, Marlene 2010, *La vigilia perpetua. Martí en Nueva York*, La Habana: Centro de Estudios Martianos.
Wacker, Jill 1994, 'Sacred Panoramas: Walt Whitman and New York City Parks', *Walt Whitman Quarterly Review*, 12, 2: 86–103.
Welty, Ward 1979, 'The Persona as Kosmos in "Song of Myself"', *Walt Whitman Review*, 25, 3, 98–105.
Whitley, Edward 2006, 'Whitman's Occasional Nationalism: "A Broadway Pageant" and the Space of Public Poetry', *Nineteenth-Century Literature*, 60, 4: 451–80.
Whitman, Walt [1840], 'Sun-Down Papers no.9', in Holloway (ed.) 1932, I.
Whitman, Walt [1841], 'Sun-Down Papers no.9 *bis*', in Holloway (ed.) 1932, I.
Whitman, Walt [1842], 'Our City', in Rubin and Brown (eds.) 1950.
Whitman, Walt [1842a], 'Life in New York', in Rubin and Brown (eds.) 1950.
Whitman, Walt [1842b], 'An Hour in a Balcony', in Rubin and Brown (eds.) 1950.
Whitman, Walt [1842c], 'A disgraceful proceeding', in Rubin and Brown (eds.) 1950.
Whitman, Walt [1846], 'Fort Greene Park, Brooklyn', in Rodgers and Black (eds.) 1920, II.
Whitman, Walt [1846a] 'Morbid Appetite for Money', in Rodgers and Black (eds.) 1920, II.
Whitman, Walt [1846b], 'Matters which were seen and done in an afternoon ramble', in Holloway (ed.) 1932, I.
Whitman, Walt [1846c], 'Slavers – and the Slave Trade', in Rodgers and Black (eds.) 1920, I.
Whitman, Walt [1846d], 'What we thought at the Institute Fair, this morning', in Rodgers and Black (eds.) 1920, II.
Whitman, Walt [1847] 'American workingmen, versus slavery', in Rodgers and Black (eds.) 1920, I.

Whitman, Walt [1847a] 'New States: shall they be slave or free?', in Rodgers and Black (eds.) 1920, I.

Whitman, Walt [1847b] 'The Sewing Women of Brooklyn and New York', in Rodgers and Black (eds.) 1920, I.

Whitman, Walt [1847?], 'Manuscript Notebook I', in Holloway 1932, II.

Whitman, Walt [1847c], 'Philosophy of Ferries', in Rodgers and Black (eds.) 1920, II.

Whitman, Walt [1847d], 'What the free-traders want', in Rodgers and Black (eds.) 1920, II.

Whitman, Walt [1847e], 'Some reflections on the Past, and For the Future', in Rodgers and Black (eds.) 1920, I.

Whitman, Walt [1851], 'Arts and Artists. Remarks of Walt Whitman, Before the Brooklyn Art Union', in Holloway (ed.) 1932, I.

Whitman, Walt [pre-1855], 'Manuscript Notebook-4', in Holloway 1932, II

Whitman, Walt [1871], *Democratic Vistas*, in Kaplan (ed.) 1982.

Whitman, Walt 1876, *Two Rivulets. Including Democratic Vistas, Centennial Song and Passage to India*, Camden, New Jersey: Authors Edition.

Whitman, Walt [1882], *Specimen Days*, in Kaplan (ed.) 1982.

Whitman, Walt 1920, *The Gathering of the Forces*, 2 vols., edited by Cleveland Rodgers and John Black, New York: G.P. Putnam's Sons.

Whitman, Walt 1975, *The Collected Poems*, edited by Francis Murphy, London: Penguin.

Wilentz, Sean 2004 [1984], *Chants Democratic: New York City and the Rise of the American Working Class, 1788–1850*, Oxford: Oxford University Press.

Wilson, Ivy G. (ed.) 2014, *Whitman Noir. Black America and the Good Gray Poet*, Iowa City: University of Iowa Press.

Wilson, Ivy G. 2014a, 'Looking with a queer smile', in Wilson (ed.) 2014.

Wilson, Ivy G. 2014b, 'Postwar America, Again' in Wilson, 2014.

Wilson, Rob 2000, 'Exporting Christian Transcendentalism, Importing Hawaiian Sugar: The Trans-Americanization of Hawai'i', *American Literature*, 72, 3: 521–52.

Wood, Ellen Meiksins 1999, *The Origin of Capitalism*, New York: Monthly Review.

Wood, Neal 2004, *Tyranny in America. Capitalism and National Decay*, London: Verso.

Ziff, Larzer 1984, 'Whitman and the Crowd', *Critical Inquiry*, 10, 4: 579–91.

Index

(The names of Walt Whitman, José Martí, C.L.R. James have been abbreviated to Whitman, Martí and James, respectively)

abolitionism
   James on   241–2
   Whitman on   163–4, 168, 171–172, 238
affirmative character of culture (Marcuse)   150–1
African-Americans
   Martí on   193–6
   Whitman on   45–7, 161–4, 166–78
   See also abolitionism, Emancipation, Reconstruction, Redemption
agape (love of strangers)
   ethics of self-fulfillment and solidarity   141–142
   socialism and   143
Ahmad, Aijaz   67–70
Allen, Gay Wilson   28, 271n34
American Revolution   157
   James on   255–6, 260
   Whitman on   86, 137, 163–4
   In *Countersong to Walt Whitman* (Mir)   255
Antebi, Susan   200n88, 207
Aristotle   141–2
Arvin, Newton   3, 84–5, 89, 144n49, 155, 162, 165, 239n107
Auden, W.H.   239n109

Blaine, James   198
Bloom, Harold   237–8
Borges, Jorge Luis   269, 271
Brennan, Timothy   220
Brooklyn Bridge
   Martí on   109–11, 124, 203, 205, 207, 210
Brown, John   164
Bucke, Richard M.   42
Buhle, Paul   243–4
Buinicki, Martin T.   119, 176–9, 180n118

capitalism   See Karl Marx on capitalism
   See also Ralph Waldo Emerson, Alexis de Tocqueville

Cherokee people   196
Civil War
   conflicts leading to   12, 157–60
   sectional and class analysis of   178–90
   Walt Whitman on   19, 74, 96, 168–71
Cohen, Jonathan   252–253
commodity fetichism
   Marx on   54–5, 56–7
   Whitman and   94–6
   Emerson and   95n111
comradeship
   Whitman on   72–74, 80–3, 86–91, 96, 137–8, 141–5, 174, 233
   in US armed forces, James on   240
Coney Island
   Martí on   108–109, 122–123, 198–199, 200, 202, 203, 204, 205, 207n112
Congress of Industrial Organizations
   James on   223–5, 242–3
Conway, Christopher   266
Countersong to Walt Whitman see Pedro Mir
Coy, Edward   195–196
Crystal Palace Exposition (New York 1853)   34–5
Cutler, Ed   34–5

Debs, Eugene   143n42
democracy
   Whitman on   40, 86, 270
   radical views on   42–5, 48–50
   workers' role in   49
   comradeship and   81, 88
   spiritualisation of   83
   labour question and   136–7
   small farms and   138–40
   important battles (abolitionism, Emancipation, Reconstruction) missed   171–2
   Martí on failure to prevent wealth concentration under   191
   James on potential of modern media in   227–8

INDEX 287

See also slavery, abolitionism, Emancipation, Reconstruction, Redemption, 'Religious Democracy', Soviet bureaucracy

Eagleton, Terry   70n56, 141–3, 233n73
Emancipation
    Whitman on   168–170, 171–172
Emerson, Raph Waldo
    Marx compared to   59n13, 65n37
    Martí and   130–31, 130n47, 211–13
    José Enrique Rodó on   204n105
    Emerson and
        poetry of the world   21n48, 99n132
        division of labour   59n13
        commodification   62n24
        commodity fetishism   95n111
        Leaves of Grass   99
        US as world leader   150n74
Engels, Friederich
    on US labour in 1886   192–193
Erkkila, Betsy   50, 71, 74, 80n50, 88n80, 96, 97, 138, 138n111, 156–7, 163, 165, 167, 169, 171, 178, 179n113, 179–80, 181

ferries
    Whitman and   14–15, 21, 22, 23n60, 110–11
Folsom, Ed   47, 167–8, 172, 178, 179n113, 181–2, 238
Foner, Eric   157, 160, 191–2, 260–1
Fort Greene, Brooklyn   20, 75–6
Freeburg, Christopher   247
free time
    Marx on   63–6, 91–2, 153–4
    Whitman on   72, 73, 91–4, 160–1
    See also loafing

Garrison, William Lloyd   164
Geffen, Arthur   110–11
George, Henry
    Martí on   183, 187–8, 190, 193, 206
    Whitman on   235
Ginsberg, Allen   83n60
Grant, Ulysses S.
    Martí on   117–20, 125, 129
    Whitman on   119–20
Grunzweig, Walter   147

Haddox, Thomas F.   141, 181, 237
Haymarket events (1886)
    Friederich Engels on   192–3
    Martí on   183, 189–90, 193
Henkel, Scott   181, 237
Herreshoff, David   59n13, 65n37
homoeroticism
    in Whitman   73, 88–9
Hunnicutt, Benjamin K.   92, 153–4

imperialism
    Marx on   66–70, 149
    Whitman's apology for   145–50, 266
    Martí on   197–8
    James on Whitman and   236–7
    In *Countersong to Walt Whitman* (Mir)   261–2
    Harold Bloom as ideologist of   237–8
    See also Aijaz Ahmad, Walter Grunzweig, Edward W. Said, Ed Whitley
internationalism (Marxist)   266

James, C.L.R.
    life to the 1950s   218–9
    James on
        rail trip across US   219–20
        contradictions and revolutionary potential in American society   221–5, 242–3
        revolutionary potential of US working class   220–1
        women in US capitalism   222–3
        Hollywood and mass commercial culture   225–8
        democratic possibilities of modern media   227–8
        C.I.O.'s radical potential   223–5, 242–3
        John L. Lewis   224–5, 228–9, 243
        US intellectuals   228–9, 241
        Max Lerner, Jr.   225
        Whitman   232–40, 246–7
            attitude to class conflict   232–3, 236
            isolation   238
            as apologist for status quo   238
            recruited for Cold War propaganda   236–7
            future of his verse   246–7

Herman Melville 220–1, 231, 240–2, 248, 249
Mariners, Renegades and Castaways (Melville)
   Moby Dick 240–1, 248, 249
     Captain Ahab and totalitarianism 240–1
     Ishmael as intellectual 241
     'Postcript' 243–6
   Wendell Phillips and radical abolitionists 241–2
   bureaucracy 229–31, 243–5
   American Revolution (1776) 255–6, 260
   male comradeship in wartime 240
   Gilded Age and the concentration of capital 260–1
  shared views with Whitman 239–40
  compared to Martí 219–20, 242
  debate on his reading of Whitman and Melville 247–9

Kaplan, Justin 20, 34
Klammer, Martin 45, 140, 176
Knights of Labor
  Martí on 185, 187–9
  Engels on 192–3

labour struggles (in the United States)
  James on 223–5, 242–3
  Martí on 184–93
  Whitman on 136–8, 165–6, 233–6
  rebellion of 1877 136
  rise of the C.I.O., 1934 to 1950 223
  course of labour after 1950 242–3
Lawson, Andrew 155–6, 165–6
Lerner, Jr., Max 225
Levis jeans 237
Lewis, John L.
  James on 224–5, 228–9, 243
loafing
  Whitman on 91–5, 153–4
  See also free time
Lomas, Laura 211–16

McCarl, Clayton 110n43
Mancuso, Luke 174–6
Marcuse, Herbert 150–1

Mariners, Rengades and Castaways (James) see C.L.R. James
Martí, José
Martí on
  American society
   Wendell Phillips 125–6, 242
   racism 193–6
   lynching of Edward Coy 195–6
   Native Americans 196–7
   political machines 184
   Wall Street and financial speculation and crises 184
   James Blaine as imperialist and expansionist 198
   expansionism and imperialism 197–8
   labour struggles 184–93
    Knights of Labor 185, 187–9
    Henry George 183, 187–188, 190, 193, 206
    Haymarket events 183, 189–90, 193, 224
    United Labor Party 184, 190, 193, 206
   monopolization of wealth 191
   commemoration of death of Marx 189
  Emerson 130–1, 130n147, 211–3
  modernity and its contradictions
   nature and the modern connected 103, 107, 120, 129–132, 204
   commitment to modernity 116–7, 123–4, 202–4, 205, 206
   city life in US 105–11
   electricity 112–3
   industry and machines 111–2
   railroads 105–6, 114, 204
   newspapers 105–6, 115, 117
   New York and US as modern Babel 113
   Brooklyn Bridge 109–11, 124, 203, 205, 207, 210
   Coney Island 108–109, 122–3, 198–9, 200, 202, 203, 204, 205, 207n112
   modern man as rebel angel 112–3
   Grant as modern leader 118–20, 125, 129

INDEX

present as preparatory stage 103,
  104–5, 106–7
anguish of modern life 106, 113–6,
  122, 123
one-sidedness and fragmentation
  120–8
art in present unsettled stage
  104–17
sense of alienation in *Versos libres*
  126–8
shared criticism of US life with
  Whitman 134
modern poetry 130–2
US as model for Latin America 117
US as a failed model of modernity
  193, 199
Cuban independence as alternative
  modernity 199
program for independent Cuba 209–
  210
socialism 187, 190–1, 209n116
Whitman 130–5, 213–6
women 201–2
compared to
  Engels 192–3
  C.L.R. James 219–20, 242
  young Marx 209–10
idealisation of capitalist present 210–11
debate on
  attitude toward modernity 199–209,
    216–7
  reading of Whitman 213–6
  reading of Emerson 211–3
Marx, Karl
Marx on
  alienation 94n110, 151–3
  'average man' and commodity production 40–2
  capitalism
    productive forces developed by
      6–7, 9
    relations of personal dependence
      dissolved in 5–6
    mobility of labour in 7
    world market and global interdependence created by 8, 9, 10,
      28
    new needs fostered in 8, 9
    United States best example of 7

history transformed into 'world
  history' by 9–10
'world-historical individuals' created by 5, 9, 11, 26, 27, 32, 110,
  113
new literature and art propitiated
  by 10
naturalization of 39, 129
notion of equality generalized by
  41–2
value and labour in 41–2, 53–4
surplus value as basis of profit in
  55–7
commodity fetishism in 54–5,
  56–7
market as alien power in 53–4, 60
imperative to accumulate and
  increase productivity under
  57–8
'clearing of estates' 58n11
exclusion of majority from property as premise of 260–1
both liberating and oppressive
  61–2
individual freedom affirmed and
  negated under 55
progress one-sided under 58–60,
  61–2
progress as emptying-out in 61
effect of division of labour and
  machinery on workers in 59–
  60
free time and working day in 63–
  6, 91–2, 153–4
class struggle required to end classes
  233n73
Hegel 138
individual liberation and collective
  action 264–5
imperialism and colonialism 66–70,
  149
revolution in backward Germany
  209–10
romantic nostalgia 62–4, 66–7, 69–
  70, 138, 149, 271–2
small commodity production 53n1
socialism 63–4, 65–6, 92
aspects of society as described by
  Whitman 11–12, 15

'variations of labour' and 'fluidity of functions' 18
network of 'varied labours' 21
new needs and a richer individuality 22–3
'world-historical' persons, events and places 26
new means of transportation and communication 28
creation of 'empirically universal individual' 29–30
manufacturing division of labour 33n106
market relations taken as natural 38–9
overthrow of all presuppositions 50
people split from each other, reduced to the pursuit of profit 72–73
progress as 'emptying-out', 'impoverishment of human nature' 77
rule of dead matter over people, dead labour over living labour 85n70, 94
labour discipline and vindication of free time 92–3
pursuit of exchange value at the expense of enjoyment use value 100
tragic sense of history 68–70, 70n56
compared to Emerson 59n13, 65n37, 62n24, 95n111
Martí on 189
Marx, Leo 31
Melville, Herman 220–1, 231, 240–2, 248, 249
Mexican War 159–60
Whitman on 166–7
Miller, Cristanne 171
Mir, Pedro
Life to the 1950s 250–1
Countersong to Walt Whitman
English translation of 252–3
aspects of 251
sections of 251–2
narrative summary of 253–64
US imperialism in 261–2
individual liberation and collective action in 264–5
idealization of American West in 266–7
internationalist, not anti-American anti-imperialism in 263–4, 265–6, 270–1
Whitman's reception in Latin America and 267–71
ideas of Edward W. Said and 265–6
Marxist internationalism in 266
Moby Dick 240–1, 248, 249
Molloy, Sylvia 88

Napoleon 120
nature
Whitman as poet of 37–40
Martí on 103, 107, 120, 129–132, 204, 212, 216
Neruda, Pablo 268
newspapers
Martí on 105–6, 115, 117
Whitman and 35–6
Norton, Charles Eliot 99, 156

Parker, Simon 35
Pascal, Richard 89, 100, 145
Pearce, Roy Harvey 151–3
Pease, Donald E. 220, 230, 243–6
permanent revolution
young Marx on 209–10
Leon Trotsky on 209, 220
Cuban Revolution and 210n120
Phillips, Wendell
Martí on 125–6, 242
James on 241–2
Post, Charles 12, 24, 157–60
'Postcript' of *Mariners, Renegades and Castaways* 243–6

racism
Martí on 193–6
James and Marxism on 247–8
Whitman and 45–7, 161–4, 166–74
See also slavery, abolitionism, Emancipation, Reconstruction, Redemption
Ramos, Julio 199–209, 216–7

Reconstruction
    Whitman and   170–3, 174–82, 238
    class and sectional analysis of   178–180
Red Cloud   197
Redemption
    Whitman on   172–3, 178
'Religious Democracy'   74, 83–6, 132, 143
Reynolds, David   50, 74, 96, 99, 144n49, 172, 238–9
Roediger, David   161–2, 173, 178
romantic nostalgia
    Marx on   62–4, 66–7, 69–70, 138, 149, 271–2
    Whitman and   71, 98, 99, 138
    Martí and   103, 106–7
Ruskin, John   25n69

Said, Edward W.   1, 66, 146–7, 149, 265–6
Santiago Pedrosa, José   258, 259
Santí, Enrico Mario   267–71
Shulman, Robert   73, 89
Sioux people   197
Sismondi, Sismonde de   138n13
slavery
    in US economy   157–60
    runaway slaves and   48, 158, 160, 163–4, 242
    Whitman on   162–8
    In *Leaves of Grass*   45–7
    See also abolitionism, Emancipation, Reconstruction, United States (economic and political evolution)
socialism
    Marx on   63–4, 65–6, 92
    Martí on   187, 190–1, 209n116
    Whitman's refusal of   137, 143–5, 233–6
    as ethics of self-fulfillment and solidarity   141–3
    See also Soviet bureaucracy
Sommer, Doris   50, 138, 141, 236, 239
Soviet bureaucracy
    James on   229–31, 240–1, 243–5
    Leon Trotsky on   230–1, 245
Stevens, Thaddeus   170
surplus value, Marxist theory of   55–7

Thomas, M. Wynn   26, 40, 87, 89, 94n110, 98, 138, 140, 145, 156, 163, 165, 166, 180
Thoreau, Henry David   26

Tocqueville, Alexis de on
    new moneyed aristocracy   192n39
    one sided pursuit of money   76n20, 60n20, 122n96
    mobility of labour, openness to innovation   7, 60n20
    recurrent crises   60n20
Trachtenberg, Alan   33
Traubel, Horace L.   143n42, 234–5
Trotsky, Leon
    on bureaucracy   230–1
    The History of the Russian Revolution   218, 219
    on permanent revolution   209, 220
    conversations with James   247

United Labor Party
    Engels on   193
    Martí on   184, 190, 193, 206
United States (economic and political evolution)
    mercantile capital, plantation economy, small commodity production before 1840s   157–8
    bi-sectional politics   157–8
    rise of manufacturing capital and market dependence and the road to civil war   12, 158–60

value, Marxist theory of   41–2, 53–4
Vázquez Pérez, Marlene   217

Wacker, Jill   20
Wall Street (financial power, speculation)
    Martí on   184
    in *Countersong to Walt Whitman* (Mir)   260–2
Walsh, Donald D.   252–3
Whitley, Edward   26, 147–9
Whitman
    occupations and trades in life   18
    poet of modern and nature   37–40
    levels and aspects of his poetry   73
    homoeroticism   73, 88–9
    writing enabled by capitalism   11–12
    centrality of New York   12–15, 19–20, 26, 36
    views akin to pre-Civil War skilled workers   155–7, 160–1

292 INDEX

as international proletarian poet (Gay Wilson Allen)   271n34
Whitman and
   affirmative character of culture (Marcuse)   150–1
   American Revolution   86, 137, 163–4
   business civilization and alternatives to it
      one-sided pursuit money   74–80, 99–100
      unease with consequences   72–3, 74–86
      social fragmentation   80–5
      emptiness, personal void   77–8
      commodity fetichism   94–96
      progress not only material   97–8
      need to vivify   73n70, 85–6, 127, 128, 136, 137, 143, 151, 239, 271–2
      comradeship   72–4, 80–3, 86–91, 96, 137–8, 141–5, 174, 233
      international "adhesiveness"   82–3, 83–6, 132, 143
      fight to save Fort Greene   20, 75–6
      free time   72, 73, 91–4, 160–1
      loafing   91–4, 95, 153–4
   capitalism
      refusal to question   137–8, 140, 141, 143–4, 234–5
      avoidance of class and apology of   144–150, 236
      poetic resolution of social contradictions   140–1, 144–5
   democracy   40, 86, 270
      radical views on   42–5, 48–50
      workers' role in   49
      comradeship in   81, 88
      spiritualization of   83
      labour question and   136–7
      small farms and   138–40
      'average man' and   40–2
      revolutionaries in other lands   48
      'Religious Democracy'   74, 90–1
   Ulysses S. Grant   119–20
   imperialism, apology of   145–50, 266
   labour movement
      labour question and struggles   136–8, 165–6, 233–6
      Henry George   235
      Levis jeans   237

   Marx's journalism   13n11
   modern, industrial world
      industry, engines, machines   15–16, 33–4
      city land rural life   20–4
      diverse labors in poems   17–18, 19, 21–2
      world trade and cosmopolitan perspective   26–30, 32
      manufacturing division of labour   33n106
      railroads   24–5, 28, 29, 31, 32–3
      Suez Canal   31, 97
      trans-Atlantic cable   31, 97
      intercontinental railroad   31, 97
      newspapers   35
      Crystal Palace Exposition 1853   34–5
   Napoleon   120
   John Ruskin   25n69
   Sismonde de Sismondi   138n13
   slavery, anti-slavery, post-slavery debates
      opposition to slavery compatible with racism   161
      extension of slavery and abolitionism   162–8
      slavery and African-Americans in 'Song of Myself' (1855)   45–7
      slavery idealized   164
      political evolution before Civil War   161–8
      abolitionism   163–4, 168, 171–2, 238
      William Lloyd Garrison   164
      John Brown   164
      Mexican War and the Wilmot Proviso   166–7
      Civil War   19, 96, 74, 168–170
      black troops   169–70
      Emancipation   168–70, 171–2
      Reconstruction   170–3, 174–82, 238
      Redemption   172–3, 178
      'Songs of Insurrection' cluster   96, 177–8
   Henry David Thoreau   26
   women   44
   C.L.R. James on   232, 240, 246–7
   Martí on   130–5, 213–6

Allen Ginsberg on   83n60
Eugene Debs on   143n42
debates on
    Whitman and Reconstruction   174–6
    Martí and Whitman   213–6
    Whitman's reception in Latin America   267–71
Wilentz, Sean   157, 160, 162
Will, George   237

Wilmot Proviso   166–7
Wilson, Ivy G.   247–9
Wilson, Rob   145–6
Women
    Martí on   201–2
    Whitman on   44
    James on   222–3
'world-historical individuals'   5, 9, 11, 26, 27, 32, 110, 113

www.ingramcontent.com/pod-product-compliance
Lightning Source LLC
Chambersburg PA
CBHW071231070526
44583CB00017B/2130